Sam Houston's Republic

second edition

Lynne Basham Tagawa

Illustrated by
Shiphrah and Evelyn Johnson

Blue Rock Press

Sam Houston's Republic
Second Edition

Blue Rock Press
5606 Onyx Way
San Antonio, TX 78222

First edition published by Xulon Press

This is a work of narrative nonfiction. Every effort has been made to be true to the historical personages mentioned or described in the text. Fictional characters are clearly described as such. Historical characters are sometimes described in a fictional way.

All Bible quotations taken from the King James Version, public domain

ISBN: 979-8-9942305-5-8 (paperback)
ISBN: 979-8-9942305-6-5 (hardback)
ISBN: 979-8-9942305-7-2 (ebook)

Illustrations: Shiphrah and Evelyn Johnson

Cover Design: 100 Covers

Library of Congress Control Nunber: 2026912258

What moths we are, and how easily we are crushed. May God by the power of His Grace, sustain us in life, and give us thro Jesus Christ, the victory in death.

—Sam Houston to his wife Margaret, March 2nd, 1856

Contents

List of Illustrations

Prologue

It was a warm, wet spring in the swampy bayou country of east Texas. A tall man with clear blue eyes sat astride a huge gray stallion; alert, both were watching what neither of them could see.

The man urged his mount slowly forward. Behind him, a scraggly army marched, silent but eager. Ahead, beyond a slight rise of tall grass, lay the unseen camp of Santa Anna and his army. The tall man, Sam Houston, knew that the Mexican dictator had received reinforcements just the night before. The men behind him were now outnumbered.

But numbers weren't everything. The Mexican reinforcements were tired; they had to be. Many of Santa Anna's men suffered from dysentery; they were far from home and their supply lines were long. It was now mid-afternoon, and the shadows were beginning to lengthen.

Houston knew about the Mexican custom of afternoon siesta, and he also knew that Santa Anna, the self-styled "Napoleon of the West," was overconfident. Perhaps the diminutive dictator was napping in his tent.

It was the Texans' only chance. Some of these men did not even have shoes, only the determination to avenge the slaughter of the Alamo. Feeling the aches of old war wounds, and knowing that bravery alone did not win battles, Houston was realistic; he had retreated many miles to find a chance for his men.

Suddenly a rider galloped through the lines.

"Vince's bridge is down! They can't get away, men! Victory or death!"

Introduction

History is about people. About their actions and the beliefs that caused those actions. At times, history can seem dry, when vast numbers of facts must be covered in a short span of time. But these were real people, who wrestled with real ideas, and I have tried to bring them to life. Themes like the rule of law are emphasized over a drill of names, dates, and places.

Sam Houston's Republic only attempts to cover early Texas history, from the time of the Amerinds to the Civil War and a little beyond. It focuses on the life of Sam Houston, a man whose life has valuable lessons to teach—whose life was both heroic and, at times, even tragic, and who only came to know Christ in his later years.

This book is written like a novel whenever possible. The people and the situations are real. Occasionally, conversations are invented, but the text indicates when spoken words are actual quotes or are merely possible. Eyewitnesses have given us the actual words of the participants (to the best of their memory) in many cases, and these are documented by endnotes.

How to use this book: just read and enjoy. For educators and parents, you can use it as a Texas History text, using the workbook (sold separately) with teacher's resources (including tests). The reading level is designed for high school; I have deliberately included challenging vocabulary, and each chapter comes with a vocabulary list in the workbook. With this help, middle-school students should be able to comprehend the text.

Proficient readers should be able to master the material in one semester. Younger students would benefit from spreading it out over a year and adding age-appropriate activities. Another option is to use the book as an add-on or enrichment to an American History class, since many of these events overlap with that subject.

Chapter 1

Tejas

TWELVE-YEAR-OLD SAM HOUSTON walked out the door of Timber Ridge Church and blinked in the sunlight. Just a hundred yards away stood his home. Built by his great-grandfather, it sported square columns supporting a classic two-story gallery.

His three older brothers walked ahead, while his elegant mother brought up the rear with Willie and his little sisters. In fact, her mere presence seemed to govern the whole caravan as the family headed toward home.

Sam's father, Major Samuel Houston, was away just now, a not-uncommon occurrence. But this year, 1805, was different. Rumors and whispers flew of possible war with Spain as well as a place called "Tejas." Frontiersmen in both Tennessee and Western Virginia were already on alert, and Major Houston had been a very busy man.

As descendants of practical Scots-Irish Calvinists, the Houstons were Presbyterians whose ancestors had often known turbulent times. Apparently, a priest named John Knox had started it all, when he studied the Scriptures, seeking the truth. In the gospel, he discovered the doctrine of salvation by grace through faith and realized that the traditions of men had obscured the truth of God.

The Houstons—a Scots-Irish Family

Like most places in Europe before the Reformation, Scotland was Catholic, its teachings espoused by the Scottish government. And because Catholicism was the only state-sanctioned religion, the message of John Knox was not welcome, but still he persisted, defying the government, in spite of the danger should he be caught.

Defying tradition, John Knox boldly dared to preach in Scotland. In great numbers, seekers heard and began to believe the gospel of Christ. In spite of the threat of punishment, the new and growing converts rebelled against the teachings of the priests and joined forces to tear down Catholic churches, monasteries, and idols. They rejected what they saw as a government-mandated bondage of the soul and refused to obey those in power when what they demanded was wrong according to the Scriptures.

Scotland was thrown into a state of chaos. John Knox and his followers, now known as "Presbyterians," were under constant scrutiny, so the preacher taught them the importance of living a life above reproach, so as not to sully the name of Christ.

Just as the persecution of believers in first-century Jerusalem resulted in the scattering of Christians to other places, so too did the turbulent times in Scotland bring about mass Scottish migration. Some immigrated to Ireland, but many of these relocated again, across the Atlantic. These "Scots-Irish" settled mainly in what was then the American frontier: western Pennsylvania, western Virginia, Kentucky, and Tennessee. Because of their ability to cope with hardship, these hardy, independent settlers thrived in the less-than-welcoming mountainous regions of America.

The Shenandoah Valley

Sam Houston's great-grandfather, John Houston, had been one of these early settlers. Apparently, even the voyage from Belfast was fraught with danger. As the story goes, the captain of the ship had planned to trick them, hoping to acquire the settlers' vast stores of gold, which had not passed unnoticed. But the vigilant and intrepid Scotsmen outsmarted the plot's ringleaders, and, putting their trust in God, eventually landed safely in the New World, their wealth still intact.

After first settling in Pennsylvania, John Houston and his family later relocated to the Shenandoah Valley, a Presbyterian stronghold, where Sam and his family now lived. John cleared land and used his wealth to construct a much-used stone church.

John Houston earned a reputation for respect and integrity while serving as a magistrate and becoming involved in the war between the French and Indians. He died at the age of sixty-five after being hit by a falling tree limb.

Upon John's death, his son Robert inherited the Timber Ridge Plantation, located in prosperous Rockbridge County. But all was not well. A new shadow appeared on the horizon, and King George III began to threaten their new way of life.

As a group, these Scotsmen believed the law of the land was superior to the will of the crown, which still held power, even in the New World. And because of their hunger for freedom, they did not hesitate to join the fight for independence. Robert Houston's son, Sam's father, Samuel Houston, joined the Continental Army.

Samuel decided he enjoyed military life. It was one he could embrace—an occupation quite well suited to his station as a country "gentleman." He married Elizabeth Paxton, daughter of one of the county's wealthiest men, Squire John Paxton.

During his military career, Samuel served the State of Virginia as brigadier inspector, and over the next twenty-three years, somehow managed to make and squander his accumulated wealth, while his godly wife, Elizabeth, whom her son Sam later described as a "heroine,"[1] presided faithfully over her household in her husband's absence.

Sam was, to put it mildly, a trial to his mother. He disliked school, played hooky, and constantly argued with his older brothers, who, by their own accounts, described themselves as good and obedient sons.

Sam did try to obey—not to please his brothers, but his beloved mother, a kind, steadfast woman, who seemed to understand him, when no one else did.

Though he hated school, Sam did like to read. He regularly pulled books from his father's bookshelves and read about faraway places and times long past, while stretched out in front of the five-foot-high mantel of the living room in Timber Ridge.

With his father gone, and war looming with Spain and a place called Tejas, it is very likely that this dreamy boy opened up his father's copy of *Morse's Geography* to look for that new frontier...

Texas before the Europeans

Tejas (later called Texas), as Sam might have learned in his reading, was a new frontier, where no man had gone before. Or almost. A huge mid-section of the American continent, it spread from the warm, moist Gulf in the south to piney forests in the east. The northwest was ruled by lush grass that, over the miles, morphed into scrub, desert and finally, mountains in the southwest. From malarial swamp to the searing dry heat of the west, from forest to grass to cactus, it was all here. From the

American point of view of the early 1800s, East Texas was the Texas farmers wanted. Forest, coastal plain, alluvial river bottoms, these were prize croplands.

San Antonio (or Bexar, as most called it) was the western rim of the land Americans would invade and occupy. But they were not the first to live there.

The Flood described in the book of Genesis obliterated all civilization and all people except for the eight on the ark Noah built. The waters prevailed and reshaped the earth, burying animals, plants, and people. After the dirt, silt, and sand settled out, the floodwaters receded and slowly leached through the sediment, replacing natural bone with minerals, ultimately resulting in the fossil record we see today.

A massive climactic shock in the upper latitudes sent yet-unheard-of subzero temperatures into the area, sufficient to instantly freeze the huge, woolly mammoth. Ice and cold crept down from the poles, while lower latitudes continued to experience the mild weather that could support wildlife.[2] Ground sloths, mastodons, giant bison, and other large mammals were among the many species migrating into Texas during that time.

Now rich with wildlife, the area was a hunter's paradise, with no lack of food to sustain early man during the long, cold winters.

But who were these men? We know they were not the Indians, or "Amerinds" of our day, because their skulls were long and Caucasoid, like the Europeans of today.[3] There is reason to believe these were men of the generations immediately following the events of Genesis 11, when the Lord confounded the language of the people, causing them to scatter all over the earth. These Caucasoid hunters, resembling Europeans, left tools and skeletons all over the New World. But they left no civilizations. What happened to them is unknown.

Rising above the Midwestern plains, the temple of Cahokia afforded a magnificent view of grain fields and the Mississippi River. Palisades surrounded the largest city in North America; its population dwarfed that of the city of London of that day. It was the Medieval Optimum period, approximately 1000 A.D., when winters were mild, and Vikings were exploring the North Atlantic.[4]

Who were these people? No one is sure today how the Amerinds, or American Indians, came to the New World, but we know they were related to peoples in Asia.

They may have migrated over a land bridge that opened up during the Ice Age, connecting northern Asia with Alaska. Sea levels were lower, and hardy hunters could have pursued game into the New World. One thing is certain: they did not bring horses or cattle with them. These Asian hunters went on to settle almost every nook and cranny of North and South America.[5]

Some bands remained nomadic, but in areas fit for agriculture, civilization flourished. The Incas built stone cities and aqueducts in the Andes; the Mayans excelled at mathematics and astronomy; and the Aztecs built cities that were clean and hygienic.

Except for the blood dripping all over the top of their temple. The Aztecs "fed" their gods with grisly human sacrifices. The Amerinds had left the region of Babel, but the religion of Babel was still in their hearts. Most remembered an invisible Creator God and a Deluge, but the important gods to be worshipped were the sun, moon, and stars. The forces of nature and even animals were revered. For this reason, many groups practiced some form of offerings, sometimes involving human sacrifice.[6]

Even their architecture remembered Babel. The temples of the Aztecs and Mayans reflected the structures of the ancient Middle East. The "Mound Builders" of North America accomplished the same with great earthen structures. These grass-covered mounds stand today, silently, as cars drive by on interstate freeways, a mute testimony to an ancient civilization that once held sway over a large section of what is now the United States.

The Mound Builders did not disappear instantly. Their descendants remembered agriculture, division of labor, and crafts. Their tribal structures recognized chiefs, sub-chiefs, and priests; some agricultural tasks were even done communally.

"Teychas" means "friend" in the Caddoan language[77]; these Amerinds inhabited the piney woods of what is now east Texas, and this term somehow stuck as the name for the entire region. The Caddoans were the westernmost group of the descendants of the Mound Builders and retained the division of labor and government of their ancestors. They also traded with other Amerind groups from as far away as the Rocky Mountains.

In the mountainous regions of the west, Amerinds never developed as high a level of civilization as the Mound Builders, but these Puebloan bands grew crops, mined turquoise, and made handicrafts.

In between, in the grasslands of Texas, nomads hunted buffalo. During the cooler period of the Little Ice Age, these buffalo roamed all the way down to the Rio Grande. Some groups, such as the Tonkawas, combined agriculture with a semi-nomadic way of life; they hunted buffalo and facilitated trade with other groups. Some groups were content to gather wild foods to supplement their hunting. These included the Coahuiltecans of south Texas and the Karankawas of the Gulf Coast. Without agriculture, the population of these groups remained small, and their cultures were simple.

This was Texas before the Europeans. But then the Spanish came; and with them came disease, and horses; and even the climate changed. Everything was different.

First Contact

Christopher Columbus squinted into the setting sun, looking for land. His men were about to mutiny. If only they could understand what he did . . . just a few more days, that's all he needed . . .

Finally. A haze on the horizon which resolved into islands. Strange people. These islands must be part of the "Indies;" therefore, these people must be "Indians." It was the year 1492.

The year 1492 was important for another reason. Cabeza de Vaca was born.

Cabeza de Vaca is Spanish for "Head of a Cow." Alvar Nunez Cabeza de Vaca didn't mind being called the "head of a cow." It was a very famous cow's head, or skull to be exact, that was responsible for his mother's family's rise in social station. In the year 1212, a simple shepherd offered to show the Spanish forces a detour around the mountain passes held by the warring Moors. To mark this route, Cabeza de Vaca's poor ancestor plunked down the skull of a cow at the detour entrance and was rewarded by elevation to the nobility, whereupon his name was changed to Cabeza de Vaca.

But now the year was 1528, and it was a very long way from Spain. Cabeza de Vaca wasn't thinking about his social station just then. He lay shipwrecked and naked on a beach on an island, just off the coast of somewhere considerably west of Florida, his original destination, where he had lost his boat, and even his clothes. Several of his companions had also survived, in the same destitute state. Desperate, they joined in prayer, calling on the Lord, and confessing their sins.

Their leader, a man sent from Spain to govern the newly claimed territory known as Florida, had perished. The whole expedition had fallen prey to one disaster after another, but somehow they managed to construct several small boats, and hugging the shoreline, made their way west, hopefully toward New Spain and the Spaniards.

They were in Tejas.[8]

Cabeza de Vaca's Amazing Experiences

Cabeza de Vaca looked up to see the Indians returning. Before the Spaniards' last disaster, which had cost them their boat, their clothes, and the lives of several companions, a band of Karankawa Indians had been kind enough to supply them with food.

This had encouraged the men to attempt a launch to continue their westward journey. They had shed their clothes in order to free the boat from the sand, but shortly after setting sail, the boat had capsized, and they escaped with only their lives. It was all they could do not to lose hope when they understood their desperate situation.

When the Karankawas returned, the despairing Spaniards felt they had no choice and asked to go home with the Indians. And although they were afraid of being sacrificed to idols, they knew they would have little chance of surviving the elements alone and unprotected. The kind natives took pity on them and took care of them, but still some of the Spaniards died.

Because the Indians themselves wore almost no clothes and lived in primitive dwellings, they had nothing to offer the explorers in the way of comfort or clothing. And to make matters worse, there was much work to be done just to survive. The Karankawas were mainly gatherers, collecting shellfish and roots from the coast and using simple nets to catch fish. Cabeza de Vaca wrote later that his life became nearly unbearable because of the pain he endured while gathering roots. But although life was difficult, he continued to trust in God, and this helped to sustain him.

Cabeza de Vaca spent eight years among the Indians of South Texas and Northern Mexico, and during that time sent reports of his experiences, which sparked outside interest in the region.

At one point, he and his companions were pressed into treating the ill and injured. When they agreed to pray for the sick, the surprised Indians shortly claimed they were healed, and de Vaca and his small group gained respect and admiration. Soon their reputation preceded them as they traveled from village to village. He became known as a "medicine man."

Finally, in northern Mexico, they met a group of Spaniards, who were trying to capture and enslave local Indians. By this time, Cabeza de Vaca must have been quite a sight, after having lived such a harsh life among the Indians for eight years.

At first the Spaniards were shocked, but they soon decided to use him to further their own agenda, entrapping Indians for use as slaves. But, as Cabeza himself later reported, this didn't work the way they planned.

The Indians knew better.

> The Indians gave all that talk of theirs little attention. They parleyed among themselves, saying that the Christians [Spaniards] lied, for we had come from the sunrise,

> while the others came from the sun sets; that we cured the sick, while the others killed those who were healthy; that we went naked and shoeless, whereas the others wore clothes and went on horseback, and with lances. Also, that we asked for nothing, but gave away all that we were presented with, meanwhile the others seemed to have no aim than to steal what they could, and never gave anything to anybody.[9]

Cabeza de Vaca was a humble man, but he wrote of his experiences. He also recorded things he heard from the Native Americans, things about cities of gold.

His readers were interested in the gold.

Chapter 2

Trojans and Spaniards

The warm spring Tennessee sun caressed the small plot of plowed earth. Next to a tree stump, a boy was stretched out on the ground, a book before him. Nearby, a team of plow horses idly nibbled the sweet and tender grass.

> Thus pondering, like a god the Greek drew nigh;
> His dreadful plumage nodded from on high;
> The Pelian javelin, in his better hand,
> Shot trembling rays that glitter'd o'er the land;

The thin grass did little to shelter Sam Houston's belly from the ground underneath, which communicated the frosty memory of a winter just past. But the lad with chestnut hair didn't notice; he was involved in the Trojan War.

> As Hector sees, unusual terrors rise,
> Struck by some god, he fears, recedes, and flies

Homer's *Iliad* was more interesting than plowing just now. The story of an enraged Achilles looking for revenge held a fierce attraction for Sam. He even had some of it memorized.

> He leaves the gates, he leaves the wall behind:
> Achilles follows like the winged wind.[1]

"Sam Houston!"

Oh, no. The Holy Apostles, he thought. Sam's blue eyes probably flashed with belligerence. He had been caught shirking by his eternally bossy brothers.

The young Houston loved to read. His heroes were Greek. How much he knew of the Spanish *conquistadores* is questionable. But they would leave a mark on his future home.

The Move to Tennessee

Part of the problem was that Sam's father, Samuel Houston, had died, leaving his older brothers, James and John, legally in charge of his upbringing, as specified in their father's will. While ailing, the senior Houston had put his shaky financial house in order before he died. To pay outstanding debts, Timber Ridge Plantation had been sold, and plans made for a move to a less expensive parcel of land on the frontier. Before he died, one of Major Houston's last purchases was a "waggon with chains and gears compleat for five horses"[2] which, along with the family's old wagon, would transport them southwest to a whole new life.

Elizabeth Houston was not raised on the harsh frontier but had always lived in an upscale and comfortable home. On the other hand, Rockbridge County high society was nothing like the tidewater aristocracy, back east. The Scots-Irish Presbyterians in the highlands of Virginia were practical and sturdy people with few social airs.

In 1807, as a widow of fifty with graying hair, Elizabeth Houston willingly obeyed her husband's last wishes and packed to leave her home, knowing she had strong sons, as well as a powerful and sovereign God.

Young Sam, by now fourteen years old, accompanied his mother while the others piled into a second wagon. They painstakingly made their way southwest, over roads that sometimes did not deserve the name. Though Tennessee had been admitted to the Union more than ten years earlier, it was still mostly an unsettled frontier, with tiny towns scattered throughout the wilderness. After finally reaching Maryville, the Houston family fought their way up Baker's Creek valley, and then up a branch of Baker's Creek, until they reached the 419 acres where they were to settle.

Wasting no time, they shortly got busy and worked from sun-up to sundown to build a simple log cabin; but as hard as the work was, at least they did not have to fear angry Indians. A cousin, Jim Houston, who lived within five miles of their new home, had reassured them that there had been no Indian attacks in the vicinity for the better part of twenty years. A band of peaceful Cherokees lived about fifty miles away.

Over time and with much hard work, the Houstons prospered and were able to purchase an interest in the Maryville general store. While the rest of the family diligently worked the land, Sam had to force himself to do his chores. The truth was, he hated fieldwork. He was the square peg, the black sheep, totally unsuited for life on the farm. Later, he took a position in the store, another occupation for which he was clearly unsuited. And while James and John did their duty to try to keep Sam in line, their efforts were probably not appreciated.

> He was a likable culprit, though, and the handsomest of Elizabeth Houston's sons —fair and tall, with wavy chestnut hair and friendly blue eyes that looked from a head full of droll humor and long words he saw in books; in fact, a hard boy to scold. . . . There were reproofs from Mother which Sam took with his tongue in his cheek, but the bossing by his brothers stirred him to rebellion.
>
> At length it was conceded that Sam was not cut out to be a planter, and so he was placed behind the counter of the store in Maryville. Here Brother James had acquired his early merchandising expertise and lived to become a successful shopkeeper in Nashville. But Sam gave promise of no such satisfactory future. His lapses increased, and he got the name of a wayward boy.[2]

There is no doubt that Sam Houston was devoted to his mother. In his writings, he described her as "an extraordinary woman. . . gifted with intellectual and moral qualities, which elevated her. . . above most of her sex. Her life shone with purity and benevolence, and yet she was nerved with a stern fortitude, which never gave way in the midst of wild scenes that chequered the history of the frontier settler."[3]

While the phrase "wild scenes" is in no way an understatement, the western frontier was not without the gospel of Christ. In fact, in the opening years of the nineteenth century, before the Houstons arrived, a gospel awakening had swept through the frontier, and preachers preached at camp meetings in the wilderness.

But the men and women who wrestled the wilderness were tough, independent souls who, by nature, had to be fearless to make their living by hunting and trapping. Though these character qualities would prove useful in taming the wilderness and defending the Alamo, they also had a dark side. This independent self-reliance often expressed itself in lawlessness, which would later prove to be a problem for Texas.

The Reverend Peter Cartwright gave this account of trouble at a gospel meeting: "They came drunk," he wrote, "and armed with dirks, clubs, knives, and horsewhips, and swore they would break up the meeting. . . .One of them made a pass at my head with his whip, but I closed in with him, and jerked him off his seat. A regular scuffle ensued. . . I threw my prisoner down, and held him fast. . . ."[4]

Clearly, Tennessee was not for sissies.

Neither was Texas.

The *Conquistadores*

The story of the conquistadores opens in the sixteenth century, before the Pilgrims came to New England. Spain was into conquest, having just ended an eight-hundred-year-long war with the Moors. It had taken them that long to drive out their former conquerors, before the fighting Spaniards, sporting Toledo steel in their armor and blades, ventured west to the New World.

In 1519, Hernando Cortés led an expedition into what is now known as Mexico. He landed on the coast with five hundred soldiers and marched into the interior. They captured the Aztec capital of Tenochtitlan and found treasure, including a cache of gold, silver, and jewels. Before long, Spaniards also discovered and plundered the ancient Inca treasure troves of South America.

News spread quickly that the Spanish Crown received rich revenues from its interests in the New World, and word of the discovery of all this gold began to whet the appetite of would-be adventurers. As the Spanish Empire grew, so did the Spanish fleet. The Caribbean eventually became known as the "Spanish Main" of legendary pirate treasure tales.

But the Crown's financial plans were not limited to plunder. Revenue could also be raised from well-managed *encomiendas*, or plantations. First in the Caribbean islands, then later on the mainland of Middle America, *encomenderos* ruled tracts of land, subjugating the native inhabitants as laborers, just as lowly peasants labored in the fields of Spain. But unlike their sturdy Spanish counterparts, the Indian slaves of the Caribbean islands tended to die under such harsh treatment, and eventually, more hearty African slaves were shipped in to work the fields.

The Spanish did not grieve over the mistreatment of the Indians, whom they now saw as potential converts to Catholicism. In fact, they believed they were right to conquer the land, if for no other reason than to bring Christianity to the Indians.

Especially after long years of war against the infidel Moors, the Spanish conquistadores did not think of conquest as merely a savvy military or political move, but rather as an advancement of the kingdom of God. Therefore, it was natural for the clergy to accompany them on these excursions.

But not all explorers had political aims.

Fray Marcos and Coronado

Cabeza de Vaca's report of the various people and places he encountered began to stir outside interest, especially those stories describing seven great cities in the north. In his travels, de Vaca had heard and written about great cities full of turquoise, copper, and emeralds, which caused the Spaniards to mistakenly envision great treasure cities like those in Mexico and Peru.

Fray Marcos de Niza was a respected man from New Spain who held the distinction of knowing what gold looked like, so he was sent with one of de Vaca's companions to explore the cities of the north. The two probably traversed parts of Arizona and New Mexico. Along the way, they heard intriguing stories told by local Indians, featuring many-storied dwellings, large cities, and cotton garments and jewelry worn by the inhabitants. They were plainly describing the Puebloans, but some of their statements gave the impression that these settlements were extremely large and prosperous. Were they exaggerations? Lies? Or perhaps descriptions of what had existed in the past?

Fray Marcos was clearly impressed and was anxious to see the beautiful city called Cibola, but his companion, having gone ahead, was captured and killed. So, because the danger was too great, he constructed a cairn of stones nearby, with a small cross on top, and claimed the region for Spain.

When Marcos arrived home with his report, it stirred up so much interest that the Viceroy Mendoza, the ruler of New Spain, put up the equivalent of two million dollars to finance an expedition to the region. Francisco Vasquez de Coronado was chosen to lead it and put up an equal amount of money to finance a small army, consisting of over three hundred Spaniards, a large group of loyal Indians, and other assorted personnel, including clergy, of which Fray Marcos was one.

With sunlight glinting off his golden armor, Coronado invaded the north in 1540 and led the band into Cibola. This description was written by a member of the expedition, Pedro de Castañeda.

> The next day they entered the settled country in good order, and when they saw the first village, which was Cibola, such were the curses that some hurtled at Friar Marcos that I pray to God that He may protect him from them.
>
> It is a little, crowded village, looking as if it had been crumpled all up together.

> There are ranch houses in New Spain (Mexico), which make a better appearance at a distance. It is a village of about 200 warriors, is three and four stories high, with the houses small and without a courtyard ...[5]

Not exactly a treasure city. Coronado must have been enraged. He wrote this to the viceroy about Fray Marcos:

"I can assure you that he has not told the truth in a single thing, but everything is the opposite of what he related except the name of the cities and the large stone houses."[6] Fray Marcos was sent home, where he then suffered a stroke and died.

A Proclamation

It was summer. The Spanish horsemen were probably sweating underneath their armor as they sat their mounts, studying the Indian village. Coronado's golden armor was probably no better ventilated than anyone else's, and his blond hair was no doubt itching underneath his fancy helmet. And to make matters worse, their food was running out. They were hungry, disenchanted, and undoubtedly very grumpy. Cibola was no treasure city. Marcos. What an idiot.

To save face and salvage what they could of the expedition, a proclamation was made to the Indians at Cibola, declaring the takeover by the Pope and Spain, but this did not go over well, and a conflict shortly erupted.

The Indians, in rebellion, retreated to their pueblos, which were admirably suited for the purpose of defense, with no doors on the lowest levels. In fact, the only entrance was an opening in the second story, accessible by ladder, which could then be drawn up into the dwelling, preventing easy access by invading troops.

But the well-trained Spaniards were not easily dissuaded and devised other means of entry, eventually overcoming the Indians. In their search, they found no gold, but by then were very hungry and grateful to find something even more precious. Food.

Frustrated by the failure of his expensive expedition, Coronado dispatched several groups of men to explore the region. One group came back, reportedly finding a huge gash in the earth, an enormous canyon. Today we call it the "Grand Canyon."

Another group reported finding a cluster of Indian villages, the main one called Tiguex. Because the villagers seemed friendly to the Spanish, Coronado decided to move the rest of his army to Tiguex for the winter.

But once they settled in, everything began to go wrong. Some of the Spaniards mistreated the Indians, stealing from them and even taking advantage of the women, and one husband became incensed, inciting a near riot in the village.

The enraged Indians lashed out, albeit ineffectively, pelting the armor-plated Spaniards with arrows from the safety of their pueblos. But the fair-skinned invaders broke through their defenses and smoked out the Indians, who then surrendered, begging for peace.

After rounding up the captives, soldiers marched the Indians to the tent of Don Garcia López de Cárdenas to recognize the Church as Mistress and Superior of the Universe and the High Pontiff, called Papa, in its name; the Queen and King, our masters, in their places as Lords, Superiors, and Sovereigns of these islands and the main by virtue of said, who was the officer in charge. Below is Pedro de Castañeda's account of what happened.

> ... They were taken to the tent of Don Garcia, who, according to what he said, did not know about the peace and thought they had given themselves up of their own accord because they had been conquered. As he had been ordered by the general not to take them alive, but to make an example of them so that other natives would fear the Spaniards, he ordered 200 stakes to be prepared at once to burn them alive....Then when the enemies saw that the Spaniards were binding them and beginning to roast them, about a hundred men who were in the tent began to struggle and defend themselves with what there was and with the stakes they could seize. Our men who were on foot attacked the tent on all sides, so that there was great confusion around it, and then the horsemen chased those who escaped. As the country was level, not a man of them remained alive, unless it was some who remained hidden in the village and escaped that night to spread throughout the country the news that the strangers did not respect the peace that they had made, which afterward proved a great misfortune.[7]

Cárdenas, by sending an envoy, attempted to make peace with the Indians of the other villages near Tiguex. But when the villagers saw them coming, they answered with a volley of arrows, having already heard about the treachery of the strange men on their strange-looking beasts.

The Spaniards laid siege, and the battle lasted fifty days. One day, the Indians asked if they could release the women and children, believing that they would not be harmed. This was allowed, and one of the officers rode up without his helmet, and, dismounting, embraced the Indian boys and girls. He then entreated the men to surrender, not wanting to attack if it could be helped. But he was driven off by another volley of arrows.

A couple of weeks later, the men of the village, with some women who had remained, attempted to escape the siege at night. There was a skirmish, and many Indians were killed. The rest fled, but a river blocked their escape route. At that time of year, the water was very cold, but the desperate Indians threw themselves in anyway. Some undoubtedly perished, but some made it to the other side. Overcome with the cold, they collapsed on the far bank, only to be rescued the next morning by Spaniards, who nursed them back to health and made servants of them.

The Spaniards were not monsters; they could be kind. But the purpose of the conquistadores was to "pacify" the country in a manner described by the requirement of 1513, a proclamation that all men everywhere should obey the pontiff of Rome, and if they did so, they should be let alone.

> But if you do not do this, and maliciously make delay in it, I certify to you that, with the help of God, we shall powerfully enter into your country, and shall make war against you in all ways and manners that we can, and shall subject you to the yoke and obedience of the Church and of their highnesses; we shall take you, and your wives, and your children, and shall make slaves of them, and as such shall sell and dispose of them as their highnesses may command; and we shall take away your goods, and shall do you all the mischief and damage that we can, as to vassals who do not obey, and refuse to receive their lord, and resist and contradict him: and we protest that the deaths and losses which shall accrue from this are your fault, and not that of their highnesses, or ours, nor of these cavaliers who come with us . [8]

One of the popes had made a gift of the islands and mainland in the New World to the Spanish Crown, and so the conquistadores operated on the basis that these lands belonged to them, and that it was acceptable to go about claiming them. The Indians, as far as they were concerned, were "vassals" or "serfs," and were treated accordingly. In fact, it was actually considered wrong for the Indians to resist them.

Texas

Despite the tragedies at Tiguex, the army of Coronado camped there for the winter, in the higher elevations of the New Mexican mountains, surrounded by evergreens and deep snow.

In the spring, the expedition traveled east after hearing rumors about a city called Quivira, which apparently abounded with gold. A Pawnee the Spaniards called "Turk," because he looked like one, described this wonderful place, and though there was some question about his veracity, Coronado let him guide them into the high plains of Texas. From central New Mexico, they traveled hundreds of miles round-trip, apparently traversing the panhandle of Texas, where all was flat as far as the eye could see. The cloudless sky appeared to be a "bowl" over their heads, and hunters were easily lost on the featureless plains. While there, they encountered large herds of buffalo, which they referred to as cattle.

Along the way, they ran across various bands of Native Americans. In one place, the Indians used dogs to drag their belongings behind them, living in tents, and relying on the buffalo for food and skins. At one time, they encountered a settlement visited earlier by the gentle Cabeza de Vaca and his companions. Thinking the Spaniards were of the same mind as Cabeza de Vaca, the Indians made a generous gift of animal skins to the Spaniards, but became upset when the soldiers greedily appropriated them and more. As Castañeda recorded, "The women and some others were left crying, because they thought that the strangers were not going to take anything but would bless them as Cabeza de Vaca and Dorantes had done when they passed through here."[9]

After traveling four days, they reached another covey of Indian settlements, but these people planted fields and tended vineyards, and Castañeda called them "Teyas." They informed Coronado that Quivera was to the north of their land.

Then the army divided. Part went north with Coronado, while the rest turned back toward Tiguex. After finally reaching "Quivira," and finding only a simple Indian village with no gold whatever, the Turk finally confessed his deceit and admitted that he had been asked to draw the strangers out into the plains, where it was hoped they would become lost and die.

The Turk was garroted, and Coronado returned to Tiguex. After various additional hardships, the troops were ordered home, and they left, no richer than before, but not entirely unsuccessful. They had claimed a significant portion of the continent for Spain.

Unknown to them, another explorer had approached Texas from the east, Hernando de Soto. This conquistadore died en route, and one of his officers continued the exploration into the piney woods of East Texas, peopled with Caddoan Indians. In fact, Castañeda wrote that an Indian woman with their expedition ran off and ended up joining de Soto's forces after a mere nine-day trek. This was only discovered after they returned home.

Coronado returned a very disillusioned man, in poor health. In making his report to the Viceroy, he had nothing good to say about Texas, since not only was there no gold or other precious metal to be found there. The Indians, who subsisted on buffalo and owned nothing, were not even good slave material. The lands were good for farming, especially to the east, but there was little that could be readily exploited, and the Spanish did not attempt to colonize Texas for another 150 years.

Don Juan de Oñate

More than a generation later, another armor-plated man invaded the Southwest who would have a greater, more permanent effect on the region than Coronado. His name was Don Juan de Oñate, and he covered much of the same territory as Coronado. But his purpose in going was slightly different. Rather than looking for gold, he was sent simply to pacify and Christianize the nation. In fact, more than one hundred soldiers took their families and livestock and settled there, since colonization was now part of the plan.

This time, the Pueblo Indians proved to be cooperative with Oñate and his band of settlers, who were also farmers. But when Oñate went east, he ended up fighting a bloody battle with the Plains Indians. Because they were mounted, the Spaniards won, but it was clear that these Indians were not going to be easily subdued.

In New Mexico, rancheros had already begun to establish a horse-centered culture, to which the local farming Indians eventually adapted. But for the Indians who hunted on the plains, the horse meant something else.

The small, Afro-Arabian Spanish mustang was perfectly suited for life on the plains. Unlike other breeds, this one was hardy and fast. Thriving on nothing but grass, they multiplied easily. Their presence changed the balance of power among the Indian bands of the plains. Previously, agricultural groups such as the Caddoans, Tonkawas, and Puebloans enjoyed relative peace, but when hunter-gatherers acquired horses, they became mobile and dangerous. The Apaches were one such group that expanded its borders and influence.

The Apaches, however, did not raise their own horses but stole them from the ranchos. As enemies of the Puebloans who had submitted to the Spanish, the mounted Apaches soon wiped out entire Pueblo villages, without any resistance on the part of the reigning Spanish government. This was too much for the besieged Pueblo Indians, who finally revolted against the government, no longer willing to submit to Spanish rule without any guarantee of reciprocal protection.

The Spanish also fled the upper Rio Grande valley, leaving livestock behind. Thus, in 1680, livestock, including horses, were widely dispersed, and the knowledge of the value of the horse spread rapidly. These horses became known as "mustangs," and feral cattle gave rise to the famed Texas "longhorns," tough and dangerous beasts.

In 1705, some Ute Indians from the Rocky Mountains obtained horses from the Spanish, who were accompanied by several members of a fruit-and-berry-picking tribe from Wyoming. The Wyoming bands gained a reputation of dishonesty and were termed "enemy" by the Utes, who also used the universal Plains sign language to refer to them as "snakes," particularly after they stole an entire herd of horses before hightailing for home.

These "snakes" would later be called the Comanches. Because they were formerly on foot, these Indians' way of life was now revolutionized, as they were suddenly able to follow the herds of buffalo. The Comanche bands abandoned the frigid Rocky Mountains, and by about 1725, these warlike people had swooped down onto the plains, where they finally had enough to eat, and their numbers began to multiply. With their small stature probably contributing to their success as horsemen, Comanches rode to war by the light of the moon, generally in the spring, when the grass grew high enough to support the horses. They quickly became masters of the lightning strike, where they would attack, kill, and take prisoners before returning home, sometimes hundreds of miles away.

When the aggressive Comanches appeared, entire bands, including the Apaches, lords of the plains, were displaced. The Apaches traveled west into New Mexico and Arizona, and some were pushed south to the very edge of the plains. In the process, the Tonkawas were displaced southward. Other plains tribes, such as the Wichita tribe, moved south, into Texas, while the Tawakonis and Wacos settled along the Brazos River.

The Comanches ruled the choicest hunting grounds, and because the buffalo did not venture south of the hill country, the Comanches had no desire to rule south Texas. But what they wanted, they took, and the Spanish were unable to do anything to stop them. The Comanches became arrogant and even boasted that they only permitted the Spanish settlements to remain on the edge of their land to provide them a steady supply of horses.

This was the backstory of Texas. How much young Houston knew of this is unknown.

Sam Runs Away

One morning, Sam Houston did not show up at his job at the Maryville store, and soon the search was on. John and James searched for weeks before finding Sam lying under a tree, reading a book.

Sam was not particularly happy to see his brothers and decided right then that he was not going home. Standing straight, he replied to his brothers that he "preferred measuring deer tracks to tape." No more measuring out dry goods for him. And the "wild liberty of the Red Men" was "better than the tyranny of his own brothers."[10]

While his brothers stood confounded by his words, he finally asked to be left alone, as he was working on a "translation from the Greek," and wished to "read it in peace."

And leave they did, probably assuming he'd be home soon. At least they knew where he was.

In fact, they had found Sam fifty miles southwest of Maryville on a forested island in the Tennessee River. This island was the home of a band of Cherokees, led by a chief named Oolooteka, a tall, middle-aged man whose name meant He-Puts-The-Drum-Away. The war drum, that is. Oolooteka was a peaceful and practical man with a group of contented followers numbering about three hundred.

Oolooteka must have been surprised the day the white man showed up. Well, perhaps not quite a man, being about sixteen summers old, but he was already as tall as the chief himself. This strange youth came armed with a knapsack full of books and guileless but mischievous blue eyes. Many white men looked down on the Red Man as subhuman, but this boy was different. He was curious but respectful.

The chief could not help liking this young man, and when he discovered this boy had lost his father, he adopted Sam Houston as his own and gave him a Cherokee name, the Raven, one of the most respected birds in Cherokee mythology.

return from Quivira
Coronado's army
return of army
route from Arizona
route to Ures
route from Compostala

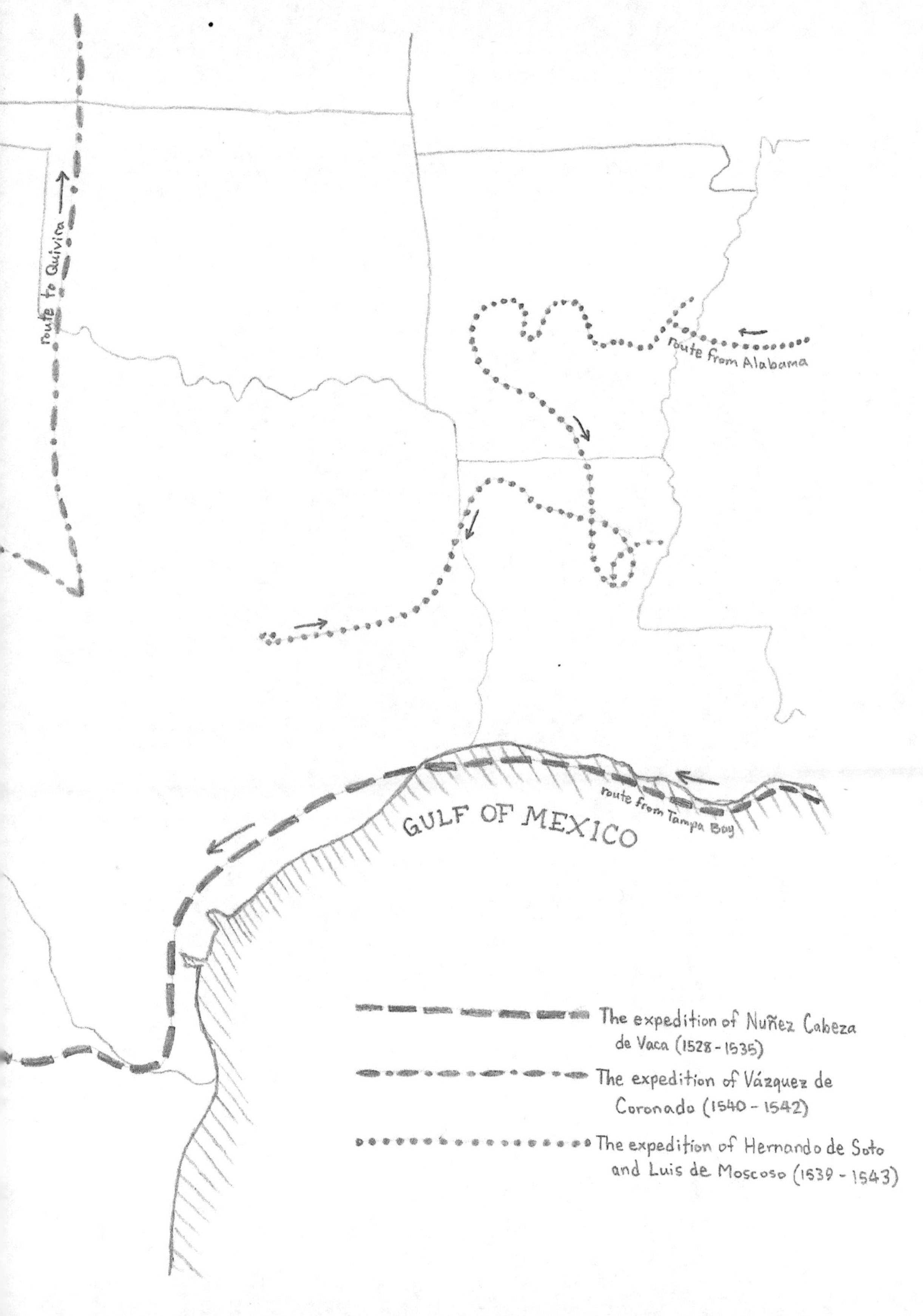
route to Quivira
route from Alabama
route from Tampa Bay
GULF OF MEXICO
The expedition of Nuñez Cabeza de Vaca (1528 - 1535)
The expedition of Vázquez de Coronado (1540 - 1542)
The expedition of Hernando de Soto and Luis de Moscoso (1539 - 1543)

Chapter 3

Celts and Comanches

Julius Caesar stared at the shoreline. A mass of armed men, some in chariots, blocked his soldiers' progress. The natives were hearty and tall, much like the Gauls of mainland Europe. They were the Celts of Britain. He signaled to his men to depart. They couldn't land here.

Modern-day France was settled by these vigorous people. Julius Caesar had a difficult time as he sought to conquer and bring under subjection these "barbarian" races. After Rome had finally succeeded in taming the unruly Gauls, it turned its attention to the isle of Britain. The Celts had prospered here, hunting in the forests and cultivating the fields. The climate was surprisingly mild for a place so far north. Unknown to the inhabitants, an ocean current from the warm Caribbean brought warmth to both the northern and western edges of the European continent.

The tall Celts towered over the Romans, but the legendary discipline of the Roman Army proved effective. Eventually Britain became part of the Roman Empire, except for the mountainous regions to the north and west, and the Celts began to learn Roman ways. Over time, unruly warriors settled down and became both farmers and craftsmen. The gospel made its way to the area, and when the Christians of Rome suffered persecution, the Christian Celts of Britain suffered too.

But the internal decay of the Roman Empire finally caused the structure to come crashing down. The Roman Legions in Britain were needed to keep the peace at home, and after their exit, the Celts were left alone to fend for themselves. Civilized now, they were susceptible to the depredations of the wild men from the hills. In desperation, they asked for government help.

In answer, Rome arranged for Saxon mercenaries, an idea which seemed logical at the time, until the Saxons themselves became a problem, when they took a liking to Britain and began to overrun the island and push the Celts into the mountains.

Early England

A man we call King Arthur lived at that time. We think. Little is known for sure. But in the confusion of Roman retreat, the idea of a heroic king appeals.

His exploits became the subjects of legends, although it is clear that medieval writers embellished them with even greater works of their imaginations.

After the departure of this Celtic warrior-king, the Angles and Saxons prevailed, and while some Celts were absorbed into this society, others fled to the mountains and became the ancestors of modern-day Scots, Welsh, and Irish.

These Germanic peoples—Angles, Saxons, and Jutes—were now the rulers of what eventually became known as Angle-land, or England. Their Germanic language, a cousin of Dutch, became known as English.

At first, these people lived as separate ethnic groups, but because of Norwegian and Danish invasions, they united under a single king, Alfred the Great. But when his descendant, King Edward, died without an heir, England was forced to choose a king.

Initially, an English earl named Harold was crowned king, but William, a cousin of Normandy's King Edward, challenged his claim to the Crown, alleging that Harold had sworn to support William's own bid for the Crown. Supporters took sides, and William's forces defeated Harold's troops at the Battle of Hastings in 1066.

How could William have been both a Norman from the region we now know as France and still have been the King of England? As often happened, royal families from neighboring countries would unite by marriage, and in this case, an English king had gone to Normandy and married the Duke of Normandy's sister. When he was crowned, he already held the title of Duke of Normandy.

William tried his best to be a just and fair king, but he was judged too strict for the Anglo-Saxons, and soon a rebellion broke out. When the battle ended, William took the rebels' land and dispersed it among his noblemen. Because of the Norman influence of that time, French became the accepted language of the courts, while the common people spoke English.

Though English was later restored to its rightful place as the language of

England, the French influence had forever altered it. And though English was declared the official court language in 1362, many French words remained in common use, such as *beauty, fruit,* and *soldier*. Between the early Latin and French influences, fully half of our present English language has a Romance, or Latin-derived, origin.

Over time, the succeeding Norman kings wrote new laws, called the king's laws, administered by circuit judges who traveled regularly to all parts of the country. In this way, the law became universally accepted in all parts of the country and became known as "common law."

The kings shared power with barons who were given their own lands to rule, including access to castles, courts, and legions of fighting men. But over time, the kings asserted more control over the holdings of the barons.

Flaunting his power, King John (1167-1216 A.D.) would presume to punish a baron for breaking the law and then go out and break that same law himself. This was odious to the barons. (At the same time, this king and his minions also got on the nerves of a certain notorious man we now know as Robin Hood, who, in rebellion, made a pointed political statement every time he stole from the king and gave to the poor.)

The barons rose up and demanded that the king obey the same law to which they themselves were subject. This determination gave rise to a document called the Magna Carta, which is Latin for *Great Charter*. It was, in essence, a bill of rights for the barons that made it clear that everyone, including the king, must obey the law. They forced the king to sign it, threatening to fight him if he didn't agree to its terms. Out of this struggle eventually came legal rights, the basis of English law, and later, the American Bill of Rights.

During the Middle Ages, the gospel of Christ spread in various places throughout England and Europe, and Roman Catholics like John Wycliffe and Martin Luther, after searching the Scriptures, found in its passages the truth of salvation through Christ. Wycliffe and later Tyndale translated the Scriptures into English, while Luther translated them into German, so the common people could read the Bible for themselves. There were always some Christians in Europe, but the Reformation—and the invention of movable type by Johannes Gutenberg—finally brought the Word of God to all.

Knowledge of the Word of God single-handedly brought Europe out of the Dark Ages. Feudalism, the class system perpetuated by the powerful on an ignorant and powerless working class, began to crumble.

European Nations Battle for Influence

Two years after Columbus landed in San Salvador, Francis I of France was born. As king, he developed an interest in the New World. This was partially fueled by the capture of a Spanish treasure ship, packed full of gold and silver objects by Cortés as a celebration of the final conquest of Mexico. Could there be similar treasures accessible through the far north passages of this New World?

Francis I found an Italian by the name of Giovanni de Verrazano to play the part of his own personal Columbus. But in his search, Verrazano found no northern passage leading to riches, and in probing the eastern coast, he learned that the Chesapeake was only a bay and not a passage at all.

Ten years later, the French king financed the trip of another explorer, Jacques Cartier, who believed Indian tales of an inland kingdom replete with gold, silver, and spices, and although he did return with some quartz crystals, for the most part, his journey yielded nothing but disappointment.

By the year 1600, the powerful Spanish were well ensconced in the Caribbean and in Florida, and the French were too busy fighting among themselves to send any more expeditions to the north. Meanwhile, however, the French fur trade continued to grow and prosper.

England's First Explorer

At this time in Europe, England, France, and Spain were the most powerful nations. England was in some ways the least influential because it was not as strong militarily. The great British Navy was yet to come.

Spain was prospering because of the gold sent from New Spain, and the Spanish fleet was by now greatly feared. But in 1588, in a conflict with Britain, the Spanish Armada was defeated, not so much by British ships as by a providential storm that suddenly crippled the fleet and opened the Atlantic to the lesser powers of Britain, France, and Holland.

By this time, the English were very interested in the New World. In 1580, the infamous sea pirate, Francis Drake, returned from a voyage around the world. Because he had received a privateering commission from Queen Elizabeth, it was considered legal and proper by the English government when he plundered Spanish treasure ships in the West Indies.

Because he brought back so much treasure, his ship, the *Golden Hind*, barely made it into port. The queen rewarded him with a knighthood, which is why we now know him as *Sir* Francis Drake.

Drake's voyage helped to engrave in the minds of Englishmen the idea that America was a land dripping with gold and precious stones. Sir Francis Drake was a Robin Hood, an English hero. But the common man may not have been as interested in gold as in land, which represented opportunity. Because England was limited in space, the sober English saw land as the real wealth of the New World.

The Role of Christianity

During that time, Christians dreamed of the wilderness for an entirely different reason: to escape religious persecution. It is difficult for modern-day Americans to imagine a world without religious freedom, but even in our world today, some Communist and Islamic countries expect their citizens to espouse the state religion, and no independent thinking or worship is allowed without terrible consequences.

Merry old England of Pilgrim days was a difficult place for "Separatists," who had separated from the "established," or state, church. Back then, most believed that the civil government should support true religion. Now, this might sound good in theory, but in practice, it resulted in horrors like the Spanish Inquisition, where all who refused to adhere to the teachings of the state religion were tortured or killed.

Protestants were those who protested against the unscriptural abuses of the Roman Catholic Church, which at one point controlled all of Britain and Europe. But these Protestants, Catholics converted to Christ, did not abandon all their Catholic traditions, but continued to baptize infants, and often believed the government should take the role in the promotion of the gospel and the restraint of scriptural error.

King Henry VIII, a licentious English monarch, proclaimed himself head of the English Church, repudiating the authority of the pope over his subjects. He wanted more liberty to divorce and remarry, and in the process, created what is now known as the Anglican Church.

But the basic situation remained the same, with nearly all the respectable people attending the Anglican Church, where things like tithing and observing the Lord's Day, which Christians today regard as a matter of personal faith and practice, were codified into civil law during that time in England.

And though the English were terrified of the idea of another Spanish Inquisition, they could not grasp the fact that the difference between their state religion and that of Spain was only a matter of degree. It was still an enforced religion without personal liberty. In fact, John Bunyan wrote *The Pilgrim's*

Progress from the New Bedford jail, where he was sent for preaching without a license.

Because of this situation, the churches were full of hypocrites. Godly Puritan preachers preached sermons against hypocrisy, trying their best to convict the unconverted of their sin. These *Puritans* were so labeled because they attempted to purify the assemblies of unbiblical doctrine and practice. The Separatists were Puritans who decided it was impossible. They thought it was time to obey the command, "Come out of her, my people, that ye be not partakers of her sins, and that ye receive not of her plagues." (Rev. 18:14)

Like Baptists, these groups chose to gather in illegal, independent assemblies. To escape punishment, some fled to Holland, and others ultimately made the famous trip to the New World on the *Mayflower*.

Later, a group of Puritans did the same, led by John Winthrop, an astute man who brought the royal charter along with him, thus relocating the seat of their government to the New World.

Six Flags over Texas

Texas, ruled by Spaniards. But today there's a place called Six Flags over Texas. *Six?* What other countries lay claim to this region?

A possible conversation at Six Flags: "What are those six flags?"

"Well, there's Old Glory, the Stars and Stripes, that's number one. There's our own Lone Star flag, that's number two. That third one is the Confederate Stars and Bars. If you remember, Texas was part of the Confederacy over Sam Houston's protests and dark prophesies, but that's getting ahead of the story. The fourth one is the Mexican flag, and number five is the Spanish flag."

"So what's the sixth flag?"

French Settlements

French fishermen had broken the trail, so to speak, to North America. Furs, over time, became more interesting than cod, and soon French trappers and traders were established in what is now known as Canada. The furs being harvested from the forests of eastern Canada became a big enough business that even the government took an active interest.

King Henry VI gave the fur trade monopoly to Samuel Champlain, who took it upon himself to map rivers, evaluate the lands they traversed for farming potential, and learn whether any of these rivers flowed from a legendary inland sea.

In 1603, when Champlain embarked on his journey of exploration, the idea of a shortcut to Asia was not quite dead. Speculations abounded. Perhaps there was a Northwest Passage that cut through to the riches of the East Indies. An inland sea could certainly have been part of such geographical imaginations. In our day of GEOS satellites, we laugh, but in 1603, an expedition into the interior of Canada was as far-fetched as a trip to the moon.

Champlain founded Quebec. He worked in alliance with the Algonquin and Huron Indians and sided with them in their conflicts with the Iroquois, the tribe Champlain judged to be the most hostile toward white settlement. This Frenchman understood the secret to successful colonization: men and women who would come for keeps, learning about the new land and working with the natives. Two centuries later, Stephen F. Austin would discover similar principles regarding Texas.

Ironically, New France suffered much in its early years, both from internal squabbling and from the Iroquois, who, in alliance with several other tribes, became known as the Five Nations or the Iroquois League. This powerful league then set about trying to destroy the French settlements. France, now the political and cultural leader of Europe, hurriedly sent help. But the Iroquois were not defeated until 1665, when a certain Marquis de Tracy arrived and decided to wage what was called "total warfare" on these Indians.

Tracy descended upon the Indians when their crops were ripe. He and his soldiers burned the fields and villages, destroying all that they had, shattering the power of the Iroquois. And just in time to pave the way for another explorer by the name of La Salle.

La Salle

Strange as it may seem, a bronze statue of Sieur de La Salle stands alone in the middle of the small town of Navasota, Texas. What on earth is this noble Frenchman of the seventeenth century doing standing across from the stores and used car lots of a Texas town? Well, this happens to be the exact spot where his companions got tired of him and killed him. And even more ironically, it seems he was in Texas by mistake.

La Salle was the explorer who claimed the entire Mississippi watershed for France. He arrived in New France just after the Iroquois problem had been settled, and prepared to explore western lands, for the benefit of both the fur trade and of France. He endured many hardships but finally made it all the way to the mouth of the Mississippi River, where he raised a cross and planted the banner of France, naming the whole region "Louisiana" after King Louis of France.

Returning to France, La Salle was able to convince King Louis to finance another expedition, and in 1684, he set sail, intending to arrive at the mouth of the Mississippi. Poor navigation landed him on the Texas coast. Now lost, he and his men wandered about, trying to make their way back to the Mississippi, but they never made it. While they were there, they built Fort St. Louis, and not long afterward, the inhabitants were killed in an Indian raid.

La Salle's last journey was tragic, but his explorations did have a lasting effect. Louisiana was claimed for France, and not just in name only. French traders and trappers settled along the Mississippi and made friends with the Indians. The next century would see the *French and Indian War* against the Anglo colonists. And French names and pronunciations lingered. Baton Rouge. St. Genevieve. Low Freight. *Low Freight?* This place started out being called L'eau Froid (cold water), but the name was repeatedly mispronounced, and the name stuck.

And what about Chicago? How is it pronounced? More French influence. And of course, the city of New Orleans, with its famous French Quarter.

And the lasting effect on Texas? Well, the eastern part was considered part of the Louisiana Territory, which was much too close to suit the Spanish, who retaliated by erecting a string of Spanish missions all the way from San Antonio to Nacogdoches, a town in modern-day East Texas.

Early American—and Texas—history is the history of Europeans colonizing a new land, where they named these new colonies New England, New France, and New Spain.

In the same way, European problems became American problems. Or sometimes, America was the solution for a European problem, like the persecution of Christians. We know that the English Pilgrims came to the New World for exactly this reason, but they were not the only ones fleeing religious persecution.

During the 1500s, the Reformation came to France, and many who were being taught falsehoods by the Roman Catholic Church embraced the truth of the gospel of grace. These French Christians were called *Huguenots* and served as a rebuke to a country where the state religion was Catholicism, and individual religious freedom was unheard of.

When these Christians, in turn, began sharing the gospel, France was thrown into a state of political and religious chaos. Finally, in desperation, King Henry IV issued the Edict of Nantes in 1685, guaranteeing Protestants freedom of religion within certain French cities. But the next king, Louis XIV, cancelled the Edict of Nantes and sent his armies after the Huguenots. During this time, more than

400,000 Huguenots fled France for other destinations. Many ended up in North America.

This was the beginning of the end for France. Just as Spain had reached a pinnacle of power in the 1500s and then declined in power, so too France began to lose her position as the ruling power of Europe.

The next king, Louis XIV's great-grandson, Louis XV, was crowned in 1715. He cared more about personal pleasure than the good of France, and consequently, made a very poor ruler. In time, France fought and lost the French and Indian War (1754-1763). In 1763, at the signing of the Treaty of Paris, France gave Louisiana back to Spain, which possessed this large territory until it was returned to France in 1800.

But the France of Napoleon did not possess Louisiana for very long before selling it back to the United States in 1803. France, at that time, needed money more than land after helping finance the American colonists in the Revolutionary War. In fact, the war effort depleted the stores of the French government to the point of bankruptcy. In the end, the French flag flew over the city of New Orleans for less than a month.

By this time, the power of Spain had waned as well. Spain had built an empire in the New World, but by 1800, its foundations were crumbling, as its possessions sought and gained independence.

When Americans looked at the political situation of Latin America, they saw a power vacuum, because Spain was no longer the world power she once was, and the newly formed independent countries were initially very fragile and unstable.

Since La Salle had originally claimed Texas for France during his explorations, many considered Texas to be part of the vast Louisiana Purchase, which had been obtained from France for $15 million. Jefferson wanted the Rio Grande to be the border of this territory, but when this did not work out, a treaty was finally made with Spain, trading our claim to Texas for Spain's claim to Florida.

But there were vigorous westward-looking Americans who still thought that Texas belonged to the United States. Or ought to.

Sam Houston's Favorite Job

One hundred dollars. In 1812, one hundred dollars was a lot of money, especially when you owed it. Sam Houston was barely nineteen at the time, and as a result of various small gifts purchased for his Indian friends at the Maryville store, he was $100 in debt. His proposition of employment for the repayment of that debt brought sudden smiles to many faces.

Sam, a teacher? Was this the same Sam Houston who had failed as a student now proposing to open a primary school?

These were the days before public schools, when an education was a cash proposition. Well, maybe not totally, at least in this case. Sam asked for one-third of the eight-dollar fee in cash, one-third in corn, and one-third in calico. This was a substantial sum for primary school tuition. The secondary school in the area, called The Academy, charged only fifteen dollars.

But Sam had brought both his Bible and *The Iliad* to the woods with him and had already read every book available for miles. Later in life, he would regret his lack of formal education, but the fact was, he could recite from memory portions of all twenty-four books of *The Iliad*, a fact garnering the respect of the denizens of Blount County. Though at first only a few pupils showed up, this unconventional professor was eventually forced to turn away many applicants.

Five miles east of Maryville, a log cabin in a clearing on John McCulloch's farm served as the schoolhouse. An oak tree shaded a spring of water nearby. The term began after corn planting in May, and with a break for the wheat harvest in July, stretched to the corn gathering in November, when Sam was finally able to repay his debt.

Years afterward, while swapping yarns on a steamboat crossing Galveston Bay, an old army comrade reminded General Houston that he had been the governor of one state, a United States senator from another, the Commander-in-Chief of the Army, and the president of a Republic. Which office had afforded him the greatest pride?

"Well, Burke," replied Sam Houston, "when a young man in Tennessee I kept a country school, being then about eighteen years of age, and a tall, strapping fellow. At noon after luncheon, which I and my pupils ate together out of our baskets, I would go into the woods and cut me a 'sour wood' stick, trim it careful in circular spirals and thrust one half of it into the fire, which would turn it blue, leaving the other half white. With this emblem of ornament and authority in my hand, dressed in a hunting-shirt of flowered calico, a long queue down my back, and the sense of authority over my pupils, I experience a higher feeling of dignity and self-satisfaction than from any other office or honor which I have since held" [1]

After his stint as a teacher, Sam Houston attended Porter Academy as a pupil. His experience shepherding his own students did not seem to help him much as a student, for his teacher described him as the most provoking student he had ever had. Dr. Isaac Anderson related, "I often determined to lick him, but he would come up with such a pretty dish of excuses I could not do it."[2]

But Sam did not stay in school long. In March of 1813, he stood on a corner in Maryville watching a recruiting demonstration for the army. The British were at it again. The War of 1812 was the result, and the governor had called for volunteers.

"Those having no rifles of their own . . .will be furnished by the State to the extent of the supply on hand. . . .It is desired to avoid the use of smooth-bore muskets as much as possible. They . . .do not carry straight. They may be good enough for Regular soldiers, but not the Citizen Volunteers of Tennessee. . . ."[3]

These volunteers were recruited during the summer of 1812, but had so far seen no action. And though Sam heard about the situation at that time, he had continued to teach in his school. But now, just after his twentieth birthday, the Regular Army was again recruiting, providing white pantaloons and waistcoats for every volunteer. For whatever reason, Houston stepped up to the drumhead and picked up a silver dollar, the token for enlistment.

Being underage, Sam had to obtain his mother's signature. Upon giving her consent, she gave him a gold ring, engraved on the inside with the single word, *honor*. So prized was the ring that he wore it until the day of his death.

Elizabeth Houston also made him a more practical gift, saying, "My son, take this musket and never disgrace it. For remember, I had rather all my sons should fill one honorable grave than that one of them should turn his back to save his life. Go, and remember, too, that while the door of my cabin is open to brave men, it is eternally shut against cowards."[4]

Sam did not commit these words to paper until years later, but they were a strict commentary on the weight his mother gave to the ring.

The War of 1812

There was a sort of rivalry between the volunteers and the regular army. In addition, Sam received some resistance from friends and family because he had enlisted in the common ranks. Didn't the son of Major Samuel Houston deserve a commission? But young Sam refused to back down, saying, "And what have your craven souls to say about the ranks? I would much sooner honor the ranks than disgrace an appointment. You don't know me now, but you shall hear of me."[5]

. . .

This was his first recorded speech. But he did not stay in the ranks for long. He became a drill sergeant after thirty days and was commissioned as an ensign, the lowest grade officer, a few months later, before being sent to the 39th Infantry. It would be almost a full year before Sam had an opportunity to prove his boast.

The War of 1812 was a kind of coda, or postscript, to the Revolutionary War. Even years after America had won her independence, Britain still had a hard time adjusting to the idea that the colonists were no longer colonists, but citizens of another country. American seamen were being impressed and made to serve on His Majesty's ships. But this war was not solely against the British, because as it soon became evident, the British were inciting certain Indian tribes to attack American settlers. When General Andrew Jackson observed that the rifle of a slain Indian possessed the imprint of a British manufacturer, he became incensed.

It did not take much persuasion to involve the Indians, as by now they had their own long list of grievances. The American government had promised much of what was now the State of Alabama to the Creek Indians, but that treaty was not being honored. With arms supplied by the British, a vengeful half-breed named Bill Weatherford led a war party in an attack on a stockade full of frightened settlers in August of 1813. The Indians prevailed and scalped four hundred white men.

Andrew Jackson took a large contingent of the Tennessee militia and tracked down Weatherford, but after a couple of successful engagements, Jackson ran into difficulties. Home-grown militiamen tended to run off when things got rough. Jackson was glad when he heard the 39th Infantry was on its way. The militia needed discipline, and this would help.

When the 39th Infantry arrived, 360 strong, Ensign Sam Houston was in command of one of the platoons. Both groups would now be under the command of General Jackson, and shortly, he would have an assignment for them.

John Woods was a fiery-tempered recruit at seventeen, who had only been part of the militia for a month. One night, this young private drew guard duty right about the time the 39th arrived on the scene. All during the cold and rainy night, he stood sentry until finally morning came. Because he was hungry, Woods obtained permission to leave his post to get something to eat, and while eating, an officer came by and told him to clean up the mess he was making.

Comprised of men of independent spirit, insubordination was a common occurrence in the militia, and a now-irate Woods refused this order outright, and was not the least shy about showing his fury. The officer ordered him arrested, and Woods threatened to shoot the first man who laid a hand on him. Shortly, news of the ruckus reached the ears of General Jackson.

"Where is the— rascal? Shoot him!" he shouted, storming out of his tent.[6]

Perhaps this got the attention of the young offender, for he now willingly submitted to arrest. But just when everyone thought that was the end of it, that maybe he would get sent home for insubordination, the unthinkable happened, making an impression no one would ever forget.

Because General Jackson was regular army, he had absolutely no use for rebellion in the ranks, and only days later, ordered the offender to be shot by a firing squad. The effect on the troops was described as *salutary*.

This was Sam Houston's first exposure to the famous general, a man who would greatly influence him and prove to be a key player in the story of Texas.

The Battle of Horseshoe Bend

Not long after this incident, the troops set out to hunt down Bill Weatherford. Cherokee scouts, including Sam Houston's friends, John and James Rogers, went on ahead until they reached a bend in the Tallapoosa River, called Horseshoe Bend, where Weatherford and the Creeks had decided to entrench themselves. Natural gullies, timber, and brush provided a good defensive position, and Weatherford improved it by ordering his men to construct breastworks out of logs. Jackson arrived with 2,000 troops, but waited to attack until the Indian women and children had been evacuated.

Taking a huge risk, the infantry charged, approaching and then scaling the breastworks, all while exposed to enemy fire.

With rifles aimed at them through holes in the redoubt, the first to scale the ramparts was courageous Major Lemuel P. Montgomery, who was killed in the fray. His name lives on in the capital city of Alabama.

Behind him charged Ensign Sam Houston, who vaulted over the barrier and plunged straight into desperate combat. His platoon soon followed and found him surrounded by Indians, beating them off with his sword. He was covered with blood when his men finally managed to overpower their enemies. A barbed arrow stuck out of Sam's upper thigh, and no matter how he tried, he could not remove it. He asked a nearby lieutenant to help, but the man had no better luck. Desperate and in pain, the tall ensign threatened his superior officer with his sword and told him to pull with all his might. When he complied, the arrowhead exited the wound with a gush of blood.

Houston lay on the ground, trying to calm himself. Even after the wound had been treated, it was clear that it might never heal completely. At this point, General Jackson rode by. He inquired about Houston's injury and ordered the ensign not to return to battle. But the impetuous youth had boasted that Maryville would hear of him, and he later admitted that it was for this reason he disobeyed the order.

Jackson's men were clearly winning the battle, except for a small band of Indians holding out at the bottom of a ravine. Jackson promised to spare their lives if they would agree to surrender, but they flatly refused. When the general asked for volunteers to storm this final stronghold, no one responded at first. Then Ensign Houston stepped up and called his men to follow him. They charged the heavily defended position, where rifles stuck out of holes in the wall. While he and his men were under fire, Sam's right arm was shattered by a ball; then he was hit in the right shoulder. And though he tried valiantly to rally his men, they fled, leaving him to climb out of the ravine alone. At the top, he collapsed, and next, General Jackson conquered the Creek stronghold using flaming arrows to burn it to the ground.

"Take a pull," the doctor might have commanded. Liquor was the only anesthetic available, but it was not enough, and two muscular aides had to hold Sam down so the surgeon could operate.

A brush fire provided the only illumination when the laceration in his thigh was dressed and his arm was splinted. Then the surgeons attempted to remove the ball that had punctured his shoulder.

"He's not going to live anyway," one may have murmured to the other. "He's lost too much blood." Resigned, they quit trying to fish out the lead and left the strapping twenty-one-year-old on the wet ground to die.

Against great odds, he somehow survived that dreadful night, but was too weak to stand in the morning, and had to be removed on a litter. It would be two months before he reached his mother's home, during which time he received little in the way of medical care. His food was coarse, and he was delirious a good part of that time. In light of the poor care and the seriousness of his injuries, it is a wonder that he survived at all.

When he arrived home, two companions helped him up the path to the front door. When Elizabeth answered the door, she was shocked at the appearance of this gaunt, ill young man. Could it really be her son?

"Don't you recognize me, Ma?" Sam asked in a weak voice.

His mother finally recognized him after looking in his eyes.[7]

Sam was taken to a doctor in Knoxville, who after one glance, refused to treat him. The practical Scotsman said it was unnecessary to run up a bill when he would not live more than a few days. Sam found a place to stay and returned to see the doctor two weeks later, at which time he finally consented to care for the young man.

As a convalescent now on leave, Houston heard of the glorious victory General Jackson won over the British at New Orleans; his former commander was now being called the "Hero of New Orleans." Finally, the war was over.

Now promoted to second lieutenant as a result of his courage at Horseshoe Bend, Houston was slowly gaining strength but still had not recovered. He was transferred to New Orleans in 1815, where an army surgeon, concerned about his shoulder, decided the musket ball needed to be removed.

Surgery consisted of whiskey, a firm grip on the back of a chair, and the surgeon's knife. Blood ran down Houston's arm as the doctor searched for the elusive lead ball. At last, it was removed, but the blood loss weakened Sam and forced him to spend the following winter in the barracks, where his full-time occupation was reading. His mother had given him a Bible, and he also soaked up *Pilgrim's Progress, Robinson Crusoe,* and *The Vicar of Wakefield.*

Slowly, Sam recovered, confused now that the war was over. But because General Jackson had not forgotten the hero of Horseshoe Bend, a new task soon awaited him.

Chapter 4

Men of Destiny

A Memorandum How To Feed A Cock
Before You Him Fight
Take and give him some Pickle Beaf cut fine...[1]

REVEREND CUMMINGS STARED at this composition, which a boarding student had so diligently copied onto the last page of his Latin exercise book. The student in question, a blue-eyed, red-haired twelve-year-old, nervously glanced at a certain willow switch that hung nearby. This lad's mother hoped to see her son trained to preach the gospel. This youngest of three sons seemed to be the brightest.

Reverend Cummins may have wondered at times at the sensibility of the widow's desire, seeing as this scrawny boy not only had no desire for said profession, but in truth, was as annoying as an unmanageable colt. Like now, for instance.

"Andrew Jackson—!" But just then an interruption claimed Cummins' attention, and the switch was forgotten. There were interruptions these days. The year was 1779.

Young Andrew Jackson and the Road to Revolution

Three years earlier, in 1776, a rider had come to the small settlement of Waxhaws, South Carolina. Then nine-year-old Andy Jackson, a good reader for his age, had been chosen to read the manuscript carried by a rider to the local inhabitants who had assembled to hear it.

"In Congress, July fourth, 1776, a Declaration by the Representatives of the United States of America, in General Congress Assembled . . .

"We hold these truths to be self-evident, that all men are created equal, that they are endowed by their Creator with certain unalienable rights . . . "

Andy struggled with the long, unfamiliar words.

"That among these are life, liberty, and the pursuit of happiness . . . "

The middle part was a list of grievances against King George III. Everybody knew that he and his minions were bad guys. Well, everybody, that is, but the Tories.

"Nor have we been wanting in attentions to our British brethren. We have warned them from time to time of attempts by their legislature to extend an unwarrantable Jurisdiction over us."

Did little Andy comprehend what he was reading? Maybe not all of it, but he did have the sense that those nasty British were doing things they ought not to do.

Undoubtedly, his audience hung on his every word as he concluded, "And for the support of this Declaration, with a firm reliance on the protection of divine Providence, we mutually pledge to each other our lives, our fortunes, and our sacred honor."

Since that time three summers ago, the war had been an underlying fact of life, but in the remote countryside of South Carolina, there was little to fear. Charleston, a busy port and the largest city, was over a hundred miles away from the fighting. And who cared about little Waxhaws? Surely no one would bother innocent farmers.

Opinions on the subject varied widely. Some of the villagers were Tories, who believed that revolution was rebellion against God. Romans 13 instructs the Christian to obey magistrates. Yet many Christians felt their legal rights were being trampled upon, and they were not required to suffer illegal tyranny. Technically, Parliament had no jurisdiction over them; the colonies were directly under the authority of the Crown.

Some people didn't know what to think, and others just didn't care. Some, especially men of wealth, were struggling under the recent acts of Parliament: restraint of trade, a tax on documents, an increase in British export taxes, and the ultimate insult, that infamous tax on tea: three pence per pound.

The rest had been major annoyances, but the tea tax was the last straw. Would a sane man rebel against the strongest nation on earth for the sake of three cents a pound on tea? No, that would make no sense, except that it was the tipping point in a long-standing and bitter conflict.

It is amazing to consider how willing the colonists were to give up their favorite beverage to make a point. Some ships sailed back to England full of tea, unable to offload it or sell it in the hostile colonial ports. In Boston, things got even more interesting, when men dressed like Indians dumped the British imports into the Boston Harbor. Hence the phrase, the "Boston Tea Party."

What made the colonists so passionate on this subject? This is an important question, because the answer is basically the same one that caused Texas to take up arms against Mexican authority sixty years later.

The thirteen colonies were not all the same. The culture of South Carolina was different from that of Maryland, which was different from that of the New England states. Nowadays, rapid communication and transportation probably tend to make us more homogenous than we otherwise would be. But at that time, each colony was unique due to the diverse nature of its settlers and their divergent opinions. Even slavery was a hotly debated issue back then.

But the colonies had some important things in common. One was the Christian faith. Not everyone was converted, but at least, most people attended church and believed God was the supreme deity. In fact, at certain times and places, churches were full of unconverted people, just like today. But in the 1740s, the "Great Awakening" began to revive sleeping churches all over the eastern seaboard, and comfortable churchgoers were shocked to realize that only the pleasure of God kept them from the damnation of hell.

Jonathan Edwards' sermon entitled "Sinners in the Hands of an Angry God," which he delivered in a quiet and composed manner (he read his sermons), did not awaken his hearers to the truth. The Holy Spirit did. And George Whitefield preached the simple gospel to thousands who gathered in farm fields when hostile clergymen denied him access to their pulpits.

But these two men were not the only ones used by God in the 1740s and thereafter. There were others, most not nearly so famous, who brought the gospel afresh to the New World, not only saving souls, but also transforming Christian thought and influence throughout the thirteen colonies. This had the effect of strengthening the second thing the colonies had in common—the belief in the rule of law.

The Rule of Law

What is meant by the *rule of law?* Well, by what is a Christian ruled? By the Word of God. A well-instructed Christian understands that when he listens to preaching or instruction, he must compare what he hears to the Word of God. No matter how much he may respect and submit to a pastor, he knows that ultimately his submission is to God and no one else. When two Christians disagree, the Scripture serves as the referee to which both must submit.

Today in the United States, the Constitution and the related body of laws serve as the referee. No man has absolute authority in and of himself, as did the ancient kings of the Medes and Persians. Now we look *above* man to a *higher* authority. Do you see how this "rule of law" is highly compatible with Christian principles?

Since the signing of the Magna Carta, during the days of Robin Hood, the English had had a long tradition of the rule of law. Englishmen knew they had rights, just as the Apostle Paul insisted on his rights as a Roman citizen (Acts 22:25-29). And since the colonists believed themselves to be Englishmen, that meant they also held the rights of Englishmen.

So what was it that engendered this conflict that finally broke out into bloodshed?

When the colonies were first founded, they were under very little rule and control by the British Crown. The first colonies, in fact, struggled for their mere existence. Think of it this way. If your entire neighborhood were dumped with provisions and tools onto an unfamiliar and deserted coastline on foreign soil, how do you think you would manage?

Hard work and mutual aid were necessary simply for survival. Under these conditions, the local government of the colonies was the only real government the colonists had, and the style of the government tended to be different than that of England. Even in the more aristocratic southern colonies, things tended to be a little more egalitarian than across the Atlantic. The Virginia colony was forced to form a legislative body called the House of Burgesses, when an inept but honest governor, Sir George Yeardley, admitted he needed help. London sent instructions that he should select two men from each borough to come to Jamestown, which was the seat of Virginia government in 1619.

This British-style governing body, patterned after the English Parliament, sweated out six days of summer heat in 1619, and accomplished several legislative purposes. They imposed the first American tax: ten pounds of tobacco from every male over sixteen. This helped to encourage even "gentlemen unused to labor" to become accustomed to working.

You see, the early American colonists, even in the aristocratic South, did not have the luxury of supporting an indolent upper class. The common need to survive tended to be a great leveler; hard-working men who were servants in England rose to prosperity and station. Your father or grandfather may have been a titled landowner back in England, but that didn't count for much in the colonies. Yes, there were "classes:" wealthy landowners at the top and indentured servants and slaves at the bottom. But except for the African slaves, a person's station was not determined by birth and could, with hard work, be changed. As Americans, we think this is normal and *the way things ought to be.*

British society possessed a more rigid class system. One rather haughty English visitor to Virginia made the comment in 1662 that not much should be expected from the Burgesses, for "they are usually such as went over servants thither, and though by time and industry they may have attained competent estates, yet by their poor and mean education they are unskilful in judging of a good estate either of Church or Commonwealth."[2] Good breeding was important in Britain, but industry—what a man did—became the deciding factor for success in the colonies.

Although Britain and her colonies were now on a divergent course, the deciding factor leading to the American Revolution was the fact that these colonists had, from the beginning, been fundamentally independent of direct British rule and taxation. Much of the "government" that affected them was locally elected. It is interesting to note that the members of the Virginia House of Burgesses were elected by the inhabitants, or those who lived there, and not by property owners, as had been the case in England.

It was not that the colonists esteemed the ideology of democracy. Rather, they feared it. Remember the French Revolution? "Liberté, Égalité, Fraternité?" In the end, it was clear that mob rule had led to the bloodbath in that unfortunate country.

It was in the American colonies where the feudal system of Europe was finally dismantled. Except for the African slaves, there was no peasant class. Even the lowliest farmers were expected to be well-informed and responsible citizens.

When Great Britain, trying to recover from the expense of the French and Indian War, attempted to get the colonies to help out by levying taxes on themselves, the passionate reaction of the colonists took the mother country by surprise. While it's true that the colonists thought of themselves as Englishmen, especially regarding their legal rights, emotionally, they regarded themselves as an independent, self-governing people who felt hard-pressed to accept the idea of British taxes. And to be taxed without representation—the colonies were not represented in Parliament, which had passed all these noxious tax laws—was a fundamental injustice, keenly felt by citizens who were, by now, accustomed to having a voice in their own affairs.

The enforcement of an unjust—and unaccustomed—rule was the ultimate cause of both the American and Texan Revolutions.

The Making of a General—and a President

Reverend Cummins, as it turned out, was not such a bad guy after all. He allowed Andy and his schoolmates to "drill" after school, using sticks for guns. They fought mock battles and soon elected Andy as their captain. He seemed to be good at strategy in their war games, and like someone you'd like to follow and obey.

But after a year, things stopped being all fun and games when Andy's brother Hugh died from wounds suffered in a battle at Stono Ferry, near Charleston. By now, Redcoats were advancing farther into South Carolina, led by General Cornwallis and a cruel officer named Tarleton, who burned homes and barns, stealing cattle, raiding and destroying everything that hindered their forward movement.

One day, a rider galloped into the settlement at Waxhaws. He quickly related the news that the Redcoats had surprised the colonial militia just ten miles southeast of town. From what he said, many had been killed or wounded, and the wounded were being taken to a nearby church now turned infirmary.

Mrs. Jackson told her boys to gather sheets, blankets, water buckets, and candles. They rushed to load the wagon and drove to the church, where they met several other women who also came to tend to the injured.

Andrew never forgot this first taste of war. Some of the wounded were dying while others cried out in pain. Thankfully, neither his Uncle Robert nor his Uncle James had been hurt. All throughout the night, Andy stayed by his mother's side while she cared for the injured and dying.

Eventually, the fiery teen was able to do something purposeful for the war effort, serving as a mounted orderly for the militia major, delivering messages to various places in the backcountry.

One day, he delivered a message and was on the way home when he spotted riders coming up the road. Redcoats! Suddenly, fourteen-year-old Andy found himself in the middle of a battle between the British and the colonial militia, amid dust, horses, gunfire, and slashing swords. Andy grabbed a rifle that had fallen to the ground, but a British officer knocked it from his hands, before calling a retreat. He ordered his men to scatter and hide.

Andy leaped into the saddle and rode off, with the British close on his heels. He headed for the creek, where his horse splashed through the water, but he could not shake the pursuing British soldiers. In a clever move, he dismounted, slapped his horse, whispering to her to go home, and ducked into the densest part of the woods, where he hid until the soldiers finally ceased searching for him.

Andy and his older brother Rob made their way to neighboring Tom Crawford's house to tell Tom's wife that her husband had been captured by the British.

But suddenly, there was loud pounding on the door and the Redcoats broke into the house. There was no time to hide, before eight red-coated men carrying sabers entered, led by a tall, cruel-looking officer, who ordered his men to ransack the cabin. Unable to keep still, Andrew protested.

"Hold your tongue, you impudent young rebel!" shouted the officer. "Take that rag in your hands, and get down on your knees and clean my boots."

"I won't! You've made me a prisoner of war, and I expect you to treat me like one."[3] Young Jackson stood by what was known as the "rule of law."

Demanding compliance, the cruel officer raised his sword. When Andy once again refused, the sword abruptly sliced through the air, and blood streamed from the teenager's head, leaving a scar on his forehead that remained until the day he died.

His brother Rob caught a sword blow to his shoulder; taken to a prison camp, they both ended up suffering from smallpox. They were released through a prisoner exchange when two British prisoners were traded for the brothers. But Rob, still in the throes of smallpox, died shortly after his release, leaving Andy as his mother's only surviving son. And if that weren't bad enough, more grief was soon to come.

Within months, his mother, who had gone to Charleston to care for some sick neighbors in a British prison, was stricken with a fever and perished, leaving Andrew Jackson an orphan at fourteen.

Uncles and neighbors had their hands full with a wild teen, who liked cockfights and horse racing better than study and work. But after several years, even Andy realized that he needed to settle down and find a profession. After a time, he finally settled on studying the law. In those days, a law student did not go to college but studied under an attorney until he was ready to take what was called "the bar exam." This Jackson did, and afterward headed for Nashville. At the time, Tennessee was not yet a state. In fact, it was only sparsely settled in the years immediately following the American Revolution.

Over the years, Andrew Jackson gained a not undeserved reputation as a hot-tempered man, though his sense of right and fairness also earned him respect. He loved children, and though he and his wife Rachel never had any children of their own, they adopted and fostered several little ones, including an Indian boy whose mother was killed in the war.

General Jackson had long wanted a fair fight with the British, ever since his injury by the cruel British officer, and he finally got his chance in New Orleans when the War of 1812 began. Jackson prayed that God would help them, and when the British Army was routed in a great victory, he went to a church the next day to give thanks to God.

The second war with the British was now over. In fact, the treaty had been signed even before the Battle of New Orleans began, but that didn't seem to stop people from cheering Jackson as the "Hero of New Orleans!"

The great General Jackson was a family man at heart, but he was not often able to enjoy his family for long. Troubles arose in Georgia when Indians from Florida began making raids across the border into Georgia, robbing and killing its citizens. Florida was a Spanish territory, but for some reason, the Spanish governor didn't seem to be able to solve the problem. As a result, General Jackson was sent to deal with the Indians, hoping to end the matter without causing an international incident.

Eventually, the governments of the U.S. and Spain came to an agreement in 1819, when the United States agreed to give up its claim to Texas in exchange for ownership of Florida. For a brief time, Jackson was assigned to serve as Governor of Florida before once again returning to the Hermitage, the home he had built for his family in Tennessee.

He had fought digestive troubles ever since the campaign against the Creeks, and he was delighted to be back at home with his family. While at home, he planted cotton, and though he owned slaves, he treated them well and called them "family." He even helped build a small church in the area, though he did not claim to be a Christian. His wife, however, was a faithful, kind and godly woman, and when she died, Jackson treasured her Bible.

Sam Houston's Early Political Career

Washington City. What a sight. Some people thought Pierre L'Enfant was crazy. This Frenchman had been commissioned by George Washington to design the capital city of the new republic. Unfortunately, not everyone appreciated L'Enfant's grand design. In the end, a modification was made to his plan, but in 1818, the word *grand* was not descriptive of the capital, where ugly red brick buildings sprouted up along wide, muddy avenues.

Lieutenant Sam Houston arrived in Washington with an entourage of Indians on February 5, 1818. One Indian elder, a man by the name of Tahlhontusky, held a place of honor within the group. He was the older brother of Oolooteka, Sam's Cherokee foster father.

This man was the chief of a group of Cherokees that wished to secede from the Cherokee Nation and be recognized independently. But their true difficulties were not with the Cherokees, but with the U.S. government. Treaty details were not being honored, and this group was suffering, a not uncommon occurrence, unfortunately. Tahlhontusky came to Washington to plead his case with President Monroe. Houston was an Indian subagent, in peacetime serving both his country and his Indian brothers. Jackson had recommended Sam for the post, recognizing his unique qualifications.

Earlier, Sam Houston had earned the thanks of Tennessee Governor McMinn, for convincing Oolooteka's band to relocate to an area on the Arkansas River. A treaty had been signed in 1816 by a small group of Cherokee chiefs, but many of the tribal chiefs had not been consulted, and the Indians with whom Sam Houston had lived three years were reluctant to leave the only home they had ever known.

What did Houston think about this situation? To be sure, he had strong loyalties to his Indian brothers, but there was no changing the treaty or the direction in which things were headed.

The Raven was welcomed by Oolooteka's band, and with the interests of the Indians at heart, he made good on some of the government's neglected promises for blankets, traps, kettles, and even rifles for the braves. Under their white brother's gentle exhortation, the reluctant Indians finally consented to the move.

In his role as Indian subagent, Houston chose to participate in Indian society as a brother, dressing as they did. Thus was he adorned when he accompanied Tahlhontusky on his journey, and when Secretary of War Calhoun received the Indian delegation.

Full of southern hospitality, Mr. Calhoun was more than gracious to his guests, but at the end of the meeting, he quietly requested that Lieutenant Houston remain behind. The courteous façade disappeared completely when the secretary of war demanded an explanation for the lieutenant's attire. What message had he meant to convey by dressing as a savage?

If that weren't enough, Houston was summoned back to Calhoun's office, where he was accused of aiding and abetting in the illegal smuggling of slaves.

Sam patiently explained that during his recent work with the Cherokees in Tennessee, he had stumbled across a band of slave smugglers illegally carrying Negroes from Florida. Without consulting anyone, he simply took the initiative and broke up its activities.

It seems these smugglers were friendly with certain members of Congress, and those same dishonest politicians, as it turns out, had conspired to accuse and entrap Houston. The young lieutenant was able to clear his name but was incensed when absolutely nothing was done to punish his accusers.

Apparently, this was too much for Houston, who, with a haste born of passion, wrote:

Washington City
March 1, 1818

Sir
You will please accept this as my resignation to take effect from this date.

I have the honor to be
Your Most Obt Servt
Sam Houston
1st Lieut 1st Infy
Genl D. Parker
A & Ins Genl.
W. City[4]

As for Tahlhontusky and his followers, they were showered with gifts and appeared pleased, even though they were unsuccessful in meeting their original goals.

Governor McMinn thanked Calhoun: "I am truly pleased to learn that the usual plan has been taken with the chiefs...corrupt as it may appear: that of 'purchasing their friendship.'"[5]

Anxious to be on his way, Sam Houston quickly finished the business of his subagency and resigned that office as well, after which he saddled his horse and rode in the direction of Nashville. What on earth was he going to do now?

A New Student

A man named Judge Trimble was alone after the Battle of Horseshoe Bend, when his law student, Lemuel Montgomery, had been killed. When was it? Three? No—four years ago now. Even his books were still here.

A shadow fell across his desk, and the old man's rheumy eyes regarded his visitor. *Houston?* Judge Trimble finally made the connection. Yes, he knew the Houston clan in Virginia. He showed Sam the books he would need to master. *Ever hear of Blackstone?*

Buckling down to the task of study, Sam Houston astonished his mentor by passing the bar in six months instead of the usual eighteen. Then he packed up and rode to Lebanon, thirty miles east of Nashville, where a man named Isaac Galladay helped Houston start his law practice. He even provided a wardrobe, and a nice one, at that. Fortunately, it wasn't long before Lebanon took to the new attorney.

Sam Houston's Popularity

The well-attired stranger was instantly popular. He was easy to remember—a perfectly proportioned, military figure considerably more than six feet tall, with a pleasant way, a pleasant word and a rich warm voice. Maidens were interested when he bowed over their hands, and the young ladies' mothers no less charmed by his careful courtesy. Men repeated his anecdotes and listened to his views on politics.[6]

The young attorney rode to Nashville often and generally stopped by the Hermitage, General Jackson's home. It is no wonder that Jackson and Houston got along so well; they had much in common. But they were more than friends. For Sam Houston, Andrew Jackson was not just a political mentor or even just a friend. Houston looked up to the elder statesman as a father figure, even calling Jackson's wife, "Aunt Rachel."

Jackson, likewise, thought highly of Houston. Perhaps he saw a little of himself in the younger man. At any rate, the general recommended his protégé for several offices, which he successfully filled: first, adjutant-general of the state militia, and then, with Jackson's endorsement, Houston was nominated for and elected to the post of prosecuting attorney of the Nashville district.

Later, Houston resigned this post to return to private practice. The officers in the militia elected him their major general, a part-time position.

Sam Houston was part of Jackson's inner circle of confidantes and one who could see political possibilities. He and other friends began testing the waters; could Jackson be elected President in 1824? Not that Old Hickory wanted the office. Or maybe he did, but perhaps Rachel's dislike of attention and high society kept the lid on such a plan.

In the meantime, because Jackson wanted to help his faithful protégé, he saw to it that Houston was nominated to Congress, and because there was no opposition, he won by a unanimous vote.

Only five years after Lieutenant Houston had received a dressing-down from the secretary of state for his Indian garb, he was back in Washington, this time as Congressman Houston—and the confidante of one of the most popular and respected men in the country. He made his way to the Capitol building, which was smaller than it is today, and found a seat in the chamber.

"Now, Butler," he remarked, speaking to a friend who was with him, "I am a member of Congress. I will show Calhoun that I have not forgotten his insult to a poor lieutenant."[7]

But things did not go well in Washington. Andrew Jackson was shut out of the presidency by an under-the-table deal, in which Clay secretly offered his support in return for the secretary of state position in the new president's cabinet. Jackson refused to make such a deal, but John Quincy Adams consented and thus became the new president. When Clay was appointed Secretary of State, the mudslinging began in earnest, and as a result, President Adams served four years under a heavy cloud of suspicion.

Worse, Calhoun managed to garner the number two spot, the vice presidency. When 1828 approached, Jackson was finally persuaded to run. He was immensely popular, seen as the people's candidate, even though many of his views were quite conservative. Sam Houston served his chief faithfully, writing articles and performing a variety of important tasks. As a part of the general's inner circle, he was stunned and infuriated when Jackson's enemies launched a slanderous campaign against Rachel Jackson, twisting the facts to make it sound like there were improprieties in their marriage.

In the end, it was a difficult campaign and took its toll. Jackson won, but Rachel had no use for the limelight. In fact, she was heard to say that she would rather be a doorkeeper in the house of her God than to live in a palace, speaking of the presidential mansion, which was not yet referred to as the "White House."

A few days after the election, Rachel became very ill and unthinkably, left her beloved Andrew for better mansions above. Jackson was heartbroken. And because she was beloved by so many, thousands made the pilgrimage to the Hermitage to pay their last respects. Sam Houston led the pallbearers to the simple grave on the Hermitage grounds, and a beautiful Christian woman was laid to rest.

As President-elect, Andrew Jackson moved alone to Washington to discharge his official duties, but the Hermitage and the simple grave and headstone were never far from his mind and heart.

Stephen Austin's Early Days

The winter storm finally let up after a singularly difficult trip west. Moses Austin surveyed his entourage, thinking. It certainly wouldn't do to present himself to Spanish officials dressed as he was, in travel-worn clothing. Surely there was a way to disguise his poverty.

The chief Spanish official, Lt. Gov. Zenon Trudeau, had a French name. This was not surprising because the Louisiana territory had been under French influence for so long before it was finally given to the Spanish. The governor now had a visitor, a man introducing himself as Moses Austin, who wore a long blue mantle, embroidered with lace, which lent him the appearance of someone of import. Austin did nothing to dispel the impression.

Trudeau wrote him a letter of introduction to the commandant of Ste. Genevieve, which helped Austin obtain a Spanish grant for land containing a large amount of lead ore. One year later, an excited Austin returned with his family and began the task of working the mine and building a home for his family. This lead mine was about forty miles west of the Mississippi, in the region we now know as Missouri. Stephen F. Austin, his firstborn son, was only five years old when the family arrived at their new home.

For a while, the business flourished, but in 1808, sales of lead began to decline. Still, during this time, Moses Austin was able to send his son to an academy in New England, and he returned home with a solid education at the age of seventeen. Over the next few years, the young Austin was given progressively greater responsibilities and finally made a trip to New Orleans on business.

When the War of 1812 broke out not long afterward, Stephen served for a short time as a quartermaster for a mounted militia regiment. But the war had secondary economic effects. Money was in short supply. The mines were struggling, and labor was scarce. Over the next several years, the Austins ended up leasing slaves to work the mines, but the business never really recovered from the damaging economic setbacks. By now, the war had taken its toll on Moses, and he became ill. He made plans to move away, leasing the whole enterprise to his capable son, Stephen.

Now twenty-three years old, the younger Austin did not lack for energy. "I shall literally bury myself this Spring and Summer in the Mines," he wrote, "and if attention and industry will affect anything I shall do much."[8]

Stephen Austin had also garnered some important connections in the militia and in the Masonic lodge, where he had recently become a member. It wasn't long before he ran for a seat in the territorial legislature in 1815 and won over three other competitors.

Though Stephen may have won the vote, the family fortunes were in deep trouble. Crippling debt hung over their heads. But Moses Austin hatched a clever scheme. He had long had an interest in New Spain (Mexico), thinking that "an adventure to that Country would be both safe and advantageous."[9]

The situation in Texas was of interest to many Americans at that time. First of all, Jefferson had claimed this region all the way to the Rio Grande. After all, it was part of the Louisiana Purchase. Then, in 1812, Spain enacted a new constitution, and businessmen like Moses Austin took immediate notice. A new constitution might help matters regarding trade in Mexico in general, and in particular, the region of Mexico known as Texas. But certain significant events began to dim Moses Austin's dream.

In 1812-1813, a man named August Magee, a former U.S. Army officer, attempted to lead Texas to independence with the aid of a private army. Magee briefly controlled Texas until royalist forces defeated him in a bloody battle, where many Americans were slaughtered.

In 1819, when the U.S.-Spanish treaty was signed, making the Sabine River the boundary between Spanish Texas and the United States, James Long enlisted a group of malcontents who still thought Texas ought to belong to the United States. They, too, briefly controlled parts of Texas before being overthrown.

This kind of political instability was clearly bad for trade, but in 1819, Moses Austin discussed another possibility with his son.

Stephen Austin later recorded:

> In 1819, he [Moses] proposed to me the idea of forming a colony in Texas. The Treaty of De Onis had been brought to a conclusion, and with the right of Spain to Texas now appearing unquestionable, grants from the Spanish authorities would therefore be valid. The project was discussed by us in Durham Hall at 'Mine A. Burton' for several days, and adopted.[10]

But this was his father's project, not his. Meanwhile, there were still severe cash flow problems.

"If I am left alone for a few years," Stephen wrote, "I may get up and pay all (of my debts) off."[11]

He went to New Orleans, where an acquaintance, Joseph H. Hawkins, had offered to help him. Stephen wrote his mother about his arrangements. "If I will remain with him he will board me, permit me the use of his books, and money for clothes, give me all the instruction in his power, until I am well fitted to commence the practice of law in this country."[12] Hawkins was clearly a true friend.

And Stephen Austin, apparently, was a likable fellow to have around. He described himself as "naturally hasty and impetuous and sensitive to a fault," but his nephew wrote: "No one would suppose so from intercourse with him, for with others he had such ways as to make every one like and be easy with him."[13]

Evidently, he made a good first impression. Handsome, he dressed well, being described by his nephew as "slender, sinewy, of graceful figure and easy, elastic movements, with small hands and feet, dark hair inclined to curl when damp, with large, hazel eyes, fair skin when not sun-burned, about five feet eight or nine inches in height."[14]

Stephen Austin was a thoughtful man who had careful manners. "His face," his nephew recalled, "was grave and thoughtful when not in a social circle—then it was animated and lit up by the gentle soul within; his voice was manly and soft, his colloquial powers fluent, persuasive and attractive, without his being conscious of it himself; his magnetic power over others gave him the great influence he possessed."[15]

This quiet gentleman did not profess to be a Christian; indeed, his father Moses opposed what he saw as religious "bigotry." But his New England education certain upheld a serious, philosophical kind of morality. Stephen F. Austin was definitely a man with a conscience.

A Providential Meeting

Moses Austin was discouraged; his worst fears had come to pass. With Stephen's slave, Richmond, he had just traveled four hundred miles in three weeks. Upon reaching San Antonio at the end of December 1820, he went to see the provincial governor, Antonio Martinez. But the unstable situation, provoked by James Long's recent expedition, had turned the hearts of the Spanish against Americans, and Moses Austin was ordered to leave Texas and not return.

What happened next can only be described as providential. It was one of those times when the destiny of a nation turns on a single "chance" event. After his disastrous meeting with Martinez, Austin walked back across the plaza. Dejected, he probably paid little heed to the figures walking about, but one familiar face caught his attention. Moses roused himself enough to strike up a conversation with this familiar-looking man.

His name was Philip Hendrik Nering Bogel, but he went by the title "Baron de Bastrop." The two had met twenty years earlier in New Orleans, when both had been there on business. As a result of their conversation, Bastrop offered to speak to the governor on Austin's behalf.

He obtained permission for Austin to remain for a time, and shortly, perhaps over tacos or the equivalent of pizza, the two put their heads together, trying to decide how to persuade the Spanish to approve of American settlers.

It seemed impossible. They knew that their only hope was to make the plan sound advantageous to the Spanish, because right now, the Americans were viewed as *diablos* (devils).

A little problem-solving was in order. What was the biggest problem Spanish Texas had? It did not take a genius to answer that. No one wanted to settle within scalping range of the aggressive and dangerous Comanche Indians.

But taking Texas away from the Comanches would be impossible without first establishing settlements—definitely a "catch-22."

Bastrop took the time to explain the facts to Austin. Governor Martinez had been there three years and had tried to develop the economy, but without success, since few people could be induced to settle in Texas. With these facts in mind, the two men approached the governor with a proposal.

Moses Austin asked permission to settle three hundred American Catholic families in Texas and establish a town at the mouth of the Colorado River. Austin was probably aware that many Spaniards were free thinkers, but a nominal Catholic presence would help reassure the government that these settlers meant to be loyal to New Spain.

Their logical arguments convinced the governor to change his mind and sign what was called an *empresario* contract, offering a restricted-use land grant. Martinez wrote that Austin was "a man of some honesty and formality, and that the proposal he is making is, in my opinion, the only one which is bound to provide for the increase and prosperity of this province."[16] Austin's application was forwarded to Monterrey, where it was eventually approved.

But Moses Austin was never to see the fruition of his plans. A thief stole his mounts, and he and the slave, Richmond, were forced to travel on foot in frigid January. Enduring the cold, they were forced to subsist on roots and berries, and by the time they arrived in Natchitoches, Austin was very ill, his health permanently broken.

He struggled to manage his affairs, but by June, it was clear that he was dying. Stephen's mother relayed this message: "He called me to his bed side and with much distress and difficulty of speech, Beged me to tell you to take his place . . ."[17]

Moses Austin died two days later.

The Three Hundred Families

Working out the details from another angle, Stephen Austin was already involved in his father's plans to some degree. His friend Joseph Hawkins was enthusiastic about the new proposal and became a partner, underwriting some of the expenses. Stephen wrote a letter intended to be widely published in American newspapers, advertising the grant to settle three hundred families in Texas. He wrote that they would be given land, and with the Spanish Constitution of 1812 "in full operation," they would retain "the most liberal privileges...both in regard to commercial intercourse and civil rights." It was decided that applicants must be "well recommended" to be considered.[18]

Stephen then set off on a journey to San Antonio, and on July 9, 1821, he and his party reached the Sabine River. The next morning, a rider caught up with them, delivering the news that Moses had died.

Writing his mother, Stephen expressed himself this way. "This news has effected me very much, he was one of the most feeling and affectionate Fathers that ever lived. His faults I now say, and always have, were not of the heart." He counseled his mother that "we must resign ourselves to the dispensations of Providence, death must finally terminate the career of us all."[19]

Returning briefly to Natchitoches, Austin consulted with a Spanish official there, who gave his opinion that Stephen would probably be allowed to proceed in his father's stead regarding the grant project.

On July 13, 1821, the young man turned his horse west and departed in the direction of Texas.

Chapter 5

La Casa Blanca

TODAY, in South Texas, there are many residents of Hispanic descent. Many are immigrants or the sons and grandsons of immigrants; others can trace their ancestry in South Texas for hundreds of years. Are they Mexicans? Hardly. They are a unique people, in food, in culture, and even in language. We call it "Tex-Mex." How did they happen to come here? And how was this *Tejano* culture woven into the history of the place called Texas?

Patricio Rodriguez was a teenage boy with gray eyes, a thin face like his mother's, and chestnut hair. He frowned. This was Tejas? Surely there was some mistake.

He looked at his father. Salvador Rodriguez had black hair streaked with gray, a thick beard, and greenish eyes, which were now taking in the details of the San Antonio de Valero compound and its environs. If his father was troubled, he did not show it.

It was March 9th, 1731. It had taken nearly a year to get here, and a few had not survived the trip. At times, only hope kept them going.

"Patricio." His father addressed him by his full name, clearly planning to say something important. At least, a conversation like this may have happened. We know the Rodriguez family was real.

"Patricio, this place may not be all that you hoped for. What the Fray just told us about the Indians is not good news. There is a reason why political exiles from the Canary Islands were sent instead of the first families from Spain. But Patricio" —his father glanced across the courtyard at his wife, Maria—"We now carry the title of nobility. Let us play the part of gentlemen. Complaining will not change anything. This place will be what we make it to be."

Salvador Rodriguez searched the face of his son. "For your mother's sake."

Patricio scuffed his toe in the dirt then met his father's gaze.

"Yes, Papa."

The Canary Islanders

The immigrants from the Canary Islands had real difficulties. In the Spanish system, noblemen supervised peasants, who did the hard physical labor. Here in Tejas, the Indians were supposed to be the peasant class, but there were few "tamed" Indians, and those who were, helped the friars run the mission.

The new immigrants had been given titles as a reward for settling Texas, and consciously or subconsciously, they saw themselves as the upper class. Many of the Canary Islanders did not adapt well and only did enough to survive. They were the complainers. But others did better.[1]

It Might Have Been LIke This

"Hey, kid, what's your name?" Patricio asked a boy he had seen around.

"Bartolome Seguín."

"How old are you?" Patricio asked the youngster. His father was inside the Seguins' house talking to the child's father.

"I'm ten years old. What's your name?"

"You can call me Pat."

"I think so." Bartolome nodded. "Wanna see my arrowhead collection?"

"Sure," Patricio agreed. He really wanted to hear what his elders were discussing, but his father had told him to wait outside, that he would not be long.

"*Hasta mañana*," he heard his father say. "Let's go, son."

After a few minutes, the teenager asked, "How did it go?"

"Santiago Seguín has lived here for twenty years," Salvador began. "He is a gold mine of information about this place, in some respects even more so than the friars."

"He will help us?"

Salvador Rodriguez was silent for a few moments. "Yes, he will help us. But there are two things you must understand. One is that in order to survive here, we must all help one another. Number two is that we must all work as if no one will ever help us. We must work like peasants."

"But we are not peasants!"

The elder Rodriguez had reined in his horse when Patricio turned his mount and faced his father.

"What does it mean to be a peasant?"

Patricio fumbled for an answer. "They. . .they. . .do the work."

"A gentleman does not work?"

The young man was silent now, sensing the drift of his father's argument, and not sure he liked it.

"It is an honor to be given a title of nobility. We ought to live up to that honor. There is nothing intrinsically ignoble about menial labor. A task has been given us."

His father made a move to leave, but then said, "Does it shame you that I have been digging in the dirt day after day?"

"No, Father," his son whispered, as a huge lump lodged in his throat. His father was the most honorable man he knew.

Setting aside their disappointment, they worked side by side to make their new place one of which they could be proud. To this day, their descendants remain in South Texas.

The Class System

Alexander the Great. Julius Caesar. Napoleon. Each of these famous generals conquered and ruled—at least for a time. But the thing is, they conquered already-civilized people groups. According to the Romans, the Gauls were barbarians, but they certainly were not savages in the same way that the Karankawas were. The Celtic Gauls grew crops and cooperated with each other to make their tribal system work, and they had rulers. So when the Romans finally conquered them, they simply accepted a new set of rulers. In this way, much of life remained the same.

When Cortés came to Mexico, he was a *conquistador* in the tradition of Julius Caesar, only more so, since the Spaniards had the additional support of the Pope. The Aztecs were *civilized*, as the Gauls once were, with rulers and division of labor. Now they had new rulers, Spanish ones, and though certain things had changed, many things remained the same.

Now the Indians were at the bottom rung of the societal ladder. They became the peasant class and were now ruled by Spanish noblemen. They were not always treated well, but the system did work, at least for a time.

Further to the north, there weren't any "civilized" Indians to conquer. Coronado had seen this problem, the lack of potential peasants. True, Oñate had begun some colonization attempts in the north, but the region called Tejas was left to itself for years. Until a Frenchman named St. Denis appeared on the scene.

The French Cause Trouble

During this time, the middle continent of North America belonged to the French. The watershed of the mighty Mississippi River, from modern-day Canada down to New Orleans, had been claimed for the French Crown by La Salle and named "Louisiana." There weren't actually that many Frenchmen in the New World, but they were influential. They disappeared into the forest, trading, trapping, and adopting Indian ways. They even sold guns to the Indians, something no other Europeans did. Naturally, the Indians regarded them favorably, and if the "French and Indian War" was any indication, the French also viewed the Indians as potential allies.

The large tract of land known as Tejas nestled beside the huge territory known as Louisiana, though for some time, the exact border between the two had not yet been determined. And what's more, no one really cared.

In 1690, a mission was established in the piney woods about fifty miles south of Nacogdoches named San Francisco de los Tejas, built with the purpose of converting the local Caddoan Indians. The relatively civilized Caddoans were somewhat cooperative but then started dying from diseases imported by the Spanish. Problems grew, and eventually the mission was abandoned.

That is, until a Frenchman by the name of Juchereau de St. Denis rode across Texas. St. Denis was a smart man who lived to make lots of money. He was also very charming, to say nothing of daring. In fact, he boldly rode into a Spanish settlement in New Spain without so much as a visa. Of course, borders did mean something, even in those days, but St. Denis was so pleasant and charming that not only was he not arrested, but he even ended up marrying a local VIP's daughter.

His plan, which he did not initially reveal because, according to French law, it was illegal, was to set up trade with the Spanish. With his sights set on the money he could make, he chose to ignore the law and soon joined his father-in-law in business, trading with the Spanish. But the man's initiative and potential for power began making the local authorities nervous, motivating them to protect their territory by developing settlements. Hence the need for Spanish missions.

The Missions

The friars had figured it out. In the north, the Indians just needed to be taught. At the missions, they would teach the Indians the Catholic faith, skills, trades, and agricultural techniques. They would civilize these savages, preparing the way for the Spanish to rule Texas. The brown-robed men calculated that this transformation would take about ten years.

San Antonio de Valera was established in 1718, two years after St. Denis had made his troubling appearance. The area was ideal. Located at the headwaters of the San Antonio River, the place had many practical advantages, not the least of which was that the local Indians, the Coahuiltecans, seemed amenable to the idea of being civilized. And at the very least, they were no threat.

Other missions were established in areas inhabited by other tribes. Three missions were planted in East Texas, since first of all, there was much hope for the already civilized Caddo Indians, and second, the French border was located there. Unfortunately, the border proved to be the undoing of those East Texas missions. The French supplied the Indians with both guns and arguments against the religion of the Spaniards. The Spanish soldiers who accompanied the friars were reluctant to round up armed Indians, and another problem occurred that made all other problems academic. Measles and other diseases, taken in stride by the Europeans, began to kill off the unprotected Indians.

The only mission that had any success was located in what is now San Antonio. In fact, a string of five missions was eventually built in this area, but they did have some major problems.

First of all, the soldiers sent to guard the mission generally chose this occupation to escape a worse fate, such as hanging or having to do real work. The padres protected their charges from these "no-goods," denying the soldiers laborers to help them build their presidio and moving the Indian women across the river at one point to remove them from harm's way. The soldiers, who were not thrilled about their assignment to begin with, did not appreciate this.

Then, the promise once shown by the Coahuiltecans began to fade; they became lazy and passive. Probably, they only flocked to the missions to escape worse enemies: the invading Comanche were now pushing the aggressive Apaches south. Life at the mission had little appeal, as it was strict, full of hard work, and, from the Indians' point of view, just another form of slavery.

When the friars requested that the Spanish settlers be sent, the King of Spain rounded up political exiles in the Canary Islands. But this caused as many problems as it solved.

And then there were the Apaches. A war-like, mounted tribe, they raided the mission, stealing horses and cattle, sometimes killing people as well. The Spanish did not realize that the Comanches had just displaced this band of Lipan Apaches, pushing them south into the hill country near San Antonio.

Despite the hardships, the friars held onto their vision for the mission.

The End of the Missions

One of the mission Indians looked up from his fieldwork and froze. Apaches! He dropped his hoe and ran away.

At some point, someone was found who could translate so the Apaches could speak with the brown robes. They had come with an offer of peace and wanted a mission of their own, to be located in the San Saba area, to the northwest.

The friars, as you can well imagine, were overjoyed at the news that the Apaches were actually asking for their own mission. And although it took several years to get the bureaucratic machinery into gear, finally, in April of 1757, a party headed northwest to found the mission of San Luis de las Amarillas.

The new mission was built out of logs, and a presidio was constructed a few miles away for use by the soldiers. But for some reason, the Apaches seemed to have lost their former enthusiasm. In fact, they repeatedly made excuses why they could not meet, and finally, they totally disappeared.

Then one morning, Padre Molina and Padre Terreros heard shrieks and shouts, and although no one saw the perpetrators, sixty-three horses were missing from the pasture between the mission and the presidio. Colonel Parilla suggested that the friars move to the presidio, but they refused, unable to believe anyone would wish to harm them.

The very next morning, a terrified yell interrupted the friars' morning routine. Terreros and Molina climbed to the parapet to see what was going on, to find that 2,000 mounted, war-painted Comanches were slowly taking positions around the mission's walls. They wore headgear made of deer antlers, buffalo horns, and eagle plumes and carried lances, bows, and French muskets, clearly prepared to do battle.

The terrified padres attempted to be friendly, but their gifts made little impression. The killing began, and only Padre Molina and a few others survived in the mission church, which, because it was made of green logs, did not burn when the Comanches set a torch to the mission complex.

From the perspective of the Spanish, this act of aggression could not go unpunished, and as a result, in August of 1759, Colonel Parilla led the largest Spanish force to date in Texas, charged with bringing retribution on the Comanches and salvaging the pride of Spain.

The plan began to fail almost immediately, when at first, Parilla's troops could not locate their prey. When they finally did run across both Comanches and other Indians, about 6,000 in all, according to Parilla, the Indians won a decisive victory, leaving the imagined supremacy of Spain in shambles. The Comanches seemed to be the rulers of the Texas plains, and over time, that reality became even clearer, as Comanche raiding parties penetrated ever farther south. Finally, even the settlers in Sonora, Coahuila, and Durango learned to dread the full moon of late spring and summer.

The mission at San Antonio de Valero was finally closed in 1793, after seventy-five years.

And though it contained only forty-three converts, it was still the most successful Spanish mission in Texas. Its lands were distributed to nearby colonists, and the buildings turned over to the military. These buildings would later be called "The Alamo."

Life on the Early Ranchos

Jose surveyed the broken ground in front of him. Old Twist, an older cow with a peculiar twist in one horn, was missing; she seemed to enjoy disappearing. This time, she had her calf with her.

Princesa shifted her weight under him. The ground ahead was rough, but the sure-footed mare could handle it easily. Jose urged her forward, barely conscious of his action. After several years together, the young man and his horse were as one, the mare now sensitive to his every movement, sometimes seemingly reading his mind.

As the mare picked her way carefully down into a ravine, Jose thought about the land. This was good land. Just four years before, the *hacendado* had received a land grant, or *merced*—literally, "mercy"—located here just north of the Rio Bravo, which would later become known as the Rio Grande. The *hacendado* owned a full mile of riverfront property, the grant extending in a long rectangle. Much of this land was only good for cattle; that much was very obvious.

The mare's ears flicked forward, a clear signal that she had heard something. Jose paid close attention since her hearing was keener than his own. He felt her interest even through the leather of the saddle and the chaps that protected his legs from chafing and thorns that grew long in some places.

Then Jose heard it too, a bleating sound—the calf. It must be stranded somewhere nearby, and if he found the calf, surely he would find the cow as well. He guided Princesa with gentle motions of his hands and knees, but she needed little guidance; she knew her job. Jose wiped the sweat that had begun to drip down his neck and then grabbed the gourd that served as a canteen. He would see to his horse as soon as this job was done.

The sound seemed to come from just over the next ridge. Princesa carried him easily over the rocky ground as he reached for the pistol under his buckskin jacket. The sound that led the way could also attract a panther. There, trapped in a thorny thicket, the three-month-old calf bawled intermittently, while its mother stood nearby, nervously tossing her head. Jose had never seen her so agitated. Then he felt Princesa go rigid beneath him. Not a dozen feet from him, a mountain lion crouched, perched above his head on the side of the ravine.

The mare had not smelled the cat because of the wind direction. Jose realized this in an instant, while his mind continued making observations, despite the possible threat of death. His pistol aimed and fired, seemingly of its own accord, as its owner wondered what would happen if he missed. Colt six-shooters had not been invented yet, so he only had one shot. After that, he would need his knife.

The great cat sprang at the same instant Jose fired the pistol, and Princesa leaped madly to the side, trying to avoid the claws and teeth of the mountain lion. The *vaquero* managed to stay mounted and drew his knife in one swift motion.

The tawny cat missed the mare, landing hard on the ground. It crouched again to spring, but Jose noticed bloody froth at its mouth. After leaping from the saddle, he plunged the knife into the animal's throat and watched as it collapsed onto the ground, where it shuddered, then was still. Apparently, the lead ball had found its mark.

Jose looked up. Princesa stood trembling a few yards away. What a good horse. Many would have bolted. Though he wanted the big cat's pelt, rescuing the calf took first priority. Before he did anything, there was something else he needed to do. He knelt and gave thanks to God.

He came in later that evening, trailing the pelt on a makeshift travois. Princesa could not abide the smell of the cat across her back, but a length of rope solved the problem.

Jose took pains to care for his mare, rubbing her down and carefully inspecting her feet. She didn't look like much, a tawny yellow buckskin a little darker than the cat's pelt, but he decided right then that she deserved her royal name.

He told his story around the cooking fire, but the other *vaqueros* seemed less than impressed, all having faced similar dangers. Jose's own father had lost his life when a *loco* bull had gored him with its long, cruel horn. These tough, rangy

Spanish cattle were essentially wild, left to fend for themselves, and their long horns were necessary for survival.

They seemed to thrive here on this *merced* above the Bravo; in fact, each year calves seemed to spring from the very earth. But there was no denying it; the life of a *vaquero* was dangerous.

Shortly Jose learned that the *hacendado* wanted to see him. Jose finger-combed his hair a bit nervously. He was a *culebra*; his father was Spanish, but he favored his Indian mother. Further south, he would be considered almost a non-person, but here, under the big sky of the *estancia de ganado*, or *rancho*, he was *a somebody*. In fact, there were places in New Spain where it was illegal for an Indian to ride horseback. But not here.

Jose stood on the veranda while waiting for the owner to appear, until finally Don Garza stepped outside.

"Jose," greeted the *hacendado*. His clothes did not mark him as wealthy; on the frontier, everyone worked.

"Jose," the man fumbled for words. "I have something for you."

Jose stood respectfully, waiting.

"I heard about the cat. Go ahead and keep the pelt. Dona Garza wanted me to bring you these when I made the trip to town."

He placed a small bag in Jose's hand, and the young man mumbled his thanks, before opening the bag. The glint of silver met his eye. Silver buttons. Every vaquero desired silver buttons on his buckskin jacket; it was practically a mark of caste, and he would be proud to own them.

"Gracias!"

The Tejano Vaqueros

Jose was not a real person, but he could have been. At the same time the missions were struggling and failing, ranchos were being established on both sides of the Rio Grande. In 1746, a certain Colonel Jose de Escandon, a Spaniard, was commissioned to plant settlements in the northern areas of New Spain, avoiding the fever-wracked coast, but bringing a number of *rancheros* and their *vaqueros* to the Rio Grande region. Large tracts of land fronting the river were surveyed, and several towns were established along the south bank. A few *merceds* extending as far as 100 miles north of the river were given to favored men. It was a controlled invasion in the feudal Spanish style.

The vaqueros of these northern provinces were unique. A man on horseback was his own master, or at least it seemed that way. For that reason, Indians had been forbidden horses in the south. But on a rancho, working with cattle, that restriction was unworkable. Indians and mixed-blood Spaniards working a ranch enjoyed a freedom and prestige that went hand in hand with hard work and danger. No wonder the saying emerged, "to be a *vaquero* was to be a hero; to be a *ranchero* was to be a king."

The missions were a failure, but to the same extent that the "cowboy" won the West, Spain has made her presence known. Do you recognize these Spanish words? *Corral, bronco, loco, arroyo, lazo, la reata, rodear, adobe, pinta, rancho.* "Mustang" comes from the root word *mesteno*, "hackamore" from *jaquima*, and "buckaroo" from *vaquero.*[2]

Things were a little different around the Rio Grande than they were farther south. The demands of frontier life and cattle ranching had modified the Spanish feudalism into something looser and more self-reliant. The *vaquero* was a new breed of man. And decades later, in the days of the Texas Revolution, the *Tejano* men of the south Texas ranchos would be well-known for their superb horsemanship.

La Casa Blanca

Don Erasmo Seguín checked over his horse. His saddlebags were already packed when he walked back to the white stone house to bid farewell to his wife, Maria. It must have pulled at his heartstrings to say goodbye, for it was not unusual for this *hacendado* and leading citizen of San Antonio to travel, not just in the performance of public duties but on business as well. It helped that they owned a home in town, and the whole family could accompany him when business in San Antonio kept him away for some time.

Thirty miles south of town was his rancho, near present-day Floresville. The white stone house on the hill perched above the outbuildings and workers' homes that served as a perimeter. Teamsters driving ox teams in from the coast rejoiced to lay eyes on the brilliant white of *La Casa Blanca*, knowing that San Antonio was finally near. And to the needy traveler, the hospitality of the Seguín family was already well known.

Seguín left the house, placing the broad-brimmed hat over his black curls; it was June of 1821, and the Texas sun would be warm in just a few hours. In the bare glimmer of the pre-dawn light, he saw his son, Juan, standing by his horse. The fifteen-year-old was excited that he would be coming along on this trip to East Texas. All was ready; the small party headed out, planning to join Juan Veramendi and his men, before following *El Camino Real*, the King's Highway, to the east.

On the way to Nacogdoches, Don Erasmo may have explained to his son the purpose of his trip. Seguín had been appointed as a commissioner to an American who had obtained a Spanish land contract. This kind of person was called an *empresario*. The colonists who would be settling this land were Americans who would become citizens of New Spain and pledge loyalty to their new country. And now they were to meet his man and bring him back to San Antonio.

Austin's Contract

Having shouldered the burden of his father's vision, an Anglo-American colony in Texas, Stephen F. Austin seemed pleased with the land before him. In the far east of Texas, there were some fever-ridden areas unsuited to farming, but as he traveled west with Seguín's party, the young *empresario* was duly impressed.

Reaching the Brazos on August 1, Austin noted that the land reminded him of the fertile Red River country at Natchitoches, though the Texas river water was of better quality. Deer and black bears were plentiful, and the river bottoms supported abundant wild grapevines. Crossing the river, the men struck the first of the large prairies that dot the region and saw their first buffalo. On August 7, they reached the Colorado, which with its clear water and clean gravel bottom reminded Austin of the Cumberland River, only bigger. He had now crossed what would become the northern width of his colony. Any doubts as to the desirability of the country were gone.

On August 10, the party reached the swift-running Guadalupe River north of San Antonio. Austin thought this "country the most beautiful I ever saw."[3]

Austin's Land for the Three Hundred

Austin's contract covered a large wedge of land located in central southeastern Texas, between the San Jacinto and Lavaca Rivers. This area included the lower part of the Colorado and Brazos Rivers, all the way to the Gulf. He had permission for 300 American Catholic families of good character to emigrate, and he had already started the process of advertising Texas land: a very good deal at only $0.125 (twelve and a half cents) per acre. At the time, the United States government had tightened its policies regarding the sale of public lands, and the smallest farm, eighty acres, required $100.00 cash up front. In Texas, a ranching family could obtain a full Mexican league—4,428 acres—at this low price, and cash up front was not required. Financially, Texas was of great interest to Americans.

But as wonderful as this land appeared to Austin and to potential settlers, the reality was that Texas in 1821 was torn and broken. Starting in 1810, New Spain had been undergoing political upheaval, including an insurrection violently quashed by the royalist forces at the Medina River. Nacogdoches was nearly abandoned, as Austin observed for himself when he passed through town. The Mexican population of Texas, once about 4,000 strong, was now down to about 2,500 people.

Independence—A New Problem

As they approached San Antonio, Erasmo Seguín sent some of his men ahead to prepare for their arrival. Later, these men returned with important news.

Mexico was now independent from Spain.

"*Viva independencia*!" rejoiced the Tejanos. Their wives sent out special dishes to their husbands and the party still on the road. The atmosphere was festive. Ten years of political turmoil had finally ended.

But the news would later cause grief for Austin, who, in speaking to the provincial governor, learned that the *empresario* contract negotiated by his father was no longer valid. The grant had been made under the auspices of the Spanish crown, which no longer ruled. He would need to renegotiate the contract.

The Problem of Language

It was a letter from Stephen. Brown Austin, the twenty-year-old younger brother of the *empresario*, was staying at La Casa Blanca while his brother was in Mexico. Juan Seguín and he must have spent time together, since the Tejano teenager was only a few years younger. But there was a problem of language. He needed to learn Spanish. Stephen wrote:

> Study the familiar phrases and lessons and *write them*, also repeat your verbs as you learn them, to Francisco or some other who can correct your pronunciation. A bad pronunciation at the start will be difficult to correct. Therefore take no lessons from any but those who are capable of giving them—Remember that it is all important to learn to write the language. . .remember that all your hopes of rising in this country depend on lear[n]ing to speak and write the language correctly. Without that, you will do nothing.[4]

Brown Austin was Stephen's right-hand man in the development of the colony and represented him while Stephen was in Mexico. The empresario was just now learning the language himself, but a diligent course of study caused him to achieve a modest degree of fluency in a very short time; in fact, other Americans in Mexico were beginning to depend on him to translate.

Mexico City was an education in itself for Stephen Austin. Not only did he devote himself to learning the language, but he also studied the people and their nation. Without relinquishing the ideals he considered American, he sincerely sought to understand his new country. His pleasant but patient and tactful manner won him friendships among high officials, even among those who may have differed with him on important issues. Austin was the quintessential diplomat.

Many years later, while reflecting on these experiences, he wrote:

> They are a strange people, and must be studied to be managed. They have high ideals of National dignity should it be openly attacked, but will sacrifice national dignity, and national interest too if it can be done in a *still* way, so as not to arrest public attention. "Dios Castiga el escandolo mas que el crime," (God punishes the exposure more than the crime) is their motto. This maxim influences their morals and their politics. I learned it when I was there in 1822, and I now believe that if I had not always kept it in view, and know the power which *appearances* have on them, even when they know they are deceived, I should never have succeeded, to the extent I have done.[5]

The immigrating colonists were supposed to be Catholic, but Austin was given the tacit understanding that this requirement would not actually be enforced, and there seemed to be a two-way understanding regarding this issue. There was a shortage of clergy in Texas to begin with, and not all Mexicans were very religious themselves. They had to maintain the appearance, at least in lip service. Austin did attempt to make a kind of enforcement when he disallowed a Protestant clergyman from establishing a church in his colony; the man taught in a school instead, the Word of God available to those who were open to hearing it.

Stephen Austin showed sincerity in his overall deportment that won the confidence of the Mexican officials. His contract was eventually renegotiated, and settlers soon began to arrive and stake claims on the banks of the Colorado and the Brazos Rivers. The colonists also developed a respect for this man, as he tirelessly worked on their behalf, settling issues and functioning almost as a parent over the endless hassles and squabbles that inevitably arose.

To the settlers, Austin continually preached wisdom and tact:

> I wrote to the settlers on the Colorado and Brazos that they ought not to meddle with politics, and to have nothing to do with any revolutionary schemes, I hope they have followed my advise [sic]—they are yet too recently established in the country to take an active part in political affairs. . .as foreigners we have a good excuse for remaining neutral without being lyable[sic] to suspicions and this is the safe course.[6]

The colonists were generally amenable to this kind of advice. They had not come for political reasons, but simply to carve out a living from the ground. They came for economic opportunity, and for that reason were reluctant to cause trouble.

By the time Stephen Austin returned to the colony and surveyed the capital of San Felipe de Austin, located in the heart of the land grant, he probably had acquired a fairly good working knowledge of Mexican politics. There were certain essential differences between Mexican and American politics that would have made themselves obvious.

First, there was no true "citizenry" in the American sense. By far, the largest group of people, the Indians, were considered peons, ignorant workers who served the upper classes. They were very poor, and the availability of their cheap labor precluded the establishment of actual slavery as had occurred in the United States.

Blue-blooded Spaniards formed the upper class, and sometimes they were able to acquire great wealth. Mixed-blood Spaniards formed a social class that floated in a kind of limbo; many were labeled as "Spaniards" as a kind of polite fiction.

The Catholic Church formed another important block of society, and although not all Mexicans were religious, the Church had political and economic power, and thus it was not wise to antagonize the clergy. Many were undoubtedly sincere and held the interests of their flock at heart, but the Catholicism of 19th-century Mexico, although declining in power, was still a religion of bondage. The rank and file were not allowed to read the Scriptures, and it had not been long since the Spanish Inquisition had employed its own prison in Mexico City. Austin was repulsed by what he saw as "fanaticism."

The military formed the other major power in society. There was very little tradition of self-government in the American style; thus these various players were kept in order by force.

Jim Bowie and Ursula

Ursula Veramendi was in love. Sometimes her cheeks felt warm from just thinking about him. At first, she had wondered—how could her father possibly consent to a marriage to an *Americano*? But her joy grew as she observed the way Jim Bowie seemed to find a place in their family. She listened when her father would discuss business with him. Soon, the huge red-haired man seemed a natural part of the large Veramendi household.

She knew of his interest right from the beginning. Ursula didn't remember the reason for his first visit to the home of the vice-governor of the province, probably something official, or perhaps business. Her father was one of the leading citizens of San Antonio, and they entertained many visitors.

Jim Bowie was a man to catch anyone's attention, and not just because of his size. He just seemed to be the sort of man who took the lead. With a genial, warm-hearted enthusiasm, he made friends easily. Others knew him as a faithful friend, valuable in a fight or other tight situation.

Jim had told her about a fight in which he had been attacked by two different men on a sandbar in Louisiana and nearly lost his life. In each case, a strong thrust with the famous knife he carried had disemboweled the man, while Bowie had been shot. He related his memories of the incident and about hearing someone say he would die, but also recalled his brother Rezin reassuring them that he would not. Well, he had proven his brother right. This same brother, Rezin, had designed the now-famous "Bowie" knife.

Ursula sat down to her sewing. It would all be done with propriety. Jim seemed to understand and to respect their ways. She wrinkled her brow. Anglo-Saxon was not a word with a positive connotation, since Americans were both hated and feared . . .but Jim Bowie, well-dressed and charming, seemed to be respected and accepted by San Antonians, at least as far as she could tell. She dismissed her doubts, certain that everything would be fine. Jim was so wonderful.

Tejas under the New Constitution

Juan Seguín listened while his father, Erasmo, sat across from their guest, Esteven Austin, the respected empresario. Juan was much too old for the local school, but he had certainly learned a lot from the discussions his father had had with this man and others.

Tonight, the subject was the new Constitution. His father had served as the representative from Tejas, helping to write the Mexican Constitution in 1824. It was a victory for the Mexican Federalists, a group fired by enthusiasm at the thought of modeling the new government after the republican principles of the United States. Educated men understood the principle of federalism: a national government supervising a lower tier of state government.

The major problem, Juan had heard, was that Tejas had been united with Coahuila, not having a large enough population to justify its existence as a separate state. But his father had succeeded in adding a provision for separate statehood when Tejas had a large enough population.

Coahuila had a much larger population than Tejas. The state legislature was composed of eleven delegates from Coahuila and only one from Tejas. Obviously, the interests of their home could be easily pushed aside by the newly formed state government.

The men continued to debate these issues while the lamplight cast dancing shadows on the ceiling. Juan may have listened for a long time before he finally fell asleep.

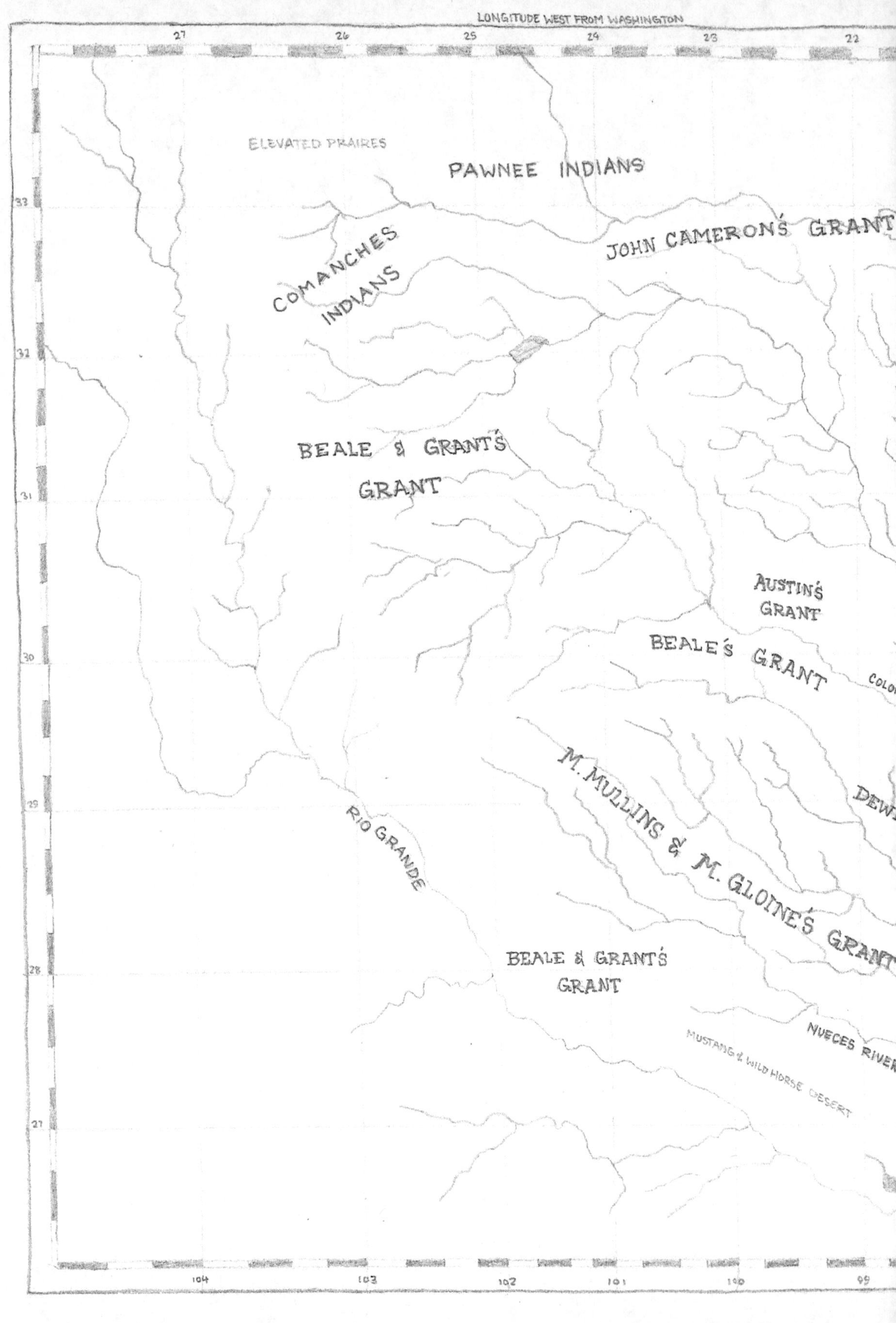
LONGITUDE WEST FROM WASHINGTON
27
26
25
24
23
22
33
32
31
30
29
28
27
ELEVATED PRAIRES
PAWNEE INDIANS
COMANCHES INDIANS
JOHN CAMERON'S GRANT
BEALE & GRANT'S GRANT
AUSTIN'S GRANT
BEALE'S GRANT
RIO GRANDE
M. MULLINS & M. GLOINE'S GRANT
BEALE & GRANT'S GRANT
NUECES RIVER
MUSTANG & WILD HORSE DESERT
104
103
102
101
100
99

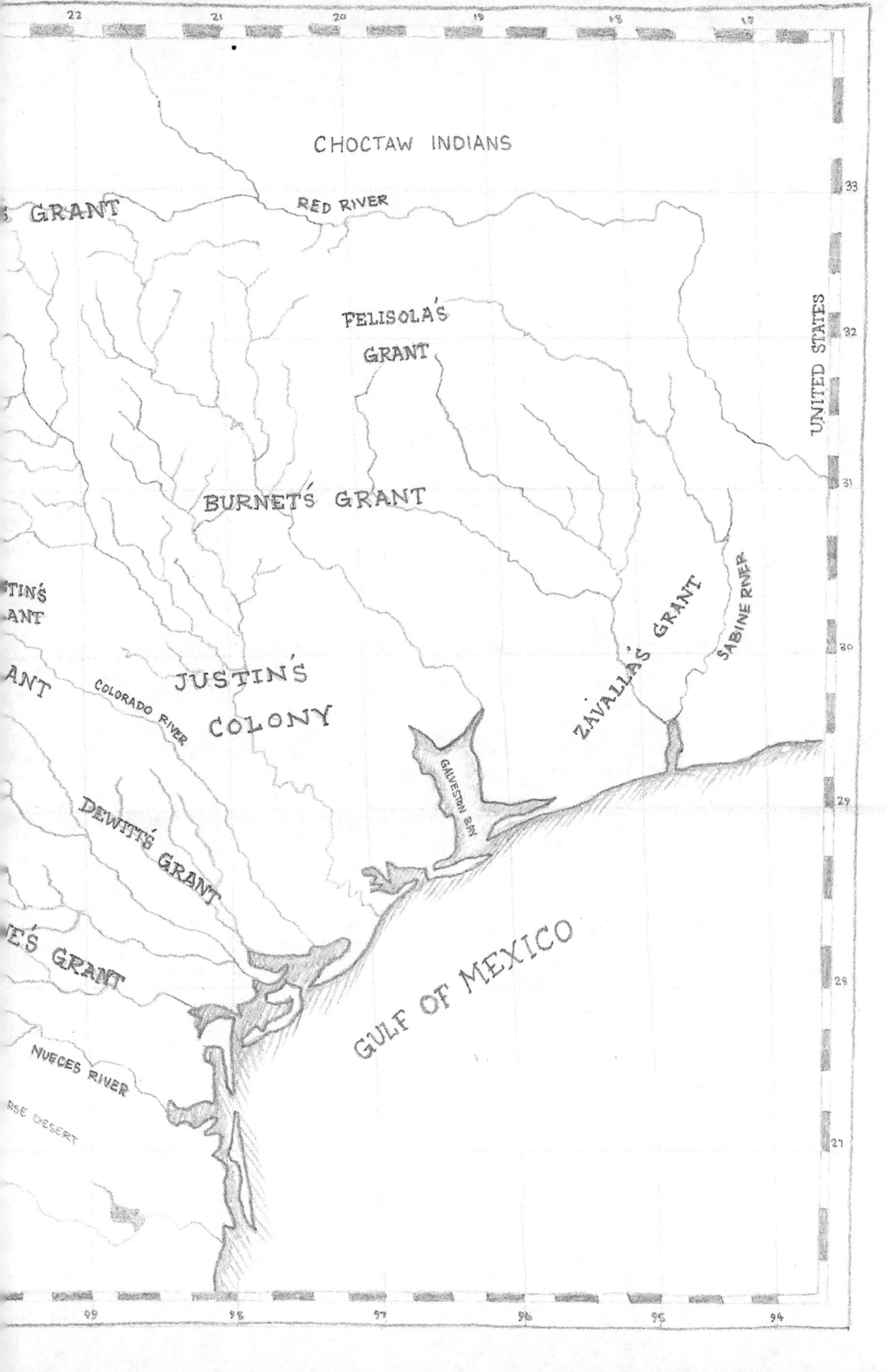
22
21
20
19
18
17
CHOCTAW INDIANS
GRANT
RED RIVER
33
FELISOLA'S
GRANT
UNITED STATES
32
31
BURNET'S GRANT
ZAVALLA'S GRANT
SABINE RIVER
30
JUSTIN'S
COLONY
COLORADO RIVER
GALVESTON BAY
29
DEWITT'S GRANT
GRANT
GULF OF MEXICO
28
NUECES RIVER
DESERT
27
99
98
97
96
95
94

Chapter 6

Trial by Fire

TENNESSEE GOVERNOR BILLY CARROLL liked his job as governor, and at one point even publicly stated that he would rather be Governor of Tennessee than President of the United States. But he had one minor problem: the Tennessee Constitution had placed a three-term limit on the office of governor, and unfortunately, Billy was now in his third term.

Billy was one of Andrew Jackson's good friends, and the two put their heads together, trying to find a loophole in the three-term rule. Finding none, they decided the next best thing was to find a man who could win the governorship and give it up after just one term, after which Carroll could legally run again. And the first name that came to mind was that of Sam Houston.

Houston Runs for Tennessee Governor

Without committing himself to anything, Sam agreed to run for governor, and, as it turned out, really took to the idea of campaigning. He was, and had always been, his own man, and certainly dressed the part of an individual.

> [He wore]... shining black patent leather military stock or cravat, incased by a standing collar, ruffled shirt, black satin vest, shining black silk pants gathered to the waistband with the legs full, same size from seat to ankle, and a gorgeous, red-ground, many-colored Indian hunting-shirt, fastened at the waist by a huge red...

> sash covered with fancy beadwork, with an immense silver buckle, embroidered silk stockings, and pumps with large silver buckles...[1]

Thus did an observer describe Sam Houston's attire at a political meeting. He owned a superb dapple-gray mare upon which he traveled from place to place, attending barbecues and barn raisings. And on election day, Tennesseans chose the warm-hearted, genial young man as their governor.

Politically, Houston's views were conservative; in his inaugural address, he maintained that the federal government should not invade the authority of state governments. (Never mind that his best buddy was President of the United States.) Overall, he was a sensible executive, a quality that carried over into his public service in Texas.

His popularity grew, making Billy Carroll very unhappy. But there was still one thing missing, one thing that Sam Houston had had on his mind for a while now: a "wee wifie."

While in Congress, he had written thus to a friend: "... I do not know yet the sweets of matrimony, but in March or April, next I will; unless something should take place not to be expected or wished for!"[2]

Houston Marries

In spite of his high hopes for marriage, Sam did not marry while in Washington, but now as governor, he made frequent visits to Colonel John Allen's home in Gallatin. Allen had two daughters, and when Houston confessed a love for the younger Eliza, her father gave his permission to court her.

John Allen was a respected leader of an aristocratic enclave of Tennessee. Wealthy, this gracious host set his table with expensive wines and delicacies from New Orleans. He kept a stable of thoroughbreds and had been host to the Jacksons when they were in town for the races.

Eliza Allen was only twenty, but had studied literature, languages, and deportment at the local academy. With blue-gray eyes and blonde hair, this young woman was also an accomplished horsewoman. As for Sam Houston, he could not have chosen better. Or so it seemed.

John Allen saw the situation as an opportunity and encouraged his daughter. This was not only the governor, but also Andrew Jackson's friend. With Jackson now in the White House, was there any reason to suppose Houston might not follow in his mentor's footsteps? Just think of it! The presidency!

Houston was now thirty-six, but his amiable, expressive heart must have found some response in the heart of the girl, since they were soon engaged to be married.

The wedding date was set for January 22, 1829. On that day, Sam mounted his shining dapple-gray mare and rode to his wedding. A curious circumstance imprinted itself on the Indian part of his mind. The Raven spotted a raven lying in the middle of the road, suffering the pangs of death. But he accorded it no meaning. How could he? This was a happy day!

The ceremony was held at the Allen residence in Gallatin, with the social elite in attendance. John Allen led his daughter down the grand staircase to the side of Governor Houston, and Eliza's hand was placed on Sam's arm. Candlelight illuminated the beautiful scene as Reverend William Hume presented the marriage vows. But the bridegroom noticed that his bride's hand was trembling.

Disaster

It was at the same time that Houston's first term was coming to an end. Billy Carroll wanted his governorship back, while Houston intended to keep it. On January 28th, six days after his wedding, he announced himself as a candidate for the upcoming August election.

Andrew Jackson had tried to prevent this collision by offering Carroll a South American ambassadorship, which the man flatly refused. Carroll had hoped that Houston would take a shot at the Senate, but the younger man had the support of his mentor, Jackson, and took the field with vigor.

Politically, Houston was riding high. Public comments during a debate held between the two seemed to favor Houston. Then the rug was pulled out from under him.

"Have you heard the news?"

"What news?"

"General Houston and his wife have separated, and she has gone home to her father."[3]

Burned in Effigy

Rumors abounded. Accusations were made against Houston, and a mob even burned the governor in effigy. Stephen F. Austin's sister Emily received this letter from a Tennessee friend who could not spell:

"There is a dreadfull stir in the country and town about our Governor... a thousand different tails afloat... I never can believe he has acted ungentlemanly untill I see him and know the trouth from himself for he was a man so popular I know it must be something dreadfull... none of his friends blame him so when you hear repoarts about him you may know they are not so. He has a good menny enemies and a great menny friends. He says time will show who is to blame. The reason he does not tell..."[4]

Carroll supporters swelled the crowds that gathered in the streets to protest Houston's supposed crimes. But the governor's friends showed themselves faithful.

The Chief Justice of the Tennessee Supreme Court, John H. Overton, stopped by, asking no questions, just wanting to support the beleaguered man.

The sheriff, also a friend, wanted to know what to tell the hysterical people filling his office.

"What can I tell them, Governor?"

"There's nothing to say, Billy."

"But you've got to say something, Governor. You owe it to yourself and your friends."

"This is a painful but private matter, Billy. I do not recognize the right of the public to interfere. I shall treat the public as though it had never happened."

"No!" the sheriff protested. "You can't do that. You'll sacrifice your friends and yourself."

Sam placed his hand on his friend's shoulder. "Remember, Billy, whatever may be said by the lady or her friends, it is no part of the conduct of a gallant and generous man to take up arms against a woman. If my character cannot stand the shock, then let me lose it."[5]

Houston's Darkest Hour

What had happened to cause the separation? Over the years, bits and pieces of the puzzle surfaced. Apparently, Eliza had been in love with another man, who had contracted consumption (tuberculosis) and had to leave the country for the sake of his health. In those days, the cause of tuberculosis was not understood, and its victims often died. All she had left were his letters.

When Eliza's father pressured her to marry Houston, she consented, thinking she could learn to love him, especially when there was no possibility of marriage to the other man. But this refined girl found Houston's uncouth manners hard to handle. And his war injuries had never totally healed. As a result, she was cold to him, and the sensitive Houston found himself reacting with jealousy.

Then on the day of the debate with Carroll, he arrived home unannounced and found his wife weeping and burning old love letters in the hearth. It must have been the final straw for the lovesick man, who accused her of infidelity. Later, when he better understood the situation, he regretted his words and made this clear to Eliza. He also seems to have said that he did not wish her to remain with him as a "slave."

Perhaps she took this last statement seriously, for only days later, Houston arrived home to find her gone and Nashville in an uproar. He jumped back on his horse and drove her hard, arriving at his in-laws' home in Gallatin with his mare drenched in sweat.

With the stipulation that his wife's aunt stay in the room with them, he was finally allowed to see Eliza and learned that she had told her parents everything, including his charge of infidelity.

Sam Houston knelt on the floor before his wife. In tears, he begged her to forgive him and come home, but she refused.

Upon arriving home, the grieving husband wrote a letter to his father-in-law:

> "That I was satisfied & believed her virtuous, I had assured her on last night & this morning. This should have prevented the facts ever coming to your knowledge & that of Mrs. Allen. I would not for millions it had ever been known to you... I would have perished first, & if mortal man had dared to charge my wife or say ought against her virtue I would have slain him. That I have & do love Eliza none can doubt, -- that she is the only object dear to me God will witness..."[6]

He continued in this heart-rending vein, entreating the Allens to forget the past. But somehow, Carroll's cronies got wind of the matter when it was leaked from the Allen household either by accident or by design. Once leaked, Houston's enemies made political hay.

Houston waited several days for a reply from the Allens, but there was no word, and the forlorn husband considered his situation. He later described these hours as the "darkest" of his life.

Then he picked up a pen and at his stand-up desk wrote a letter to the Speaker of the Tennessee Senate, General William Hall:

> It has become my duty to resign the office of Chief Magistrate of the state... that veneration for public opinion by which I have measured every act of my official life,

> has taught me to hold no delegated power which would not daily be renewed by my constituents... And although shielded by a perfect consciousness of undiminished claim to the confidence & support of my fellow citizens, yet delicately circumstanced as I am, & by my own misfortunes, more than by the fault of contrivance of anyone, overwhelmed by sudden calamities, it is certainly due to myself & more respectful to the world, that I should retire from a position which, in the public judgment, I might seem to occupy by questionable authority.—[7]

The letter was delivered, and a week later, wearing an Indian blanket over old clothes, Sam Houston boarded the Red Rover, a steamship on the river, traveling to Arkansas under an assumed name. His heart was empty, and he was searching for something... perhaps he even searched the Scriptures for answers. Before he left town, he had spoken with a minister, hoping to be baptized, but was refused. His heart turned toward his foster father and his Indian brethren.

On the riverboat, his thoughts gave way to despair, and he reproached himself for lashing out in jealousy. Later, he revealed to someone that at that point, "I was in an agony of despair and strongly tempted to leap overboard and end my worthless life. At that moment, however, an eagle swooped down near my head, and then, soaring aloft with wildest screams, was lost in the rays of the setting sun."

Taking it as a sign, his thoughts of suicide left him. "I knew then that a great destiny waited for me in the West."[8]

Troubles in Texas

Tall pines in red clay soil stood guard over the remnants of Nacogdoches, a village in East Texas, which had once boasted a population of over six hundred but was now only a shrunken, pathetic shadow of its former self. There remained now only a church and a few houses in what was practically a ghost town, though over the years various individuals had settled in the area around it. While some had titles to their land, and some were "squatters," the most certain thing that can be said is that an interesting composition of people lived there. A polyglot mixture, it was home to Spanish, Indians, French Creoles, and finally Anglos from the United States, with a few planters of substance among them.

On a warm day in the late spring of 1825, two men stood at a street corner, examining a notice, one of several identical notices posted in and around Nacogdoches, and their conversation went something like this:

"Juan, what in tarnation is this?"

"*No sé.*"

"Yeah, I *no sé* either. Haden Edwards. Have you ever met this here man? He says he military commander! Juan, this is a strange world we live in."

"*Es Tejas.*"

"Yeah, well, who does he think he is?"

Juan frowned at the notice.

"Look at this. He says here that all who claim land in this territory must present titles or documents . . . why on earth do we have to prove our claim to this Edwards fellow?"

"Empresario."

"What is an . . . empre—what?"

"*Como* Stephen Austin."

"You mean this man went and got some kind of contract from the Mexican government?"

"*Si.*"

Juan's neighbor was speechless, but only momentarily. "My claim is good, and I don't intend to give it up. It says here that the lands that don't meet Edwards' requirements will be "sold to the first person who occupies them." Well, I'm that first person, and I ain't moving."

Juan said nothing, but he was thinking.

A Title Dispute

Stephen Austin was disturbed. He held a letter from a man named Haden Edwards, a man who with his brother had obtained a contract and now was empresario of a large tract of land east of Stephen's own colony. Apparently, Edwards had sold a piece of land now occupied by a Mexican without a title to an American. The Mexican had petitioned the legislature, and the resulting controversy had the unfortunate effect of dividing the people. Mexicans now sided with the Mexican plaintiff, while some of the Americans sided with Edwards.

In this letter, Edwards boasted, "I came out in a Herricane... Sounded the trump all around bidding defiance to all their threats and bidding them leave the lands or... make arrangements to pay for them."[9]

Austin couldn't help but worry. From the beginning, the colonization project had required tact and discretion. This was not the United States, and they were under the authority of another nation. Foolishness could ruin everything.

He picked up his pen. "You do not understand the nature of the authority with which you are vested... " Austin wrote. "Continuation of [your] imprudent course... will totally ruin you, and materially injure all the new settlements."[10]

And he was right. Before long, the squatters took matters into their own hands. Forty men rode into Nacogdoches and seized Edwards. They took him to court, but no one would testify against him, because they were afraid of reprisal.

Desperate to make a point, these men tried and "convicted" several of Edwards' associates, in a kind of community lynching, which, fortunately, did not go as far as actual hanging.

Not long after this, the controversy between Edwards and the displaced Mexican was decided in favor of the Mexican. Edwards' brother appealed to the governor of the combined state of Coahuila-Texas, and was amazed and angered when the governor replied:

> "In view of such proceedings, by which the conduct of Haden Edwards is well attested, I have declared the annulment of his contract, and his expulsion from the territory of the [Mexican] republic... He has lost the confidence of the Government, which is suspicious of his fidelity... you will first evacuate the country, both yourself and Haden Edwards... "[11]

What the brothers did next boggles the mind. At any rate, it is a good example of the sinful pride of man. Appealing to other colonists to join their cause, on December 16, 1826, they declared Texas to be independent of Mexico and named it the Republic of Fredonia. The Edwards brothers appealed to Austin to help them, but the empresario refused.

In January, three hundred men under Colonel Mateo Ahumado marched east to put down the rebellion. On his way, Ahumado marched through San Felipe. Stephen Austin and several hundred armed colonists joined the force and approached Nacogdoches, where the Fredonians were stationed.

Discouraged, the Fredonians retreated, crossing the Sabine on January 31, 1827, and thus ended a revolution so pitiful that it would have been funny if it had not had other consequences. It left suspicion in the minds of all Mexican officials toward Americans. Despite the clear wrongdoing by Edwards (he was bound under the terms of his contract to protect the claims of prior owners), doubts rose in the minds of many who now believed the Mexican government had dealt unfairly with the Edwards brothers and could not be trusted.

The Young Santa Anna

Antonio Lopez de Santa Anna was eighteen, a daring young cadet in the royalist army. Spain ruled, but times were troubled. The poor and ignorant were exploited, and recently, rebellion had erupted, led by Catholic priests. Father Miguel Hidalgo y Costilla, a public-spirited but immoral clergyman, was the leader of the most recent incident. When finally he was betrayed, captured, and hanged, other priests rose up in his place, and blood flowed freely.

Now, in August 1813, young Santa Anna marched with others under General Joaquin de Arredondo, sent to quash a certain General Toledo. Another uprising had occurred, this time on the Medina River in Texas.

A large number of Anglo-Americans joined in the fray and were trapped by an ambuscade and summarily slaughtered.

Erasmo Seguin, now postmaster of San Antonio, must have been shocked at the cruelty. He tried to intervene to save the lives of the Americans, but it was of no use. Seven hundred fifty were killed. As a result of his intervention, Seguin was deposed from office, his property confiscated, and he was charged with treason. It took five years to be acquitted.

Santa Anna returned with his army to Mexico, where there was still work to be done, routing the stragglers from the Hidalgo rebellion. The young man showed great persistence and courage in this task, so much so that he was promoted to captain.

That Santa Anna was a genius, there is no doubt. Even Sam Houston recognized in him elements of genius and greatness. But his great talent was channeled into one primary goal: achieving power. And like the cat with nine lives, he refused to stay down when defeated, and over the years, won the position of leader of Mexico nine different times.

His earliest successes were associated with slaughter and bloodshed, quashing rebellion with brute force. During the political turmoil of the early 1800s, power was up for grabs.

The Emperor of Mexico

A new face appeared on the Mexican political scene, in the person of Augustin de Iturbide. Described as a "handsome, dashing man with brown hair and reddish sidewhiskers,"[12] he was clearly an opportunist. He had already offered his help to Hidalgo, but when the wise priest did not trust him, he simply exchanged loyalties and fought on the royalists' side. By deception and political maneuvering, he managed to garner support, including that of Santa Anna, who, by this time, was a lieutenant with a significant following.

On February 24, 1821, Iturbide declared Mexico's independence from Spain. Riding into Mexico City on a black charger, he was cheered by the people as "the

Father of Independence." Later, on July 21, 1822, he proclaimed himself "Emperor of Independent Mexico."

But this emperor did not rule long. In fact, his ally Santa Anna turned against him, and with a charisma that attracted followers, he provoked a revolution. Besieged, Iturbide's generals abandoned him, along with the rest of Iturbide's following. Now alone and hunted, the red-whiskered emperor fled the country.

A Mexican Republic?

But Santa Anna, at twenty-four, was too young to take command himself. He promoted a "republican" type of government, not out of conviction, but out of expediency. He helped set up a regency of three men; then he went on to establish a Congress, which met on November 7, 1823, to write a constitution.

Among educated Mexicans, there was support for the "republican" ideal of government. After all, their neighbor to the north, the United States, was a successful experiment in liberty, and *liberty* was a sweet-sounding word just now.

The only problem was, these Mexicans had no practical experience with republican government. The American colonies had sought to preserve a long-standing inheritance of political freedom through their revolution. And what was more, the United States Constitution was a document whose gestation had occurred over the centuries as a result of the English tradition of the rule of law. And finally, the truth of the gospel had ignited and tempered this tradition, giving the founding fathers wisdom they would not have otherwise possessed.

Mexico had no such tradition, nor had the gospel swept the country the way it had up north. And in fact, many Mexicans who theoretically supported republicanism did not even understand it. On the contrary, intrigue, tyranny, and treachery were the most salient characteristics of Mexican politics, and it was unlikely that things would change overnight.

Their congress did meet and form a constitution. But unlike the United States Constitution, which could not be amended or changed easily, because it held a place above normal statutory law, there were no such stipulations in the fledgling Mexican Constitution.

In fact, the new constitution could be easily changed or repealed by the Mexican Congress. And it did not provide for certain civil rights that Americans take for granted, such as trial by jury or the right to assembly.

Erasmo Seguin was part of the body forming this new document, representing Texas. One thing that Seguin wanted—that Anglo colonists opposed— was an amendment to unite Texas with Coahuila to the south, a much more heavily populated region. Texans feared their interests would be buried in the government of this larger state. But Seguin was able to add a provision for the establishment of Texas as a separate state at such time that it became able. This gave Texans the hope that they could eventually become independent.

With the new constitution in place, a man named Guadalupe Victoria was elected President and inaugurated on April 1, 1825, ushering in a time of peace for the Mexican people. Except for the Fredonian Rebellion and ongoing Indian troubles, Texans prospered as well.

But Santa Anna was still around, biding his time.

Houston with the Cherokee

Anticipating a good time, Diana Rogers prepared herself to go to the Green Corn Dance. She was a member of the important Rogers family, half-sister of James and John Rogers, Sam Houston's boyhood friends. Though more white than Indian by blood, she saw herself as Cherokee.

Tall and beautiful, Diana was alone. Her two children had died, and her husband had been killed by the Osages, on Osage hunting grounds, in a conflict that had occurred after Ooleteka's band had been relocated to Arkansas.

The Green Corn Dance was an important time for Cherokees. When the new corn crop approached maturity, the entire tribe gathered to celebrate and cleanse themselves from evil and disease. They would drink a bitter substance to purge both their bodies and their souls and entreat the Great Spirit to bless their crops. It was a chance to begin again.

The seven-day celebration was the most important annual event for the Cherokees. More than simply a religious event, it was a major social event as well. Upon her arrival, Diana greeted old friends and noticed a familiar face. Sam Houston.

Undoubtedly, Diana had heard Houston was back, but their paths might never have crossed in the year since he had arrived.

Still grieving over his lost love, Houston was welcomed by his foster father and eventually became a Cherokee citizen.

It is almost certain that Diana knew Sam from his youth. She may have wondered at the changes she saw in him. Sam's suffering must have etched itself on his face. Older now, his thick head of chestnut hair may have already begun to thin on top. He grew it long, braiding it down his back in a queue. He dressed as an Indian, though his flamboyant personality could not be hidden. He was extravagant even in Indian dress: a white embroidered doeskin hunting shirt, yellow buckskin leggings, beaded moccasins, and turkey feathers or a Cherokee-style turban on his head. He preferred to speak the Cherokee language; only his fair skin and blue eyes marked him as a white man.

There was something else that Diana must have already known, because it was common knowledge: Sam's heart was elsewhere. In Texas. Well, that was not entirely true. Right now, he had two passions: the Cherokees and Texas.

The Chief had received his foster son with these words:

> "I had heard that a dark cloud had fallen on the white path you were walking, and when it fell in your way you turned your thoughts to my wigwam. I am glad of it—it was done by the Great Spirit... We are in trouble and the Great Spirit has sent you to give us council, and take trouble away from us. I know you will be our friend, for our hearts are near to you, and you will tell our sorrows to the great father, General Jackson. My wigwam is yours—my home is yours—my people are yours—rest with us."[13]

Making every effort to help his Indian friends, Sam served as peacemaker between Indian tribes. He also worked as a kind of Cherokee ambassador to the federal government and fought against the corruption that was common among Indian Agents. Sadly, it was not unusual for Indians to be fleeced by the very ones appointed to see to their welfare.

But from the time he arrived in Arkansas, Sam Houston had Texas on his mind. A chance meeting with Jim Bowie on his trip down may have stimulated his interest, but he had been drawn to Texas since 1822, when he joined a group of investors trying to purchase land there.

With the Indians in Arkansas, the still-grieving Houston sought comfort in a bottle. He had long been a drinker, as many men were, but in exile, his intemperance became well known. Hurting and broken, he gave himself to the "flowing bowl."[14]

He was not the type to stay depressed for long, however, and his mind began to churn with possibilities. He believed in Providence, having a general faith in God from his Christian upbringing and exposure to the Scriptures, and the Indians' religious beliefs only reinforced his feeling that he had a special and yet unfulfilled destiny.

He saw himself like an ancient Roman named Marius, whom he had learned about from his reading. Caius Marius had repeatedly suffered setback and defeat, but gathered an army of rabble and peasants and was victorious in the end. It is said that when Houston was drunk, he quoted Marius, and he later asked to be painted as Marius in a portrait. This painting of Houston as Marius now hangs in the Austin Capitol building.

Identifying with Marius, he saw his setbacks as temporary. Always on his mind were the Cherokees and Texas, and after a while, almost everyone knew he wished to be President of Texas. And the Cherokees? He couldn't help but wonder if there was a better place for them, a place where he could protect them from the scourge of the white man. In his grieving and often drunken state, it is difficult to know how many of his remarks were truly serious.

But far away in Washington, his friend, President Jackson, was taking things seriously. He wrote to Houston:

> "It has been communicated that you had the illegal enterprise in view of conquering Texas; that you had declared that you would, in less than two years, be emperor of that country, by conquest. I must have really thought you deranged to have believed you had such a wild scheme in contemplation, and particularly when it was communicated and that the physical force to be employed was the Cherokee Indians."[15]

Houston had already denied wrongdoing in a previous letter. But it is clear, that even while still in Nashville, the ex-governor had voiced hope of leading a little "two-horse republic" in Texas. Jackson appeared mollified by Houston's assurances, but continued to be watchful. President Jackson was in a unique situation at the time, looking out for a dear friend, but at the same time trying to protect his reputation and see to the needs of an entire country.

Diana Rogers may not have known all of these details, but when she met Sam at the Green Corn Dance, it would not have taken her long to understand the direction of his heart. She was attracted to this tall man with turkey feathers in his hair. She must have seen past the heavy drinking and the frontier manners—all the Cherokees did. In spite of his behavior, they loved and respected him, even when he acquired the nickname, "Big Drunk." There must have come a point when Diana asked herself if she could join herself to such a man. And what would she do when he must leave... ?

During the dance, Houston did not participate in the ceremonies but sat and watched respectfully. At some time during the evening, he was introduced to Diana, and not long afterward, they were married.

Changes in Mexico

Meanwhile, the political house of cards that was Mexico was about to topple, and it would fall right on Stephen Austin's head. At first, this didn't seem likely; in fact, after the Fredonian Rebellion, things seemed to settle down. Then, in 1829, a revolt replaced Mexican President Vincente Guerrero with Vice President Anastacio Bustamante.

At first, the situation didn't seem likely to cause problems, because, for one thing, Bustamante was Austin's friend. Plus, the new President was centralist in his leanings, a healthy development for Mexico; its constitution resembled the unworkable Articles of Confederation the United States later replaced with the stronger federal Constitution.

Mexico was a weak country with a very large poor working class. Only a few at the top levels of society were wealthy. The Constitution of 1824 had divided the country into states, further decentralizing the government at a time of great national instability. It was a house of cards that would eventually collapse.

Austin was hopeful that perhaps Bustamante could keep things together. In Austin's opinion, he was ambitious, but overall a "very good man."[16]

Stephen F. Austin certainly did not need trouble right now. The care of the colony and worry over his family in Missouri had taken their toll. Wrinkles were appearing on his face, and his health was on the decline, though he was only thirty-six years of age. Those close to him became concerned, and someone remarked that Stephen was "now nothing but a mere shadow, and if he does not quit his desk, ride about and take more exercise, his life will be but short."[17] A deep sense of melancholy plagued his spirit.

Bustamante took office on the first of January, 1830, and his administration set in motion a sequence that led straight to the Alamo.

The Danger of the *Americanos*

General Manuel Mier y Terán didn't like the American colonists. To put it bluntly, they were foreigners. True, they had sworn allegiance to the Mexican government, and they were supposedly Catholic, but that didn't change the fact that they were still foreigners, Americans. They *thought* like Americans. In an unstable political situation, General Terán instinctively knew that these people could be turned against their government. They were a danger.

Terán's convictions were only strengthened as he traveled through Texas to do research. He had been commissioned to write a report on what Mexico must do to save her Texas territory. The colonists were not the only problem.

Twice now, once in 1825 and then again in 1829, the United States had offered to *buy* Texas. The U.S. was faced with a largely ungoverned territory at her back door, clearly a refuge for desperadoes. The offer to buy Texas was not fundamentally motivated by aggressive imperialism. It was more like the situation with Florida, where a powerless Spanish government could not restrain the Indians from raiding Georgia settlers. Taking over Florida had helped. Maybe taking over Texas would help bring peace to the region.

But Terán and others did not appreciate this point of view. These Mexicans knew that the U.S. was the stronger nation, and this made them feel defensive. General Terán was certainly not the only Mexican official who was suspicious of Americans. He needed to compose a report for his superior, Lucas Alamán.

Picking up his pen, he wrote that the Mexican government needed to secure Texas. And it had to be done now. If events kept unfolding as they were, Texas might well break away—and once that happened, reconquest without a local base of operations would prove to be difficult, if not impossible.

General Terán was thinking like a general--a general who was taking his own country's weakness into account. The Americans were, in his eyes, the "enemies."

He proposed to establish numerous military posts in Texas, even suggesting that the Mexican population could be increased if convicts, when released from jail, were to settle in Texas.

Bustamente's Law

Alamán read the report and agreed. He formulated a policy that eventually gave birth to Bustamante's Law of April 6, 1830. The law provided for the military occupation of Texas, settlements composed of Europeans and Mexican convicts, new customs duties, other trade restrictions, and a cancellation of all unfulfilled empresario contracts. Further, American immigration was also prohibited.

For Stephen Austin, Bustamante's Law was a trial by fire. He wrote both Bustamante and Alamán, protesting that the law was unwise. He hoped for repeal, but for the time being, argued for his own interests and the interests of his colony by giving the law an expansive interpretation. He argued that his own unfulfilled contracts—only the original contract of 300 families was totally settled at that point—were actually fulfilled in the sense that he had already contracted with the settlers planning to immigrate. This was a blatant lie. The truth was that when immigrants to Texas heard about the empresario's contracts, they loaded their wagons and came. Austin simply welcomed those who showed up, with no idea who was coming. In the end, he signed blank certificates and had them sent to the border for immigrants to fill out and present to Mexican officials.

But Austin had another problem. The settlers. They not only thought like Americans, they were independent, frontier types who did not take kindly to the idea of military occupation. And the customs taxes! The Anglo-American settlers liked their local autonomy and did not want to give it up. The stage was set for another "Boston Tea Party."

In accord with his nature, Austin sought peace. He assured the colonists that the Mexican troops were there for their protection. That was not exactly true either. At the same time he was trying to pacify the settlers, he was also writing the Mexican government on their behalf:

> "I have informed you many times, and I inform you again, that it is impossible to rule Texas by a military system... From the year 1821 I have maintained order and enforced the law in my colony simply by means of civicos [civil decrees], without a dollar of expense to the nation [Mexico]... Upon this subject of military despotism I have never hesitated to express my opinion, for I consider it the source of all revolutions and of the slavery and ruin of free peoples."[18]

Despite Austin's efforts at diplomacy, trouble broke out. A hot-headed young lawyer from Georgia, William Barret Travis, led a small group in punishing a couple of Mexican soldiers for bad behavior. They were arrested and confined in the brick fort at the mouth of the Trinity River, where the incident occurred.

Word spread, and colonists gathered from miles around. They elected Frank W. Johnson as their leader and marched on the fort, where they demanded the release of Travis and others. The Mexican commander, an Anglo adventurer named Colonel John Bradburn, decided to exchange his prisoners for the captives Johnson had taken.

This was Texas's own interpretation of the "Boston Tea Party." Real trouble was yet to come.

Houston and Stanberry

Attired in a rumpled buckskin coat, Sam Houston arrived in New York City. It was March of 1832, and he had come to see James Prentiss, a financier involved in selling land in Texas. Houston was beginning to sound out the ways and means to accomplish his dreams, and thought perhaps a survey trip was in order.

Shortly, Houston traveled south to Washington. Three days after he arrived, he picked up a copy of the April 3rd edition of the *National Intelligencer*, containing the report of a speech by Congressman William Stanberry of Ohio. In it, the Congressman had asked the question, "Was the late Secretary of War removed because of his fraudulent attempt to award the contract for Indian rations to Governor Houston?"[19]

The smear was directed against the Jackson administration generally and against Houston in particular. Apparently, Houston's efforts in exposing corruption had garnered enemies. Stanberry put a slanderous spin on a situation that had occurred in 1830, in which Houston had sought a contract as a provider of Indian rations.

The charge was specious, but it prompted Houston to write to Stanberry: "The object of this note is to ascertain whether my name was used by you in debate, and if so, whether your remarks have been correctly quoted... I hope you will find it convenient to reply without delay."[20]

Stanberry replied that he did not recognize the right of Mr. Houston to make this request. Infuriated, Houston made it known that he planned to chastise the congressman at the first opportunity. For this purpose, he carried a heavy walking stick cut from a hickory tree at the Hermitage wherever he went.

The Beating

One evening, Houston and two friends paid a call on a senator, and later, after leaving, were walking along Pennsylvania Avenue, only to see Stanberry approach. One of their party, a congressman, fled, anticipating trouble. The other companion, Senator Buckner, was later to testify to what happened next.

Stanberry, a large man of impressive physique, strode up, and Houston asked politely, "Are you Mr. Stanberry?"

The man answered that he was.

"Then you are the d—d rascal!" Houston exclaimed and struck the congressman over the shoulder with his hickory cane.

"Oh, don't!" Stanberry tried to escape. Houston leaped on the large man from behind, but was unable to simultaneously hold and strike him because of his war injuries. Finally, Stanberry tripped and fell, and Houston chastised the congressman's posterior while the man yelled.

Then, Stanberry pulled out a concealed weapon and tried to fire it, but it apparently did not discharge, and Houston seized it before continuing to whack the man's backside.

When Houston stopped, the congressman fled.

Houston was later asked how he felt while punishing Stanberry, and he replied, "Meaner than I ever felt in my life; I thought I had gotten hold of a great dog, but found a contemptible whining puppy."[21]

Arrested

From his bed, Stanberry brought charges against Houston, asking the Speaker to lay the issue before the House. Houston was arrested and brought before the House of Representatives.

Wearing his shabby buckskin coat and carrying the cane, Sam Houston was escorted down the aisle by the sergeant-at-arms. The arraignment was read, charging that Houston had "waylaid" Stanberry, a charge Sam denied, though he did admit to a spontaneous assault. He was given forty-eight hours to prepare his defense. What happened next became a turning point in his life.

At first, things did not seem to be going well. Stanberry lied, saying he had not intended his statement to accuse Houston of fraud. To make matters worse, Houston's attorney was not in good form; his arguments were worse than pathetic.

Anti-Jackson newspapers had a field day when the trial dominated the news. One newspaper reported that Jackson wished for a "dozen Houstons to beat and cudgel members of Congress."[22] What the feisty president had actually said was, "After a few more examples of the same kind, members of Congress will learn to keep civil tongues in their heads."

After a week, Jackson sent for Houston. He was in a worse rage than Houston had ever seen before. "It's not you they wish to injure, Sam," he said. They wish to injure your old commander."[23] Wanting to help Houston, Jackson insisted that he accept money, most of which went to a tailor, who made him a fine set of clothes, including a white satin waistcoat.

From then on, because it was important for him to clear his name, Houston handled his own defense. In front of the court, he touched upon a more fundamental issue than his behavior.

> "When a member of this House, entrenched in his privilege, brands a private citizen in the face of the whole nation, as a fraudulent villain he... renders himself answerable to the party aggrieved... Gentlemen have admitted that the power they claimed is not in the Constitution. Then where is it?"

The House chamber was, that day, packed with socialites, dignitaries, the press, and, of course, numerous members. Houston's oration gripped them all one way or another; his enemies were furious while his friends rejoiced.

He continued,

> "But while standing at this bar, have I not been branded with the epithet of assassin?... I bore no dagger when I met my accuser!... I could not but think of the... rebuke administered to the high priest of the Jews by the Apostle Paul, when he stood in bonds before him; the high priest ordered him to be smote upon the mouth. 'God shall smite thee, thou whited wall, for sittest thou to judge me according to the law, and commandest me to be smitten contrary to the law?'"[24]

Houston understood the rule of law and accused the House of tyranny and illegality in the case before them. They had stepped well beyond their bounds in trying him in this manner. Then he paused, and a hushed silence fell on the chamber.

Continuing, Houston first reminded his audience of his voluntary pledge to abide by the judgment and penalty of the House, however illegal the proceedings. Then he brought up a matter that had been stricken from the Congressional Record because of its impropriety. Apparently, during the trial, the prosecution brought up Houston's former marital troubles. He then proceeded to remind them that he was not on trial for his marital difficulties and tragic suffering.

The distinguished man in the white waistcoat straightened his shoulders. "That man Stanberry," he roared, "has slandered me through the columns of a newspaper, and refused to answer even a polite note, and I chastised him as I would a dog, and I will visit the same punishment on the shoulders of anyone who insults me, even though it be on one of you who now sits in judgment of my conduct."[25]

Houston's speech brought down the house, while the Speaker pounded his gavel, but it was no use. Finally, when it was quiet, a young woman in the gallery rose and tossed a bouquet at Houston's feet. She cried, "I had rather be Sam Houston in a dungeon than Stanberry on a throne."[26]

The defendant stooped down and retrieved the flowers, then bowed in thanks, and added, "Though the ploughshare of ruin has been driven over me and laid waste my brightest hopes... I have only to say to those who rebuke me... when they see adversity pressing upon me...

"I seek no sympathies, nor need; the thorns which I have reaped are of the tree I planted; they have torn me, and I bleed."[27]

He finished his oration with an emotional appeal.

> "Though it may have been alledged that I am a man of broken fortune and blasted reputation, I never can forget that reputation, however limited, is the high boon of heaven. Perhaps the circumstances of adversity, by which I have been crushed, have made me cling to the little remains of it which I still possess, and to cherish them with greater fondness."

Then Houston quoted a poem he had written, without naming the author.

There is a bright undying thought in man,
That bids his soul still upward look
To Fame's proud cliff;
And longing, look
In hope to give his name
For after ages to admire
And wonder how he reached
The dizzy dangerous height,
Or where he stood, or how.

Then he pointed to the American flag hanging in the House chamber, and concluded,

> "So long as that flag shall bear aloft its glittering stars... shall the rights of American citizens be preserved safe... till discord shall wreck the spheres... and the grand march of time shall cease—and not one fragment of all creation be left to chafe on the bosom of eternity's waves."[28]

Sam took a bow, and the gallery rose in standing ovation, while once again, the Speaker's gavel cracked in vain.

Although in the end, Houston received a reprimand, he scored a win in the court of public opinion. Also, when the ration matter was investigated, the final report stated, "John H. Heaton [the former Secretary of War mentioned by Stanberry] and Samuel Houston do stand entirely acquitted from all imputation of fraud."[29]

For Houston, this was a huge personal victory. He had stood his ground, fought, and won. The shabby coat was gone. Big Drunk was gone, and now it was time to rejoin the living. And that meant Texas.

Chapter 7

Come and Take It

PATIENTLY, Jack put one foot in front of the other, enduring two burdens: the weight on his back and the occasional flies to which his tail-less condition rendered him vulnerable. Jack was a small yellow Spanish mustang, carrying a rather large man whose long legs dangled on either side of him. Yet in a single trip, this homely but hardy creature managed to transport to Texas that state's own future general, president, senator, and governor, albeit in a slightly ridiculous fashion.

Sam Houston entered Texas with very little to call his own. He had left his good horse with Diana. In fact, he'd left her everything, including their home, with its wonderful backyard orchard, nestled beside the long main road that led to Texas.

He never made a public statement about his Cherokee wife, but rumors sprang up, flourishing over the years. One rumor said that Diana died before Houston left for Texas. This, however, seems unlikely. In another story, this one much more likely, it is said that he begged her to accompany him to Texas, but the beautiful Cherokee woman refused, instead choosing to remain with her own people. At any rate, divorce among the Cherokees consisted of "dividing the blanket," and apparently, Houston gave her most of it.

Houston Arrives in Texas

When Houston arrived in Nacogdoches, he reacquainted himself with some of his old friends. He then packed up and turned his horse onto the *Camino Real*, the

King's Highway, which ran from Nacogdoches to San Antonio and beyond. It was full of weeds and sometimes difficult to follow. Then he took the Middle Road to San Felipe de Austin, the headquarters of Stephen Austin's colony.

It was December of 1832, and the air was crisp and the sunshine bright, when Houston rode his mount along the main thoroughfare of the frontier town, looking for Stephen Austin. On paper, San Felipe had been laid out with some care and hope; in practice, it was a sorry-looking place, including crude homes, saloons, the village "smithy," the alcalde's office, and a hotel, all strung out unevenly along one main road. The sign at the Virginia House Hotel promised no rats or fleas.

Jim Bowie

After a short search, Houston located Austin's home, but the empresario was not there. Instead, he found a man who was almost as tall as he was: James Bowie, who was also looking for Austin. Jim Bowie must have noticed the change in Houston, who was now clean-shaven and alert, in contrast to the broken man Bowie had met once before. This man, he could believe, had once been the Governor of Tennessee.

Jim Bowie must have shared his adventures with Houston as the two rode together to San Antonio. He probably explained how he had met and fallen in love with the elder daughter of the vice-governor of Coahuila-Texas, Ursula Veramendi. They had married, and Bowie now had a precious little daughter. Now the owner of a textile mill in Coahuila and a land speculator, he was prospering financially, after purchasing property in Austin's colony as well as a nice home near Saltillo.

Bowie liked making money, and apparently, he was good at it, but the warm-hearted man was also given to gambling, like many other Texas adventurers. The muscular man with the reddish mane loved excitement and adventure. He may have told Houston about a recent adventure in which he almost lost his life.

Bowie, it seemed, had always been fascinated by tales of old silver mines that were supposedly located just north of San Antonio. On an expedition financed by his in-laws the year before, he had taken along his brother, Rezin, and nine other men to investigate the San Sabra area. Six miles from San Saba, a band of Indians attacked them. Camped in an oak grove, they fought for their lives. They were greatly outnumbered, but after thirteen hours, the Indians departed, leaving forty of their warriors dead and thirty more wounded. Of Bowie's men, only one was killed, though several more were injured, before the adventurers finally returned home.

Skirmish at Nacogdoches

As the two men wended their way along the king's road, Bowie may have talked about the battle at Nacogdoches, about which the future Texas general may have already heard, after visiting with his friends in town.

Ironically, the battle at Nacogdoches had only occurred because the Mexican garrison commander was trying to avoid trouble. Col. Jose de las Piedras, officer in charge of nearly 300 men at Nacogdoches, had visited Anahuac, where the "tea party" episode involving William Travis had occurred. Piedras had tried to quell the antagonisms between the colonists and the government in that area before returning to Nacogdoches. Upon his arrival, he demanded that the inhabitants surrender their weapons. A sensible precaution. The Mexican commander certainly wanted no uprisings in *his* jurisdiction.

The settlers, however, refused. The ayunamiento of Nacogdoches organized a militia and sent word to others, desperately demanding help. Jim Bowie was one of those who had responded as part of a hastily gathered group that elected James W. Bullock as its senior captain.

On August 2, 1832, Bullock made two demands. First, that Piedras rescind his order, and second, that the colonel declare for Santa Anna. The colonel refused on both counts.

Bowie may also have explained to Houston something of the confusing political situation in Mexico at the time. Santa Anna had been opposing President Bustamante, whose hated law of 1830, prohibiting immigration, had triggered the unrest in Texas. Santa Anna was a federalist, who would undoubtedly bring more liberal policies to bear regarding Texas, and for that reason, many Texans favored him. Col. Piedras symbolized the Bustamante regime and the law that had called for the establishment of military garrisons in the first place.

It wasn't long before fighting broke out. Texan losses were very light; Piedras lost thirty-seven men. The Mexican commander decided to evacuate and left with his men during the night.

Jim Bowie joined a small group of men who pursued the Mexican column. They ambushed the fleeing soldiers, who then turned against their commander and turned him over to the Texans. Bowie eventually escorted these soldiers to San Antonio, where they were released. Piedras was taken to San Felipe and turned over to Austin, who released him on parole. The colonel returned to Mexico, and Nacogdoches was finally free.

As the former Louisiana man described these events, Houston listened with interest.

A Scout for President Jackson

After arriving in San Antonio, Jim Bowie took Houston under his wing and introduced him to his family. Entertained by the Veramendi family, Houston explored the town of San Antonio with its stone and adobe dwellings. Don Veramendi introduced his guest as Don Samuel Houston, who was undoubtedly polite and even charming to his hosts. But there was another task at hand: Don Samuel was a secret emissary for President Jackson.

Houston had two tasks, one overt and one covert. On the surface, his mission was to meet with Indian chiefs, which he did. He met with Comanche chiefs north of San Antonio, relaying messages from Jackson and informing them of a peace conference with other tribes scheduled for three months hence in Arkansas.

But that was only one of his tasks. The other was to scout out the country for President Jackson, who, in those turbulent times, needed eyes and ears he could trust. Houston eventually wrote a letter, reporting to Jackson that Texans were determined to have a separate state government. He also wrote that nineteen-twentieths of the people would be in favor of the acquisition of Texas by the United States.

He went on:

> She can defend herself against the whole power of Mexico, for really Mexico is powerless and penniless...Her want of money taken with the course that Texas must *and will adopt*, will render a transfer of Texas to some power inevitable...
>
> My opinion is that Texas, by her members in Convention, will, by 1st of April, declare all that country [north of the Rio Grande] as Texas proper, and form a State Constitution. I expect to be present at that Convention, and will apprise you of the course adopted...I may take Texas as my abiding place . . .[but] *I will never forget* the country of my birth...[1]

A Convention

Houston seemed very confident that Texas would separate itself from Mexico and that such a move would be successful. How did he come to these conclusions? Some say that he absorbed these notions from Texas radicals, who believed along these lines. Maybe, but Sam Houston was always his own man, thinking for himself.

The "Convention" he referred to was not the first held in Texas. A couple of months before Houston arrived in Texas, in October 1832, a convention had been held in San Felipe. Stephen Austin presided and helped to squash the more radical elements calling for war. The grievances of the colonists were expressed in a petition to the Mexican government, demanding a separate government for Texas and free immigration.

Then the colonists got the good news. The hated Bustamante had been deposed! Santa Anna had led a revolt against the Mexican president and had been elected in his stead. He was to take office on April 1st. The colonists called for a new convention, hoping they would have more success. Santa Anna was now the champion of the people. He would hear their cry!

Nacogdoches chose Sam Houston as its delegate to this convention. He was a newcomer, but the citizens of that small hamlet seemed to esteem "Don Samuel."

Austin's Trials and Sufferings

Stephen F. Austin was a man who enjoyed the finer things in life. Good company, fine clothes, and he had occasionally spoken of a desire to "hunt a jolly old widow" to marry. Austin was not truly old, being only in his thirties, but he was looking careworn. He had even commented that he was a "kind of slave" with Texas as a master.[2]

He was a man capable of entering the highest levels of diplomacy, and so he did, corresponding and meeting with high-level Mexican officials, always seeking a peaceful solution to the whirlwinds that now surrounded Texas. He was not one to join in the gambling and revelries that served as entertainment in San Felipe.

Austin had promised and worked to ensure that the settlers in his empresario grant would be of good character, and most were exactly that, living and working diligently on their farms. Some of those in town were tradesmen, such as Noah Smithwick, who had ridden into San Felipe a few years before and had set up his blacksmith shop. Others who straggled in were outlaws and adventurers or insolvent debtors, who were either trying to escape debtors' prison—some states still put debtors in jail—or were simply trying to start a new life.

Noah Smithwick later wrote that, "It was the regular thing to ask a stranger what he had done, and if he disclaimed being guilty of any offense, he was regarded with suspicion." He went on to explain, "Historians, however, fail to discriminate between the true colonists—those who went there to make homes, locate land, and so far as the unfriendly attitude of the Indians permitted, were able to reside on the land and improve it—and the outlaws and adventurers who flocked into the towns."[3]

The Problem of Outlaws

The riffraff were illegal immigrants. The Anglo colonists of Texas had been granted permission to live in Texas according to the terms of their empresario's contract with the government. These requirements included Mexican citizenship and a pledge to support the Mexican government. Stephen Austin and most of the settlers entered this agreement with sincerity. The colonists were also supposed to be Catholic, but this requirement was only loosely enforced. In any case, Americans who came to Texas and lived there apart from the empresario system were not only illegal invaders in the eyes of the Mexican government, but they also tended to have very little loyalty to the established authorities.

When Bustamante's government forbade further immigration by that hated law of 1830, the only people who actually obeyed that law were the law-abiding, while outlaws and adventurers continued to come to Texas as before. And so, in the end, the law of 1830 worsened the situation for the Mexicans.

The Problem of Factions

Stephen Austin was not especially enthusiastic about the upcoming convention. For one thing, there would be a group of hotheads in attendance. Collectively, these men were labeled the "War Party."

For another thing, Austin had yet to secure the active involvement of the Tejanos, though he knew that many of them were like-minded with the Anglo colonists. The *empresario* understood the delicate nature of the situation. He knew that to have petitions submitted only by Anglos would paint a picture he must avoid at all costs: the takeover of Texas by Americans. Mexicans and Anglo colonists must present a united front in protesting wrongs. But San Antonio, a Tejano stronghold, had sent no delegate to the first convention.

The new convention met at San Felipe on April 1, 1833, the same day Santa Anna took office as President of Mexico. Austin must have been greeting the arriving delegates when Sam Houston rode in from Nacogdoches. William Wharton and his cronies were there: the "War Party." One of them, David G. Burnet, an attorney practicing in San Felipe, was barely over five feet in height, but he made up for it in other ways: scorning alcohol, he carried a pistol in one pocket and a Bible in the other. Austin's friend Erasmo Seguin had come from San Antonio. With these and other delegates present, the first order of business was to elect a presiding officer.

Austin's heart probably sank when Wharton of the War Party was elected. In the first convention, Austin had been elected and managed to keep a lid on the hotheads, but what would happen now? And what did Austin think of Sam Houston, who had supported Wharton?

Houston knew that his constituents in Nacogdoches were dissatisfied with the results of the first convention. They had hoped for more forceful results from the first convention. For this reason, he supported Wharton over Austin, though he did respect the *empresario.*

Austin, however, need not have worried, as the assembly did nothing radical. It prepared a new plea to the Mexican government, again requesting a separate state government. But this time, the convention went ahead and formed a committee headed by Houston that actually wrote a constitution for the proposed Mexican state of Texas. The resulting document was well crafted, according to Houston, who wrote most of it.

Three individuals were chosen to take these documents to Mexico City: Austin, Seguin, and another man, James B. Miller. Houston supported the choice of Austin for the mission and later spoke to Austin privately, assuring him of his support. He did not want Austin to think evil of him, knowing that after he supported Wharton for presiding officer, the *empresario* might suspect him of intrigue in his absence. Houston promised that there would be no intrigue but affirmed that he would support and sustain him in his absence.

Austin Goes to Mexico City

On April 22, 1833, Stephen F. Austin mounted a mule and rode west, probably taking the *Camino Real.* It was springtime, and rain and muddy roads made the trip to San Antonio miserable. He slogged along for a week without any hotels along the way, but Texas settlers proved to be a hospitable group, more than willing to put up travelers for the night.

"This is my last effort to save Texas," he wrote a cousin at the time. "If I succeed I shall be happy, and will try to enjoy some comfort in [the] future and have nothing to do with politics or public business. If however I fail, and war is the result, I will take a hand in that, and enter the ranks as a soldier of Texas."[4]

Before journeying to Mexico City, Austin wanted to meet with the Texan leaders in San Antonio. Their support was crucial.

But Austin was disappointed. After much debate, the principal citizens of San Antonio refused to endorse the convention's petition. Not because they disagreed in principle, but because they were afraid. The convention itself was illegal, according to Mexican law; only state legislatures had the right to petition Congress. These Mexican citizens also had a better sense of what could happen to revolutionaries than these Anglos did. Erasmo Seguin remembered the slaughter in 1813. In the eyes of the Mexican government, Austin's petition was at best irregular, at worst, seditious. It was dangerous. Seguin stood with Austin in endorsing the plan but asked to be excused from the trip to Mexico City.

In the end, Austin went alone.

Stricken by Cholera

On July 18, 1833, Stephen F. Austin arrived in Mexico City, just before the cholera did.

Cholera is rare in modern countries with good sanitation. That is because it spreads through contaminated water. The bacteria attach themselves to the intestinal wall and proceed to produce toxins. These toxins cause diarrhea, which can be so bad that the victim dies of dehydration and electrolyte loss in only a matter of hours.

On August 12, Stephen Austin was stricken. He described his symptoms. ". . . excessive purging of a white mucos nature, great pain in bowels, cold feet, hands, etc, pains over the body—no cramps—moderate vomiting." He recovered, although he mentioned that "others have died in less than one hour whose simptoms [sic] were similar to mine."[5]

People were dying all around him. "[I]t was horrible," he reported. He estimated the death toll at eighteen thousand in Mexico City alone.[6]

Then he received devastating news. The epidemic was also raging in Texas. In October, he learned that his widowed sister's young daughter had died.

"I am so much afflicted by accounts of the deaths by cholera in Texas that I can scarcely write anything," Austin wrote to an associate. "I am too wretched to write on this subject or any other."[7]

The same day, he wrote another letter, to the ayuntamiento of San Antonio. Austin's efforts in the Mexican capital were not very promising. "... in my opinion nothing will be done... Therefore I hope that you will not lose one moment in sending a communication to all the Ayuntamientos of Texas, urging them to unite in a measure to organize a local government independent of Coahuila, even though the general government withholds its consent." Normally Stephen Austin closed his letters with the expression, *Dios y libertad*. But this time, he signed it, *Dio y Teyas*. God and Texas.[8]

The depressed man probably did not realize what this letter would cost him.

Illness Strikes Bowie and His Family

Bowie felt his head. It hurt. His muscles hurt. And he felt so cold ... surely, hopefully, this wasn't what he thought it was. Then he threw up. Bowie stared. "Black vomit" was another name for the dreaded yellow fever.

No one knew what caused this disease, although there were speculations. It tended to come and go in epidemics. Years later, the mosquito would be shown to be the vector for this African disease that had come to America on ships bearing slaves.

No wonder this disease kept reappearing around the coastal bayous of Louisiana and Texas. Mosquitoes.

Bowie was in Louisiana, visiting his family and conducting some business. But now he lay in pain, on a bed at his mother's home. He was glad now that he had left Ursula at home with their little daughter. Especially in her condition... would it be a boy this time? Delirious, Bowie's mind drifted. The creak of the Spanish moss in the mattress reminded him of his youth.

Days passed, and finally, Jim Bowie regained his strength.

Then one day, he received a letter from Texas.

When he opened the letter and began to read, this famous knife fighter was pierced to the heart. His wife, both children, and both of his in-laws were dead. Cholera had swept through Texas and stolen from Jim Bowie all those he cherished the most.

Austin Imprisoned

The building was made of stone, the walls three feet thick. It was originally a Dominican convent. Later, it was used in the Spanish Inquisition to incarcerate heretics. Stephen Austin sat inside a cold stone cell, sixteen by thirteen feet in size, with a high ceiling and a small skylight which did little to dispel the gloom. Austin had been condemned to solitary confinement and sat miserably, staring at snakes and landscapes scrawled on the wall by a prisoner during the Inquisition years before.

He was allowed no books or writing materials, but had managed to smuggle a small notebook and pencil in his clothing.

"What a horrible punishment is solitary confinement, shut up in a dungeon with scarcely light enough to distinguish anything," Austin scribbled in the notebook.[9] Although he was lonely, he did manage to make friends with a mouse, feeding it crumbs from his dinner. Thankfully, the guards were not cruel, and he was able to have food brought in from outside.

Austin's letter to the ayuntamiento of San Antonio ended up in the wrong hands, after which he was accused of sedition and arrested. Austin had never been hot-headed, even in his depressed state, but he had heard of further developments in Texas, including plans to hold another convention to declare Texas independent from Coahuila. Austin knew he could not restrain the Anglo colonists. Events had progressed beyond the *empresario's* gentle persuasion. But if he could convince the ayuntamientos, the town councils, to take matters into their own hands, things might be seen in a better light. Austin had always been the diplomat. *Sigh*. Now a diplomat in a dungeon.

There was one good result of this imprisonment as far as Mexico was concerned. After an initial wave of outrage, the inhabitants of Texas quieted down for a while. They didn't want anything to happen to Austin.

The Napoleon of the West

"Were I made God," said Santa Anna, "I should wish to be something more."[10] This statement was a good summary of the personal philosophy of Mexico's new president. He wasn't satisfied with being president; he wanted more.

At first, he relegated most of his presidential duties to Vice-President Farias, while he busied himself putting down dissension and other tasks related to gathering power. Santa Anna portrayed himself as the champion of the people, a tactic common to those who wished to become dictators.

Tall and thin, with "brilliant and restless eyes,"[11] this cunning demagogue styled himself the "Napoleon of the West." He even surrounded himself with Napoleonic bric-a-brac. Santa Anna's fascination with the French emperor was so complete that one of his generals, Filisola, observed that he wanted to do nothing that Napoleon himself would not do.

And like Napoleon, Antonio Lopez de Santa Anna wanted to be Emperor.

On January 1, 1835, the power-hungry man made his move.

Bleeding Zacatecas

The reeling man stumbled in the door, his back covered with the red wheals of a lash. He groaned, and someone came to his aid. Santa Anna's men had beaten him.

The men of Zacatecas received the newcomer. They were engaged in a battle for their liberty, which had now become a battle for their very lives.

Several months earlier, in January, Santa Anna had proclaimed himself dictator. Abolishing the Congress, he established a new legislative body, composed of members of his own loyal following. This new Congress did everything he wanted, rewriting the Constitution of 1824, until the Napoleon of the West was finally satisfied. Power was his. When Vice-President Farias protested, he was called a traitor and banished. Santa Anna then found a more tractable vice president.

Santa Anna then moved to abolish all state legislatures, including that of Coahuila-Texas. He appointed governors who would be directly responsible to him. Most of Mexico submitted out of fear. What else could they do?

The brave citizens of Zacetecas, however, organized for resistance, refusing to surrender their weapons, esteeming their civil liberties more than their safety.

But they did not account for the treachery of Santa Anna, who sent several of his trusted officers to infiltrate the ranks, pretending to join the insurgents. The patriots of Zacatecas received these men, only to be betrayed.

To make an example of them, the "Mexican Napoleon" massacred them as traitors. But not too quickly. Rape and torture came first, followed by burning, looting, and pillaging. Not only men, but also defenseless women and children were slain.

Elsewhere, others saw through their leader's vicious hypocrisy. Brave Mexicans protested, calling Santa Anna the "worthy son of the father of lies," an "unrivaled chameleon," who possessed "...the tranquility of a tiger, which, sated with the flesh of its prey, reposes on what it does not wish to devour..."[12]

Amazingly, Santa Anna preached that his life was entirely devoted to the freedom and happiness of the people and the preservation of the federal system. He knew that with many people, the word "freedom" was enough. He could give them that.

Texas—the Next Target

The variegated, motley mob, twenty-five concerned citizens of San Felipe, gathered to discuss recent events on this June day. Assembled in the barn-like alcalde's office, an unfinished building with a dirt floor, the group had met to discuss Captain Antonio Tenorio, the Anahuac customs collector, who had thrown Andrew Briscoe into jail in January. Briscoe hadn't done anything horrible. Just played pranks on the guards. Should they help him?

Then a fellow arrived with a mailbag that had been captured from a courier. It contained letters from General Martin Perfecto de Cos, Santa Anna's brother-in-law, who had been assigned to rule Mexico's northern provinces, including Coahuila-Texas. With Santa Anna's blessing, Cos had abruptly disbanded the legislature at Monclova and arrested the governor. The Texans who were there at the time fled, and now Cos ruled. Former Americans, accustomed to civil liberties, were now living under martial law. The colonists had sworn allegiance to the Mexican government, true, but they would never have sworn allegiance to *this*. And the adventurers had no such oath to worry about.

They opened the bag and explored its contents. Here was a letter addressed to Captain Tenorio, the very fellow they had been discussing! What did it say?

It was from General Cos. He acknowledged Tenorio's complaints against the settlers, and promised that more troops would be coming, as the beleaguered customs collector had requested. That wasn't good news.

Pulling out another letter from Cos, the citizens read:

"In a very short time the affairs of Texas will be definitely settled, for which purpose the Government has ordered to take up the line of march a strong division composed of the troops which were in Zacatecas... These [Texas] revolutionaries will be ground down... "[13]

Troops which were in Zacatecas! They knew what had happened in Zacatecas. Fugitives had trickled across the border several months earlier, confirming the gruesome rumors about Santa Anna. The truth sank in--they were to be the second Zacatecas.

Word spread quickly, and the very next day, a group of two hundred men gathered and organized a force to go to Anahuac and take care of Tenorio. The customs collector wasn't Santa Anna, but for the angry men, he was good enough.

The Impetuous William Travis

William Travis took charge of twenty-five firebrands, a group that eventually swelled to 250. They seized a ship, put a cannon on it, and proceeded to load it with the one available cannonball. Taking the ship to Anahuac, they aimed the cannon at the Mexican fort located there. Someone lit a match. *Boom!*

A hit! But a cloud of dust obscured their vision, and when it settled, the men on board were probably bitterly disappointed. Unfortunately, the shot had done no discernible damage to the fort.

But the impetuous Travis was not discouraged. He proceeded to demand immediate surrender, and when Captain Tenorio asked for a day to consider, Travis gave him one hour. Based on one cannonball and chutzpah.

Tenorio was outnumbered and knew it could get worse. He surrendered, and he and his men were paroled, being forced to pledge never again to fight against Texas. Those captured were sent to San Antonio.

But most of Texas disapproved. Not sure of what course to take, the colonists generally regarded this action as rash or premature. Certainly dangerous.

William Travis defended his actions.

> "I discharged what I conceived to be my duty to my country to the best of my ability. Time alone will show whether that step was correct or not. And time will show that when this country is in danger that I will show myself as patriotic & ready to serve her as those who to save themselves have disavowed the act & denounced me to the usurping military."[14]

Santa Anna's men demanded the arrest of Travis and several other troublemakers, but the colonists responded that the whereabouts of these men were unknown. *So sorry.*

Austin Returns

Then, about a month later, Stephen Austin arrived after being released from prison. At the same time, news reached the colonists that Santa Anna had gathered three thousand men and was preparing to invade Texas. Austin spoke to the citizens of Brazoria, stirring them to action; it was time to decide whether they would continue to submit to tyranny. He blamed the turmoil on the actions of the Mexican government.

This was new. The advocate of peace was preaching resistance. He also proposed another convention, calling it a "consultation." Translated into Spanish, "convention" referred to a plan for military insurrection. So he used a different word. Stephen Austin was still a careful diplomat, but his intentions were clear. He asked each municipality to send at least one man who could remain and be part of a new state government, a clear rejection of General Cos' authority.

Feisty Nacogdoches wasted no time, calling a meeting and electing Houston chairman. They supported Austin's proposal, while Houston went even further.

Houston's Letters

Knowing what they were up against, the former army lieutenant wrote a letter to a man who then carried the missive across the Sabine into Louisiana.

> War defense of our rights... is inevitable, in Texas! If volunteers from the United States will join their brethren in this section, they will receive liberal bounties of land... Let each man come with a good rifle and one hundred rounds of ammunition, and to come soon.
>
> Our war cry is: 'Liberty or Death.'
>
> Our principles are to support the constitution, and *down with the Usurper!!*[15]

Houston's general orders to the Nacogdoches troops were also personally hand-carried to the United States to raise support and volunteers for their cause:

> The time has arrived when revolutions in the interior of Mexico have resulted in the creation of a dictator and Texas is compelled to assume an attitude defensive of her rights, and the property of her citizens.
>
> Volunteers are invited to our standard...
>
> The morning of glory is dawning upon us. The work of liberty has begun. Our actions are to become part of the history of mankind... Let your valour proclaim to the world that liberty is your birthright. We cannot be conquered by all the arts of anarchy and despotism combined. In heaven and in valorous hearts, we repose our confidence.[16]

Sam Houston's flashy words hit a chord with the citizens of the young republic. Just as a few years earlier, blood had been spilled to maintain their independence from Britain; did not many of the southern states still celebrate January 8th, the anniversary of Jackson's victory at New Orleans? And their fathers, including Houston's own, had fought in the Revolutionary War. It was a day when liberty was more than just a word.

Men responded to the call. One fellow in particular raised enough money to outfit two whole companies of infantry: the "New Orleans Grays," so called because of the gray uniforms they wore.

Individuals continued to trickle in from such states as Kentucky, Louisiana, and Georgia. Some were not well-equipped but came anyway.

General Cox Arrives

The "consultation" to form a new government was scheduled for November 1, but General Cos decided to show up sooner. On September 22, he landed on the coast with four hundred men and marched them toward San Antonio. The Texas he invaded was a confused, leaderless mass of stubbornness. Just as the American colonists had been divided in their opinions on the eve of the American Revolution, so Texans differed in their thinking. There were "Tories": some of the Tejanos of south Texas even ended up serving under Santa Anna. There were Tejanos and Anglo colonists who counseled caution, either out of wisdom or fear, or both. Then there were firebrands who possessed less wisdom or fear. But by the time General Cos arrived, even conservative heads of families were checking their rifles. Texas was a powder keg. Cos supplied the match.

One Worthless Cannon

Dr. Launcelot Smither heard the news while in San Antonio. His hometown of Gonzales had been ordered to surrender a cannon given to them by the Mexican government several years earlier, for self-defense against the Indians. But apparently, General Cos had instructed Colonel Ugartechea, military commander of San Antonio, to get the thing back. In any case, Ugartechea sent some men to Gonzales, who were then escorted out of town. The citizens of Gonzales had no intention of giving up their cannon, even though it wasn't the greatest cannon, and even though it didn't work very well. It did make noise.

Now, what was the big deal about a nearly worthless cannon? And what is the big deal about the Second Amendment to the Constitution? Why do people get so upset about gun control laws? Why do we have the Second Amendment in the first place?

Think about the principle of the "rule of law." Austin told Mexican officials that Texans must be governed by *moral* force, not military force. Military force, he told them, would not work. Why not?

The nature of "republican" government is not compatible with a dictatorship whose authority is derived from force of arms. If the settlers at Gonzales gave up their cannon, they would be consenting to martial law, to powerlessness. In a sense, they would be giving up their rights and would become like serfs of the Middle Ages.

Suddenly, that stupid cannon took on new significance.

It was important to Colonel Ugartechea, too. If he were to rule this area, his demands must be complied with. It was the principle of the thing. He asked Cos for reinforcements, and the general sent him some troops under Lieutenant Castañeda, whose job it was to demand the cannon, but to avoid confrontation if at all possible. Being a new arrival in Texas, poor Castañeda may not have known how impossible such an order would be.

But Dr. Launcelot Smither knew. He went to see Ugartechea, and the Colonel told him that his men would not take hostile action if he could convince the settlers to give up the cannon. Dr. Smither got on his horse and left for Gonzales.

Meanwhile, volunteers were arriving in Gonzales, where the second-class cannon had been *buried* for safekeeping. A frustrated Castañeda was parked with his men across the river from the colonists. He had already tried to give his message to the alcalde, but the men across the river were stalling for time. He was beginning to realize what a mess he was in.

Then Dr. Smither rode up with a few escorts from Ugartechea, and Castañeda spoke with him. The Mexican officer was clearly frustrated.

Look. See on the opposite bank. Three mounted scouts. I just need to send these men a message. I didn't come to fight these settlers. I just want to speak to their commander, but so far, my requests for communication have been denied.

The doctor spoke with one of the mounted men whom he recognized: Matthew "Old Paint" Caldwell, an Indian fighter. Caldwell told Smither that Castañeda could not be bothered that night, but that in the morning, communication would be possible and the Mexican officer would be treated with the respect due a gentleman.

Caldwell meant well.

A Bloody Nose

Lieutenant Castañeda remained in place, guilty of no hostile action except for being there with his men. A few miles away, the leaders of an impromptu militia held a council of war. They decided that although the Mexicans had done nothing except ask for the cannon, these volunteers had come from a long way. It was not sensible to send them home without a fight. They were probably unaware of Caldwell's promise.

Preparing for war, a group of men dug up the cannon. Because they didn't have any cannonballs, they gathered metal scraps with which to load it.

Geared up for battle, the Texans made their way toward Castañeda's camp. At midnight, a fog settled in, and though they couldn't see, they continued to advance. They were hoping to surprise the Mexicans, but at three o'clock, the yapping of a dog alerted the camp.

Shots were fired. None of the Texans was injured except one man whose horse reared, throwing off his rider. Landing on his nose, this fellow shed the first blood by a Texan in the cause of liberty.

They were fighting for principle. Mostly. Noah Smithwick wrote years later,

"Some were for independence, some were for the Constitution of 1824, and some were for anything, just so long as it was a row."[17]

After this skirmish, the Texans took over. While waiting for morning, they ate watermelons from a nearby patch.

Dr. Smither was irritated. The attack, if it could be called that, by the Gonzales militiamen, had resulted in his arrest by the Mexicans. In the morning, after another brief skirmish, Lieutenant Castañeda sent for him, wanting to send a message to the commander of the Texans.

"Don't shoot, don't shoot!" Smither had cried, approaching the militia's hide-out. He repeated Castañeda's message, asking for a parley. But his fellow Texans thought this man too friendly toward the Mexicans, and he was arrested again.

This, then, was the reason for the doctor's irritation. He had been arrested by both sides. Maybe one day he would laugh about it, but right now, he was mainly interested in getting back the belongings and money the Mexicans had confiscated.

Finally, a parley was arranged. Castañeda met with Colonel John Henry Moore, leader of the Fayette militia, who had been elected as overall commander of the group. The doctor stood by, indignant. The conversation went something like this:

"Why have I been attacked?" Castañeda began.

"Your troops are acting on behalf of the usurper, Santa Anna, and are defying constitutional authority." Moore was pleading constitutional grounds.

Castañeda was tired and probably irritated, but he did his best to be conciliatory. "My orders were to request the cannon, not seize it. I have no wish to fight American colonists, and besides, I am also a republican."

"If you are truly a federalist, sir, then you wear the wrong uniform and are fighting on the wrong side. If you are sincere, you and your troops should join us in our fight for the Constitution of 1824."

Castañeda was shocked. Moore had just invited him to mutiny.

"Sir, as a soldier, I am obliged to obey orders."

There was nothing more to say.

Is it ready? Good! Raise it! A white banner now floated above the Texans. The outline of a cannon was painted in black, along with the words, "COME AND TAKE IT."

After Moore returned to the camp, the disputed cannon was used to fire on the Mexican position. Well, at least it made a big *Boom!* Then the Texans charged.

But what had happened? Where was the enemy?

Gone. Castañeda had left. He later explained to his commander, "since the orders from your Lordship were for me to withdraw without compromising the honor of Mexican arms, I did so."[18]

Thus concluded the famous "Battle of Gonzales."

The powder keg was ignited.

A Ragtag Army

The next logical step was for this informal army to immediately march on San Antonio. Noah Smithwick, the blacksmith, was there.

> Our plan was to rush on to San Antonio, capture the garrison before it could get reinforcements, and then—on to Mexico and dictate terms of peace in the capital of the Montezumas...
>
> What days those were! So full to the brim with busy preparation, excitement and eager anticipation, without one misgiving as to the outcome. Looking back on it now, from my snow-crowned summit of my ninety-one years, it seems like a piece of egregious foolhardiness, and I find it hard to identify myself with the hotheaded youth who entered into it with such ardor. Our whole available force could not have amounted to more than 250 men, while Mexico had an organized army of several thousand, and there were thousands of Indians eagerly watching for an opportunity to swoop down on us and wipe us from the face of the earth and thus regain their lost hunting grounds, which they had always been able to maintain against the Mexicans. That one bushed cannon was our only artillery, and our arms were Bowie knives and long single-barreled, muzzle-loading flintlock rifles, the same our fathers won their independence with... But the Mexican soldiers had not shown themselves brave; the army, indeed, being largely composed of peons and convicts—men who had no incentive to patriotism or bravery, and over whom it was necessary to keep a strong guard to prevent them from deserting. Then, too, the seat of war was a long way from the Mexican base of supplies; a weary waste of desert infested by hostile Indians intervening, and no means of communication except by courier.
>
> Perhaps, too, we unconsciously relied on the active sympathy of the United States, whose offspring we were; still, as a rule, I do not think we apprehended the remotest possibility of such assistance being necessary... No prophet had arisen to warn us of disaster and experience had not yet taught us that cowardly foe might also be a cruel foe when opportunity offered...
>
> Words are inadequate to convey an impression of the first Texas army as it formed in marching order... Buckskin breeches were the nearest approach to a uniform, and there was a wide diversity even there,... A fantastic military array to a

casual observer, but the one great purpose animating every heart clothed us in a uniform more perfect in our eyes than was ever donned by regulars on dress parade.[19]

Houston Finds Austin and the Militia

Houston's mare picked her way along the streets of San Felipe de Austin. Arriving at the empresario's home, Houston handed the reins of his mount to a servant. Austin himself was not at home; he had been in Mexico for two full years, in prison for much of that time, and despite having returned to Texas, his property was not in good condition. Weeds brushed the feet of the delegate from Nacogdoches as he walked to the veranda, where he found a dozen men sitting around, talking in small groups.

It was late October 1835, and the "consultation" slated for November 1 had been gathering. Then word had come that the volunteers marching on San Antonio needed a general. Stephen Austin knew he was not qualified, by nature or by experience, for military command, but the need was there. So he had decided to take command. Every delegate in his house wanted to leave with him and join the "Volunteer Army of Texas," as the militia called itself.

But Austin refused to allow them all to come. Some needed to stay behind and conduct the business of the consultation. The men Houston found on the veranda were not delegates legally able to conduct business or form a government. Texas had gone to war, but Texas did not have any sort of established government, except for General Cos, and his martial law was the cause they were fighting against. Consequently, there was no one in charge.

Of course, many independent, self-reliant Texans didn't fret too much over this. But Houston knew they needed a government as much as they needed soldiers to fight. He opened Austin's pantry and found food he would need for the trip to San Antonio. He stuffed it in his saddlebags and went to find his horse.

Houston caught up with the army twenty-five miles east of San Antonio. He greeted Austin, then turned his mount around and searched for the front of the line. From the side of the road, he inspected the ragtag militia as it passed. As a man who had led others into combat, he liked the spirit of the men, but he worried about their lack of equipment and the lack of discipline.

That night, Houston sat at Stephen Austin's campfire and listened to the commanding general. Austin had given out commissions, but couldn't remember them all. Let's see, Smith, Fannin, Wharton, Travis, Grant, Burleson. Oh, yes, Jim Bowie just joined us with some others from Louisiana. I made him a colonel or a major, I don't remember which. Bowie and Fannin left with some men to scout, but it has been reported to me that they have had a disagreement. I don't know where they are now.

Houston heard Austin coughing and watched as the empresario drew his coat around him. It wasn't cold; autumn evenings were usually mild in South Texas. Prison had broken Austin's health, and he obviously shouldn't be here.

Houston wasn't sure about the wisdom of assaulting San Antonio in the first place. But he held his peace and instead asked Austin about the delegates. He needed to retrieve enough delegates to conduct business. The worn empresario agreed.

A group of men left with Houston the very next day.

In San Felipe, fifty-one delegates met in the alcalde's office, their body heat warming up the drafty, unfinished structure, congregating around a long table made of rough boards. A large number of them had just arrived with Sam Houston, after traveling many miles, but after a while, the confined delegates probably didn't even notice the horse smell.

It was November 3, 1835, and after much discussion, William Wharton rose and moved that Texas declare itself an independent nation.

Lorenzo de Zavala quietly opposed him. Zavala was short and chubby with small hands and tiny feet. He was a well-educated man who had extensive experience in government, even having served as governor of the State of Mexico. But he had suffered at the hands of Santa Anna. In fact, his Yucatan estates had been seized after he had signed a protest against the conduct of Santa Anna in Zacatecas. With his family, he had fled to Texas.

Zavala maintained that Wharton's suggestion would alienate those Mexicans who were sympathetic to their cause. By establishing themselves as a Mexican state instead, they might attract support from other Mexicans.

Houston rose to speak. His views were closer to Zavala's than to Wharton's, and he suggested they fight for the Constitution of 1824. He proposed that they carefully record and explain all their grievances against the Mexican government in a document.

Houston was thinking globally. Their actions would have to be justified before the court of world opinion. Plus, it would clearly be unwise to declare independence now. It would be an invitation to instant annihilation, the equivalent of adding 10,000 men to Santa Anna's army.

Houston's views carried the day, and he would later come to regret it.

The Army Arrives in San Antonio

After Houston left, the volunteer army soon reached the San Antonio River. Bowie and Fannin took a group north along the river and finally found a defensible position about a quarter mile from the old mission of Concepcion, near the present-day intersection of Highway 90 and Interstate-37. Because the Mexicans had already spotted them, the Texans climbed down the bank at the bend of the river, which provided a natural defense. Noah Smithwick was there:

> The Mexicans now opened on us with cannon, but we lay low and their grape and canister crashed through the pecan trees overhead, raining a shower of ripe nuts down on us, and I saw men picking them up and eating them with as little concern as if they were being shaken down by a norther. Bowie was a born leader, never needlessly spending a bullet or imperiling life. His voice is still ringing in my deaf old ears as he repeatedly admonished us, "Keep under cover, boys, and reserve your fire; we haven't a man to spare," and had he been obeyed, not a man would we have lost... Excited and eager to get a shot, some of the boys [after receiving an order to change position] mounted the bank and cut across, exposed to the fire of the whole Mexican army. They got there before we did, who went around, but the first man I saw as I came around was Dick Andrews, lying as he had fallen, great drops of sweat already gathering on his white, drawn face, and the life blood gushing from a hole in the left side, just below the ribs. I ran to him and attempted to raise him. "Dick," I cried, "are you hurt?" "Yes, Smith," he replied, "I'm killed, lay me down." I laid him down and put something under his head. It was the last time I saw him alive....
>
> "Fire!" rang out the steady voice of our leader, and we responded with a will... Three times they charged, but there was a platoon ready to receive them. Three times we picked off the gunners, the last one with a lighted match in his hand; then a panic seized them, and they broke... With a ringing cheer we mounted the bank and gave chase. We turned their cannon on them, adding wings to their flight...
>
> Having no knowledge of civilized warfare, the poor wounded wretches thought they were to be summarily dispatched, and it was painful to hear them begging for the miserable lives that no one thought of taking. We had no means of relieving them, even if we had had an opportunity... The utmost we could do was to give water to those who asked for it, which no one was brute enough to refuse. How our humanity was repaid, let Goliad and the Alamo testify...[20]

The volunteers' rifles had a longer range than the Mexicans' Brown Bess muskets. This was partly because the Mexicans' powder was of inferior quality, which the Texans discovered when they scavenged the enemy's ammunition. Following European tactics, the Mexican soldiers advanced together, but they never had a chance. The longer-range Texan rifles picked them off before they were even in range to fire.

The militiamen may have been encouraged by the easily won battle of Concepcion, but they were developing an unwise disdain for their enemies.

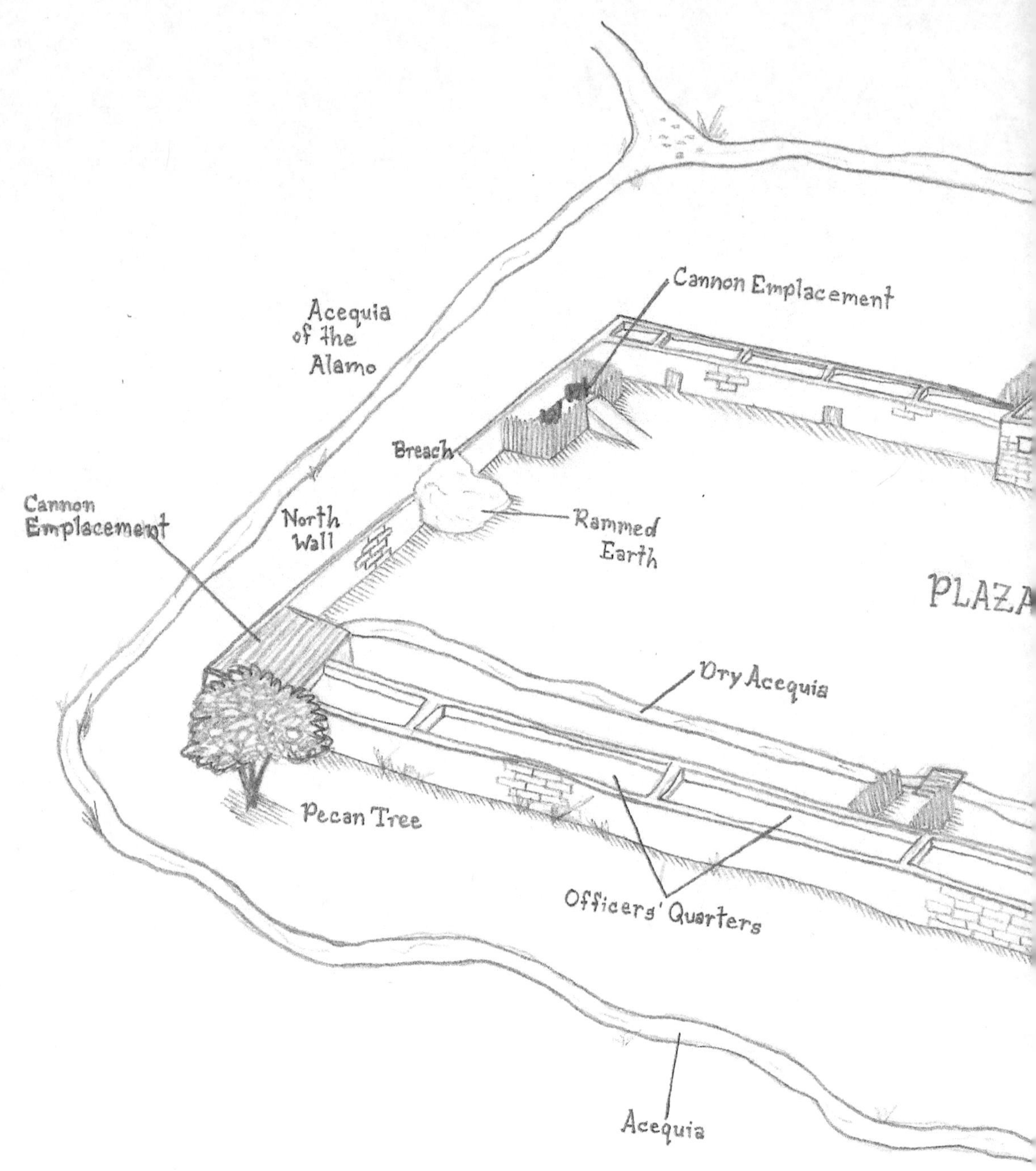
Cannon Emplacement
Acequia of the Alamo
Breach
Cannon Emplacement
North Wall
Rammed Earth
PLAZA
Dry Acequia
Pecan Tree
Officers' Quarters
Acequia

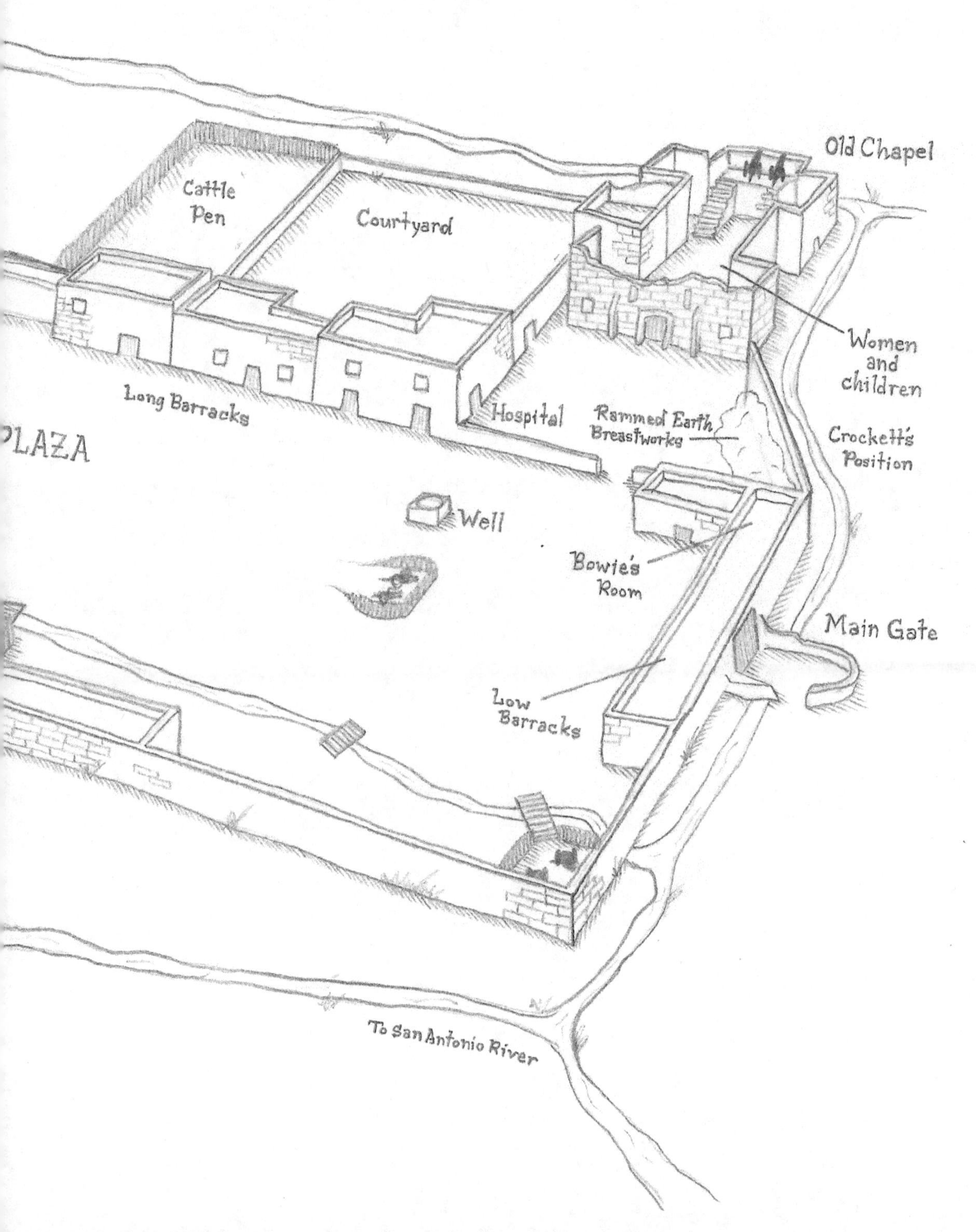

Old Chapel
Cattle Pen
Courtyard
Women and children
Long Barracks
Hospital
Rammed Earth Breastworks
Crockett's Position
PLAZA
Well
Bowie's Room
Main Gate
Low Barracks
To San Antonio River

Chapter 8

Victory or Death

STUDYING his reflection in the mirror, Sam Houston adjusted his velveteen jacket, proud of his new look. At his request, the landlady of the Virginia House Hotel had sewn impressive loops of gold braid (were they from a doily?) onto the jacket, so he could command the respect he deserved in his new occupation as major general and commander-in-chief of the army.

The delegates to the "consultation" in San Felipe had written up a basic framework for Texas's provisional government. Henry Smith, a feisty man who habitually wore a black coat tightly buttoned up to the neck, was the governor-elect. A council was appointed to serve the legislative body, and Houston was elected commander-in-chief of all forces called into public service—that is, the regular army.

The volunteer army of Texas was not "regular army," but militia, which meant that Houston, unfortunately, had no authority whatever over Texas's only army. The Council had made elaborate plans, designing a regular army and even ordering some armaments, but the ranks were empty, empty, empty. And although only the General Council had the authority to appoint officers, Houston, never one to sit idle, got the ball rolling with a letter-writing campaign, and one of those letters was addressed to James Walker Fannin.

A Sad November Rain

A blue norther drenched the town of San Patricio in cold, driving rain. Captain Ira Westover and his men were nearby, having just defeated a small force of Mexicans. As at Concepcion, the superior range of the Texans' rifles had proved deadly to the *soldados*. The Mexicans sustained twenty casualties, either wounded or killed, but only one Texan was hurt, with three fingers torn off by a bullet.

Now they stood freezing in the frigid November rain. After tossing captured Mexican artillery into the Nueces River, Captain Westover led his men into San Patricio, where the citizens willingly housed the dripping volunteer soldiers. Philip Dimitt, commander of the troops at Goliad, had sent Westover to capture a Mexican post not far from San Patricio. The capture of the tiny fort was deemed essential because it would be a way station for any soldiers coming to invade Goliad. Plus, they could capture arms, ammunition, and horses, which Texan rebels desperately needed.

Unfortunately, they had only managed to capture fourteen horses and two cannon. Make that zero cannon, since the artillery presently rested at the bottom of the river. But at least Westover's men were now dry and warm.

When dawn filtered into the wet sky, someone spotted a man approaching San Patricio, carrying a makeshift white flag. The captain of the Mexican force had sent a messenger, asking permission to bring his miserable, wounded men into town after enduring the night out in the rain.

Captain Westover readily agreed, and the injured Mexicans were either helped or carried into town. John J. Linn, Westover's aide, recognized one of the casualties as an old friend, Marcellino Garcia, who was dying of his injuries.

Linn did what he could to ease his friend's suffering. Garcia gave Linn his horse, and with his last breath, deplored the situation that had arisen because of Santa Anna's ambitions. Being a federalist, he confessed that he was "at heart a sympathizer with the Texans; but being an officer of the regular service, had no option in the premises."[1]

Garcia died soon after and was mourned by both sides.

By the Merest Accident under Heaven

Erastus Smith must have helped the artillerymen direct the cannons, set up west of the Alamo, as part of a siege of San Antonio by the Volunteer Army of Texas. "Deaf" Smith, so called because he was hard of hearing, was a recent addition to the force. He was a forty-eight-year-old family man who lived nearby with his Mexican wife and four children. But after the army had begun the siege, a group of Mexican soldiers had tried to capture him as he headed home to his family. One man struck him in the head with a saber, but thankfully, Smith's hat took most of the impact. That did it. If a man couldn't go home to his family without being accosted, well, he would just join the rebels. And he did.

Smith was watching the inexperienced volunteers handle the artillery. And listening—he wasn't *totally* deaf.

"A hundred neat and handy musket balls against twenty," one wagered, "that I hit the old barracks between the third and fourth windows."[2] The other man took up the challenge. *Boom!* He missed.

Another offered, "My pistols—by the way, the best in the place—against the worst ones in camp." Now that was a very tempting offer for Erastus Smith, who accepted the wager and, a moment later, was the proud new owner of a fine brace of pistols.

"Look here, friend," Smith conceded, "I will also fire the gun once. If I miss my aim, then I'll return your pistols." He took careful aim and touched off the gun, but his aim was dead-on.

Erastus Smith was a careful observer, and he probably took note of the problems that had beset the volunteer army in its siege of Bexar. Austin was trying his best, but even by his own estimation, he was a weak general. Also, the men in the ranks were uncommitted volunteers who came and left at will. As fall turned to winter, some went home for warm clothing or to care for their families, and ranks that had once swelled to more than eight hundred rapidly dwindled. Many of those who had joined were thrill-seekers from the United States, who had come to find adventure, but over time, became disillusioned and bored, enduring seemingly endless rain and miserably cold temperatures, which left them restless and irritable. The most popular form of entertainment was finding the bottom of a jug.

In a letter, Austin begged the General Council, "send no more ardent spirits to this camp—if any is on the road turn it back, or have the head [of the barrel] knocked out."[3]

Almost completely without leadership, in a state of chaotic disorder, and infested with no-good adventurers, it is no wonder that this army brought William Wharton to despair. In a letter resigning his post, he wrote, "No good will be atchieved [sic] by this army except by the merest accident under heaven."[4]

An Unhappy Fannin

A tall, dark, loose-jointed man dismounted in front of the Virginia House Hotel in San Felipe. After tethering his horse, he went inside, where the landlady, a large, motherly soul, directed him to General Sam Houston's office.

James W. Fannin introduced himself to his commander-in-chief. A nervous man with shifty eyes, he had come to protest the rank being offered him by Houston: inspector-general with the rank of colonel. An ambitious, overbearing man, Fannin believed he deserved the rank of brigadier general, though he had little to recommend him—only two years at West Point, and even worse, a reputation as a smuggler and slave-runner.

Houston had specifically requested that the Council make the thirty-one-year-old a colonel, which meant that Fannin was very unhappy with Houston.

Old Ben Milan and Henry Karnes

Ben Milam could not believe his eyes when he gazed about the camp outside of San Antonio. Returning from a scouting expedition, Milam did not like what he saw and heard. The army was a mess, disorganized, leaderless, and now, he had heard, about to give up and go home. *Now?* When the enemy had been weakened by a month of siege? The Mexicans' cavalry horses were probably starving by now.

Milam found Colonel Frank W. Johnson, who agreed with him, but said that the order had already been given. So? He could countermand it!

The two men walked to Edward Burleson's tent. Burleson had taken Stephen Austin's place as general, while Austin had been sent to the United States by the General Council to help raise support and money.

Though Burleson was sympathetic, he explained that most of the officers did not want to continue the campaign. It seemed prudent to them to withdraw to Goliad. Milam and Johnson insisted they should at least try to hold the line.

Shortly, Milam walked out of the tent. "Who will follow old Ben Milam into San Antonio?"[5]

Out of the five hundred men remaining in camp, three hundred volunteered. Plans were made; Burleson was to stay behind with the others as a reserve force, and J.C. Neill was to make a diversionary attack on the Alamo, while Milam and Johnson led the larger force into San Antonio. The attack on the Alamo was simply a distraction.

Several men were chosen to serve as guides, including Erastus Smith, his son-in-law, and Jesus Cuellar, a Mexican officer who had deserted. Before daylight, the next morning, December 5th, they all got into position.

In the pre-dawn stillness, the men listened. Even "Deaf" Smith was probably listening intently for the sound of Neill's cannon.

"*Centinela alerta*," cried the sentry. All's well.

The only other sound was the moan of the cold wind.

Then they heard it. *Boom!* Now, the question was, would the Mexicans take the bait?

One of the men later recorded, "The hollow roar of our cannon was followed by the brisk rattling of drums and the shrill blasts of bugles. Summons, cries, the sudden trampling of feet, the metallic click of weapons mingled in the distance with the heavy rumblings of the artillery. Our friends had done the trick."[6]

Milam led a group of men down Acequia Street, headed for the Garza house. Johnson took a group of men to Soledad Street, headed for the Veramendi house, a large residence with a Spanish-style central courtyard. The Mexican soldiers, distracted by Neill's attack on the Alamo, were not yet aware of their presence.

Erastus Smith and others of Johnson's group had almost reached the Veramendi house before a Mexican sentinel spotted them and began firing. Smith aimed his weapon and shot the man, suddenly raising the attention of the entire Mexican army.

Grapeshot, the cannon's version of shotgun pellets, filled the air, and the Texans flew for cover, but there really wasn't any. The men hid in houses, whose shocked inhabitants took to the streets in their nightclothes, unarmed.

The easy part of the attack was over, but now the Texans faced house-to-house and even room-to-room combat. Still, they persisted. Though the Mexicans put up sustained resistance, the Texans were confident. And so far, their casualties had been very light.

The Texans captured the Veramendi house, the same house to which Jim Bowie had once brought Sam Houston. Only now the Veramendi family and Bowie's wife and children were all dead of cholera, and the mourning husband was drinking so much that he might soon join them.

Ben Milam stood inside the Veramendi home, holding a pair of field glasses. He stepped into the courtyard, hoping to get a clear field of vision, attempting to scan the enemy's defenses. *Crack!*

Old Ben Milam had been shot neatly through the head. Someone saw a puff of smoke from the direction of the trees, and the enraged Texans fought back, instantly aiming for the sharpshooter, who fell dead from a tree. The rebels were learning. Not all Mexican soldiers were stuck with muskets; some had Baker rifles, at least equal to those of the Texans.

Over the course of the next several days, the Texans continued to advance, and General Cos was worried. His men were fighting bravely but were losing ground. Where was Ugartechea? If only the colonel would show up with reinforcements, they would certainly be in better shape. They already outnumbered the Texans two to one, but these barbarians fought like devils!

On the third day of the battle, a twenty-three-year-old Tennessean, Henry Karnes, hunched low with the rest of his company, while cannon fire "poured an incessant storm of shot,"[7] pulverizing the adobe walls around them, looked for cover. If they could find a house made of stone, they would be much better protected.

Just a few yards away stood a large stone house, but muskets protruding from its windows proved that the house was full of Mexican soldiers. Some could even be seen on the roof.

More cannon fire. Karnes made his decision.

"Boys, load your guns and be ready. I am going to break open that door, and I want you to pour a steady hot fire into those fellows on the roof and hold their attention until I can reach the door, and when I break it in I want you boys to make a clean dash for the house."

Someone protested. "That building is full of Mexicans; don't you see the muzzles of their *escopetas* in the windows?"

Not normally a swearing man, Karnes exclaimed, "D—n the Mexicans and their *escopetas*. It's that house or retreat. You men do as I tell you."[8]

He sprang over the barricades, with his rifle in one hand and a crowbar in the other. Mexican fire poured down on him as Karnes crossed the street; onlookers later said that they did not know how he survived. But he arrived at the door unscathed and desperately worked to pry it open. The brave Tennessean soon forced open the door and entered the house, but not alone. His company, by now inspired, had crossed the street after him.

The Mexican soldiers fled. Their hearts failed at the sight of such crazy, reckless courage.

On the fourth day, December 8th, Col. Ugartechea arrived with reinforcements and somehow managed to get past the Texans' mounted scouts. It may not have been that difficult, because many of the local Texan horsemen who had joined the volunteers were now fighting on foot in San Antonio. But entering the Alamo, the new troops were shocked. They saw starving horses chewing desperately on clothing and equipment. Had they been brought here to die?

General Cos was dismayed. The soldiers Ugartechea brought were convicts with no experience and very little incentive to fight for a few adobe walls in the middle of nowhere. They only added to the confusion. What was he to do now?

It was a no-brainer. Supplies were low. Morale was low; as many as three hundred of his men had already deserted. If Cos ordered his men to fall back behind the walls of the Alamo, surrender would only be delayed by a few days. And he had no hope of help any time soon.

Cos sent an officer to the plaza with these words: "Sanchez, by reason of cowardice and perfidy of many of our companions all is lost... I authorize you to approach the enemy and obtain the best terms possible. Save the dignity of our Government, the honor of its arms and honor, life and property of chiefs, officials and troops that still remain even though I myself perish."[9]

On December 9th, Burleson met with emissary, Lt. Col. Jose Juan Sanchez-Navarro, and discussed terms until the early morning hours. For Sanchez, it was a very uncomfortable situation. "We were surrounded with crude bumpkins, proud and overbearing," he later remembered. "Whoever knows the character of North Americans may well appreciate the position in which we found ourselves."[10] Upper-class Mexicans were disdainful of uncultured frontiersmen and knew of their lack of army discipline. It was a humiliating defeat.

General Cos and his men were granted generous terms, being allowed to leave Texas with enough arms and supplies to see them safely home. Texans rejoiced. They had ejected the military governor of Texas.

One recalled, "We hoped that in a brief lapse of time reports would carry to the other Mexican states the news of our success against the Usurper's troops, and that once more the whole nation would rise in revolt to overthrow Santa Anna and his administration."[11]

Many Texans assumed that the war was over; the volunteers desperately wanted to go home. But Santa Anna was coming.

Houston's Letters

Sam Houston sat writing a letter at a rough-hewn board table that matched the general decor of his office. He sat at one end of a large, unfinished barracks-like structure that probably let in a good deal of the January cold. "Rough-hewn" was the general description of both the building and the whole town of Washington-on-the-Brazos, to which the commander-in-chief had recently been exiled by the General Council. The members of that body were tired of his pointed requests for action regarding the regular army. They had better things to do, such as choosing new names for towns and giving money to shady men who were never heard from again.

But these were minor issues compared to the way the council members were plotting to undermine Houston's authority. They appointed James Walker Fannin as "military agent," a new kind of office they had illegally created. According to the terms of the provisional government, all officers the Council appointed would be under the command of Sam Houston. "Military agent" was an inspiration appreciated only by the council members and James W. Fannin.

Houston had obediently loaded his things on the back of a sturdy mule, the rough equivalent of a pickup truck in those days, and traveled forty miles north to a raw hamlet just hacked out of the wilderness, tree stumps still in evidence. Before he left, Governor Smith, disgusted by the actions of the Council, made a suggestion. Just go and collect troops. Then you will be given orders to disperse the Council and put an end to its subversive activities.

But Houston could not do that. It would put Governor Smith and himself on the same level as Santa Anna. Sam Houston believed in the rule of law, treasuring liberty enough to abide by the decisions of the civil government, even when they were stupid.

So he went to Washington-on-the Brazos, where the Council had sent him to get rid of him. But because he couldn't sit idle, when men were going to die, he sat at this table in a drafty building and wrote letters.

Idiocy

Dr. James Grant had been injured in the Battle of Bexar, but not seriously. Scottish-born, his brogue seasoned the stories he told. The volunteers were rejoicing after the victory over Cos and feeling invincible. Grant told them about the lands south of the border, hoping to stir their interest. He had just lost several rich estates in Coahuila and knew that the only way to reclaim any of his wealth was by armed force. He lobbied for an immediate assault on Matamoros, a Mexican town in Coahuila.

Grant convinced Frank Johnson of his scheme, and they presented their case to the General Council. They knew better than to ask Houston. In fact, the audacious Grant had even called for Houston's removal as commander-in-chief.

Upon hearing these things, Sam Houston formulated his own plan to invade Matamoros, sending word to his friend Jim Bowie to make preparations. If he could put himself at the head, perhaps they could avoid disaster. Unknown to him, the Council illegally authorized both Johnson and Fannin to command the invasion. Then, Governor Smith ordered Houston to go to Goliad and take charge of the proposed offensive.

Johnson managed to convince many of the volunteers at Bexar to head south, leaving J.C. Neill in charge of the garrison there. The departing volunteers had callously stripped the garrison of its provisions, leaving only one hundred destitute men, including those recently wounded in the battle. Neill wrote Smith and the Council.

"The clothing sent here by the aid and patriotic exertions of the honorable council was taken from men who endured all the hardships of winter and who were not even sufficiently clad for summer," the officer complained. Many of the remaining men had "but one blanket and one shirt, and what was intended for them [had been] given away to men, some of whom had not been in the army more than four days, and many not exceeding two weeks."[12]

Meanwhile, Johnson was making patriotic declarations. "To arms! then Americans, to aid in sustaining the principles of 1776, in this western hemisphere... Our first attack shall be upon Matamoros; our next if Heaven decrees, wherever tyranny shall raise its malignant form."[13]

Johnson had turned the defense of liberty into a rant that had no basis in reality. The ill-equipped Texas volunteers were not exactly capable of putting down tyranny wherever it raised its head. Governor Smith, not a man gifted with tact, lost his temper. He denounced the Matamoros expedition as idiocy; anyone who supported it was a fool or a traitor. For a long time, Smith had endured the machinations of a self-seeking Council. Now that this august body was sending the sons of Texas on an insane crusade, the governor let loose with an eloquent description of the "scoundrels" with which he had to deal. That is, the scoundrels in the Council.

The governor announced that the council was dissolved. The General Council responded in kind, impeaching Governor Smith. Neither had the right to get rid of the other, and both decisions caused mass confusion. Which of them represented Texas's lawful government? Governor Smith or the General Council?

Volunteers were marching, ill-equipped, in a southerly direction, to where Santa Anna waited somewhere with his troops. Then there was Neill and the poor men in the Alamo, who murmured and muttered among themselves, hoping that relief would arrive shortly. Where on earth was Bowie?

Unaware of the Council's latest actions, Sam Houston prepared to leave Washington-on-the-Brazos in response to Smith's command to go to Goliad. He saddled his horse and, knowing the danger ahead, planned to take charge. But he had been kept on the sidelines by the political maneuverings of his opponents or perhaps just by Providence. He believed in a kind of Destiny for himself, and this helped him to remain patient. He was now forty-two years old, his chestnut hair thinning on top, no longer a young man. Experience and suffering had tempered his natural ambition and flamboyance. He had discovered the wisdom of keeping things to himself—the same kind of wisdom he had observed in the stoicism of many Indians.

But the Raven was feeling the pressure. The leaders of the Matamoros expedition were blinded by ambition and greed, and their followers would most likely end up like Mexia's, that fool of a federalist who had recently invaded Tampico, with thirty-one Americans. Except for Mexia himself, who somehow managed to escape, everyone else had died. Twenty-seven Americans had been shot without the benefit of a trial.

As commander-in-chief, Houston had carefully thought out a military strategy, but things were far beyond his control. Well, he would do what he could.

January 8th was cold and windy when Houston mounted his horse, probably feeling the ache of his old war injuries. He was glad to have with him a friend, George Hockley, who accompanied him to Goliad.

Fannin's Foolish Notice

The two men arrived at the Goliad mission on January 14th and found many volunteers preparing for the Matamoros expedition, but neither Dr. Grant nor Johnson was present. In fact, Grant had left with some men for Refugio, and Major Morris, who was now in charge, was supposed to follow with the rest of the men the next day.

Houston read a notice posted for the troops: an appeal signed by Col. Fannin, "Military Agent" of the General Council, calling for volunteers to "reduce Matamoros." He promised: "The troops shall be paid out of the first spoils taken from the enemy."[14]

Truly, Fannin knew better than this. He should, with two years at West Point! There was no excuse.

Houston clambered up onto the gray stone wall of the mission. Standing there, every man could see him as he spoke, sharing his heart with his customary skill.

What would it mean to pay them out of the spoils of the enemy? What would this look like to the civilized world? It was piracy. Furthermore, it was useless to expect any help from the citizens of Mexico to the south.

Houston's Call for Independence

> Since it is impossible to call forth any sympathy from our fellow Mexican citizens... and as they let us, the smallest of the provinces, struggle without any aid, let us then, comrades, sever that link that binds us to that rusty chain of the Mexican Confederation... A general convention of the representatives of the People will be held at Washington on the first of March of this year. It is the duty of the army to send several representatives; and I hope that my comrades will elect only men who will vote for our independence, will fearlessly proclaim our separation from Mexico, and what they decide upon, comrades, we will defend with our arms...[15]

Houston had seen his earlier mistake and now preached independence. The previous fall, he had counseled that to declare independence this soon would not be wise, that it would be inviting annihilation by Santa Anna's troops. But Santa Anna was coming anyway, and without a clear goal of independence, the men would be easily distracted by visions of plunder.

Momentous Decisions

Even as Houston spoke, he was interrupted by the arrival of a courier from Neill at the Alamo. A scout had returned from the border, reporting to Lt. Col. Neill that two of Santa Anna's generals had led troops across the Rio Grande. In his dispatch, Neill asked for help to defend the Alamo and for permission to leave and take care of his sick family.

Then Jim Bowie rode up. He had come to lead any volunteers who wished to help him defend the Alamo.

General Houston now wrote out an order for Bowie to deliver. He granted Neill furlough and gave him instructions to remove the artillery from the Alamo and demolish all fortifications. Houston knew that this tiny force bottled up in that old mission would be very vulnerable to Santa Anna. He wanted the place abandoned when Neill left for home, but Houston included a statement at the end that the colonel should use his own judgment, since he was there and knew the situation best.

Houston then left and traveled to Refugio along with Morris and the volunteers. He met with Johnson, who showed him some papers, stating that the Council had dismissed Houston. Instead, Fannin and Johnson had been elevated to joint supreme commandership. Johnson asked him if he would try to interfere with his authority, and Houston answered that he had no such intention. It was not hard to give up authority in such a potentially disastrous situation.

But he did address the troops, reading them his commission from the governor and explaining, "But now, orders have been issued by the Council that conflict with the governor's. The Council, in my opinion, does not have the authority to issue such orders. I intend to recognize the authority of Governor Smith. Your new leaders—military agents—on the other hand, recognize the authority of the council. You must decide for yourselves which you accept."[16]

About half of the men went home. The others would pay dearly for their decision to stay.

General Council vs the Governor

In the evening, after the talk with the troops, Houston started out for San Felipe, along with Hockley and two officers. From one of the officers, Houston learned about the General Council's impeachment of Governor Smith. Already laboring under discouraging conditions, this news crushed his heart. He later described his feelings, writing of himself in third person:

> All the way to San Felipe, he was troubled by the most painful suspense—whether to withdraw once more from the treacheries and persecutions of the world, and bury himself deep in the solitude of nature, and pass a life of communion with the Great Spirit and his wonderful creations—or whether he should boldly mark out a track for himself, and in leading a new people to Independence, trample down all opposition. During most of the [following] day he rode along in silence, and none of his companions disturbed his reveries. Towards evening he addressed them... and dwelt with enthusiasm upon the prospects of Texas...[17]

Everything had fallen apart, but this time Sam Houston wasn't going to run away.

Santa Anna's Push North

Santa Anna pushed his troops northward. Seasoned veterans marched alongside new conscripts, who formed the bulk of the army. It was a difficult trek. Houston expected the dictator to travel with "the rise of grass" in the spring; historically, this was the custom, since cavalry horses needed grass to eat. But Santa Anna changed his pattern and departed late in December in spite of the hardships of winter. His men suffered from the cold, short rations, and lack of water.

Even as far south as Mexico, Comanches were a danger. As the army advanced, it discovered that its supply depots had been raided by Indians. Any army stragglers were in danger of being scalped.

Then in February, a blizzard dumped over a foot of snow on the soldiers, and some of those unaccustomed to cold weather died.

The Mexican soldiers pressed stoically on, their leader single-mindedly fixed on one objective: San Antonio. Santa Anna favored the old Spanish town as a base of operations in any case, but there was more at stake here than mere expediency. General Cos had been defeated there, and the honor of Mexican arms must be validated. The Napoleon of the West had something to prove; he needed a victory, a glorious victory.

A Desperate Message

The delegates shivered in the late February cold. In the town of Washington-on-the-Brazos, which had been fixed up for the occasion, the rough-hewn barracks-like building was now finished, and a few tree stumps removed. The representatives had gathered to form a new government. The same norther that had dumped snow on Santa Anna had passed through Texas on its way south. Finally, things warmed up a bit, but food was beginning to run low. One observer theorized that imminent starvation might motivate the delegates to accomplish something, but that did not seem to be the case. They were waiting—for Sam Houston.

But someone else, a courier, did come, dashing in with a letter dated February 24, 1836, from the commanding officer of the Alamo, Col. William B. Travis. The impetuous Georgian had been transferred to the Alamo after Neill went on furlough. The letter was a cry for help.

> To the People of Texas & all Americans in the world—
>
> Fellow citizens--& compatriots—I am beseiged, by a thousand or more of the Mexicans under Santa Anna—I have sustained a continual Bombardment & cannonade for 24 hours & have not lost a man—The enemy has demanded a surrender at discretion, otherwise, the garrison are to be put to the sword, if the fort is taken—I have answered the demand with a cannon shot & our flag still waves proudly from the walls—I shall never surrender or retreat. Then... come to our aid, with all dispatch... If this call is neglected I am determined to sustain myself as long as possible & die like a soldier...

> VICTORY OR DEATH
>
> P.S. The Lord is on our side—when the enemy appeared in sight we had not three bushels of corn—We have since found in deserted houses 80 or 90 bushels & got into the walls 20 or 30 head of Beeves—[18]

The delegates wanted to help, but what could they do? Where was Houston? The respect this man had shown for the civil government assured them that he would be the best choice for commander-in-chief. They would look to him for leadership.

Inside the Alamo

Jim Bowie was impressed. Commander Neill had accomplished a lot. The Mission San Antonio de Valero, now known as the "Alamo" after the "Alamo de Parras" battalion once stationed there, was a rectangular structure enclosing about three acres of ground. Because the old adobe walls would never hold up against siege cannons, Neill and his men had put in much effort to fortify them further. Bowie wandered into a barracks building. Ditches were dug into the dirt floor, and the north wall, which formed part of the outer wall, was buttressed with breastworks made of hides and filled with dirt.

Despite their privations, the men here were cheerful and optimistic. Neill had managed to keep morale high despite the hardships they suffered due to the lack of supplies. Jim Bowie talked to the commander: Houston wanted them to abandon the place, but Neill was authorized to make his own decision. In the end, Jim Bowie had his way. They would stay. How could things be so bad? After all, hadn't a former Congressman, the great David Crockett, just arrived with some tough men from Tennessee? Crockett had even refused any special rank, preferring to join their cause as a private. Maybe others would join them as well.

But there was one difficulty. William Travis was made commander in place of the departing Neill and had a formal commission, while Bowie was simply a volunteer officer. The men weren't certain of Travis, but they were sure of Bowie. The men held an election, and Travis was defeated in favor of the large knife-fighter. Bowie celebrated by getting drunk, and while intoxicated, became obnoxious.

Waking the next morning, February 13, Bowie had a bad hangover. He felt guilty for his bad behavior and perhaps humbled for the fool he had made of himself. He sought out Travis and proposed that they share command: Bowie over the volunteers, Travis over the regulars.

Then, one of Juan Seguin's mounted scouts rode up to report that Santa Anna had crossed the Rio Grande. The men in the Alamo had been hearing many rumors and wondered how seriously they should take this one. They continued to work, shoring up the defenses of the fort. At one point, near the chapel that tourists now identify as the "Alamo," there was no adobe wall, just a short palisade. The troops cut down trees and sharpened their limbs. These were arranged outside the palisade, limbs outward, to discourage would-be invaders.

On February 23, a lookout spotted troops and sent the Texans scurrying to gather as much food and water as they could carry into the fort. Santa Anna was here!

Troops poured into San Antonio, while atop the nearby San Fernando Church, the Mexicans hoisted the flag of no quarter, sending a stern message to the defenders of the Alamo.

> "The Mexican army cannot come to terms under any conditions with rebellious foreigners to whom there is no recourse left, if they wish to save their lives, than to place themselves immediately at the disposal of the Supreme Government from whom alone they may expect clemency after some considerations are taken up."[19]

Seguin Sent with an Appeal for Help

Travis possessed nineteen pieces of artillery left by General Cos, and he used one of them to deliver a pointed answer to Santa Anna's demand for surrender. The dictator was probably not disappointed at the response; he had, after all, come for a glorious victory in battle.

Shortly, the Mexican artillery was set up and soon pounded away at the old adobe walls of the mission. But for some reason, Santa Anna's army lacked heavy-duty siege guns; there were some on the way, but they would not arrive for several weeks. The Mexicans commenced the siege using small cannon. Given enough time, even these guns would demolish the old walls of the fort.

Both Travis and Bowie understood their vulnerability and sent appeals for help. They wrote Fannin in Goliad: "We have but little Provisions, but enough to serve us until you and your men arrive. We deem it unnecessary to repeat to a brave officer, who knows his duty, that we call on him for assistance."[20]

Because he was familiar with the area, Col. Juan Seguin was chosen to take the message to Goliad, and he had a good chance of getting past the Mexicans. Seguin borrowed Bowie's horse, and after giving what must have been an emotional farewell, departed with his orderly. Riding past a company of Mexican dragoons camped for the night, Seguin responded to their hail: "We are countrymen."[21] They were able to escape the siege.

Santa Anna was disdainful, calling the Alamo an "irregular fortification hardly worthy of the name."[22] But he did place mounted scouts on the roads to watch for Texans attempting rescue or reinforcement.

But Fannin did not come.

Houston's Challenge

It was raining in Washington-on-the-Brazos, and the delegates were discouraged. But then they heard a shout: Houston had come! Men converged on the figure on horseback. One observer remarked, "General Houston's arrival has created more sensation than that of any other man... He is much broken in appearance, but has still a fine person and courtly manners; he will be forty-three years old on the 3rd [2nd] of March—looks older."[23]

Governor Smith had sent Houston to some Cherokees in east Texas who had been riled by Santa Anna's agents. Already, he had been engaged in combat, the combat of careful diplomacy, which could not be rushed.

The delegates got to work, and soon Texas had its own Declaration of Independence, with Sam Houston's large, flowing signature added along with others. Then the group received another dispatch from Travis:

> I look to the *Colonies alone* for aid; unless it arrives soon, I shall have to fight the enemy on his own terms. I will, however, do the best I can under the circumstances; and I feel confident that the determined valor and desperate courage, heretofore exhibited by my men, will not fail them in the last struggle; and although they may be sacrificed to the vengeance of a Gothic enemy, the victory will cost the enemy dear, that it will be worse for him than defeat... Their threats have had no influence on me or my men... *God and Texas—Victory or Death!*[24]

One thousand copies of this appeal were ordered printed for distribution. The delegates themselves wanted to depart en masse for the relief of the Alamo, but Houston stood up.

> "This proposal is mad. We have declared ourselves independent but have no organization. There must be a government. It must have organic form. Without it we would be nothing but outlaws, and can hope neither for sympathy nor the respect of mankind. The country is in peril... While you choose to sit in convention I

promise you the Mexicans will never approach unless they march over my dead body. If mortal power can avail I will relieve the brave men in the Alamo."[25]

Because, even now, the rule of law had to supersede expediency. Without a government, they would be bandits in the sight of the world. Houston departed, leaving the delegates with pen and paper.

Setbacks at the Alamo

Jim Bowie was sick; his health had finally broken under the combined strain of grief, hard drinking, and the stress of war. He was suffering from some kind of respiratory ailment, possibly pneumonia. William Travis now had sole command of the troops.

By now, the men behind the adobe walls of the Alamo were discouraged. The constant bombardment of the cannon unnerved them and robbed them of needed sleep. They had enough to eat for the time being, and a well for water, but it would not last forever. Thirty-two volunteers from Gonzales had somehow managed to get past Santa Anna's sentries and had joined the 150 or so inside the fort, but what were these against so many?

The artillery positioned about the fort required many men to operate; the number of defenders was simply too few to adequately defend a full quarter mile of perimeter. Sharpshooters did inflict damage on the Mexican army but exposed themselves to danger with every shot.

Then on March 3rd, Travis received word that Fannin would not be coming.

A Sad End to a Misbegotten Expedition

A cold, driving rain drenched San Patricio. Colonel Frank Johnson and thirty-four of the remaining Matamoros expedition waited in the town while Dr. Grant and another group of men were out looking for mustangs. It was late, or rather very early on the morning of February 27th, and most of the men were asleep.

Suddenly, there were Mexicans everywhere. The Texans fought bravely—or ran. Johnson and five others managed to escape. By dawn, it was all over; eighteen were taken prisoner, nine or ten were dead. Mexican General Urrea had taken the town when he learned that Grant's group was returning to San Patricio.

Grant and twenty-six men were driving a herd of several hundred horses when suddenly, sixty mounted Mexican soldiers rode out of the woods beside them, cutting between Grant and most of his men. Placido Benavides, riding with Grant, wanted to go back and help the other men, but the Scot told him to ride to Fannin and tell him of the Mexican General's advance. Benavides rode off, and Grant rode with another man, Ruben Brown, to the aid of the others.

But as the two men rode near, they saw that most of their comrades were already dead. A Mexican rode up and killed Brown's horse with his long lance. Brown grabbed another animal at the same instant that a large herd of mustangs stampeded. The Texans saw their chance and urged their mounts onward. They tried to escape amid the rush of the stampeding horses.

It might have worked, but the Mexican cavalrymen pursued them stubbornly. Finally, one of them managed to drive his lance through Brown's arm. Grant shot and killed the man, but just as he did so, the Scot was thrust through with several lances. Brown was lassoed and dragged but lived to tell the tale. Before he was taken to Matamoros for interrogation, the captured Texan watched the Mexicans run their swords through Dr. Grant's dead body. Some of them had known the unscrupulous opportunist in Mexico and "had a bitter grudge against him."[26]

Thus ended the Matamoros Expedition.

Fannin at Goliad

"Military Agent" James Walker Fannin listened to Benavides describe the hair-raising ambush. General Urrea was to the south of him, and Santa Anna was to the northwest. Commander of several hundred Texans at La Bahia, now renamed "Fort Defiance," he evaluated the situation.

Cold reality had, by this time, stripped the tall, dark man of his self-confidence. He wasn't sure what to do, and he finally saw his own inadequacy. He wrote, "I am a better judge of my military abilities than others, and if I am qualified to command an Army, I have not found it out."[27]

He thought that he should withdraw from Goliad, but vacillated. He asked for orders, explaining that he wasn't really acting as commander-in-chief; he had never received orders to that effect. Thus he rambled in a letter to the government.

Just the day before the arrival of Benavides, Fannin had started out with his men for the relief of the men at the Alamo. But an oxcart had broken down within a mile, forcing them all back to Goliad.

The Impatient Napoleon

Santa Anna's officers sat silently, horrified. The "Napoleon of the West" had called them together to discuss an assault on the Alamo. It was March 5th, the twelfth day of the siege, and the heavy guns hadn't even arrived yet. Everyone knew that once the walls were demolished, taking the fort would be child's play. Why throw away the lives of their men?

But Santa Anna insisted, saying that "an assault would infuse our soldiers with that enthusiasm of the first triumph... "[28] but in reality, he wanted his glorious victory, and conventional strategy would not give him that.

His officers knew better than to oppose him. They prepared for an assault to begin at five o'clock the next morning.

How many would die?

The Assault

It was quiet, wonderfully quiet. Ominously quiet, now that the Mexicans' artillery was no longer assaulting their senses. The tired men inside the Alamo must have wondered why the continuous barrage had ceased, but they were so tired that it didn't seem that important anymore. They slept; even the sentinels on duty dozed off.

So nobody noticed the columns of Mexican soldiers advancing silently, the moonlight illuminating their march toward the Alamo. A few sleeping sentinels never woke again, thanks to the quick thrust of a bayonet.

"*Viva Santa Anna!*"

"*Viva la Republica!*"

Adjutant John Baugh was jolted awake. He ran across the plaza toward Travis' quarters. "Colonel Travis! The Mexicans are coming!"

Travis woke and jumped to his feet. "Come on, boys, the Mexicans are upon us... !"[29]

In a mad scramble, the Texan gunners raced to their cannons, which were loaded with scrap metal, chopped up horseshoes, nails, whatever they could find—they lacked proper canister shot.

By now, the columns of Mexican soldiers were so close that the gunners could not miss, and shards of metal tore through the soldiers' flesh. Then came round shot—a nine-pound ball of iron that made a sickening thud when first contacting human flesh. The Mexicans were being systematically mowed down, but their comrades deep in the ranks could not see what was happening, though they could hear the awful screams.

There was no escape. Santa Anna's lancers were deployed around the area for the dual purpose of defense and to prevent the desertion of their own men. The monster of Zacatecas was sacrificing his own soldiers to satiate his lust for glory.

The columns broke down under the deadly barrage of artillery and the accurate aim of Crockett's riflemen. But the surviving soldiers hurriedly regrouped and somehow managed to scale the walls.

A few of the Texans, seeing their enemies pour over the walls, begged for mercy and asked to surrender, but the Mexican soldiers had just witnessed the horrible deaths of scores of their friends and countrymen. They were in no mood for mercy.

Jim Bowie lay on a cot, feverish and possibly delirious. The Mexican soldiers went from room to room on a killing spree, sparing only a woman, her child, and a black slave. They did not spare Bowie.

A Sad Morning

Houston was tired. He had spent much of the previous six weeks in the saddle and had been fighting malaria to boot. But he had pledged his word, and the men of the Alamo were under siege. He did not know how he could save them, but surely he would if at all possible. He and several others rode hard toward Gonzales, over a hundred miles away.

They camped for the night on the open prairie, and early the next morning, Houston walked alone for some distance to listen. Travis had written that as long as the Alamo could hold out, the men inside would fire a cannon at dawn. This signal could be heard for a hundred miles, and Houston had been told that the day before "a rumbling murmur had boomed over the prairie like distant thunder."

But when Houston heard "not the faintest murmur floating on the calm morning air,"[30] he knelt and pressed his ear to the ground, the way the Indians had taught him, knowing sound travels better through the ground than through air. But the general heard absolutely nothing. It was the morning of March 7th.

Houston said nothing to his companions, but the possible fate of his friend, Jim Bowie, must have burdened his heart.

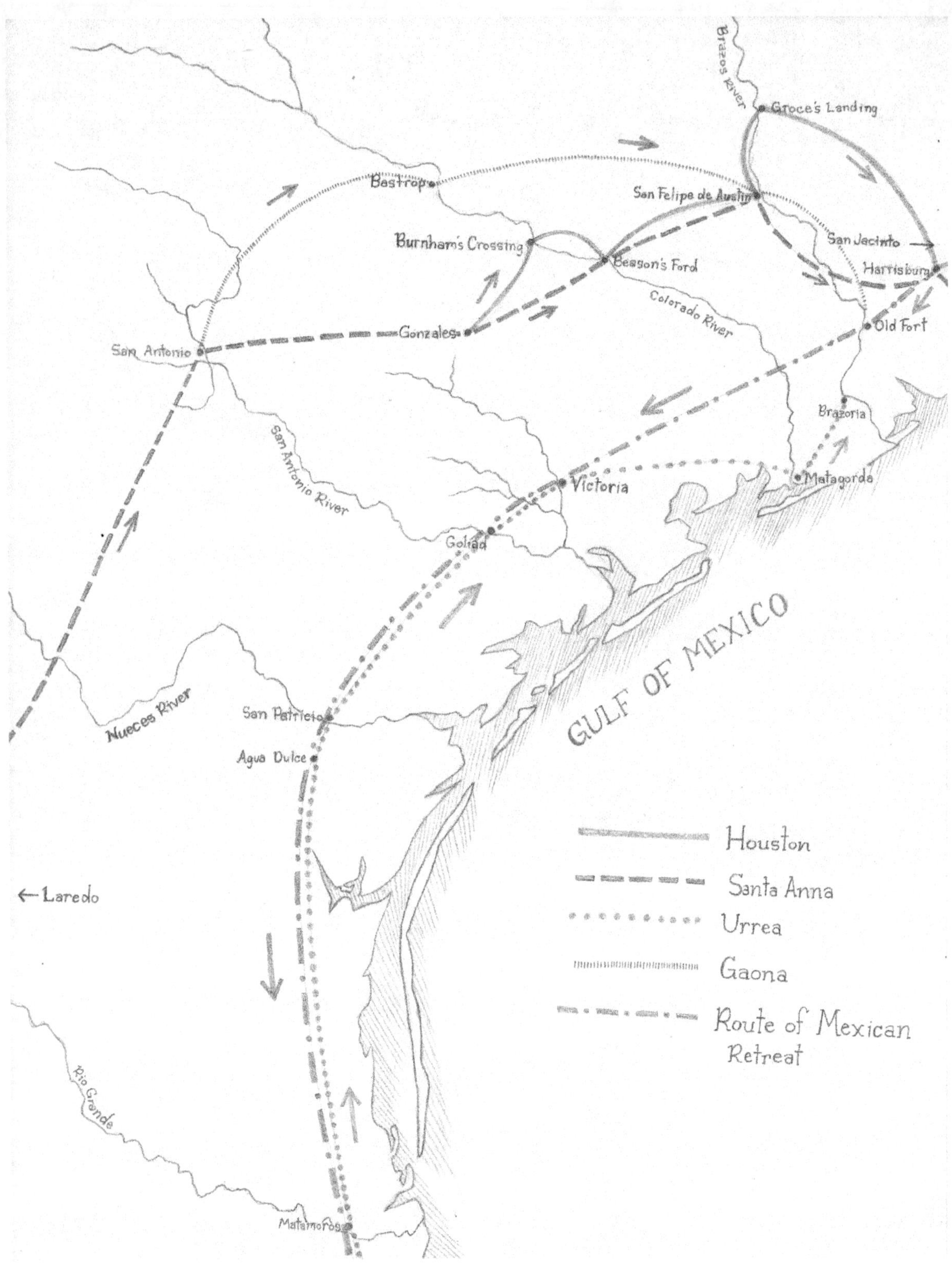

Brazos River
Groce's Landing
Bastrop
San Felipe de Austin
Burnham's Crossing
San Jacinto
Beason's Ford
Harrisburg
Colorado River
Old Fort
Gonzales
San Antonio
Brazoria
San Antonio River
Victoria
Matagorda
Goliad
GULF OF MEXICO
Nueces River
San Patricio
Agua Dulce
Houston
Santa Anna
Urrea
Gaona
Route of Mexican Retreat
← Laredo
Rio Grande
Matamoros

Chapter 9

Retreat to Victory

SANTA ANNA SURVEYED the carnage inside the walls of the Alamo. "These are the chickens. Much blood has been shed; but the battle is over. It was but a small affair." He later dictated a report to his Secretary of War: "The fortress at last fell into our power with its artillery, ammunition, etc., and buried among the ditches and trenches are more than 600 bodies, all of them foreigners."[1]

Santa Anna's secretary recorded these lies over his own protests. The alcalde of San Antonio, Francisco Ruiz, reported 182 defenders dead; among these were seven Tejanos.

Ruiz also recorded over fifteen hundred Mexican casualties; there were so many bodies that some of the corpses had to be disposed of in the river. And no field hospital had been set up before the battle. According to one, "more than a hundred of the wounded died afterward as a result of the lack of proper medical attention and medical facilities in spite of the fact that their injuries were not serious." It was reported that those who lay suffering envied those who had been instantly killed.

Jose Juan Sanchez-Navarro remarked, "With another such victory, we will all go to the devil."[2] Santa Anna had lost one-third of his best battalions.

Houston Arrives in Gonzales

Spring in Texas meant rain. Sam Houston and his companions pushed westward despite muddy roads and swollen rivers. They passed a number of people fleeing east, of which Houston wrote later, "None turned about, joined our party and faced the hazards of the westward journey."[3]

He sent a dispatch to Col. Fannin, instructing him to abandon the Goliad fort and march to Cibolo Creek, twenty-five miles east of San Antonio. Houston included information about his new commission from the Washington Convention: Fannin had not recognized his authority earlier, but maybe he would now.

On March 11th, 1836, Houston rode into Gonzales. He was not much to look at, wearing a Cherokee coat over a rustic buckskin waistcoat, trousers that clashed with the coat, a saber at his side, and a feather in his hat. Apparently, the velveteen coat with the improvised braid had not survived long.

The men who had gathered in Gonzales were not much to look at either. Some had no weapons, while others had no ammunition. They only had about two days' worth of foodstuffs. Just fifty of the 400 men were mounted. Houston read to them the Texas Declaration of Independence and his commission. Then he began to organize them.

The shadows lengthened and finally darkness fell. What was that sound? Wailing and crying floated through the air. Houston received word that two Tejanos had arrived in town, bearing word that the Alamo had fallen, and Sam knew that thirty agonized women had just discovered their widowhood. Hearing the lamentations of these women and their children, those in the army became upset. Emotions ran high.

Houston gave the command to arrest the Tejanos as spies and commanded his officers to spread the word that the stories were lies. In spite of this, twenty men left, saying they needed to look after their families. Houston called them deserters.

The commander-in-chief sent another message to Fannin, telling him to go to Victoria, east of the Guadalupe River, where they could be a support to each other. He also continued to organize the army; officers were elected, and the men were instructed in drill and tactics. Then he heard about two talented men, Captain Henry Karnes and "Deaf" Smith, who had by now become friends. Houston wanted them for scouts, sending both to San Antonio. But where was Fannin?

Santa Anna's Plan

Santa Anna took the little girl into his lap. He wanted to send her to Mexico City, where she could be brought up properly. Mrs. Dickerson protested. The dictator had been kind to her, but her daughter was going nowhere with him.

Well, this woman could be useful. Santa Anna provided her with a horse and an escort. He also sent along a proclamation, offering pardon to all insurgent

Texans who would lay down their arms, but also promising that those who did not would meet the same fate as those who had fallen at the Alamo. Mrs. Dickerson mounted and deliberately made her way east, the baby slowing her down.

Then the widow saw two horsemen approach. It was Erastus Smith and Henry Karnes who stumbled across the woman and her escort less than twenty miles from Gonzales. After hearing Mrs. Dickerson's account of the fall of the Alamo, Karnes galloped back to camp; Smith accompanied the small party at a slower pace back to Gonzales.

Houston Hears the News

> Houston was walking alone, a few hundred yards from the camp, the moment this stricken and bereaved messenger arrived. He returned soon after, and found that her fearful narrative of the butchering and burning, with some of the most stirring details of that dark tragedy, had already struck the soldiers with a chill of horror; and when she told them that 5,000 men were advancing by forced marches, and their artillery would soon be heard at Gonzales, the wildest consternation spread through the camp. Their alarm soon reached a pitch of desperation. Some were stunned with silence—others with wild lamentations...
>
> He then addressed the soldiery in the most fervid manner, and they all gathered around him, except for a few, who had the first impulse fled for their horses. He detached a guard instantly to intercept fugitives, and more than twenty were brought back to camp. But a few good runners made their escape to the settlements, and carried panic in every direction.[4]

A Slight Change of Plan

Fear. Because it was such a powerful and useful motivator, Santa Anna ruled by fear. It was his most powerful ally. Now that the dictator had made his point at the Alamo, the rest was a mere clean-up action. There was no Texan Army of any real size, and now that news of the Alamo's fall had spread, fear and panic would prevail, stealing the strength of the people. He was the Napoleon of the West: fear was the key to his power, and fear would conquer Texas.

It was time to return to Mexico; there was a disturbance to the south, and it needed his attention. His trusted generals could handle Texas. Santa Anna explained his plan. General Urrea, who had entered the country separately, was having good success south of them on the coastal plain. The rest would split into several groups and go in different directions, with General Gaona taking a northeasterly route toward Nacogdoches and General Sesma leading his force right through the midsection of the Anglo colonies, towards San Felipe.

Most of the population of Texas resided to the east of San Antonio, and so Santa Anna sent his men east. Three armies would plunge through the fear-stricken land; every rebel with a gun was to be killed, even if he surrendered. As for the others, well, they would long for the chance to flee beyond the Sabine River.

Santa Anna had done this before in Zacatecas.

The Texas Declaration

> *When a government has ceased to protect the lives, liberty and property of the people, from whom its legitimate powers are derived, and for the advancement of whose happiness it was instituted, and, so far from being a guarantee for the enjoyment of those inestimable and inalienable rights, becomes and instrument in the hands of evil rulers for their oppression;...*

So began the Texas Declaration of Independence, which was speedily composed in one night, using the American Declaration as a template, and then signed by the delegates on March 2, 1836.

This document was written before Houston left for Gonzales. The rest of the delegates in Washington-on-the-Brazos settled down to the task of writing a constitution for a new republic, all the while conscious of the fact that thousands of Mexican soldiers were already doing their best to make sure that nothing they were planning would ever come to pass. And, of course, just putting their signatures on the Declaration was probably an automatic death warrant as far as the Mexican government was concerned.

Under such pressure, the assembly of Texans formed a government in only two weeks, adopting a Constitution on March 16 and electing David G. Burnet, the short, teetotaling attorney, as president; Lorenzo de Zavala, the former Mexican governor, as vice-president, and Thomas Rush, secretary of war.

But were they safe? Where were Santa Anna's men?

A Few Good Men

Houston considered his men. Teenage boys, farmers, and volunteers from the United States; these were men who had gathered under J.C. Neill, who had purposed to return to the Alamo. But Travis, Bowie, and Crockett were all dead; the bodies of the 182 defenders had been burned and their ashes thrown into a common grave. What were they to do now?

With only 374 "effectives," Houston knew he could not meet the enemy, except on his own terms. The men were spoiling for a fight; some of them didn't care a bit about the odds. But Houston had to care, because this was Texas's only army, except for Fannin's men, and Houston didn't know if he could count on Fannin. If this little group at Gonzales was massacred, there would be no more Texan army and no more Texas. And this collection of men was no army, really; they had no understanding of army discipline, drill... nothing. They would be easily slaughtered by experienced troops.

But there were good men here; he had learned he could count on Henry Karnes and Erastus "Deaf" Smith, a short, stocky man with a peculiar squeaky voice. In his respect for the man, Houston referred to Smith as "the wonderful Mr. E." And there were others; Juan Seguin and a whole group of Tejanos; Sid Sherman with a company of Kentucky and Ohio volunteers; Edward Burleson, a respected Indian fighter, and the man who had taken over after Austin left; and of course, J.C. Neill, a reliable man in his own right. Making use of this vast pool of talent, Houston appointed officers and organized the men into companies and battalions.

Houston had arrived in Gonzales on Friday, March 11th. Saturday evening, he told Ed Burleson that the army needed to be ready to leave at 11:30 that night.

Fannin's Delay

Col. James Walker Fannin was worried. He had sent Colonel Ward to relieve Captain King, who had been trapped by some of General Urrea's advance guard. He did not know what was happening to those he had sent to help with the evacuation of American settlers, and he certainly could not just abandon them.

But General Houston had ordered Fannin to withdraw to Victoria. That seemed sensible to him. South Texas was becoming a dangerous place, and he had difficulty getting information because of the loyalist rancheros who had taken Santa Anna's side. As in the American Revolution, Texas was not fully united in rebellion; there were "Tories," especially here in South Texas. What had happened to King? Fannin waited for news, not knowing his delay would cost him dearly.

Big Drunk Smashes the Poisoned Whiskey Bottles

"Move on! Step lively!"

Some of the volunteers grumbled, wondering about the townspeople. Were they abandoning helpless civilians to Santa Anna?

They didn't know that Houston had sent Juan Seguin and his men to help the remaining civilians get out of Gonzales to follow the fleeing army. Houston heard their complaints but ignored them.

Several miles east of Gonzales, the ground underfoot became sandy. Few of the men had horses, and all the available wagons were being used to evacuate townspeople. The one remaining wagon left to the army carried ammunition and other essentials. Their only artillery, two brass cannon, had sunk in the river behind them. The men had to carry everything else themselves, and they stumbled along, sinking to their ankles in the sand.

Then the ammunition wagon got stuck in a sand trap. General Houston rode back to the rear to help. He still had one good shoulder.

They made ten miles before nightfall, then set up camp and slept.

A Strategic Retreat

The men were awakened by the sound of explosions. Santa Anna's artillery? No. The sound was that of whiskey bottles exploding. In fact, General Houston had ordered the destruction of all liquor left in town after he learned that the townspeople had poisoned it and left it for Santa Anna's soldiers to drink.

They camped at a place called Peach Creek, where the men ate brittle tortillas made with flour and water prepared by the women of Gonzales. The civilians had finally caught up with the army. Hungry, the volunteers didn't even notice the lack of shortening in their breakfast.

Juan Seguin had a new job, and he gathered his associates to make plans. Houston had appointed the Texan his commissary officer, since it was a well-known fact that every army traveled on its stomach. One of their main tasks would be to locate beef cattle to slaughter, and for that, the horsemen were well-suited.

The army broke camp, and the mixed multitude, soldiers and townspeople, animals and crying babies, resumed their flight east. Houston rode along the column, his sharp eye on the caravan, and when one young officer saluted him in a peculiar fashion, he stopped to investigate. Maybe not all of the ardent spirits had been left behind in Gonzales after all. Sure enough, several jugs were found in a wagon, and Houston ordered that they be broken on the rim of the wagon wheel.

"Big Drunk" watched as the liquor spilled onto the ground. He saw alcohol as a friendly enemy, promising joy and comfort; but he had felt its mockery and bore its scars within. Houston vowed not to drink a single drop on this campaign, and to help in moments of weakness, he carried a vial of hartshorn, whose ammonia vapors helped to take away the desire. He needed to be on the top of his game in this crisis, and so did his men.

The general had a lot on his mind. What about the delegates in Washington, who were forming the government? He had pledged to protect them. Would they understand his retreat? They were politicians; few were military men. With this in mind, he composed a letter:

> We could have met the enemy [at Gonzales] and avenged some of our wrongs; but, detached as we were, without supplies for the men in camp, of either provisions, ammunition, or artillery, and remote from succor, it would have been madness to hazard a contest... By falling back, Texas can rally, and defeat any force that can come against her...
>
> I am fearful Goliad is besieged by the enemy. My order to Colonel Fannin, directing the place to be blown up, the cannon to be sunk in the river, and to fall back on Victoria, would reach him before the enemy could advance. That they have advanced upon the place in strong force, I have no doubt; and when I heard of the fall of the Alamo, and the number of the enemy, I knew it must be the case...[5]

Disaster Strikes

Colonel Fannin knew he needed to leave and finally gave the orders. Houston had directed him to get rid of his cannon so that his men could move quickly, but perhaps that was not really necessary. His men prepared to move the next day, packing a large amount of personal belongings and five hundred spare muskets. Nine cannon were prepared for the march.

The next day dawned gray and foggy, perfect for an early, sneaky getaway. But it took forever to get going, much like a family packing their car for a vacation trip; there were all kinds of last-minute details. Then, when everything was finally ready, Fannin told his men to burn everything left behind, so the Mexicans could not use it. The pillar of smoke that rose above the fort served as an announcement to the enemy that the troops were now on the march.

In spite of their careful planning, everything that could possibly go wrong *did* go wrong. The oxen pulling the artillery had not been fed, and only four miles from their starting point, the hungry animals stopped to graze and could not be dissuaded.

One man recalled that "several wagons were broken up or merely abandoned and their teams hitched to the remaining carts. After crawling on a little farther, disgust at the creeping pace of our column induced us finally to abandon all our equipment."[6]

Then someone realized that the food had been left behind and was burned by mistake. They could only be grateful that no one was chasing them. More than three hundred men, mainly volunteers and adventurers from the States, enjoyed the beautiful spring day.

Until the Mexicans showed up, that is. Fannin's column was caught in open prairie, and the enemy cavalry split up and galloped into position, blocking any attempt at flight into the timber. The Mexicans had learned how deadly American sharpshooters could be behind cover, and they weren't eager to make that mistake again.

The Runaway Scrape

Austin's colonists had not come to Texas to fight a dictator. They had come to till the soil, feed their families, and earn a living that might result in a suitable inheritance for their offspring. But in the muddy spring of 1836, they had to make a decision. Would they stay and fight for what they believed was right? For the land into which they had poured sweat and labor? And for liberty?

Some packed their wagons and headed east and kept going until they crossed the Sabine. Others cleaned their rifles and kissed their families goodbye; they were joining Houston's assemblage. Yes, it was an army in retreat, but it was the army of Texas. Fathers and sons joined together; they weren't hot-blooded adventurers. They were farmers defending their families.

The whole of Texas was on the move. Women whose husbands had gone off to war soon realized they weren't safe at home. The Mexican army was coming, and rumors were spreading about the horrible slaughter of the men at the Alamo. Some knew of what Santa Anna's men had done in Zacatecas. Many panic-stricken families threw their belongings into wagons and headed east, leaving their chickens to fend for themselves.

The "Runaway Scrape," as the flight of Texas refugees became known, poured eastward, through the spring rain and thick mud. But swollen rivers hindered this eastward flow of humanity.

"Eliza! Eliza! Where are you?" Shouts such as these must have rung out at

Burnham's Ferry, on the Colorado, where chaos reigned. Babies cried, husbands called for wives, and mothers searched for children. A thousand people milled around on the muddy bank of the Colorado River, frantic to cross.

Houston's army was growing. One by one or in small groups, colonists were joining his unlikely band as they marched eastward, still giving assistance to the settlers from Gonzales. General Houston had purposed to get to the Colorado River, now only a few more miles away. Maybe there he would find that place and that time where he could make a stand against the enemy and win.

After a twelve-hour march, Sam Houston and his caravan arrived at Burnham's Ferry, where the general's tired eyes regarded the scene: crowds of frantic people, children wailing, tempers flaring, and animals bleating. The mob of refugees was not encouraged by the arrival of Houston's army. They thought the volunteers would insist on cutting to the front of the line. It was taking forever to get across the river as it was, and nobody felt like waiting. They were terrified.

Sam Houston rode his horse into the middle of the mayhem. Calmly, he addressed the people with soothing words. Not one member of his army would cross the river until every civilian was safely across. He directed his soldiers to man the ferry and kept his promise. Every single civilian was safely across before any soldier boarded the ferry. Then, when his men had landed on the other side, he stationed them on the east bank of the river for two days, serving as a shield for the frightened refugees traveling before them. Plus, his tired men needed the rest after marching for four long days.

While there, he wrote another letter to the delegates, lamenting, "It pains my heart that such consternation should have been spread by the deserters from camp..."[7] Houston knew that if Texans were ruled by fear, the battle was already lost.

Fannin Exposed and Outnumbered

James Walker Fannin didn't feel the pain right away. He felt the force of the impact as the lead ball entered his thigh, and he knew he had been shot, but at first it was just a burning pressure. Then the pain came.

Colonel Fannin had organized his men into a defensive square out in the middle of the prairie, while Urrea's *soldados* had the benefit of timber several miles away; they advanced first with cavalry, then on foot. Fannin and his men had some success using their artillery, but their position was too exposed. They were sitting ducks.

Finally, night fell, and a cool shower helped to relieve the suffering of the feverish wounded among them. Fannin's men dug ditches and constructed breastworks using the bodies of dead horses and oxen and whatever else they had on hand. They dug, then slept, then dug some more. At least that helped them keep warm. The wounded continued to cry out and moan all night long.

When morning came, the American volunteers were assailed with grape and canister shot from the Mexican artillery. Then it stopped. General Urrea, it seemed, had no desire to slaughter a group so hopelessly outnumbered and outgunned.

Colonel Fannin and his men had fought bravely, but there was no point in continuing. Surrender might preserve the lives of his men. Fannin took a white flag and limped out to meet the enemy.

Depressing News

Strategy was everything. With a small, untrained, inexperienced force, Houston knew that he had to seize every advantage he could. He turned the army south on March 19th, and they marched along the Colorado until they reached Beason's Ferry. This was better ground. Not only did he have the command of three crossing points on the river, but he also had good high ground behind him, to the east, in case he needed to retreat toward San Felipe.

But Houston kept his ruminations to himself. He did not debate strategy with his officers but simply gave commands. Some of his men began to murmur. *Why do we keep running away? Why didn't we fight at Gonzales?* These volunteers were not accustomed to unquestioning obedience, and they didn't like being reproved. *Who does he think he is, anyway?*

But others served without complaint. Captain Henry Karnes and Erastus Smith proved their worth as scouts. The day after the march to Beason's Ferry, Karnes and five others encountered a Mexican scouting party from General Sesma's army. They pursued the Mexicans, killed one, and captured another. They also captured a saddlebag that contained an article of clothing belonging to a man killed at the Alamo.

Two days later, Karnes and Smith had a new report: Sesma was here. The Mexican General was located on the opposite bank of the Colorado River, just a few miles away.

In Washington-on-the-Brazos, the new government of Texas received some distressing news: Santa Anna's cavalry was on the east side of the Colorado River. They had no way of knowing that the information was false. They decided to go south, down the river. Maybe Harrisburg would be a safer place. Not knowing about Santa Anna's three-pronged strategy, and that Harrisburg lay in the path of the middle prong, they left.

Terms of Surrender

Colonel Fannin asked for terms. General Urrea replied, "If you gentlemen wish to surrender at discretion, the matter is ended, otherwise I shall return to my camp and renew the attack."[8] Fannin accepted the terms.

"Surrender at discretion" meant no guarantee. Urrea was not promising to spare the lives of Fannin's men, but as was the tradition in "civilized" warfare, it was not considered honorable to butcher men who had laid down their arms. Fannin told his men that their lives would be spared. Perhaps he just made that assumption.

General Urrea's officers made that assumption as well. In fact, they took Fannin to the coast to make arrangements for the transport of his men to New Orleans.

But Urrea was concerned, after learning Santa Anna wanted all captured foreigners executed. Urrea wrote a letter—surely that was not necessary in this case.

Houston Writes to Rusk

Houston received several distressing pieces of news. For one thing, the government had fled to Harrisburg, and for another, the Mexican Army had attacked Fannin and his men, and the result of the battle was still unknown. The general wrote Thomas Rusk, the Secretary of War, a long, anxious letter.

> You know I am not easily depressed but, before my God, since we parted [at the Washington Convention] I have found the darkest hours of my past life! My excitement has been so great, that, for forty-eight hours, I have not eaten an ounce, nor have I slept. I was in constant apprehension of a rout; a constant panic existed in the lines... All would have been well, and all at peace on this side of the Colorado, if I could only have had a moment to start to express in advance of the deserters [from Gonzales]; but they went first, and, being panic struck, it was contagious, and all who saw them breathed the poison and fled...
>
> The retreat of the government will have a bad effect on the troops, and I am half-provoked at it myself... If what I have heard [of] Fannin be true, I deplore it, and can only attribute the ill luck to his attempting to retreat in daylight in face of a superior force. He is an ill-fated man...[9]

A Courier Comes With Orders

The Mexican officers struggled with their consciences. They had heard the news: a courier had arrived from Bexar, where Santa Anna still made his headquarters. The prisoners were to be shot.

The next morning, March 27th, one of these officers came into the room where two American surgeons, who had offered to care for Mexican wounded, were being held. He was pale.

"Keep still, gentlemen, you are safe; these are not my orders, nor do I execute them."[10] Because they were useful to the Mexican Army, the doctors would not be executed.

One officer hid several of Fannin's men, as did the wife of another officer. The rest were told they were being taken to Matamoros.

Thinking that they were going home, the men willingly marched out onto the road. Actually, they had been divided into three groups and were marched out onto three different roads.

"*Pobrecitos! Pobrecitos!*" Some women watching them knew. Poor fellows!

The guards marched on either side of the prisoners; then they stopped. The guards on one side filed around to join those on the other.

Someone shouted, "Boys, they're going to shoot us. Run for it!"[11]

Muskets fired. Those who were not hit ran; many were shot as they ran, but a few escaped into the woods.

Later, the wounded who had been left behind were dragged out onto the road and shot. Fannin was blindfolded and seated in a chair before he was shot in the face.

A Mexican officer, who commanded one of the firing squads, wrote this in his diary.

> This day, Palm Sunday, March 27th, has been to me a day of most heartfelt sorrow. At six in the morning, the execution of... American prisoners was commenced, and continued till eight, when the last of the number was shot... what an awful scene did the field present, when the prisoners were executed, and fell in heaps! And what spectator could view it without horror! They were all young, the oldest not more than thirty, and of fine florid complexions. When the unfortunate youths were brought to the place of death, their lamentations and appeals which they uttered to Heaven, in their own language, with extended arms, kneeling or prostrate on the earth, were such as might have caused the very stones to have cried out in compassion.[12]

Houston Drills His Men

The news that had discouraged Houston was having the same effect on his men; they were grumbling, and a few even left camp. Now that they were no longer helping civilians, the general warned his men; any man who left camp without permission would be treated as a deserter. They were in for the duration of the war, and they needed to learn how to fight. Houston drilled his men, and although self-reliant farmers and volunteers were not used to this kind of thing, they obeyed orders. For now, at least.

Houston confiscated the drum used to beat the morning and evening tattoo in order to beat the signal himself; that way, no one could use it to beat an alarm in panic. He had no tent or any luxuries but chose to sleep under a tree, beside the drum.

One day, "the wonderful Mr. E." and Captain Karnes brought a couple of prisoners and captured communication to General Houston's tree. It reported that Sesma had received reinforcements. A few other things also became clear, and Houston sat as if working a puzzle, putting pieces together in his head. Apparently, Santa Anna had several generals working together. One was across the river, one north of him, and one south of Houston's position. But where was Santa Anna? Had he gone back to Mexico?

The position on the Colorado had, by now, become quite precarious. Houston knew his men would not want to retreat farther, but he could take no chances.

The commander-in-chief sent scouting parties across the river, towards General Sesma's position. He wanted the Mexicans to believe that he was going to attack. Then, as darkness fell, he instructed his troops to build huge campfires. With the fires burning brightly, the men withdrew under the cover of darkness.

Fearing an attack, Sesma withdrew and stayed put. Two days later, Houston's men arrived in San Felipe, on the Brazos River.

Houston Handles Mutinous Behavior

Captain Mosely Baker was tired of retreating, and he knew that he was not the only one who felt that way. He suggested that if Houston ordered another retreat, his successor would take over the next day. Perhaps what he saw at San Felipe provoked this mutinous behavior; watching escaping colonists making their way east, he literally broke down and wept at the sight of the refugees. Texas was coming unraveled before his eyes; women and children were suffering, babies were dying.

They had to fight! Couldn't anybody see that?

Then their commander-in-chief ordered another retreat, up the west bank of the Brazos. Several officers, including Baker, balked. Houston could have court-martialed them but took another course: he gave them assignments he knew they would accept.

Baker, go across the river and entrench. Remain behind with your company to delay the enemy's advance.

Captain Mosely Baker obeyed.

Horrifying News

Houston found a piece of good ground on the west bank of the Brazos. The never-ending spring rains had flooded the rivers and creeks, and this high spot was surrounded by water like a castle with a moat. Defended by water all around, the general started school again, basic training in the middle of a real war. He taught his men subordination, since the key to victory was clearly in obeying orders.

That's when they heard the horrifying news from Goliad, regarding the massacre of Fannin's men.

After the fall of the Alamo, Houston had tried to keep the news under wraps, in hopes of avoiding an all-out panic. Now, he chose another tactic. He encouraged his men to talk about Goliad. Walking through camp, his men asked him questions. How could this have happened?

The rank and file was full of bitterness and hungry for vengeance. They had a deep respect for "Old Sam," as he was sometimes called. Houston wrote to Secretary of War Rusk: "Will not our friends rush to the conflict, and at once avenge the wrongs which have been inflicted on our dauntless comrades! The day of just retribution ought not to be deferred. Send expresses to the coast and to the United States."[13]

A Loss of Confidence

General Gaines of the United States Army surveyed his campsite. He had marched his men within a short distance of the Texas border. With war at their doorstep and refugees pouring across the border, the United States was justified in sending in troops to secure its territory. At least, that was the official reason he was here. There was an unofficial reason, too. Somehow, it became known that "deserters" who found themselves crossing the border into Texas and fighting in General Houston's army would not be punished. General Gaines would look the other way.

On the Brazos, the ranks swelled; a few of the colonists wore the remnants of a U.S. Army uniform they had tried to disguise.

But not all had confidence in Houston, including the new President of Texas, David G. Burnet, who wrote:

"The enemy are laughing you to scorn. You must fight them. You must retreat no farther. The country expects you to fight. The salvation of your country depends on you doing so."[14]

Houston wrote back, with just a hint of sarcasm:

> To D. G. Burnet Esq., President of the Republic of Texas:
>
> Sir: I have kept the army together under the most discouraging circumstances, and I hope a just and wise God, in whom I have always believed, will yet save Texas, and that confusion and dismay may yet seize upon her enemies, and chastise them for their cruelties and oppression. I am sorry that I am so wicked, for "the prayers of the righteous shall prevail." That you are so, I have no doubt, and hope that Heaven, as such, will help and prosper you, and crown your efforts with success in behalf of Texas and humanity.
>
> I am very truly your friend—Sam Houston.[15]

Later, another cutting letter was received from Burnet. In his response, Houston reminded the president "on *whom* to rely, and on *whom*, for a while, the burden must rest..."[16]

In Harrisburg, David G. Burnet was irritated, frustrated, and scared. The president of the new republic could not fully appreciate the military situation, and he tended to blame Houston. Why did he keep retreating? Sam Houston had always rubbed Burnet the wrong way, and now this drunkard was telling him to trust in God. He had a spy in Houston's army already; maybe it was simply time to replace him. They had elected him commander-in-chief, and they could unelect him.

But Lorenzo de Zavala and Thomas Rusk wanted no part of such intrigue. They left Harrisburg, seeking Houston's camp. Might as well join the army and fight.

Santa Anna Decides to Come East

General Filisola had approached Santa Anna's most trusted aide for help, Colonel Almonte. What did he think of this three-pronged strategy? Personally, he thought the plan less than brilliant. Santa Anna thought the war was essentially over, but Filisola disagreed. And the dictator was too stuck on himself to listen.

Almonte agreed with Filisola. Together, they tried to persuade Santa Anna that the men they would be dealing with in East Texas were men defending their homes, not adventurers from the United States. The fighting would be desperate. The armies should be consolidated.

But the Napoleon of the West was contemptuous of Texans. He was not convinced by Almonte's arguments. He did change his mind about one thing; perhaps he really did need to oversee this thing himself. The problems in the south would just have to wait.

On March 31, 1836, Santa Anna left San Antonio. With a small force, he hurried east, catching up with General Sesma a week later. Filisola, his second-in-command, was to follow.

A Gift of Cannon

The lessons were over, and hopefully, the Texas army was now prepared, because the Mexicans were once again advancing on their position. Houston ordered a retreat across the Brazos to a farm owned by a certain Mr. Donoho. But Mr. Donoho, a Mexican sympathizer, protested. The army was cutting his timber for firewood!

The general explained to his men that they could not use the man's timber and marched them to a long rail fence. The army took the hint and used Mr. Donoho's fence for firewood instead.

About this time, the army received a welcome gift: two fine cast-iron cannon from the citizens of Cincinnati. The men promptly named them "The Twin Sisters." At Donoho's farm, Houston supervised a blacksmith who cut up horseshoes and old iron to use as ammunition.

A new and misinformed recruit approached Houston and asked him to repair a broken lock on his rifle. After taking the rifle, the general told him to return in an hour; later, the recruit returned shamefacedly, now understanding that he had given his gun to his commander. "I was told you were a blacksmith," he explained.

"You were correctly informed. I am a very good blacksmith, and here is your rifle with its lock in good order to prove it."[17]

Soon the men heard the word that the tough, inscrutable general could take a joke.

But when Houston ordered the men to break camp and assume marching formation the next morning, a group of men who had just come in from Fort Bend were upset. They hadn't had any breakfast and refused to march on empty stomachs. General Houston told them to fill their bellies and then leave, but not with him; they could either go east and try to revive the courage of fugitives there, or they could go plumb to (a much hotter place). The grumblers chose East Texas.

While this was going on, scouts came into the camp, bringing with them a man who had a message. Houston took the letter. It was from Santa Anna.

By that time, the Napoleon of the West had overtaken his armies and was striking ahead with a small force. He knew of Houston and his army but was not terribly concerned; this Houston was just one more incompetent rebel leader, whom he planned to destroy along with the rebel government, which he now knew was located in Harrisburg. He hoped these rebels were armed, because then he could legitimately execute them. Now, where was Harrisburg? The land was unfamiliar and swampy, and the rain was a nasty hindrance.

Santa Anna wrote to the Texan commander, whom he knew was north of him. He informed the rebel general that he was going to return and smoke him out as soon as he had finished with the government at Harrisburg.

The dictator had shortly resumed his march when his men came upon a creek, but a fallen tree bridged the stream nicely, and the infantry passed over without incident. But the mules weren't so lucky; they would have to swim across the rain-swollen stream. Santa Anna was in a hurry; he didn't want the Texas government to escape from his grasp. He ordered the baggage and commissary mules to cross fully loaded; unloading them would take more time than he wanted to spend.

That decision proved to be a costly mistake. The mules plunged into the stream heavily loaded and almost made it across safely, but had trouble getting a foothold on the opposite bank. Ultimately, they slid back into the water, causing a traffic jam of mules, horses, and men. Several men fell into the water, and two of the mules drowned.

Watching, Santa Anna was thoroughly amused; he stood on the bank and laughed and laughed.

Borden and the Texas Government Evacuate

Gail Borden, who one day would achieve fame for condensed milk, disagreed with his printers. Borden was the editor of the *Texas Telegraph* in Harrisburg; the printers wanted to remain with their equipment. But the editor had already decided to leave with the members of the Texas government who were now in the process of evacuating.

Finding that he had just missed capturing the government, the Mexican dictator burned Harrisburg, then set off in hot pursuit, but heavy rain and boggy ground hindered his advance. As it turned out, Borden, along with President

Burnet and the rest of the Texas government, had already boarded a boat and sailed for Galveston Island, escaping the pursuing dictator by mere minutes.

A Strategic Move by the Raven

Houston wondered. Was that letter genuine? Was Santa Anna with the Mexican Army south of him? It was a military opportunity ...

His troops moved out in a downpour, one the men said was unlike any since the time of Noah. A dark sky threw diagonal sheets of rain, drenching the men as well as the already soggy ground. The storm thrashed the army, but the men continued their dogged advance, slipping and sliding in the mud. Shortly, a wagon became mired, its wheels sinking above their hubs into the sucking muck.

Houston dismounted, took off his coat, and lent his one good shoulder to the task, something he would repeat eight times in the next few hours.

Somehow, Houston's men made good time, covering fifty-two miles in two and a half days. They arrived at the Buffalo Bayou, across from which stood Harrisburg, or rather, the remnants of Harrisburg. The Mexican Army had beaten them there. But where was it now? And was Santa Anna with it? The men camped and slept while Houston consulted a dirty map.

With his faithful scouts feeding him information, the general made his move the next day after only a few hours' sleep. The army crossed Buffalo Bayou, a difficult operation. The ferryboat had to be repaired before it could be used, and all the men worried over their vulnerability, knowing the enemy was not far away.

Finally, they were all across.

Houston's Address to his Men

Then the commander-in-chief addressed his men. Until now, the inscrutable Raven had said little, but now he wished to stir their souls for battle. He explained that a single man, Santa Anna, was responsible for their troubles and sacrifices. He told them that this man and his army were now cut off from support (which was not exactly true, but Houston was known to use subterfuge for the sake of morale). A decisive battle was at hand; anyone who was afraid should leave now.

Houston paused. Not one man moved.

"This is our battle cry," their commander announced. "Remember the Alamo! Remember the Alamo!"

In his memoirs, Houston wrote, "This watchword... was caught up by every man in the army, and one simultaneous shout broke up into the sky... and the green islands of trees in the prairie sent back the echo."[18]

Seguin's Tejanos

Juan Seguin felt the blood rise to his face. *No.* He understood Sam Houston's concern, and in the corner of his mind, he appreciated it, but no. The suggestion to remain behind, guarding the baggage and wounded in Harrisburg, was meant to protect the Tejanos from the dark mood of the Anglo volunteers. After hearing about the massacre at Goliad, the rage of the men had morphed into hatred toward all Mexicans.

The handsome young Texan stood straight in his classy but mud-spattered uniform and faced his commander. "No one has more reason to hate the Santanistas than we do. And plus, we can't even go home until this usurper is ejected from this country; we are all from Bexar." Respectfully yet forcefully, Juan Seguin demanded the right to fight Santa Anna.

"Spoken like a man,"[19] replied Houston. He had one request--that Seguin's Tejanos must put a piece of cardboard in their hats, so that his men would be better able to distinguish them from the enemy.

Tricking Santa Anna

Santa Anna was coming. After the Texas government escaped by boat to Galveston, the dictator gave up the chase, turned his men around, and headed north.

Information from his scouts and his crumpled map could lead Houston to only one conclusion. They needed to get to Lynch's ferry before Santa Anna did. The Mexican Army was marching north on a piece of land bordered by several bodies of water—the Buffalo Bayou to the north and the San Jacinto River to the east. Because Lynch's Ferry was the only way to cross the San Jacinto, they had to beat Santa Anna to the ferry.

As the men marched, the general's tired, sleep-deprived mind considered his options. What was in the mind of his adversary? A captured courier, courtesy of Erastus Smith, had confirmed his belief that Santa Anna was at the head of that force just a few miles away. He could make another deduction based on the boastful letter he had received earlier: the Mexican dictator had a proud contempt for the Texan army and its leader. The fact was that no commander would inform his enemy of his plans without a sure assurance of victory.

The more Houston thought about it, the more he liked the idea—of using this information and playing his enemy for his own ends. He could pretend to be "trapped" by Santa Anna, whose contempt for the ragged force before him *might* just cause him to be careless... the Buffalo Bayou led into the San Jacinto near Lynch's Ferry. A position near the ferry would give the appearance that Houston's men were "cornered."

The Cavalry Sent to Reconnoiter

After pushing hard, Houston's army beat Santa Anna's men to the ferry by just a few hours. A thick grove of oaks grew along the bayou, and here the men made camp. South of them, the Mexican force approached, making its way over soggy and swampy terrain. They made camp about a mile away from the Texans, in a rather exposed position, but *El Presidente* did not seem the least bit concerned.

His scouts reported the presence of two pieces of artillery near the oak grove. Santa Anna knew his enemy must be camped among the oaks, and he decided to provoke them. He wanted to test the mettle of this backwoods drunkard, who presumed to call himself a general.

Skirmishers moved up, along with only a single cannon. In response, J.C. Neill prepared the Twin Sisters, and soon the artillery was blasting away at each other. Neill fell when a piece of grapeshot broke his hip, but otherwise, casualties were light.

The Mexican artilleryman realized that his cannon was no match for the Twin Sisters, and he withdrew. But the Texans didn't want to quit. Their nerves were like tightly coiled springs, and they lusted for blood. With a shout, Sidney Sherman challenged Houston; he argued that a cavalry charge could capture the Mexican artillery. We could send them all running!

Houston knew his cavalrymen were little more than mounted infantrymen, while the Mexican cavalrymen bore lances and sabers that could make short work of a man who had to dismount to reload his long rifle. He finally let Sherman go, warning him not to bring about a full-scale battle. He was only to reconnoiter.

Secretary of War Thomas Rusk joined Sherman's group of mounted riflemen, who rode off toward the enemy lines. Contrary to orders, Sherman charged the enemy, and Mexican cavalrymen galloped up to meet them.

The Texans learned quickly that they were out of their league; they were facing Mexican lancers who had no need to stop and reload. Rusk was surrounded and nearly killed, but then a private named Mirabeau Lamar rode up on a huge stallion, and by literally knocking aside a smaller Mexican horse, cleared the way for Rusk to escape.

The rest of the men watched from the safety of the oaks, and seeing their comrades in trouble, marched to support them, against Houston's express orders. Sherman finally saw the handwriting on the wall and ordered his men to retreat.

But what was this? Everyone thought that poor Walter Lane was dead. The nineteen-year-old had been thrown from his horse by a Mexican lance, but now here he was getting up and stumbling to safety. The Mexicans saw him, too, and several charged with their deadly lances aimed for the teenager. Lamar, on his stallion, rode interference and, pulling a pistol, shot one horseman dead. The brave Henry Karnes then galloped up, grabbed Lane, and pulled him up behind him. As these Texan horsemen then turned to follow their departing comrades, some of the Mexicans applauded the brave rescue. They appreciated good horsemanship. Mirabeau Lamar, who was a poet, turned his stallion and bowed.

Lamar was now a hero among his men, making Houston the unpopular spoilsport who tried to stop the infantrymen from aiding their comrades. The assumption was that if it weren't for Houston, they could've whipped the Mexicans. This belief caused dissension in the ranks.

That night, April 20th, the contentious and grumbling soldiers went to bed, while their commander kept his thoughts to himself.

A Sign

What was this? The morning tattoo had not been beaten by Houston himself, as was his custom. In fact, the men discovered that he had given express instructions that he was not to be disturbed. Was he going to sleep all day? They honed their knives, all the while grumbling and complaining.

After his first good sleep in many days, Sam Houston opened his eyes to see an eagle circling in the sky above him. *An eagle.* The Raven arose, refreshed. This was the day. It was April 21, 1836.

He consulted his scout, "Deaf" Smith, who reported that Santa Anna had received reinforcements. Apparently, his brother-in-law, *El Presidente*, had convinced General Cos that his oath never to set foot in Texas again was meaningless. The Mexican army, now only a mile away, greatly outnumbered Houston's nine hundred men.

"This sounds a good deal like a fight," squeaked Mr. "E." Smith was given the task of destroying Vince's Bridge, which would hinder the arrival of further reinforcements. His commander sent him off with the remark, "Unless you hasten, you will find the prairie changed from green to red on your return."[20] Smith set off with six volunteers.

At noon, Houston called a council of war. He listened to his officers wrangling, but did not respond, and finally dismissed them. Then, at 3:30 in the afternoon, he gathered his restless troops. It was time to fight.

Santa Anna Retires

Santa Anna's men were tired. They had spent much of the night constructing breastworks, but the expected dawn attack did not materialize. Then General Cos arrived, but his troops were hungry and tired from a long march. The day wore on, and finally, in the afternoon, Santa Anna commanded his men to stand down. It was siesta time, and now they needed the rest; their muskets were stacked in piles. The rebel army would not attack; now that Cos's reinforcements were here, they would surely think twice. The confident dictator retired to his fancy tent.

The Battle of San Jacinto

There was nothing but grass between the Texans and the Mexican line. Only a swell of ground hid them from each other. Houston, astride a huge gray stallion named Saracen, led his troops toward the enemy, instructing them to hold their fire. The mounted riflemen were on the right of them, now led by Colonel Lamar, promoted after Houston had deposed the rebellious Sherman. The Twin Sisters were positioned across from the enemy artillery. A few musicians had been gathered; they consulted and found a song they all knew how to play.

For a while, the enemy seemed unaware of them. Had they posted no sentries? Finally, a shout rose from the Mexican camp. They had been spotted. The Twin Sisters erupted, and the enemy returned fire. Still, Houston and his men advanced silently, under fire; their muzzle-loading rifles took time to reload; it was imperative that the first volley be effective.

"Deaf" Smith galloped onto the field, riding behind the line, waving his ax and yelling, "Vince's Bridge is down!"

A few Texans let loose and fired their weapons, and Houston cursed. "Hold your fire! Keep low, men! Hold your fire!" The men crouched and moved rapidly through the tall grass.

The Mexicans, by now, were fully alert, scrambling about in confusion.

His steed's light coat shining like a banner in the afternoon sun, Houston signaled to the musicians. The sound of "Will You Come to the Bower?", a popular love song, floated on the breeze, in counterpoint to the glint of firearms. It was the only tune all the musicians knew.

A stone's throw from the barricade, Houston gave the command. "Kneel! Shoot low! Fire!" A deadly rain of bullets poured forth from the ragged army of Texas. Then the general waved his hat, the signal to charge.

"Forward! Charge! Remember the Alamo! Remember Goliad!"

Lacking bayonets and lacking the time to reload in their frenzy, the men used their rifles as clubs. Bowie knives flashed. They poured over the Mexican breastworks.

The confused *soldados* broke in terror. Some stood and fought, including General Castillon, a brave old gentleman who reported to his men that he "had been in forty battles and never showed my back. I am too old to do it now."[21] Observing the man's bravery, Rusk tried to save his life, but others rushed up and shot him down.

The Mexicans did manage to get off one concerted volley. Saracen took several lead balls in the breast, and one struck Houston an inch above the ankle, shattering the leg bone. The stallion shuddered beneath him, but responded, and the general galloped to a point in the line that seemed to be in confusion.

What is the cause of the delay? Houston asked an officer.

The Texan colonel looked at Houston's horse. Your horse is wounded. The beautiful stallion then collapsed.

Hand-to-Hand Combat

Jimmy Curtis had never gotten along with his son-in-law, Washington Cottle. But Wash Cottle had gone with a group of men from Gonzales to assist the men in the Alamo, and now Curtis' daughter was a widow. Wanting revenge, he grabbed a Mexican officer and shoved his Bowie knife in front of the man's face.

"You killed Wash Cottle. Now I'm going to kill you and make a razor strap out of your hide!"

On the swampy ground next to the Santo Jacinto River, Mexican resistance had lasted only eighteen minutes. Officially, the battle was over, and General Houston had ordered his men to take prisoners. But many were not listening. They were here for revenge.

Colonel Wharton galloped up and rescued the Mexican officer from Curtis' hands. "Men, this Mexican is mine," he shouted, indicating that the man was a prisoner. He pulled the officer up behind him on his horse.

Not willing to take no for an answer, Jimmy Curtis raised his rifle and shot the Mexican dead. Walking away from the enraged colonel, he was heard to mutter, "Remember Wash Cottle."[22]

The fleeing Mexican soldiers soon discovered that Vince's Bridge was down. They threw themselves into the water to escape the crazed Texans. Coming up on the bank, Houston's men fired on the men in the water, and soon, the water was red with their blood.

One man, S.F. Sparks, discovered another rifleman threatening a woman, one of the Mexican camp followers or *soldaderas*.

"No," Sparks enjoined, "she is a woman and not armed."

The other man made a lunge at her with his bayonet, which Sparks parried with his rifle.

"You can't knock off a bullet," the man warned, cocking his weapon.

Sparks glared and insisted, "If you kill her, I will kill you."

The man paused, "Are you in earnest?"

"Yes, I am in earnest."[23]

Sparks watched his comrade run off in search of other prey.

Houston Led to a Tree

Houston, astride a new horse, gazed down at the horror before him. He had ridden along the route that many fleeing Mexicans had taken; bodies littered the ground all along the way. Now he sat his mount, looking into the water.

> ...multitudes, in their desperation, had rushed to this spot as a forlorn hope. They had plunged into the mire and water with horses and mules, and, attempting to pass, had been completely submerged; every one who seemed likely to escape soon received a ball from the murderous aim of a practiced rifleman, and the morass was literally bridged over with carcasses of dead mules, horses, and men.[24]

Houston stood there gazing, dazed from loss of blood and fatigue. His men called to him, and he reined in his mount rather sharply. The horse collapsed and fell down dead, and the general narrowly missed getting pinned underneath. The men saw that he was wounded and helped him onto a sturdy roan.

On the way back to camp, the soldiers began to gather about him, with no more complaining or disputing. He returned their show of affection, saying that this day they had covered themselves with glory and would receive the spoils as a reward for their valor.

Not long afterward, a soldier's hand inadvertently bumped against the injured general's boot, provoking an exclamation. The boot was wet with blood, and soon everyone knew that Houston had been wounded.

The procession finally arrived at the tree that served as Houston's headquarters. A few orders were given. A completely exhausted Houston fell from his horse, only to have his faithful friend, Hockley, catch him and lay him at the base of the tree.

An Epic Conversation

At the start of the battle, Santa Anna was in his tent, only partially dressed. Emerging, he attempted to give orders, but soon saw his army dissipate before his eyes. He grabbed a horse and quickly made his escape.

The next day, some of Houston's scouts came upon a Mexican, hiding in the tall grass near the remains of Vince's Bridge. He was dressed rather strangely, wearing ordinary pants but a fancy, though soiled, shirt. They took him prisoner.

When he was brought into camp, some of the other Mexican prisoners exclaimed, "*El Presidente!*"

What? This small, complaining man was the cause of all their troubles? Without delay, he was marched to Houston's tree.

The general was dozing under the influence of pain medication when he looked up and saw an oddly dressed prisoner being brought before him.

"I am General Antonio Lopez de Santa Anna, President of the Republic of Mexico, and a prisoner at your disposition." He stood bold, but nervous, as hard eyes watched him from all sides.

Houston was now fully awake and sat up. He indicated a box nearby, and Santa Anna sat down.

Then Secretary of War Rusk approached with Lorenzo de Zavala, Jr., the son of the Texan Vice-President, who had fled from Santa Anna's scourges.

Santa Anna recognized the young man. "Oh! My *friend*, my *friend*, the son of my *early* friend." He embraced de Zavala, and a tear slid from his cheek.

De Zavala looked the dictator full in the face. He was not moved. "It *has* been so, sir."

As reported by Rusk, his look seemed to "wither" Santa Anna, who seemed to shrink before his eyes.

Colonel Almonte, now also a prisoner, was brought to serve as a translator. Santa Anna embraced him, then said to Houston, "That man may consider himself born to no common destiny, who has conquered the Napoleon of the West; and now it remains for him to be generous with the vanquished."

"You should have remembered that at the Alamo."

"You must be aware that I was justified in my course by usages of war. I had summoned a surrender, and they had refused. The place was then taken by storm, and the usages of war justified the slaughter of the vanquished."

Houston rejected his argument. "That *was* the case once, but it is now obsolete. Such usages among civilized nations have yielded to the influences of humanity."

Santa Anna sidestepped. "However this may be, I was acting under orders of my government."

"Why, YOU *are the Government* of Mexico."

"I have my orders in my possession commanding me to act."

Houston replied, "A Dictator, sir, has no superior."

Santa Anna turned the discussion again, saying that the Texans had no government and no flag.

"So far as the first point is concerned, the Texans flatter themselves they have a Government already, and they will probably be able to make a flag."[25]

Then Houston became agitated. His eyes flashing, he continued, "But if you feel excused for your conduct at San Antonio, you have not the same excuse for the massacre of Colonel Fannin's command. They had capitulated on terms offered by your General.

"And yet, after the capitulation, they were all perfidiously massacred, without the privilege of dying with their arms in their hands."

Santa Anna formed an excuse, saying he was ignorant of it. He laid the blame on Urrea.

Angry soldiers gathered around, and the dictator grew nervous. He offered to make a treaty, but Houston refused, on the grounds that only the government could make a treaty. But he did agree to an armistice and demanded that Santa Anna direct his generals to withdraw their men from Texas. Almonte wrote out such an order to Filisola under his leader's direction.

Later, Colonel Almonte asked Houston why he did not attack the first day. By way of explanation, he continued, saying that their men were expecting it and were anxious for the fight.

"Well," replied Houston, "I see I was right. I knew you expected I should bring on the battle that day, and were consequently prepared for it... I will say *that was just the reason I did not fight...*"[26]

Upon overhearing the conversation, Santa Anna wanted to know Houston's response, and Almonte translated. Infuriated, the dictator cursed Almonte for losing the battle. But it was Houston who had actually provoked him.

The backwoods drunkard had outsmarted him.

Chapter 10

Sam Houston's Republic

ANDREW JACKSON CLOSED Rachel's Bible. Even years after his wife's death, the president still cherished this volume, but it had ceased to be a mere memento. Somewhere along the line, the aging Jackson had found peace and strength in these pages. But he refused to announce his faith in Christ publicly while still in office. The scoundrels here in Washington would surely turn it into something *political*, and the white-maned statesman refused to give them that opportunity. Later, when he was back at the Hermitage, his beloved home, he would join the assembly that gathered nearby, in the little church he had helped to build.

And that would be soon. This year, 1836, was the last year of his second term as president, and age and infirmity had taken their toll. He would soon be able to leave behind the bickering and fighting that defined Capitol Hill, especially now, as a dark and dangerous undercurrent seemed to be slowly rising, spilling out into the Senate and House and influencing everything.

Dark Political Currents

Slavery. It used to be that abolition societies were only found in the South, but no more. Jackson owned slaves himself, but few people he knew were actually interested in *promoting* the institution; it was just "one of those things" that hopefully would work itself out. But now that radicals in the North were pumping out anti-slavery literature, some in the South felt backed against a wall and defended something they otherwise never would have. John C. Calhoun of South Carolina was their voice in the Senate. What a rascal. Jackson feared that he was giving strength to a growing dissension that might one day— God forbid— tear the Union apart.

This political division had even cast its shadow on Texas. Much of the West, including his own state of Tennessee, was interested in Texas, and thousands of emigrants had streamed across the Sabine; some interested in cheap land, some in other things. Could Texas be annexed as a state? Well, first she would have to come loose from Mexico, and much as Jackson sympathized, he could have no part in that. There was a treaty to be honored.

But *if* she did win her independence, what sort of state would she become? Slave or free? Everyone knew that Texas colonists had emigrated primarily from the South and West and had brought their slaves with them. There was no doubt in anyone's mind that she would weigh in on the pro side of the slavery question. It was actually kind of ironic. This issue would put Jackson and Calhoun, his old adversary, on the same "side." If Texas became a state, Calhoun and his clique would have two more votes in the Senate. Obviously, those in the North saw this too and opposed the whole idea.

Right now, Texas had not even won her independence yet, so it was a very big *if*. But Jackson's old friend and protégé, Sam Houston, was down there in the thick of things, and if anyone could pull it off, he could. Houston's old commander followed the reports with keen interest, and one day he received another bit of news from Texas.

A Letter from Sam Houston

Sitting in his littered study in the White House, Jackson pulled out a map. He had observed that Houston was retreating east, and some were saying that the Texas general would march all the way to the Sabine and safety. But the Hero of New Orleans disagreed. Studying the map, he pointed at Galveston Bay. He would turn and fight—there. Or *there,* he thought, pointing to the Buffalo Bayou.

A few days later, a lieutenant arrived with dispatches from General Gaines—and from Sam Houston. Andrew Jackson's eyes lit up, and he grabbed the papers from the young man.

Over and over, he exclaimed, "Yes, that is his writing. I know it well. That is Sam Houston's writing. There can be no doubt about what he says."[1]

Writing from the shade of the oak tree, his painful wound wrapped in rags, Houston had penned a letter to his former commander. The news was incredible.

The Mexicans had been routed, with only a handful of Texans lost, and Santa Anna, the supreme dictator of Mexico, was now a *prisoner?*

Jackson asked for the map. San Jacinto. Where is it? San Jacinto? The small river did not seem to be marked. "It must be there! No, it must be over there!"[2]

The news spilled out into Washington, and everyone rejoiced. Government officials held parties and celebrations, and the Mexican envoy to the United States recorded his "shock and astonishment at this intemperate joy."[3]

The News Spread

Near San Jacinto, the news spread rapidly. A little girl named Dilue Rose later remembered, "We travelled nearly all night, sister and I on horseback and mother in the cart... We were as wretched as we could be, for we had been five weeks from home, and there was not much prospect of our ever returning."

But a rider approached, waving his hat. Were the Mexicans coming? But "... when the rider got near enough for us to understand what he said, it was 'Turn back! The Texas army has whipped the Mexican army and the Mexican army are prisoners. No danger! No danger! Turn back!'"[4]

The tide of refugees turned, and many returned to their homes, or what was left of them.

The Mexican Army in Retreat

General Filisola sighed. Well, he had been right after all. He finished reading the letter from His Excellency instructing him to order General Gaona and his own troops to retreat to Bexar to await further orders... Santa Anna had been captured. Well, at this point, it didn't make much difference. His troops were bogged down by mud, rain, dysentery, and lack of supplies. At the moment, they were all on half rations.

He wrote back, indicating his willingness to obey orders; he would now be withdrawing over the Colorado. He gave the missive to the peculiar man with the squeaky voice, and "Deaf" Smith rode back to the battlefield of San Jacinto, accompanied by his guard.

"The Hand of Providence"

Near the San Jacinto, Houston's men rejoiced. One man, W.C. Swearingen, wrote his brother, "To see the number, the position, and the termination and the time in which it was done, (time 18 minutes) it at once shows that the hand of Providence was with us."[5]

From the Mexican baggage, spoils were distributed, including clothing, weapons, and even money. A chest containing $12,000 in silver was found, and General Houston directed that it be equally distributed among his men, as partial payment for their services in the army.

When he took nothing himself, the men insisted he accept Colonel Almonte's fine stallion. But the magnificent animal was later returned to its original owner, a settler with Mexican sympathies.

Colonel Delgado, captured along with seven hundred other prisoners, later wrote, "It was hard to see them breaking our trunks open and everyone of them loaded with our shirts, trousers, coats, while we remained with what we had on our bodies."[6]

And what was to be done with them? After the Alamo and the massacre at Goliad, the Mexican prisoners were understandably frightened.

The captives were all marched into the woods where a large fire was burning. *Are they going to burn us to death?* Delgado considered that it would be an act of mercy to be shot before he was tossed into the flames. Understandably, he did not approach the fire. He was surprised when he was prodded with the butt of a rifle and told to get closer to the flames, where he could warm himself and dry his clothes.

But the Texans still possessed an enmity toward the Mexicans. Houston must not have known of a cruel joke some of his men played on the prisoners, lining up with rifles, as if preparing to execute the terrified men.

Houston's Missives

The same day he wrote Jackson, Houston wrote a note to a certain Anna Raguet of Nacogdoches, for whose affections he had been unsuccessfully laboring. He also wrote a detailed report to the Texan government, although he was uncertain as to its location. He praised the bravery and actions of various officers, and reported the numbers of Texan and Mexican casualties, as could best be determined. To the courier taking this letter to Galveston, (the last reported location of the government), he wrote instructions, "Tell our friends all the news and that we have beaten the enemy... tell them to come on and let the people plant corn."[7]

Burnet's Plan

The stench was horrible. David G. Burnet, President of Texas, could smell the battlefield even before he could see it. Houston's letter had reported 630 of the enemy killed, and now he could believe it. No wonder he had moved his headquarters a mile and a half away.

Houston. It was painfully obvious that the rank and file now worshipped the man who had somehow managed to pull this off. Well, the men were the ones who had won this battle. That self-serving Houston was getting a lot more credit than he deserved.

At first, Burnet was cautious. With an army this devoted, Houston could do whatever he wanted. After meeting with the general, the president and members of his Cabinet began to make arrangements. So *this* was the great and terrible Santa Anna. A treaty needed to be made.

Well, it didn't look as if Houston desired to make himself dictator or anything of that sort. In fact, he couldn't even stand up. The short, slightly rotund president relaxed a little.

Perhaps these men would worship Houston a bit less if they knew a little more about him. With this in mind, Burnet began to spread some details of their commander's personal life, but the plan didn't work. The rank-and-file contingent was just not impressed, though there were some officers who didn't seem to think much of their general. President Burnet already had most of his cabinet on his side, but he needed to drag Houston's name through the dirt publicly. Otherwise, after having opposed him all this time, the president would look really stupid in the face of this wonderful victory.

A Piece of Shirt

Dr. Alexander Ewing was worried about Sam Houston. While the general lay on his cot under the tree, attending to this and that detail, writing letters and giving orders, his injured leg was not improving. Obviously, there were circulation problems, plus infection. He needed surgery, not to mention basic supplies for dressing to replace the piece of shirt that presently bound the wound. The truth was, he needed to get this man to New Orleans soon, or he might well lose him. Dr. Ewing advised Houston that it was imperative that they leave immediately.

Houston wrote an affectionate farewell to his troops. The Texas government was preparing to leave on the *Yellow Stone*, and preparations were made for the general to leave with them, but the government refused him passage; instead, he was informed that his place was with his troops. When the captain of the boat found out, Dr. Ewing heard him exclaim in salty language that his boat was going nowhere without General Houston.

After the government officials and the more important Mexican prisoners boarded the boat, Houston was carried on board by Rusk, who was now in charge of the army, with Rusk's brother and Dr. Ewing accompanying them.

Mirabeau Lamar, who had made the transition from private to colonel to secretary of war in just a few short days, approached Ewing. "You are not authorized to leave the army. If you do, you will be discharged from service."

Hearing this, Houston said to his doctor, "I am sorry, my dear fellow, for I have nothing to promise you in the future, and you know I am poor, so you had better not incur the displeasure of the new Secretary of War."[8]

Ewing chose to remain with his patient.

The Tribute

They floated away from the dock; some of those on board watched as the battlefield came into view. Colonel Pedro Delgado, one of the Mexican prisoners being transported to the coast, stiffened. His eyes widened at the sight of Houston's troops. This irregular rabble was in formation, drums beating, facing the river and the steamship which carried their injured commander. He marveled.

Burnet's Plot Backfires

Lying on the cot, Houston shook his head no. The kind captain of the *Liberty* had offered to transport the general without the knowledge of the Texas government, which had refused to give passage to the wounded man.

Houston needed to get from Galveston to New Orleans for treatment. But how many times had Houston preached subordination and obedience to the civil government to his men? He could not break his principles now. Taking the captain's offer would look like disobedience to the government. After a search, he found another ship, the *Flora*, a leaky vessel that was barely seaworthy, making ready to sail.

The captain of the *Liberty* waited for the *Flora*. At least he could sail with her, watching out for the little ship. He heard shouts coming from somewhere. *He deserves a dunking in Galveston Bay!*

Weak and feverish, Sam Houston probably could not hear the commotion as he lay in a small berth in the dirty schooner, waiting to depart. But Dr. Ewing came aboard and sought out his patient.

He explained that Burnet was telling stories about him, and the people here didn't like it a bit. Especially the men from the army—they were really riled up. Something could happen!

At that point, Dr. Ewing probably wouldn't have minded if David G. Burnet got thoroughly soaked, but after thinking it over, Houston wrote a directive to his men to be posted publicly:

> ...[The Commander-in-Chief] has heard with regret that some dissatisfaction has existed in the army. If it is connected with him, or his circumstances, he asks as a special favor, that it may no longer exist... Obedience to the constituted authorities and laws of the country is the first duty of a soldier. It will adorn his virtues and qualify him for the highest rights of citizenship.
>
> The General in taking leave of his companions in arms, assures them of his affectionate gratitude, and enjoys an assured confidence that they will not neglect the advice of a fellow soldier, who will be proud to reunite with them, at the first moment when his situation will permit.[9]

Arrival in New Orleans

I don't believe it. Yes, it's true! General Houston and his men *captured* Santa Anna!

The news filtered through the West, the East, and the South. In New Orleans, the excitement grew.

Then word spread around the city that Sam Houston had arrived on the *Flora*, and crowds gathered about the dock. Among them, a dark-haired seventeen-year-old girl, Margaret Lea, waited and watched. Friends of the general boarded the boat; so many people clambered aboard, in fact, that the little vessel began to list. Several men seemed to be trying to move the injured man, who was lying on deck.

Then Margaret saw a disheveled, bearded man lift himself using a pair of crude crutches. He was going to try to get off the boat under his own power. Was this Houston? The image of this gaunt, sickly man burned itself into the mind of the teenage girl. He wore a tattered leather jacket, and as he climbed over the gunwale, she could see that a bloody shirt was wrapped around his ankle. Shortly, some kind of cot or litter was brought to the dock, but as he tried to lie down on it, he fainted.

There was something about this man... how could it be? Would he somehow become part of her own *destiny*? Margaret kept these things in her heart.

God was gracious to this man, who, once again, stood at death's door. In fact, the same surgeon who had removed a lead ball from Houston's shoulder twenty-one years earlier now removed numerous bone fragments from the injured leg. Once treated, the wound began to heal, and slowly, the Hero of San Jacinto began to regain his strength.

A Preacher Comes to Texas

"Oh, yes! Oh, yes! Oh, yes! Everyone who wants to buy, without money and without price, come this way!"[10]

Nacogdoches was astonished. Preachers were almost non-existent in Texas; even Catholic priests were hard to come by. The curious gathered around a man who was now singing in the corner of a large, unfinished building, open to the air.

Sunday was also election day in that particular district, and there was a large crowd in town of every type and description: Mexican, Indian, and American.

The preacher, who seemed to be frail in some way, now opened his text: "The wilderness and the solitary place shall be glad for them; and the desert shall rejoice and blossom as the rose." (Isa. 35:1) For one hour, the crowd remained and listened with rapt attention, and in the most unlikely place, hearts were stirred, and tears were shed.

Afterward, many came forward to shake the preacher's hand. Zechariah Morrell, a "canebrake" preacher, had come to Texas. Because Morrell was afflicted with hemorrhage of the lungs, his physician had informed him that continued preaching would kill him; a warmer climate would be helpful. On his way west, Morrell bucked the tide of east-moving refugees, being upbraided by all he met, and finally arrived in Texas. Over time, his condition improved, and seeing a field white unto harvest, almost bereft of gospel laborers, he left for home to fetch his wife and children. This was the place for him.

Houston Back in Texas

Sam Houston wanted to return to Texas. Rumors of misbehavior in the army had reached him, and he needed to get back and put things in order. But he could barely sit up, much less stand. Then he heard crazy talk about invading Mexico. Matamoros again. Against the advice of doctors, Houston set out for Texas. Somehow, he made it over the border to San Augustine, but when it became clear that he could go no farther, he made arrangements to stay with an old friend.

While there, Houston heard more troubling news. First of all, in the two treaties the Texas government had made with Santa Anna, the dictator had been promised a safe return to Mexico; Houston knew this was a mistake. With the Napoleon of the West back in Mexico, there would be no leverage to force the Mexican government to *ratify* the treaty. He had proposed that the dictator be held hostage until it could be ratified, but this suggestion had evidently been ignored.

What was worse, the continued influx of volunteers from the States was causing another, more serious problem. Angry adventurers who had just come to Texas were demanding that Santa Anna be executed.

Burnet's Choice

What am I going to do now? President Burnet heard the mob shouting in front of his house, demanding that Santa Anna, who was at that moment aboard the *Invincible*, bound for Mexico, be turned over to them. Two men, Thomas Jefferson Green and Memucan Hunt, were stirring up the crowd with their inflammatory speeches.

The office of president was beginning to get a little old, from David Burnet's perspective. Feeling desperate, he finally stepped outside and waited for the crowd to quiet before speaking.

He explained that Santa Anna must be returned to Mexico. The terms of the treaty demanded it.

The crowd was not impressed. Burnet reluctantly agreed to sign a requisition authorizing a small force to return the dictator to shore. Green led some men onto the ship and seized Santa Anna, who was then marched through menacing crowds to Velasco, and later moved to Columbia, after a plot to poison him was discovered.

An Injured Houston's Correspondence

Houston read the letter from Tom Rusk, reporting that two army colonels were demanding that Santa Anna be tried and executed. Once again, The Raven was forced to sit on the sidelines while things fell apart. He wrote to Rusk:

> "...disregard if you will our national character and place what construction upon the rules of civilized warfare we are compelled by every rule of humanity and morality,... execute Santa Anna and what will be the condition of the Texans, who are held as prisoners by the Mexicans?... Texas, to be respected must be considered politic and just in her actions..."[11]

His letter seemed to have the desired effect; the fervor subsided for a time.

In Washington D.C., President Jackson was closely following every development. He wrote Houston:

> Nothing *now* could tarnish the character of Texas more than such an act [Santa Anna's proposed trial and execution] at this late period. It was good policy as well as humanity that spared him... He is the pride of the Mexican soldiers and the favorite of the Priesthood and whilst he is in your power the priests will not furnish the supplies for another campaign, nor will the regular soldiers voluntarily march when their reentering Texas may endanger or cost their favorite Genl. his life, therefore preserve his life and the character you have won.[12]

Santa Anna seemed safe for now, but the adventurers flooding to Texas were stirring up the army, wanting to invade Matamoros. Houston again used his pen in the hope of restraining this foolish, lawless spirit, telling his soldiers that such a "mad, impolitic, and hazardous project"[13] could lead to disasters like the one at the Alamo and Goliad.

This appeal worked for the time being, but the whole country was in chaos. Refugees were gathered in camps, seeking to have their land restored. Stealing and looting were common occurrences, and Indians were killing and scalping settlers with renewed fervor. And to make matters worse, Texas was in over its head financially, more than one million dollars in debt because of the war.

Desperate for relief from the stress of office, David G. Burnet desperately wanted someone else to assume leadership. He called for an election to take place on September 5, 1836.

Cynthia Ann Parker's Capture

The whole thing was a nightmare. The Indians, streaked with slashes of war paint, looked like human wraiths in the firelight as they screamed and danced about, pausing only to kick or stomp their prisoners. Nine-year-old Cynthia Ann lay on the ground, her face tear-streaked, her brown hair tangled and mussed. Her hands and feet with tied with plaited thongs; all the captives were bound and helpless. She could hear little James whimpering next to his mother, Mrs. Plummer. Cynthia's little brother began to cry. She winced, knowing what would happen next. *Thump.* A tremendous blow silenced him. Cynthia could only hope her brother was still alive.

The little girl tried not to think of the raid. Uncle Benjamin had been mutilated, with arrows protruding from his body like pins in a pincushion. The commotion, rifles firing, women screaming, the whoops of Indians, even her *father*... tears began a new path down the side of her face. But she would not make a sound; she had learned that lesson already.

The next morning, the Comanches strapped their prisoners onto horses and rode north, finally splitting up at Grand Prairie, in the area where Dallas and Fort Worth stand today. Several bands had joined together for this raid upon Parker's Fort, and now they went their separate ways. Cynthia Ann and her brother went with one group, while the other prisoners went elsewhere.

Finally, the Indians arrived at their camp. It was not a true village; Comanches were nomadic and did not stay long in any one place. They did not plant corn or anything else, but subsisted almost entirely on game, principally the buffalo. Cynthia Ann must have been weak and dazed from the trip, having been given only enough food and water to sustain life.

Thankfully, she had not been beaten after the first night. Now she was being taken to a tent of sorts. Was this a wigwam? There were hard stares all around, but some seemed curious, especially the children. The little boys ran around entirely naked, something to which she was not accustomed.

A woman emerged from the tent. Her eyes were gentle.

Cynthia Ann Parker was the daughter of Silas Parker, an officer in the Texas Rangers, a group organized a year earlier to protect settlers, while the main body of men gathered with Sam Houston to fight the Mexicans. Hundreds of mounted, war-painted Comanches showed up at Parker's Fort, probably the northernmost settlement in Texas, in May of 1836. Hopelessly outnumbered, Silas, his brother Benjamin, and a few other men bravely defended the women and children. The fort was pillaged, stock was slaughtered, a few useful items were stolen, and then the Comanches returned from whence they came. Indian raids were not new, especially in settlements to the north and west, the hunting grounds of the Comancheria. But 1836 was a particularly bad year.

Men Coming for Plunder

Blacksmith Noah Smithwick was now a Ranger, part of a group of Rangers that was presently attached to General Rusk's army. As the Mexicans retreated, the army moved west from San Jacinto, following them. Smithwick and his group guarded the baggage, strung out in a line ahead of the wagons.

The colonists, who had formed the greater part of Houston's victorious band at San Jacinto, had melted away, wanting to see to their families and fields, a move the general had approved, including in one public proclamation, the instruction that the people of Texas "plant corn." Replacing them were volunteers from the States, who were still coming, not realizing that the war would be over by the time they arrived.

Of these men, the blacksmith would later write that they seemed to be "actuated by no higher principle than prospective plunder... and acknowledged no authority, either military or civil."[14]

They would bring grief to themselves and to Texas.

Houston Meets with Morrell

Sam Houston looked up. A visitor had come to this refuge in San Augustine; a loaded wagon and ox team stood outside.

Zechariah Morrell. Sam remembered this man, a Baptist pastor from Tennessee. "What brings you to Texas?" he must have asked.

After Morrell had explained the events that had brought him to this new field of labor, the two discussed the future of Texas, and the preacher left encouraged, later writing, "[Houston] entertained no doubt of the success of the 'little two-horse republic' that he had seen with prophetic eye years before, while yet in Tennessee."[15]

Morrell had brought his wife, two sons, and young daughter to Texas. After purchasing cattle from a band of Cherokees then living north of Nacogdoches, the preacher and his family resumed their journey, planning to settle near the falls of the Brazos River.

Houston Lays Down His Sword

Stephen Austin was glad to be home in Texas. After months in the United States, addressing crowds and speaking to individuals, attending to the interests of this place he called home. Now he was back.

With large, sad brown eyes, a lined, careworn face, and thinning hair, the forty-three-year-old man waited patiently beneath the huge live oak tree, which had been selected as the site for the inauguration ceremony. Columbia was the capital of the new republic, at least for now; that honor would be shifted several times, before finally remaining on a municipality named after Austin, an honor the man would never know.

Sam Houston was about to be inaugurated as president. At first, the general had stayed out of the presidential race, thinking that the problems of the army demanded too much of his attention, but then a petition had been passed around, and finally, Houston agreed, writing that: "the crisis requires it."[16]

After defeating Stephen Austin by almost ten to one at the polls, the former empresario graciously conceded, having run for office at the mandate of others, never able to shirk what he saw as his duty. But by this time, Austin's health was poor. He hoped he would be able to adequately perform his duties as Secretary of State. Actually, it had been an honor when Houston asked him to take the position, that office being the highest and most prestigious cabinet post of all.

It was the afternoon of October 22, 1836, when Austin watched the crowds begin to assemble. The official inauguration date for the presidency was set for the second Monday in December, according to the Constitution so feverishly composed in Washington-on-the-Brazos. Because President David Burnet had just resigned, the hastily conceived ceremony could not be delayed.

Hopefully, it wouldn't rain; the sky was threatening. Stephen Austin watched Sam Houston approach, limping badly, but at least he no longer needed crutches. The president-elect wore a broadcloth suit over a maroon brocade waistcoat. Head and shoulders taller than most of the crowd, he was noticeably thin, his face lined, and his chestnut hair streaked with gray. It was four o'clock when the ceremony began.

At first only a few sprinkles of rain spattered on the live oak leaves, but it soon began to pour, and the crowds departed *en masse* for the shelter of a barn-like store building.

Inside, Sam Houston delivered his impromptu inauguration speech. He referred to a vote taken during the recent election, asking people whether or not they desired annexation by the United States, a question that had been overwhelmingly answered in the affirmative.

"Will our friends disregard it [the vote]? They have already bestowed upon us their warmest sympathies. We are cheered by the hope that they will receive us."[17]

He wore his sword to the ceremony, the same sword he had carried at San Jacinto, and now he took it in his hands. The words that follow in brackets were inserted by the stenographer recording the speech.

> "It now, sir, becomes my duty to make a presentation of this sword—the emblem of my past office. [The President was unable to proceed further; but having firmly clenched it with both hands, as if with a farewell grasp, a tide of varied associations rushed upon him;... his countenance bespoke the... strongest emotions; his soul

> seemed to have swerved from the hypostatic union of the body... After a pause... the president proceeded:] I have worn it with some humble pretentions in defense of my country; and, should... my country call... I expect to resume it."[18]

A roaring applause honored the man who had just fittingly symbolized the rule of law. Texas would not be ruled by the sword.

The Armed Preacher

Thirty-five miles south of Parker's Fort sat a tiny colony of six or eight families at the falls of the Brazos, attended by a nearby garrison housing twenty or thirty soldiers. Z. N. Morrell arrived with his family and his wagonload of possessions.

It was a small group perched on the frontier of Texas; all of Texas was a "frontier," but areas to the north and west were more likely to be attacked by Comanches, whose hunting grounds encompassed the entire north and mid-section of the new republic. Because of that, Indians were certainly a major concern to the newcomers.

Morrell preached once a week to the little group. But he carried a rifle too.

> About the first of January, 1837, I was notified by the commander of the fort that the ammunition was almost exhausted; that there were not five rounds to a man; that the government had neither money nor lead. We were of course in imminent peril. This was *our country*, and *our fight*; and although it was painful under the circumstances to leave my loved ones, exposed as they would be, my sense of duty to the land of my adoption required that I should go alone to the town of [New] Washington, one hundred miles south on the Brazos River, in search of powder and lead, at my own charges.[19]

Morrell started out. Arriving in the tiny hamlet named Nashville, he preached to the six or eight families there and spent the night. The next night found him in the town of New Washington, where again he had the opportunity to preach.

In the morning, the Baptist preacher went looking for powder and lead. Some lead was found and loaded into saddlebags, even strung across the horn of the saddle. But no powder could be obtained.

The return trip commenced, and he held out hope that Jackson's store, eight miles from Nashville, would have the needed powder.

Upon his arrival, it was a cold, wet, exhausted preacher who stepped into the crowded establishment. A shipment of powder had just arrived from Colombia, but those present had already bought and paid for it. Shivering in his wet clothes, Morrell explained the precarious situation at the Falls and eventually took possession of six canisters of powder, duly bought and paid for with his own money.

The next night, he arrived home, having traveled 240 miles in four days, and the soldiers were very relieved and grateful for the ammunition.

Houston Sends Santa Anna to President Jackson

Where are we going to sit? The Senate of the new Republic of Texas stood around in a dingy shack that constituted their duly appointed meeting place. The House possessed a similar structure and had a similar problem—no furniture. Some had been promised by local settlers, but none materialized. Substitutes for the missing chairs were hurriedly built, along with a board table.

Lodgings were another problem. In good weather, some of the members of the government slept outdoors under the inauguration tree.

Nearby, after being offered a room in the home of a certain Mrs. Sledge, the new president searched for a pen. He needed to sign some commissions; everything needed to be done at once, and with some urgency. It seemed they were constructing a nation from scratch, and a multitude of details demanded Sam's immediate attention. Finally, he located a "suitable" pen.

He also needed a seal. As of yet, there was no "seal" representing the Republic. Sam Houston took a look at one of his personal cuff links, a modification of an ancient coat of arms of the Scottish barons of Houston (Hugh's town.) There was a dog's head, a rooster and inscribed at the top: "*Try me.*" This would do.

Houston appended, "signed and affixed my private Seal, there being no great Seal of office yet provided."[20] He dipped the cuff link in the hot wax.

On to the next item on the agenda—Santa Anna. He had asked the Senate for approval to release the Mexican dictator and his aide, Colonel Almonte, in accordance with the Treaty of Velasco. But the members of the Senate in the nearby shack were not in accord with Houston's point of view.

Thankfully, Secretary of State Stephen Austin had been in communication with Santa Anna, and a proposal had been broached which might just do the trick. Houston wrote Jackson, and before long, the plan was set in motion.

The new president gave Santa Anna a fine horse, and another individual lent him some money with which to buy clothes. The dictator and a few trusted men were then sent off to Washington, D.C.

President Jackson received Santa Anna for dinner, where the "butcher of Zacatecas" made a good impression. He spoke only that which would be agreeable to Jackson, saying that Mexico would never conquer Texas, and that if he were home, he would immediately put a stop to the invasion then being proposed by Generals Urrea and Bustamante.

Jackson was not deceived by the smooth talk but arranged for the Mexican ruler to be escorted to Norfolk, where he boarded the *Pioneer*, a naval vessel bound for Veracruz. Santa Anna was going home.

Austin's Last Acts

"The prosperity of Texas," wrote Stephen F. Austin to a friend, "has been the object of my labors, the idol of my existence."[21] The Secretary of State was now working diligently toward the goal of annexation by the United States, and the first step of that goal was official recognition. But even that simple step was mired in politics.

William Wharton, Texas agent in Washington, reported events from the capital. He wrote:

> "The Northern Abolitionists and fanaticks will of course always oppose annexation... [but] When the North has... lost her political ascendency she will not object to indefinite extension of the agricultural interests of the south and West... I believe that this Union will dissolve should the North obstinately oppose the annexation of Texas..."[22]

Slavery was the issue. In the House, John Quincy Adams had denounced Jackson for conspiring to bring about recognition of Texas. In the Senate, Calhoun welcomed Texas with open arms, a move that northerners interpreted as a desire to acquire more slave-holding territory. The Congress was split down the middle.

Secretary of State Austin considered these matters in a half-open shack, heated by a small fireplace, his official office. He sent instructions to Wharton.

Then he went out for a walk. It was Christmas Eve, 1836, and chilly. By the time he returned, his teeth were chattering. By the next day, Austin was desperately ill, lying on a pallet on the floor, delirious. A doctor was summoned. During a rare moment of consciousness, he spoke. "Texas recognized. Archer told me so. Did you see it in the papers?"[23]

On December 27, the former empresario breathed his last.

Houston wrote:

"The father of Texas is no more. The first pioneer of the wilderness has departed. General Stephen F. Austin, Secretary of State, expired this day at half past twelve at Columbia."[24]

A twenty-three-gun salute was ordered, one for each of the twenty-three counties of the Republic of Texas.

The Problem of Huston

Albert Sydney Johnston arrived in San Antonio with orders from President Houston. He was to replace the temporary commander, Junior Brigadier Felix Huston. Apparently, this Huston—a distant relative of the president—was stirring up trouble. This temporary commander was painting pictures of the spoils south of the Rio Grande; sinking the "do-nothing Houston government" in the Brazos River was another of his proposals. The volunteers listened; they were comprised of ne'er-do-wells who had just arrived in Texas. They had no loyalty to Houston.

Johnston presented his orders to Huston, a tall, blond, handsome man with one peculiarity: he had a cast in one of his gray-blue eyes that gave him an air of mystery. The junior brigadier promptly abused Houston and the Texas Senate and refused to yield the command.

A duel ensued. Johnston felt that honor compelled him to fight, and alongside the LaVaca River, the two brigadiers were able to get off five shots between them before Johnston fell, seriously wounded.

Huston rushed to his side. He expressed regret and acknowledged Johnston as his superior officer, promising his loyalty, a promise he soon broke.

In the meantime, drunken troops were causing problems in San Antonio.

President Houston ruminated over the problem of how to get rid of Huston.

The Tent City

"Pa, what are we going to do?" The twelve-year-old boy trembled with discouragement. "You said when we got here, we would get something to eat; we have had no bread since yesterday; there is no boat, no canoe. Our skillet is lost, and we can't even get a place dry enough to bake an ash cake."[25]

Zechariah Morrell, traveling with his oldest son, was in search of supplies for their little community in the spring of 1837, when even getting across the river had been a daunting task, and now even cooking proved problematic. But the inventive father hewed a block ten inches wide from an ash tree, which served as a crude skillet, and soon father and son were enjoying a meal of "johnny-cake," broiled meat, and coffee.

Resuming their journey, they finally reached the new city of Houston, their destination.

> Houston, in 1837, was a city of tents; only one or two log-cabins appeared. John K. Allen's framed building was raised, covered and partly weather-boarded. A large amount of goods in tents, a large round tent, resembling the enclosure of a circus, was used for a drinking saloon. Plenty of "John Barley Corn" and cigars.... Upon inquiry I found that there had never been a sermon preached in that place. It was a quite a novel thing to hear preaching, and some, to enjoy the novelty, and some no doubt with purest motives, went to work, and very soon seats were prepared in a cool shade on that beautiful spring morning. The sermon was preached to an attentive, intelligent audience....[26]

Sam Houston viewed his namesake. The "city" stretched out before him was largely composed of mud and tents. The Allen brothers, land developers, had presented the idea to the Texas Congress: a capital on Buffalo Bayou, near the battlefield of San Jacinto. Alligator-infested swampland was not Houston's first choice, but it seemed to be the choice of Congress, and he was not about to fight them on every issue. At that moment, he was there on Main Street, looking around.

Shortly, Houston reached the office of Major John Kirby Allen, who cordially received the President and conducted him to the "executive mansion": a two-room shack with a dogtrot in between.

Soon, the rest of the government made the move to Houston City. The conditions in Columbia had been insurmountable, and hopefully this would be an improvement. There was already a capitol building of sorts, definitely an improvement on the shacks in Columbia, though they had to wait a few days, until the addition of a covering, in place of a roof, was erected to keep out the glaring sun. But on May 5, 1837, the Texas Congress was ready to convene.

President Houston spoke to the assembled legislators. Referring to recognition, he said, "We now occupy the proud attitude of a sovereign and independent Republic; which will impose upon us the obligation of evincing to the world, that we are worthy to be free."[27]

The Plan

The birds began to chirp at dawn when Dr. Ashbel Smith finally met Sam Houston's gaze. Seated on moss-covered cots inside the executive "mansion," the two men had talked all night.

Dr. Smith was a new arrival in Texas, a short, wiry man or thirty-two, who had studied both law and medicine. So far, he liked what he saw.

Houston confided that there was a problem with the Texas "army." It was composed mainly of adventurers from the States, and the head of that "army," Junior Brigadier Felix Huston, who had broken his promise to defer to Johnston, had even appointed a certain Colonel Rodgers to take charge while he went to Houston City.

Even now, Huston was in town, trying to stir up San Jacinto veterans with his ideas of conquest below the border, and speaking to members of the government, arguing that it would be easier to raise money from Mexican spoils of war than from the taxation of Texan citizens.

Sam Houston finally came up with a strategy. "Dr. Smith, will you help me?" he must have asked.

"Of course. What do I do?"

"Well, I'm going to invite Huston to stay here... will you stay, too?"

Soon, Huston was installed in the president's room, and Houston and Dr. Smith shared the other. During the day, when the president was away, Dr. Smith encouraged Huston to speak of his ideas for invading Mexico and the logistics of the situation: how many men, how much in the way of supplies, and so forth.

General Huston was hopeful. *The president must be seeing things my way.*

That night, when everyone was asleep, Sam Houston got up, quietly sneaked out of the "mansion," and walked down the road to the one-room cabin occupied by his Secretary of War, William S. Fisher.

Roused from a deep sleep, Fisher lit a candle. Dressed in a long nightshirt, he rubbed his eyes. What was Houston doing here in the middle of the night? He soon found out.

I want you on your horse by daybreak. I need you in San Antonio as fast as you can. I'm sending orders for the army.

Orders?

I want to furlough the entire army except for six hundred men. Give them a thirty-day furlough, with the instruction to really enjoy it, because when they get back, they will be given arduous and unaccustomed duties. There is work to be done. Marshland to be drained and railroads to be built.

Fisher left, and Houston's orders had their desired effect. Except for six hundred faithful men, the rest of the "army" took off for the Sabine. They didn't come to Texas to work!

In a rage, Felix Huston left immediately for New Orleans.

But Dr. Ashbel Smith was so impressed that he decided to stay in Texas, and Houston nominated him to the position of Surgeon General of the Army.

Texas Recognized

It was the last day of the Jackson Presidency, a man who served eight years without great personal ambition for the office. His character had stamped so great an impression on the nation that historians would refer to this entire era, as the "Jacksonian" era. "The man of the people" was in fact a ruler of the people, who did what he thought was right without testing the current of public opinion. And the "people" loved him for that.

Sam Houston was like a son to him, and yet this matter of Texas was a thorny one indeed.

William Wharton, Houston's emissary to Washington, had labored for weeks. Texas must be recognized, despite the problems. He was on Capitol Hill when he wasn't at the White House and saw to it that a provision was made in a certain congressional bill that would innocently provide for a minister to Texas, "whenever the Executive is satisfied of her independence."[28] Somehow, the bill was passed with that provision intact.

Now William Wharton stood in Jackson's study, its contents strewn about in wild disarray. In fact, the whole White House was being stripped of eight years' worth of Jackson's presence in preparation for his move back to the Hermitage. It was the evening of March 3, 1837, and tomorrow, Martin Van Buren would be sworn in as the new president.

But that very afternoon, Jackson had sent a nomination of Alcee La Branche, of Louisiana, to the Senate floor. His post would be "to be Chargé d'Affairs to the Texas Republic." The Senate approved the nomination.

Now as the hands on the clock approached midnight, Jackson and Wharton toasted the Texas Republic.

The white-maned Jackson lifted his glass to propose one more toast. "To Sam Houston's Republic."[29]

A "Wee Wifie"?

Houston wrote a friend in Nacogdoches, Dr. Irion:

> You will have learned that we are Independent, and recognized by the U. States... the last official act of Gen'l Jackson's life. This alone is a cause for joy, but annexation wou'd have rendered me truly happy, and secured all that we contended for. My only wish is to see the country happy—at peace and retire to the Red Lands, get a fair, sweet "wee wifie" as Burns says, and pass the balance of my sinful life in ease and comfort (if I can)... [30]

Houston was lonely. Would he ever find the one to whom he could truly open his heart?

Chapter 11

Margaret

Sam Houston stepped outside. Behind the "executive mansion" sat a bucket of water, above which perched a piece of broken mirror supported by pegs. Vivid strokes of red and orange painted the morning sky as the President of the Republic of Texas performed his morning rituals. He was quite capable of shaving without a mirror, military style, but had to agree that civilian life had its advantages. The mirror also revealed the extent to which his hairline had receded. What hair he still had was beginning to gray, and Sam Houston, the realist, had already instructed Sam Houston, the romanticist, that the chances were slim indeed that young Anna Raguet would respond to his suit. In fact, he was the oldest in a wide field of competitors, which included his own secretary of state, Dr. Robert Irion.

Not long before, Miss Anna had heard disturbing reports about his divorce from Eliza Allen. Though their divorce had been filed in 1833 and approved on the grounds of Eliza's desertion, the paperwork had been lost, and the attorney who had filed the papers had since died, which meant the paperwork had to be redone. It upset Anna to realize Houston had been courting her before he was legally free to remarry.

For once in his life, Sam Houston was at a loss for words. Even dealing with the great Santa Anna was not as hard as this. Last night, he had tried to address Miss Anna's concerns. Dated June 4, he wrote,

> "Miss Anna, Having learned that by some agency you were induced to believe that I had presumed to address you at a time when I must have been satisfied in my own

> mind that legal impediments lay in the way of my union with any lady. This may have been the fact as to your belief, and yet the result as to my hopes and my attachments [was] not changed so far as your choice was concerned and my wishes or destiny involved... Then had I addressed you or sought to win your love when I was aware that the same must have taken place at the expense of your happiness and pride and peace and honor in life, I must have acknowledged myself a 'lily liver'd wretch!"[1]

The letter didn't make a lot of sense, but maybe she would respond to the heart behind it. It was Houston's last-ditch attempt to warm the heart of a young lady who, so far, had not given him much encouragement.

He peered into the mirror and saw a weary and aging forty-five-year-old man. Dr. Irion *did* stand a better chance than he did.

Standing for the Gospel

Not all of the furloughed soldiers had left the Republic. Some of them remained in Texas, and since many of them were young men unaccustomed to hard physical labor, they ended up spending their time drinking and gambling in nearby towns. Zechariah Morrell noticed such a band of young men in the town of New Washington, where he and his family had settled.

A small group of eight Baptists in the little town joined and formed a church, and Z. N. Morrell was chosen as pastor. At first, meetings were held in a house while a church building was under construction. The idle soldiers in town took an interest and began to attend the meetings, but after the service, they would take an interest in the saloon. At times, they could be overheard mocking the Christians, which would only provoke the Christians to pray harder for the souls of these lost young men.

Two Cumberland Presbyterian preachers arrived in town, Roark and Andrew McGowan, and plans were made to hold a series of special meetings. On the second night of the meetings, the young men attended, already partly intoxicated. They purposed to mock the proceedings, stationing a man outside the building holding a live chicken. When the congregation would sing, the man would make the chicken squawk. Then another man would stick his head in the window and shout, "Glory to God! Others would mockingly reply, "Amen and amen!"

Z. N. Morrell was sitting with his wife and daughter near the window where the man had stuck in his head. Being crippled in some fashion, he carried a walking cane made of stout hickory. Standing, he approached the window with his cane, waiting for the man to repeat his prank. The next time the man stuck his head in the window, the preacher struck him solidly above the left ear, giving him a scar the man carried to his grave.

"There are more dangerous weapons than this stick," Morrell stated. Constantly under threat from hostile Indians, the men brought their firearms to church.

After the sermon, Morrell stood and made a short but pointed speech to the assembly.

> "Before me are sons from the battle-field of San Jacinto, coming from the various parts of the United States. For what did you traverse the prairies of the west, under the command of the gallant Houston? And for what did you charge the enemy's cannon and burn the bridges behind him, unless it was for civil and religious liberty? Santa Anna has been captured, and priestcraft driven from the land; and yet, in less than two years, you have commenced to pull down what you have built up by so much toil and sacrifice. We are determined, as ministers of the gospel, that we will not be run out of Texas, nor out of this town. For one I can say, let Texas rise or fall, live or die, her fate shall be mine; and I believe God will yet overrule all this to his glory. I have looked for something in the Scriptures to justify my hasty conduct [striking the man] on this occasion. The Savior, driving the thieves from the temple, is the nearest I can find. In this case the house of God was made a house of mockery."[2]

Col. Matthew Caldwell was present with his family, a well-known Indian fighter who had distinguished himself on the battlefield. He spoke. "Gentlemen, I have a wife and daughters here, as well as Mr. Morrell, and this state of things shall be broken up. If there is any fighting to be done, you can put me down on the side of civilization and religious liberty."[3]

From that time on, the disbanded soldiers no longer molested the meetings.

An Angry Buffalo

Noah Smithwick rode his horse along the river bottom. Probably wearing a hunting shirt, buckskin trousers, and moccasins, the Texas Ranger scouted the area for game. Venison and buffalo meat formed the main source of sustenance for these Rangers, who were stationed on the frontier to protect the settlements from Indian raids.

Built of logs, their crude fort was located near the present site of Austin. At the moment, things were pretty quiet, Indian-wise, so the major occupation was hunting.

Smithwick heard his dog begin to bay. There was something out there in the brush. What was it? The man dismounted and tied up his pony; the tangle of brush was too thick to navigate on horseback. Grasping his rifle, Smithwick advanced towards his dog's baying, but had only taken a few steps when a snort and then a crash of brush revealed what kind of creature the dog had flushed. A very large creature.

Smithwick lunged for a fallen tree. Grabbing a branch, he swung himself out of the way just as an old buffalo bull rushed into view, closely followed by the dog. The huge animal was brought to bay right underneath the Ranger, perched precariously in the little tree. Sometimes the bull would strike the tree as it lunged about, almost knocking Smithwick off. But the man managed to get off a shot, bringing the animal down, and a second shot finished him off.

At that point, Noah Smithwick probably took a deep breath. An angry buffalo bull was no joke.

Houston Pivots

John Quincy Adams, former president and now U.S. Congressman, stood up in the chamber. It was July 7, 1838. Everyone knew what would happen next, because it had happened every morning of the past five weeks. Perhaps a member here or there drew a deep breath or stifled a frustrated groan. Not again.

Representative Adams began his denunciation of the Texas Revolution. Everyone knew what he was going to talk about. Slavery. It was the issue. The entire nation was polarized.

But today was the last session of Congress. So it was Adams's last speech on the subject, and undoubtedly, even some of his friends were glad. Well, one thing was certain; if Texas were to be annexed, it wouldn't be in 1838. The United States had sent a "chargé d'Affaires" to Texas, effectively recognizing it as a sovereign nation, but the annexation plan had gone nowhere.

Sam Houston, in the summer of 1838, was faced with two questions of honor: would he continue to court a girl who gave no evidence of romantic interest toward him? And would Texas continue to beg for admission to the United States?

Instructed by the president, Dr. Anson Jones formally withdrew the request for annexation. Scorned by the United States, Texas would blaze her own trail. In truth, her needs, both financial and trade-wise, could be met by another. Perhaps Great Britain?

And though Sam Houston still had occasional contact with Miss Anna Raguet, his manner toward her was kind but decidedly reserved, an appropriate response for the woman who had denied him her heart.

Noah Smithwick's New Post

Injuns!

A small party of Indians, waving a white flag, approached the fort. The Rangers discussed what to do. Comanches didn't understand English, but they did generally possess some knowledge of Spanish. Any discussions would have to be conducted in that language.

Who here speaks the most fluent Spanish? The Rangers deliberated. Noah Smithwick, who was the most fluent of the lot, finally left the fort, accompanied by a few other men. He approached the small group of Indians, which included two older men, probably chiefs, while six warriors, who guarded them, stood silent but alert.

The two chiefs explained to Smithwick that their tribe desired to enter into a treaty with the white men. Might a commissioner be sent to the tribe to discuss the matter?

The Rangers escorted them into the fort, where the matter was laid before Captain Andrews. The Rangers embraced the treaty idea with delight, although they generally viewed the Indians as treacherous. As a result, few coveted the post of commissioner.

The Comanches, upon seeing Smithwick's capability as interpreter, requested that he be named the commissioner and pledged that no harm would come to him. The Ranger yielded "to the stress of circumstances," knowing "that there is a degree of honor even among Indians, touching those who voluntarily become their guests,"[4] and agreed to accompany them back to their camp. But some of Noah's friends worried, wondering if this would be the last time they would see him alive.

A Token for Good

Morrell was discouraged. As a Baptist pastor, he was alone, faithfully ministering to the little flock in New Washington, and now, in the summer of 1838, his family was sick. His little daughter was quite ill with a fever that was common at that time.

He had just received an invitation to preach at a camp meeting about twenty-five miles away. His friend, Dr. Manly, who was both a medical doctor and a

Methodist preacher, had been coming to the house every day to see to the needs of the sick, and now he agreed to care for Morrell's family in the preacher's absence. Morrell later wrote, "I considered this a good opportunity for me to go and preach Jesus."[5]

At the meeting, Morrell opened his Bible to Romans. "The wages of sin is death, but the gift of God is eternal life, through Jesus Christ our Lord." Even as he read, he felt cast down.

His ministry in Tennessee had been fruitful, but two years had passed in Texas, and nothing. Not a single soul had been converted. At least his motives were right.

> My line of argument drawn from the text was, that while death was the wages of sin, God was a just pay-master, and would always pay wages where and when they were due. A fervent appeal was made, showing that it was a fearful thing to fall into the hands of such a God as our God, without the righteousness of his Son.
>
> A man by the name of Jackson was sitting right in front of me, who attracted my attention by his fine appearance and marked interest in the discourse. He had come some distance to the meeting, with his saddlebags loaded with whiskey, and confidently expecting to have a mery time around the camp with his friends. Greatly alarmed at the judgments of God declared respecting the sinner at the great day of account, he sat trembling for a moment, and fell on his face in the aisle. The friends who gathered round him were admonished of the fact, that the mind for the time being had overpowered the body, and that God would take care of his soul. Very soon he professed a hope in Christ, and lived a consistent Christian to the close of his life, some years afterwards.
>
> At the conclusion of the sermon old sister Hall, a Baptist from Missouri, who had not heard a sermon for six years, and several others, praised God aloud, as we are informed they did in ancient times. To God be all the glory. A great burden was lifted from my mind, and I determined more resolutely than ever to "spend and be spent: among the people of Texas. This was the first testimony, clear and decided, that God had given in the wilderness of the west, of salvation wrought under my ministry. My sick family demanded my presence at home, and Sunday night found me watching with the loved ones there. God saw fit in his providence to spare life and restore health.[6]

Smithwick with the Comanches

Because the name, "Noah Smithwick," was too hard for the Indians to pronounce, they found a new name for him, choosing the name of an old chief who had died. "Juaqua."

Juaqua met with the chief, an older man named Muguara. Strangely, he was bald, the only bald Indian Smithwick could ever remember seeing.

The camp was smaller than he expected, about fifty lodges and not more than one hundred warriors. There were six prisoners in camp: one white woman, two white boys, and three Mexicans.

The white woman had been captured when small and now had an Indian husband and several children. The boys did not remember anything about their homes; in fact, one of them, now about eighteen, Smithwick recognized. He had been rescued twice, but each time returned to the Indians, along with several stolen horses.

The other boy was only five or six years old, and Smithwick, not wanting the boy to grow up as a savage, offered a fine horse in exchange, but the squaw who had adopted him refused, insisting, "He is mine, my own child," which was obviously a lie. At least the child was loved, which was some consolation to the frustrated white man.

For three months, Smithwick lived with the Indians. He managed to learn some of the Comanche language and observed their customs with great interest.

> I could never discover anything analogous to written language; the nearest approach to it being diagrams, or more properly maps, which they sometimes marked out on the ground to convey an idea of locality. They were peculiarly expert in sign language, however. Some idea of drawing they had acquired, their work at times evincing a remarkable degree of skill.[7]
>
> Not wishing to give the least occasion for offense, I ate with them, but I laid in a supply of coffee before I went out, which I boiled myself, drinking it from the cup in which it was prepared. In order to be sociable, I offered old chief Muguara some coffee, for which he soon contracted quite a liking, thus cutting my supply short. The Indian mode of cooking meat — roasting it on sticks — was excellent, but they had become so far civilized as to possess a pot in which, perhaps out of deference to me, they sometimes boiled their meat; but I much preferred the roasted, that seeming a little less filthy...[8]

Smithwick observed their children's play, which resembled the play of children anywhere, right down to the construction of dolls. Women worked hard at processing the game that the men brought in; skinning, tanning, and making clothing took large amounts of time.

> They had some kind of religious belief which seemed akin to sun worship. Judging from outward manifestations there was some power which it was necessary to propitiate by offerings. When out on a hunt as soon as game was killed they struck fire and roasted meat, and always before eating a bite the chief would cut off a morsel and bury it; the first fruit of the chase, I suppose.
>
> A similar ceremony was observed when the chief lit his pipe; the first puff of smoke was blown toward the sun and the second to the earth... They evidently believed in a hereafter, but whether the conditions thereof depended on their conduct in this life is not certain. One thing I know, that though they would fight desperately to rescue the body of a fallen comrade so long as his scalp was intact, the moment he lost it he was abandoned; they would not touch the body, even to bury it. ...
>
> But taking them all around they were the most peaceable community I ever lived in. Their criminal laws were as inexorable as those of the Medes and Persians, and the code was so simply worded there was no excuse for ignorance. It was simply the old Mosiac law, "an eye for an eye and a tooth for a tooth." "Whoso sheddeth man's blood, by man shall his blood be shed."[9]

Lamar's Influence and Houston's Ruminations

Someone knelt beside a pile of cast-off lumber and brush, and soon the flames danced over the top. In a few minutes, the bonfire was giving off welcome heat, here in the middle of the street, in front of a Houston City saloon. People gathered around and swapped yarns or talked politics. The weather was turning, and in the boomtown of Houston, where crude shacks were the norm, chilly weather could feel downright frigid.

In November of 1838, the weather was turning, in more ways than one. Mirabeau Buonaparte Lamar had just been elected President of the Texas Republic, and his friend David G. Burnet vice-president. Sam Houston could not succeed himself as president, according to the Texas Constitution, and for some reason, the first term was only two years long. Lamar and successive presidents would have three years at the helm.

But there was more going on than just constitutional technicalities. A lot of people were tired of Houston. He was too conservative, truly a "do-nothing" president. He had refrained from getting tough with Mexico, which was still officially at war with Texas. Santa Anna's speeches were not sweet now that he was safely back at home in Mexico. And add to that the fact that Houston was an Indian lover. There was no doubt about that, especially after he had repeatedly hosted Indians in his yard, even sitting around a campfire with them. Lamar understood that Texans needed to be protected from those he thought of as red vermin.

Plus, Houston had spent most of his time either chasing annexation or some other scheme involving Great Britain, or maybe France. Texas could stand on her own. Who knew? Texas might one day encompass the entire western half of the continent, a new American Republic. Why not? If the United States wanted to destroy herself over the slave issue, and reject the bounty Texas represented, then maybe...

The conversation around the bonfire might have included thoughts like these, especially as Lamar's speeches contained many of these themes and were enthusiastically received by the people. The dark-haired poet and violinist had declared that he would give Texas a "new character." His administration would make it easier to make a living; he would reduce taxes and get tough with the Indians. All of Houston's policies would be swept away. The hero of Sherman's failed cavalry charge had great visions for Texas—a Texas that could stand on her own.

Sam Houston stepped into a puddle. Oh, well... there had been times when he had walked through ankle-deep water just to get to his house. But overall, Houston City was doing well. Immigration had swelled the population to several thousand, although members of the gentler sex were still few; men outnumbered women about ten to one. The health of the populace had improved after several cypress cisterns had been purchased in New Orleans and installed to catch rainwater; the practice of drinking water from the Buffalo Bayou had made people sick.

Houston rode along the street, approaching the executive "mansion." His namesake city was a true smorgasbord of nationalities and occupations. One hundred of the Mexican soldiers captured at San Jacinto were still here, having opted to remain in this raw country, full of possibilities.

Lawyers abounded, seeing the possibilities for legal strife. Gambling and drinking were an important part of the city's economy. But there were plenty of honest and even talented folk who cheered Sam Houston's heart, like Dr. Smith, his new friend and surgeon general, and Dr. Henderson, who had done such good work overseas. Thanks to bold but discreet diplomacy, Henderson had arranged a trade agreement with Great Britain. Not the same as recognition, but it was a good start. And warming up to Great Britain might just cause a nearer kinsman to reconsider...

Houston planted a foot on his porch, then stepped up. He might not have totally regained all the weight he had lost, but anything close to his normal weight of 230 pounds would certainly be a challenge to the porch, which was now beginning to sag. Fortunately, Esau, his black body servant, was coming and could help with several other repairs. There were floorboards that needed to be replaced; a few had been pried up and used for kindling on cool nights when the conversation was too good to be interrupted. The mud chinking had fallen out in places. There was plenty of work to be done to get the place ready for the incoming President Lamar.

Lamar. A "new character." Houston probably had ambivalent feelings about the situation, wanting the best for Texas and Texans, yet...

The inauguration was scheduled for December 1st, and Houston was supposedly "in charge" of the ceremony, yet there was no opportunity for him to speak. He had said nothing during the campaign, but now he wanted a chance to explain, to defend his policies. Perhaps there was a way.

Smithwick—a Sacrifice?

One day, a group of war-painted Waco Indians approached the Comanche camp. Old Muguara and some others spoke with them, but Noah Smithwick could understand very little of the "mongrel jargon" they employed in their discussion. But the white man noticed the vindictive glances the Wacos sent in his direction, and catching a few words of Spanish, soon realized that the conversation was about him.

Smithwick called one of the young Mexican captives, who by now was fluent in the Indians' language, and asked him to interpret. Apparently, the Wacos had been on a horse-stealing expedition among the white settlements, and one of their braves had been killed, necessitating a blood sacrifice, for which the white man was the perfect choice.

Smithwick later wrote, "The Comanches and the Wacos were for the time being allies and I can assure you that I felt as if my chances for life hung on a slender thread, and I made up my mind then and there that if the Comanches yielded to the demand of the Wacos I would fight to the death; I would not be taken alive to be slowly tortured to death by the merciless fiends."

But old bald Chief Muguara refused. He drew up his tall form before the Waco chief, and towering above him, decreed in tones of thunder, "No! This man is our friend, and you must walk over my dead body to reach him! Hurt but one hair of his head, and not one of you shall get away to tell the tale!"[10]

The Comanche warriors gathered around their chief, weapons in hand. Smithwick watched in awe, wondering if they might battle over *him!* Finally, the Wacos withdrew, muttering threats under their breath.

Muguara took precautions against a reprisal by stealth, even giving Smithwick a bodyguard on those occasions when he needed to visit the settlements.

Throughout his visit, Smithwick held long discussions with Muguara and the older men regarding a treaty, for which purpose he had come. During these long, earnest talks, Smithwick could not help but admit the justice of some of their contentions.

Their main concern had to do with their hunting grounds. Old Muguara explained:

> "We have set up our lodges in these groves and swung our children from these boughs from time immemorial [not true, but one hundred years may have seemed as such for a people with no written history]. When game beats away from us we pull down our lodges and move away, leaving no trace to frighten it, and in a little while it comes back. But the white man comes and cuts down the trees, building houses and fences, and the buffalos get frightened and leave and never come back, and the Indians are left to starve, or, if we follow the game, we trespass on the hunting grounds of other tribes and war ensues."[11]

Smithwick suggested adopting the ways of the white man, cultivating the ground.

"No," the chief replied emphatically, "the Indians were not made to work. If they build houses and try to live like the white men they will all die. If the white men would draw a line defining their claims and keep on their side of it the red men would not molest them."[12]

When Noah Smithwick and an envoy of Comanches finally journeyed to Houston City to formalize a treaty, the Texas Ranger remembered what the old bald chief had said. He spoke with President Houston, explaining the Indians' desire for a definite line of division between the red man and the white.

Sam Houston sadly shook his head. "If I could build a wall from the Red River to the Rio Grande, so high that no Indian could scale it, the white people would go crazy trying to devise means to get beyond it."[13]

Smithwick knew he was correct. And in this particular situation, the treaty that was formed did not protect the peace, for neither side fully complied with it, and seeing the bad faith on the part of the whites, the Indians lost what trust they had in the commissioner, saying Smithwick had lied to them. Also, some among the whites distrusted him, thinking that the Ranger was now on the "side" of the Indians because of the time he had spent with them.

Noah Smithwick consoled himself, observing that he was in good company, since Houston and General Burleson had been accused in the same way. And he wondered if these Comanches would remember him for good if they ever met in battle. He had a hunch they might just remember "Juaqua."

Old Sam's Speech

A huge crowd had gathered in front of the Capitol Building in Houston City. It was December 10, 1838, Inauguration Day. Standing a mere five feet seven inches, with black wavy hair, Mirabeau Buonaparte Lamar fingered his inner coat pocket, where he had placed his carefully prepared inauguration speech.

Sam Houston arrived and took the chair of state.

What? A low murmur issued from the crowd, taking in the odd dress of the outgoing president. He wore a silk coat, knee breeches with silver buckles, pumps with buckles, and a *powdered wig!* This old-fashioned costume instantly reminded one and all of George Washington, which, of course, was the intended result.

The crowd responded with murmurs that broke into loud cheers for "Old Sam!" Other voices demanded a speech.

And Old Sam had come prepared. Standing, he proceeded to review his policies, including those for which he had been so viciously attacked during the campaign.

Certainly, no one was bored. Houston's oratorical skill included both wit and satire, sometimes good-natured, sometimes sharp. He begged Congress to treat his successor better than it had treated him, describing the presidency as "a pillow of thorns." He concluded his long address by expressing his sincere goodwill for the incoming administration that was to give Texas "a new character." He beckoned to President Lamar.

But Lamar was having problems. Intestinal problems. Beset by weak digestion, Houston's long oratory had played havoc with his innards. He stood up and withdrew his speech from his coat pocket, but internal affairs were not cooperating. He handed the paper to the clerk of the Senate, who read Lamar's speech in an uninspiring monotone.

But the crowd, though already worn out after the first speech, still responded to Lamar's themes. "The white man and the red man cannot dwell in harmony together. Nature forbids it."[14] This statement elicited thunderous applause. Clearly, Texans wanted strong leadership against the Comanche threat.

Houston's Trip East

Now what? What was Sam Houston going to do now that he was a private citizen? He first decided on a land development venture with some of his friends.

Then he agreed to enter into a law practice with John Birdsall, an attorney with a more systematic education than his own. Perhaps he could benefit from such an association.

But before Houston could start up his law practice, he needed to take a trip to the United States regarding the development venture. He also wanted to buy blooded horses for a ranch he owned on the Trinity River. Plus, this trip would also give him a chance to stop by the Hermitage and visit with his old commander, Andrew Jackson, who was now in retirement. The Hero of San Jacinto probably had no idea how providential this trip would prove to be.

Margaret Prepares Strawberries

Margaret Lea helped her sister as she prepared for guests. Her eighteen-year-old younger sister, Emily, had married a businessman named William Bledsoe. Vivacious and beautifully dressed, the young Mrs. Bledsoe was preparing to entertain the ladies of the Baptist Church. Their father, Temple Lea, had pastored the church until he died in 1834. Now Margaret's older brothers helped to keep an eye on the family, and their mother, Nancy Lea, served as a pillar of strength for them all.

It was strawberry season, and Margaret, taller and more plainly dressed than her younger sister, helped to prepare the strawberries for their guests.

Houston Arrives at the Bledsoe's

Houston arrived in Mobile and found the office of William Bledsoe, a merchandise broker who received him cordially. They discussed the land project Houston was promoting. Because Bledsoe was interested, and believed that his mother-in-law, Nancy Lea, might also be interested, he invited Houston to his home in nearby Spring Hill.

At his home, Bledsoe introduced his guest to his wife, Emily, and to his mother-in-law Nancy Lea. Houston was normally good at remembering names and faces, but there were a great number of ladies present.

When served the strawberries and cream, which were being served by Margaret,

Houston found that the strawberries were not nearly as interesting as the lovely girl with violet eyes. He bowed low over her hand in the way men did in those days.

When he said he was charmed, he meant it. Ever since she had watched the injured Houston climb over the gunwale of the *Flora* that day in New Orleans, she had wanted to meet him, and now here he was. But the poised twenty-year-old continued her duties, helping her sister.

At one point, she once again passed near Sam Houston, and he noticed her, saying to another guest, "If she were not already married, I believe I'd give that charming lady a chance to say 'no.'"

"But that's not Mrs. Bledsoe," came the answer. "That's the older unmarried sister. So you're free to give her that chance, General."[15]

Margaret finished serving her sister's guests, and somehow she and Houston ended up outside, standing among the azaleas. Emily was amused. She saw little more of them that afternoon.

Sam Houston stayed with William Bledsoe a full week. He attended to his business interests and found time to spend with Margaret in the azalea garden.

Could this be the one for him? She was twenty-six years younger than he, and her health did not seem robust. Could she stand up to the conditions she would face in Texas? During their time together, he explained things very candidly to Margaret.

Sam pointed to a star perched low in the heavens. He called it the star of destiny, and asked Margaret to look at it after he had gone—to think of its significance. To remember what he had told her about life in Texas—not only the hardships of primitive conditions, but also the hardships that might come by being married to a man whose life seemed destined for strife. He was going to Nashville, but promised she would hear from him soon, and he would be anxious to know how his message was received.

Houston departed, and Margaret stayed up late that night, writing a poem. This man had won her heart.

At the Hermitage

Jackson was glad to see his old protégé; he and Houston had much catching up to do. They talked about Horseshoe Bend, the Battle of New Orleans, and San Jacinto. The old general wanted the details of the retreat from Gonzales. He was proud of Houston for not killing Santa Anna and thought he was clever, surprising them during their siesta.

Andrew Jackson's hair was almost pure white, and when he read, he had to hold it close to his right eye. He was by now quite thin and weak, his face deeply etched with lines. But he was still strong in spirit. He consoled the discouraged Houston, convinced that the annexation issue would work itself out in time. The United States would not want another British-dominated country on her borders. One Canada was enough. He knew of the political game Houston had conceived.

Sitting with his old friend in the bedroom of the Hermitage, Houston must have cheered Jackson's heart when he said he would always regard his success at San Jacinto a direct result of his familiarity with his old commander's tactics in the campaign against the Creeks.

Truly, he had learned much from "Old Hickory." He had served his political apprenticeship under the eye of the master. Was there such a thing as an honorable politician? This frail old man before him had certainly run the race with honor. "Western" honor, to be sure: at the close of his presidency, Jackson had admitted two regrets: that he had been unable to shoot Henry Clay or hang John C. Calhoun.

And now his old friend spoke of the life to come. Houston could see Aunt Rachel's grave from the bedroom window, and he must have remembered the beauty of her faith in Christ. A path he had not taken, that he needed to take...

Margaret. Shortly after his arrival, Houston had written her, forming in gentle prose *the question*—perhaps Margaret could help him find that path of faith.

He was a sinner and didn't know how to change that.

Margaret's Response

Margaret wrote back. "...however, I have heard from you and the tidings are quite welcome I assure you. My answer may be taken as strong evidence of that, for it is the first I have addressed to any gentlemen."

She went on to write, "Last night I gazed long upon our beauteous emblem the *star of destiny*, and my thoughts took the form of verse, but I will not inscribe them here, for then you might call me a romantic star-struck young lady..."

At the end, she signed, "Forever thine own Esperanza."[16] The one hoped for. That was what he had called her.

Margaret set down her pen. She was seated in the library, a favorite place, filled with old friends, heroes and heroines... the decision to marry Sam Houston was not made in haste. She loved him. Perhaps she could be a *help* to him.

When Houston returned to Alabama, his "Esperanza" received him joyfully, and they spent time in the azalea garden. She tucked her hand inside his arm and smiled up at him. Sam Houston had finally found that one to whom he could entrust his heart. He took her in his arms.

But Nancy Lea was not as certain as her daughter about this man. She had heard about a failed first marriage and about his drinking. He did not profess to be a Christian, though he knew the Scriptures well. Was Margaret simply infatuated with the Hero of San Jacinto? But in spite of herself, Nancy Lea couldn't help *liking* this man. *Well, we'll see.*

Lamar's Devious Move against the Cherokee

John H. Reagan was a deputy surveyor for the Republic of Texas. Originally from Tennessee, Reagan was only twenty-one this fateful summer of 1839.

He knew from the beginning that surveying was a touchy issue. In fact, there were land disputes between white men and the Cherokees who lived in the area north of Nacogdoches. Old Chief Bowl's band had lived in Texas for a while now, having been granted, by the Spanish, a strip of land 130 miles long and about sixty miles wide. Sam Houston had negotiated a treaty on behalf of Texas in February 1836, just before traveling to the meeting in Washington-on-the-Brazos and signing his name to the Declaration of Independence.

The agreement guaranteed this land to the Cherokees, in return requiring peace on the part of the Indians. But during Houston's presidency, the Senate had refused to ratify the treaty, the terms of which the Cherokees were faithfully honoring.

Reagan may not have known all the details, but the fact was, the land these Cherokees were parked on was very good land. And Americans had never really recognized the right of Indians to possess the land.

Sure, they formed treaties "guaranteeing" land, but those treaties were often broken or conveniently forgotten. Houston's idea of giving legal title to these Cherokees sounded almost weird. So simple. But it was never done. The red man was not the equal of the white, even while he farmed the land, raised cattle, and built homes as these Cherokees did. His "rights" were not respected.

President Lamar had decided to take a stand against the Indians. He provoked wars in the west against the Comanches. And here in the east, he had decided that the peaceable Cherokees must go.

The truth was that some of his friends held land claims overlapping the Indians' territory. He tried unsuccessfully to provoke war by sending surveyors into their land, and while they objected, no fighting resulted. *There has to be a way to get rid of those Indians.*

Then it was discovered that some Cherokees had joined up with Manual Flores, a Mexican bandit with a mischievous reputation. A few renegade members of Chief Bowl's band had been captured on the Colorado River, and charges were made against them. There were probably agents of Chief Bowl, gone to Mexico to confer with Santa Anna for no good purpose. Peaceable indeed.

Lamar had his excuse. He chose men to negotiate with the Cherokees, and while they talked, the president arranged for troops to be made ready.

A group of men, including David G. Burnet and John H. Reagan, was sent to the Cherokees. Chief Bowl received them courteously and invited them to meet beside a spring near his home.

The president's commissioners charged the Cherokees with murder, theft, and treachery, referring to the renegades who had been captured. Old Chief Bowl denied the charges, explaining that his people had instructions to kill these renegade Cherokees wherever they were found. The chief was every bit as interested in justice as the whites.

Reagan reported these facts to Lamar, but the president had already determined his course. He stationed troops on Cherokee land, answering the chief's protests by charging that the region had become a refuge for conspirators.

In further negotiations, Chief Bowl defended himself until he was weary. Finally, he explained that he was eighty-three years old. Whatever came of this could not matter to him personally, but he feared for his three wives and children.

He was caught between a rock and a hard place. If he fought the whites, he would die. If he refused to fight, his own people, provoked beyond measure, would kill him. Chief Bowl concluded by stating that he had led his own people for a long time and would stand by them.

John H. Reagan was impressed by Bowl's dignified behavior and frankness, and he was grieved when an action was ordered against the Cherokees, one in which he nevertheless participated.

On July 15, 1839, the fighting began, and two whites and eighteen Cherokees were killed. The next day, the conflict continued.

Reagan watched as Chief Bowl rode up and down in the rear of his line, mounted on a paint horse. The old man wore a black military hat, a silk vest, and carried a sword—probably an old sword Houston had given him. He exposed himself recklessly, encouraging his men.

But heavy fire shattered all encouragement, and the Indians were forced back. Chief Bowl took a lead ball in the thigh, and his horse was injured. He dismounted and attempted to limp off the battlefield, but then he was shot in the back. The old

Indian walked a short distance but shortly collapsed. Somehow, he managed to raise himself to a sitting position.

Reagan ran toward the old chief. He couldn't bear to see this dignified old man killed. He saw another man, Captain Robert Smith, approaching Chief Bowl, pointing a pistol.

"Captain, don't shoot him,"[17] the young surveyor pleaded.

The captain aimed the pistol and fired at the old Indian's head, still capped by the black hat. The battle was over.

Shortly afterward, in Arkansas, Chief Ooleteka received the news. Members of Chief Bowl's band had arrived, distressed and needy. What had happened? The whole band, including its sick and wounded, had been driven over the Texas border by attacking white men. His heart must have grieved when he heard of Bowl's death. Where was his son Colonneh? *The Raven?*

Bad News

Sam Houston rode into San Augustine after returning from his trip to the States, and he met with some friends, who gave him the news. Mostly bad news.

John Birdsall, his new law partner, had contracted yellow fever. More followed. Had he heard that the capital had been moved out to some dangerous place on the western frontier? It was named after Stephen Austin. The legislative act that accomplished this feat of insanity also precluded, for all time, the possibility of relocating the capital back to Houston. Lamar was keeping his campaign promises. Everything connected with Houston's leadership was being summarily swept into the dustbin.

Then his friends informed him that they had elected him as their representative.

Despite the fact that such an office required Houston's presence in the new and dangerous western capital, the general felt complimented that the citizens of San Augustine should so honor him, especially when Nacogdoches was actually his home.

Then Houston found out about the Cherokees and felt sick at heart. He searched out the details, speaking to a number of participants. Chief Bowl had been his friend, a friend to whom he had made promises, and he couldn't stop hearing the promises that still echoed in his head.

"The words of good men should never be forgotten... I have given an order that no families or children of Indians shall be disturbed or have troubles, but that they shall be protected and even the Mexican families, and property shall not be troubled!

"That war may cease everywhere is my wish... Tell my Sister, the children, and all my red brothers to sleep in peace."[18]

He had written that to Chief Bowl just one year ago. And this summer, while Houston had been speaking with Andrew Jackson about the principles that bring honor to a nation, President Lamar and his cohorts had brought dishonor upon Texas. They had disregarded the fundamental principle of American civilization, the rule of law, and had taken by force what they were powerful enough to take.

Houston mounted his horse and rode to Nacogdoches, where the citizens there called a meeting at the town hall, eager to know what their former president would say about Lamar's action against the Cherokees.

Houston faced an audience of old friends and acquaintances. He told them the truth, that the Cherokee War was an act of bad faith, and expressed indignation over the action, probably also giving vent to his personal grief.

His friends did not understand, however, and his speech angered them. In fact, it was years before some of them forgave him.

Houston got back on his horse and embarked on a journey to Austin to take his place in the House of Representatives.

A Gruesome Memorial

Hugh McLeod, Lamar's Adjutant General, approached Houston on the floor of the Texas House. He held out a large, black military hat, which he presented to the representative from San Augustine. McLeod explained that this was to be Houston's share of the spoils of the Cherokee War. The Raven looked at the gruesome memorial he held in his hands. A bullet hole now disfigured Chief Bowl's hat.

Up to this point, Houston had been arguing the right of the Cherokees to their land and trying to convince those in power that it would behoove them to use restraint and moderation instead of brute force. But now he lost his temper, charging that the government was a tool of land speculators, and mentioned Burnet by name.

Then he brought his speech to a passionate end. He had introduced a bill that would cause the confiscated Cherokee land to be regarded as government property, instead of letting it go to the land speculators who had initially provoked the war. He said that he doubted if he had convinced the House of the justness of the bill, but he expressed the honest convictions of his heart, and believed his own integrity would be upheld in the future, no matter which way Congress chose to vote.

Houston won. Even though his friends disagreed with him on the Indian issues, this time the line being drawn was too glaring to ignore. Land speculators versus public interest; the bill passed almost unanimously. It was a victory, but not big enough to compensate for the hat he held in his hands.

A Trousseau

Nancy Lea and her son-in-law, William Bledsoe, stood on deck, surveying the scene. Galveston Harbor in the morning was thought by some to be a charming place. Seagulls swooped overhead, curlews sang, and cranes screamed. Houses destroyed by a hurricane provided visual interest near the wharf. Elsewhere, shipwrecks provided the decor.

They had come from Mobile, via New Orleans, to investigate the possibilities in Texas land. Sam Houston was supposed to be meeting them.

Was that him? A dory was approaching, and after a second look, they knew that, yes, it was him.

Boom! Nancy Lea jumped. "What was that?"

Houston quickly explained that the cannon shot was not a sign of hostility, but of honor. His friends were using that means to announce their pleasure at the arrival of his bride-to-be. Was Margaret indisposed?

"General Houston," Mrs. Lea replied firmly, "my daughter is in Alabama. She goes forth into the world to marry no man. The one who receives her hand will receive it in my home and not elsewhere."[19]

Sam must have been bitterly disappointed, having expected to see his *Esperanza*, but the Hero of San Jacinto immediately bowed his acquiescence.

Meanwhile, in Alabama, Margaret occupied herself in sewing a trousseau that included a white satin dress, a purple silk, and a blue muslin.

A Devoted Heart

Finally, the day arrived. In view of his "temperament" and "his terrific habits," one friend had implored Houston to "resort to any expedient rather than *marry*,"[20] but he had not succeeded in changing his mind.

Sam Houston arrived at the home of Henry Lea, Margaret's brother, on May 9, 1840, just in time to see the minister and the guests arriving, while the musicians tuned their instruments.

Then one of Margaret's brothers took Houston aside, demanding an explanation of his separation from Eliza Allen. If this were not forthcoming, he said, the ceremony could not take place.

Houston felt as if he had been ambushed. He replied in a courteous tone that he had not before and would not ever reveal the cause of the estrangement, and if the wedding depended upon his telling now, then he should "pay the fiddlers" and call the wedding off.[21]

But the difficulty was somehow overcome, and the musicians began to play, allowing this melancholy man of destiny to now be blessed with a beautiful young wife. It seemed almost too good to be true.

A few months later, Houston would write to Margaret that he never imagined such a "perfect companion and one who wou'd be capable by her wisdom and prudence to sustain me, or one who wou'd endear life to me and blot out the infelicity of the past."[22]

Margaret had made known her wish that her husband refrain from excess in drinking, something he had already intended to do, especially now that he had a strong motive to please this love of his life. In the same letter, Houston encouraged his wife's hope in her Redeemer. "This reflection will sustain you in the trials of your earthly probation! You will find no conduct of mine a stumbling block to your path. The study of my life shall be to render you happy in temporal & spiritual affairs!"[23]

From the beginning, their marriage endured frequent separations, as Margaret's health was unable to withstand the rigors of his frequent and often dangerous travels. The young wife received many letters from the new capital of Austin, where her husband continued in his duty as the representative from San Augustine.

By now, public life distressed him. Houston wrote to his wife, "To see men in Congress, who have not been in the country for one year, and they assume to become law givers distresses me! The Sages of antiquity dictated wisdom, and young men listen to the wisdom of others. As it now is the young men governed by passion, decided according to feeling, to interest, and to passion."[24]

He missed her desperately when they were apart.

> From day to day, I read and peruse your letters. They are to me a solace, and when I peruse them, I feel, at moments, as tho' I were in sweet communion with you; and hear my Margaret's voice. Then I feel again, that I am far distant from the spirit of my earthy hopes! I can not & will not, stay one hour longer than I can avoid. My love, I will fly to you, as the weary dove wou'd return to the Ark of old, when it was weary and desired rest! Such my love, is the condition of my devoted heart.[25]

Houston's friends were amazed. One friend wrote, "I have never met with an individual more totally disqualified for domestic happiness..."[26] Perhaps they worried that this marriage would fail as the first had done, and plunge Houston into deep depression and more heavy drinking.

But their fears were not being realized. They watched. Had he given up his bachelor habits? Houston seemed the model husband.

Early in their marriage, the Houstons stopped in Nacogdoches, the place where Sam had recently offended so many good friends. But Margaret's smile took the edge off an awkward situation. In fact, feelings were warmed enough for the citizens of Nacogdoches to throw a barbecue in their honor.

Normally, liquor was served at a Texas barbecue, but people had noticed that Houston only drank cold water. They also noticed the impressive poise and happy confidence of his wife.

Then the couple visited San Augustine and were guests at a number of barbecues and dinners, where everyone observed Margaret's charm and the general's abstinence.

Houston's friend, George Hockley, was dumbfounded at the change he saw in Sam. He had thought that marriage would be the general's ruin, but, over time, he was forced to change his opinion. He wrote to Ashbel Smith that if Sam's reformation could be accomplished by anyone, it would be by Houston's estimable wife.

Houston confided to Margaret his deepest secrets. He told her about Eliza Allen, explaining what had happened, something he had told no one. Later, he wrote, "My Love, what I told you of Miss E. ... was correct. You may think of the matter—but let it be kept a profound secret—be always guarded—you are "Houston's Wife" and many would joy to dash our cup of bliss. My joy is in your life!"[27]

There was no bitterness in Sam Houston's heart toward Eliza Allen. In spite of everything, he still chose to guard her reputation. But now he had an additional care—his new wife's happiness—and knew that the political attacks that sometimes descended upon him could affect her. He wished to protect his "wee wifie" and their happiness together.

He couldn't help but imagine how wonderful it would be if he could retire from public life. Then they could enjoy each other and the normal "cares" of life.

But that was not to be. Texas was falling apart.

Chapter 12

Blood and Tears

YOUNG, redheaded Henry Karnes had seen much in his wartime service, but this was new. The three Comanche chiefs before him wanted peace. It was January 9, 1840, and these three chiefs on horseback had trotted their mounts into San Antonio as though they owned the place—and they had when Spain ruled Texas. At that time, one lone Indian entering a town could take what he wanted, because all the inhabitants were too terrified to put up a resistance.

But that was then. Now, Lamar's policies had put pressure on these warlike Comanches and had driven them to talk peace. Karnes was now a colonel in charge of a group of Texas Rangers, and being the military authority on hand, he had to make a decision.

He told the Comanches that peace would be contingent upon the return of all the white captives, of which there were currently about two hundred. The Indians listened and promised to return in twenty days.

The Terms of Peace

Then Colonel Karnes wrote a letter to General Albert Sidney Johnston. He requested that commissioners meet with the Indians. He also requested troops, not having any faith in Comanche promises. He proposed that if the Indians did not return the prisoners, then those who came to San Antonio could be held as hostages as a guarantee for their return.

Johnston gave assent and sent troops under Lt. Col. Fisher to Bexar, instructing him to seize the Indians if they did not return the captives. Terms to be given to the Comanches also included certain boundaries that the Indians must not pass.

On March 19, 1840, a group of Indians, many colorfully painted for council, rode into San Antonio. Among them were twelve chiefs; the old bald chief Muguara seemed to be the spokesman. Accompanying these chiefs were several women and children, including two captives: a sixteen-year-old girl named Matilda Lockhart and a Mexican boy.

Mrs. Samuel Maverick, a citizen of San Antonio, was horrified. The appearance of the girl, Matilda, shocked everyone.

Her head, arms, and face were covered with bruises and sores, and her nose had actually been burned down to the bone—the fleshy end was entirely gone, and a large scab had formed on the end of the bone. Both nostrils were wide open and denuded of flesh. She told a pitiful tale of being beaten and awakened from sleep with a fiery stick to her flesh, most often to her nose. Burn scars covered her body.

In a move of compassion, Mrs. Maverick and several other women helped to gently bathe and dress the abused captive. Matilda, who understood some of her captors' language, told them of the Comanches' plans: they hoped to get a higher price for the captives by bringing them back a few at a time.

Chief Muguara's behavior seemed to confirm this story as he bargained with the commissioners. He requested ammunition, vermillion, blankets, and bangles in return for the rest of the captives. The commissioners, while meeting with the Indians in a one-story limestone courthouse, known as the "Council House," asked why all the captives had not been returned. Muguara replied that they were with other tribes but could be bought back.

Muguara did not seem to be intimidated when he asked, "How do you like that answer?"[1]

Having seen Matilda Lockhart and heard her story, the three commissioners were pale with fury. Lt. Col. Fisher responded to the chief by ordering soldiers to come into the room. He told the interpreter to tell the Indians that they would be imprisoned until the rest of the white captives arrived.

The interpreter did not want to translate this. He whispered that the Comanches would fight. Finally, he relayed Fisher's message, then turned and ran from the room.

Hearing this ultimatum, the Indians in the room responded with war cries, and when they turned to find the door blocked by a soldier, one Comanche thrust his knife into the man, as the Texans opened fire. Amid the chaos, smoke, and screams, the Indians fled the building. They tried to flee to the river but never made it. All the Indians were either captured or killed; all twelve of the chiefs, including Muguara, perished, and about thirty tribe members, half the total, were imprisoned.

A captured squaw was given a horse and told to tell the Comanches that the prisoners would be killed unless all the white captives were returned within twelve days. This grieving woman, the wife of one of the dead chiefs, rode into her camp. Hearing of the massacre, the Comanche band mourned, with women cutting off their fingers in their grief. Horses were sacrificed. Then the thirteen remaining captives were killed in slow and revolting ways.

Twelve chiefs had been killed during a council of peace, and there would surely be revenge.

Morrell Makes a Decision

Zechariah Morrell knew what the smoke meant. Indians. Traveling across their trail between the Guadalupe and Lavaca rivers, the preacher worried. The tracks in the ground before him had not been made by a small band; no, there had to be four or five hundred Indians advancing toward the settlements below.

A few miles ahead, Morrell came across an injured man hiding in a thicket. He and his companion had been attacked by a small group of Indians straggling behind the main band. He had escaped by crawling with his gun into a thicket, a defensive position, which the red men were loath to charge. His companion had fared worse, being chased down and captured, after which time the soles of his feet were cut off. After being forced to walk back to the site of the attack, he was killed with his own gun, and his body mutilated.

Knowing that the citizens of the Colorado valley must be warned, Morrell returned home, borrowed a good horse, and then raced for Colonel Burleson's home.

Buffalo Hump's Revenge

Buffalo Hump led the multitude southeast. Comanche warriors, family members, Kiowas, and Mexican guides formed an army of about one thousand. The only remaining chief of the southern Comanches' blood was still warm, his heart grieving over the treacherous murder of Muguara and the other chiefs in San Antonio.

Behind him, the bodies of pale faces and their dark slaves watered the earth with their blood. The Indians also stole horses along the way, and 1,500 animals now accompanied them on this vengeful raid.

The sun was high on August 8, 1840, when the huge band of Indians reached the settlement on Lavaca Bay. Linnville was a way station for goods coming to San Antonio from the Gulf, and a schooner was presently anchored just offshore.

The residents of Linnville observed the approach of a great commotion and many horses. Mexican horse traders—that must be it. Comanches were unknown in these parts, and it took a few moments before someone realized who these people were.

Indians! Run for the bay!

Judge John Hays grabbed his shotgun and took off with the others. They grabbed the small boats at the edge of the water and pushed off, with men helping women and children to climb in.

Comanche war screams chilled the blood of the people as they ran for safety. But the customs officer, Hugh Oran Watts, decided to return for his gold watch, unwilling to leave such a valuable keepsake for these savages, who were already looting homes and stores. But he paid dearly for that decision.

Watts's new bride, Juliet, watched in horror as the Comanches killed her husband. Several others were also killed, but most of the residents of Linnville watched the commotion from the safety of the bay, sitting in small boats or on board the schooner.

Throughout the day, the Indians plundered the town. A warehouse full of goods for San Antonio merchants proved an interesting discovery, with the Comanches breaking open full boxes of hats and umbrellas destined for James Robinson's shop. With fire consuming the buildings of the village, Indians galloped about, arrayed with top hats, umbrellas, and other décor, whoops and hollering punctuating the chaos.

Judge Hays couldn't bear it any longer. Grasping his shotgun, he splashed through the surf toward shore. Undoubtedly, others called to him to stop, as he would surely be killed. He had no ammunition, but he couldn't just stand back and watch. Reaching shore, he yelled at the Indians, waving his empty shotgun. And though Comanche warriors turned their horses and encircled this strange man, they never harmed him. They had what they had come for.

Finally, the Indians gathered up the loot and loaded it onto pack mules. A few captives were likewise strapped onto mules, and more stolen horses were added to the herd, which now totaled about 3,000 head. Satiated with the spoils of war, the Comanches turned and headed for home.

A Message

Zechariah Morrell arrived at Burleson's home and quickly related his story. The colonel immediately ordered his war horse, and before mounting, showed Morrell some marks on his saddle—bullet marks, one on the inside of the horn, one on the outside, and one on the back of the tree.

"All these," remarked Burleson, "were made while I was in the saddle."[2] These were badges from the battle of San Jacinto, where his horse had been shot out from under him.

Mounting their horses, the men saw a rider quickly approaching. A paper in his hand fluttered in the breeze. The message read:

> "General: The Indians have sacked and burned the town of Linnville; carried off several prisoners. We made a draw-fight with them at Casa Blanca,--could not stop them;--we want to fight them before they get to the mountains. We have sent expressmen up the Guadalupe.
>
> (signed) Ben McCulloch."[3]

This hastily penned note revealed that the Comanches had abandoned their usual guerrilla tactics. Normally, small groups would converge on a place, kill, scalp, and steal, then separate to elude pursuit. They didn't attack and burn whole *towns*. Until now.

Burleson and Morrell rode up the Colorado valley, telling everyone the news as they went. At Bastrop, Burleson called a council, and the men agreed on a plan. They would try to intercept the retreating Indian army at Plum Creek, twenty-seven miles below Austin.

Morrell was asked to go to Austin to help gather volunteers. Returning from the Texas capital with a company of men, he discovered that Burleson had just left for Plum Creek. Riding hard, the Baptist preacher and his companions caught up with the main group just as the men encountered Buffalo Hump's vast army.

At first, the Indians didn't seem interested in fighting and would ride up and haphazardly shoot arrows, doing no damage, then wheel their horses and withdraw. They were garishly dressed, in a combination of Comanche costume and the spoils from Linnville. Morrell recorded the appearance of one who caught his attention.

> One of these daring chiefs attracted my attention especially. He was riding a very fine horse, held in by a fine American bridle, with a red ribbon eight or ten feet long tied to the tail of a horse. He was dressed in elegant style, from the goods stolen at

> Linnville, with a high-top silk hat, fine pair of boots and leather gloves, an elegant broadcloth coat, hind part before, with brass buttons shining brightly right up and down his back. When he first made his appearance he was carrying a large umbrella outstretched.[4]

The reason for these feints was soon discovered. The Indians were trying desperately to get their huge cavalcade of stolen horses and heavily packed mules past this point. If they engaged in an all-out battle here, they would forfeit all their spoils. Burleson, Caldwell, and McCullock saw immediately that charging the enemy right there was their best chance. They convinced Felix Huston, commander, to order a charge.

The Texans howled like wolves as they charged into the Comanche flank. Shooting and screaming, they stampeded the huge horse herd, and the Indians who were dispersed around it were carried off with the charging animals. Thick, choking dust rose into the air; the summer had been dry.

For fifteen miles, the Texans chased the Comanches through the dust, killing over eighty, while only one Texan lost his life.

When the Texans finally called a retreat, Morrell heard a woman screaming from some nearby bushes. When he approached the spot, he found a lady trying to extract an arrow from her breast. Someone called for a doctor, who removed it.

Then Morrell unsaddled his horse and set down the saddle for the woman to use as a pillow. Interestingly enough, a whalebone corset was responsible for saving her life; the stiff undergarment had prevented the arrow from doing much damage. It was the newly widowed Juliet Watts who had thus escaped death; after the looting of Linnville, she had been captured and strapped to the back of a Comanche mule.

Mrs. Watts rejoiced at her escape, sincerely believing the fate of captivity to be worse than death itself. Other captives were found nearby, their dead bodies bristling with arrows. Apparently, when the Texans charged, the Comanches had taken out their fury on their prisoners.

Later, as the Baptist preacher made his way home, he pondered the events of the long day. Weary and careworn, he wondered, *how long shall these things be?*

Out of Their Minds

Sam Houston sat in his seat in the Texas House of Representatives and looked at the chunk of soft pine in his hand. A horse head? An Indian? Briefly he pondered, then withdrew a pocketknife and commenced whittling.

There were children in Austin who were already favored with the products of Houston's restless hands and heart. While his colleagues held forth in oratory, Sam would whittle or write letters to his beloved Margaret, now residing with friends in Galveston, while he occupied his seat in the Fifth Congress of the Republic of Texas.

Houston was troubled, and he took it out on the wood, which was slowly taking shape. Just being separated from his beloved wife was a hardship in itself, but there was no way he could bring her to Austin. Even if her health were robust, the location of the new seat of government, poised on the very edge of the Indian frontier, was dangerous in the extreme.

The new settlement possessed fewer than one thousand inhabitants, and the buildings were crude, having been hastily constructed under the gaze of curious Indians who watched from nearby hills. Hopeful surveyors had laid out wide avenues, which during the rainy season became a muddy morass, so that just getting from one side of the street to the other became an adventure. Plus, the stinginess of Mr. Bullock, proprietor of Bullock's hotel, where Houston resided, caused his patrons some suffering during the cold winter nights. No, Maggie definitely could not come here.

The state of affairs in the infant Republic also weighed heavily on his heart. Even the trip here had been troubling, as the Hero of San Jacinto heard rumors of Indian raids and atrocities along the way. Lamar had sown war and reaped bloodshed; what else did he think his policies would produce?

And economically, the situation was wretched. Lamar's administration had responded to the money shortage by simply printing more. This was not so terrible in itself, but Lamar's ventures were putting a strain on the delicate young economy that had caused the value of the "redbacks," as they were called, to plunge precipitously. Trade was at a standstill, except for bootleg whiskey, which continued to enjoy a market but brought in no tax revenue.

From the beginning, even under Houston's own administration, Texas had spent money she did not have, and the government had become heavily burdened with debt. The great needs and expenses associated with the war and the establishment of the most basic government services—mail, courts—could not be fully met by the taxes, which were often difficult to collect. Texans did not like taxes. But now, under Lamar's rule, grandiose schemes were being proposed, which could not possibly be paid for, while the government payroll continued to grow.

And then there was Mexico, which had never recognized the independence of Texas. Recently, Texans had been disturbed by threats of invasion, and Houston had written his wife about the situation, explaining that, "Panic makers are to be found in every country. They now exist in Texas & are in full meridian and beaming splendor... You may rely upon this fact that you will never be disturbed by the approach of a Mexican force."[5]

But President Lamar thought differently, requesting Congress to declare war on Mexico. He wanted to send troops south, and while Texas legislators seemed amenable to this idea, Houston argued against it on the floor of the House. Texas needed peace!

He wrote to Margaret, "We are so poor as a nation that we can not procure stationary. How then can we invade a nation with mines and eight millions of souls?"[6]

When a vote was taken, Lamar's plan was defeated, but the insanity birthed by ambition, pride, and greed continued to erupt and trouble Houston, who doubted his own ability to fight it. Wood shavings dropped to the floor as he listened in frustration to the current session of the Texas House.

What was this? Houston's whittling slowed. Santa Fe? President Lamar had hatched a new proposal—an expedition to Santa Fe.

This was not a new idea. In fact, last year, Lamar had proposed sending an expedition to the west to secure Texas's claims to that region and open up trade. Technically, according to the Treaty of Velasco, which Mexico had not even ratified, a large region to the west of Austin belonged to Texas. Last year, good sense had prevailed, and Congress had refused to cooperate.

But this year... the same undercurrent of belligerent ambition that had fed Lamar's desire for war with Mexico now concocted a new and insane idea—to send an army across the west Texas plain. And Lamar, desperate to hold things together economically, was preaching that this project would be the salvation of Texas. If the duties charged by Mexico on the goods carried over the Santa Fe Trail could be diverted to the Texas treasury, the new Republic would be saved from insolvency!

President Lamar knew that some members of the House and Senate would fight his plan, most notably the big drunkard, Sam Houston. His flowery and often sarcastic speeches always swayed the opinions of many people.

Members of the public, including ladies, would crowd the hall when they knew Houston would be speaking and leave when he had finished. Lamar and his supporters, including his vice president, David G. Burnet, bitterly resented the influence of this man, but there was nothing they could do but deal with it.

So, Lamar decided to frame his plan in the best possible light to win over Houston's crowd. He described the expedition to Santa Fe as a "peace mission."

Sam Houston sat and listened to the details of this proposed "peace mission" as described to the Fifth Congress. He thought that "peace mission" was a disingenuous description of a movement of troops intended to subjugate territory occupied by another country.

With pine shavings clinging to his pants, Houston stood and spoke to his colleagues in the House. These gentlemen would be out of their minds to take this proposal seriously. An unsupported expedition, one thousand miles through wilderness, prairie, and mountains, would, in all likelihood, endanger the already shaky future of Texas.

The men listening to the General's speech were reluctantly convinced, and the measure was defeated. But that did not stop Lamar.

A Humble Revival

Zechariah Morrell marveled. Robert Emmett Bledsoe Baylor, former Congressman from Alabama and now judge in the Republic of Texas, possessed a spirit so like his master's that he had no problem associating and working with a "cane brake" preacher with limited education.

Both Morrell and Judge Baylor were part of a small group of Baptists who had come together to form an association; they represented a number of small churches dotting the Texas countryside.

As the population of Texas swelled with immigration from the United States, men of God came too, sent as missionaries or simply coming to settle as Morrell did. And so the little churches were provided with pastors and the association with officers.

Judge Baylor was elected president of the association, and Z. N. Morrell served on the board of managers. God had blessed amid scenes of struggle and toil, blood and tears, and small churches thrived under the care of godly and faithful men who preached the truth of the gospel in a land formerly dominated by priestcraft and ignorance.

Soon, the Lord was pleased to encourage His people by a special visitation. In the little town of New Washington, the members of the church pastored by Morrell had dispersed to other places, and Morrell ended up shepherding a flock in Gonzales.

But in 1841, another brother, William M. Tryon, a godly man and able expositor of the Scriptures, reorganized the church in New Washington. Judge Baylor was also in town, serving in his official capacity at court.

One Lord's Day, Brother Tryon was unable to preach because of family afflictions, which kept him at home. Elder Baylor preached in his stead, and the Spirit of the Lord attended His Word with unusual power. The brethren asked Baylor to continue preaching, and for two weeks the meetings continued, with the Lord giving the substitute preacher strength and wisdom.

A deep interest took hold of almost the entire population of the town, and a large number professed hope in Christ. Almost every night, the brethren followed the meeting with a baptismal service on the banks of the Brazos River.

> The baptismal scenes were of the most interesting and impressive character. The moon was shining on these occasions beautifully. The congregation marched in procession, singing the songs of Zion, from the place of worship to the river. The noise went abroad of the mighty displays of God's power to save, and also of the beauty and sublimity of the baptismal scenes, and from twenty-five miles people came, and were themselves baptized before they returned. Forty-two were baptized during that meeting, and some of them yet live, to bless the church with their influence and to tell of the power and willingness of God to save sinners in 1841.[7]

The Santa Fe Expedition Departs

George Wilkins Kendall of the New Orleans *Picayune* was ready. He watched the troops as they readied for departure from the fort here, some twenty miles north of Austin. General Hugh McLeod was the military commander of Lamar's Santa Fe Expedition, with several hundred volunteers filling the ranks.

None of them expected much resistance from the inhabitants of that community. After all, last night a letter from someone in Santa Fe had been circulated, explaining that most of the inhabitants would welcome the Texans and that the Mexican governor of the province would not resist, having not the means to do so even if he desired.

Kendall carefully recorded the departure of excited men, clad in new uniforms and mounted on fine horses. A number of merchants were also coming, their goods stashed in ox-drawn wagons. More wagons contained the expedition's supplies. The newspaperman also made note of the presence of an artillery piece, drawn by a team of mules. Interestingly, the cannon was inscribed with the name *Mirabeau Buonaparte Lamar* on the breech.

It was June 19, 1841. Kendall and another man, an attorney from Britain named Thomas Falconer, had received permission from President Lamar to accompany the expedition and record their discoveries along the way. As Kendall wrote, "...the country was a perfect *terra incognita*, untrodden save by wild and wandering Indians, and all were eager to partake of the excitement of being among the first to explore it."[8]

No one feared to take a 1,300-mile journey across the west Texas prairie under the hot summer sun. And no one knew that the Mexican guide was a spy.

Challenged to a Duel

Dr. Branch T. Archer stood at the door. Sam Houston received his caller, who seemed to be on a formal mission. And he was. Archer had come as the "second" of David G. Burnet, who was challenging Houston to a duel. A certain etiquette and formality surrounded the custom of dueling, which was still fairly common in the South and West.

Houston had exchanged shots in this manner only once, in his youth, and after wounding the other man, sincerely regretted it. Now he opposed the practice altogether.

But what message to give to Burnet? Houston's name had been proposed as the next president, an office for which he would again be eligible when Lamar's term expired. David Burnet was desirous of that same office and had begun a slanderous campaign against Houston, calling him a "half-Indian," which, in those days, would have been considered derogatory.

Texas politics was fought in the mud. Houston had responded by calling Burnet a "hog thief," and it was this appellation that had sent Archer on his Saturday evening call. The slightly rotund, five-foot-one Burnet was offended and challenged Houston to a duel the next morning.

The Hero of San Jacinto formulated a detailed excuse, mentioning that the next day was Sunday, and no good could come by fighting on that day. Then he stated that he never fought "down hill."

Archer went home and delivered this answer to Burnet, whose disposition had once been described as "snarlish as a half starved dog."[9] Not much of a sense of humor.

The campaign launched into full swing, with Burnet producing reams of slanderous attacks against Houston, aided by several newspapers that retained an anti-Houston view of the world. The Houston *Telegraph and Texas Register* referred to Houston as a drunkard, although it seemed to show compassion when in May it described him as "a noble wreck of humanity-great even in ruins."[10]

Houston did not turn the other cheek. He wrote publicly to Burnet. "Now, *about your honesty*. I could inform the public that you had made over all your property to your brother. ...by way of dafrauding just creditors out of their lawful demands against you. ... Is this honest?... You prate about the faults of other men, *While the blot of foul unmitigated treason rests upon you*."[11]

But Houston's heart was not in it. His heart was with Margaret, whose company he now enjoyed as they fixed up their little house at Cedar Point. The pocketknife that had seen service in Austin now came to his wife's aid, fashioning household items out of pine or cedar.

His health was returning, his complexion clearing due to his near abstinence from alcohol. He had not felt so good in years, and the "sweets of the fireside" now delighted his heart.

Even his candidacy for president was placed in his wife's hands. Before returning from Austin, Houston had written,

> "The affection and happiness of my endeared Margaret are more to me than all the Gewgaws of ambition or the pageantry of Royalty. Shou'd she desire me to do so [run for president], I will consent but not otherwise! My Love must decide and let her regard her own happiness. Mine will consist in Her felicity. The determination of my Love I will abide by. Thy people shall be my people and thy God shall be my God!"[12]

Apparently, Margaret saw the need Texas had for her hero. Other Texans were beginning to see it, too. With her currency only worth twenty cents on the dollar, Texas was falling apart. Houston's sensible strength was needed for such a time as this.

The Ill-Fated Expedition

Captain Damasio Salezar handed a bundle of papers, obtained from a vanguard of the Santa Fe expedition, to Governor Armijo, who had been expecting them. Spies had kept the governor informed, and he had sent Captain Salezar to watch for the approaching Texans.

Later described by Kendall as a veritable mountain of fat, the governor had been handsome once. Now this man, who had made his start in life by stealing sheep, gazed at the handbills before him. His eyes opened wide as he read President Lamar's invitation to the citizens of Santa Fe to join the Republic of Texas as "fellow citizens." The imperfect Spanish translation did not hinder Armijo from gleaning Lamar's purpose. The Texans were invaders come to wrest Santa Fe and the whole area from Mexican dominion.

The irate governor gave orders, and soon an army of one thousand men was ready to leave, with Armijo leading them himself, with a beautifully caparisoned mule supporting his weight. On the way, the governor met Captain Salezar, who, with a modest force, was bringing back a small party of captured Texans. Few of them could speak Spanish.

One man who could, a Captain Lewis, insisted that he and his men were American merchants who had lost their way. Armijo rejected this explanation, seizing Lewis by the collar. He pointed to a button on the man's dragoon jacket that was decorated with a single star and the word "Texas."

"What does this mean? I can read— Texas! You need not think to deceive *me*. No merchant from the United States ever travels in a Texas military jacket."[13]

The others were sent to prison, while the governor and his men sought the main body of Texans, dragging Lewis along as an interpreter.

Finding General McLeod's main force, Governor Armijo stared. These men were in no condition to fight; the large force of Mexican soldiers with him was clearly unnecessary.

After traveling under the hot summer sun and becoming lost several times due to the misdirection of the Mexican spy, these men had been reduced to scavenging lizards for food. They were half-starved and weak; many had jettisoned their arms as too much of a burden to carry. Several small groups, like the one Lewis came from, had been sent ahead to procure food, but the Mexicans had captured them all.

Lewis translated the governor's words to the discouraged men. If they surrendered without resistance, they would be permitted to return to Texas or the United States. When the weary Texans had surrendered their weapons, Armijo's men tied the men together with lariats and marched them into the plaza of Santa Fe.

There, General McLeod was stripped of his uniform, now a prized souvenir claimed by Governor Armijo. Soon McLeod stood shivering, dressed in ragged clothing that some resident of Santa Fe had cast off, in favor of new garments procured from the merchants' wagons.

The goods that had survived the haul across the west Texas prairie were now in the hands of the citizens of the town. That night, the volunteers shivered in the cold, at that high elevation, with their once fine uniforms reduced to rags by the ill-fated trek.

What would happen to them now? The forlorn Texans expected execution. But instead, they were rounded up and taken south. Captain Salezar had received orders from Armijo to take the prisoners two thousand miles to the capital, Mexico City, and he obeyed, except in the matter of keeping them tied together. Salezar had his own cruel method of control: to keep his prisoners so weary that they could not even try to escape.

He fed them just enough to keep them alive. Well, most of them. A few died, and then one man, John McAllister, whose ankles had become inflamed and swollen, declared that he was unable to go on.

"Forward, or I'll shoot you on the spot," declared Salezar.

"Then shoot!" replied the suffering McAllister, "and the quicker the better!"

The newspaperman from the New Orleans *Picayune*, George Kendall, recorded what happened next. A single shot accomplished Salezar's purpose, then the officer followed Armijo's macabre procedure for accounting: McAllister's ears were cut off. Also, "... his shirt and his pantaloons were stripped from him, and his body thrown by the roadside as food for wolves."[14]

After two days of walking through the desert, without an overnight stop, an experience later labeled the Dead Man's March, the ragged Texans came upon the Rio Grande, which they forded, the cold water reaching their chins.

Thin and ragged as scarecrows, the appearance of the prisoners shocked the citizens of El Paso. The Mexican women poured out their hospitality upon the starving men, feeding them meat, eggs, and tortillas, as much as they could eat. The men were allowed to bathe and sleep, and generous citizens gave them money for clothes.

But this wonderful paradise was only a temporary refuge, and after three days, the Texans resumed their march to Mexico City. But they would always remember the kindness of the people of El Paso.

Houston's Election

The Republic of Texas sported an interesting mix of inhabitants, including adventurers and lawyers, who had sniffed out the possibilities of quick advancement in the infant nation. There were also many responsible small farmers who were too busy settling a frontier to write letters to the editor. And on the warm, wet alluvial soils of east and southeast Texas, well-to-do men planted cotton and managed Negro slaves, an extension of the Southern traditional lifestyle.

Not surprisingly, these planters and farmers tended to be more conservative and responsible than the adventurers who came merely for the excitement.

Sam Houston was a pragmatic man who realized that the most important issue in Texas was planting corn. He believed that the industry of the people themselves would lift the Republic out of its worst problems. In agreement with Houston's ideas, the planters and farmers stirred themselves, and when the election of September 6, 1841, took place, they elected Houston president by an overwhelming majority—7,508 votes versus 2,574 for Burnet.

Leaving Margaret in Houston with her mother, the new president journeyed to

Austin. Before leaving the old capital, Houston had spoken to a large crowd, preaching economy: "Instead of millions thrown away on swarms of useless loafers... we shall find the expenses of government reduced to three hundred thousand dollars per annum instead of three millions."[15]

On a cold and windy day, December 13th, Houston was inaugurated president. He dressed that morning in a linsey-woolsey hunting shirt, an old pair of pantaloons, and an old, wide-brimmed fur hat. Underneath a canopy behind the Capitol, he spoke to the people about industry and economy, his modest clothing serving as a kind of visual aid.

At first, Congress seemed amenable to Houston's direction. They cheerfully cut their own salaries and then sliced their president's in half, and shortly, followed their leader's suggestion to cut taxes. But unfortunately, they reduced taxes so low that they were not even worth the expense of collection. The unruly Congress tended to legislate in great leaps and bounds, like an untrained horse given oats.

Then the real debate ensued. Houston was surely not the only one who wished to move the capital of Texas to some safer spot, away from the threat of Indian depredations. But the citizens of Austin, who had benefited financially from the presence of the government, stubbornly resisted the move, and over time, the issue became quite controversial.

Throughout the winter, Houston wrote warm letters to his wife, speaking of his love for her and how much he looked forward to the day Congress adjourned so that he might return to her. Margaret was highly esteemed in the republic's capital, even though absent. Everyone could see the improved health and sober habits of their president and correctly attributed his "reform" to their marriage.

A Pig Disturbs International Relations

What was the matter now? French Chargé d'Affaires Saligny stared at his filthy groomsman. The story was told him: a troop of vagrant hogs had partaken freely of the grain fed to the French delegation's horses.

The groom couldn't take it anymore. Grabbing a pitchfork, he lunged for the nearest pig, impaled it, and threw it over the fence. The disturbance came to the ears of the landlord, who assailed the groom. How dare he kill the pig?

Saligny marched to the landlord. He would have satisfaction! Favoring filthy hogs over his fine, blooded horses! *Incroyable!*

But as his complaint circulated around the frontier town of Austin, it soon became apparent that satisfaction would *not* be forthcoming. Too bad. Texas wanted a loan? Well, a lien against all of Texas's public lands was attractive, but maybe not all that necessary. Time to go home.

Noah Smithwick wryly recorded:

> Thus the amicable relations between the sister republics were disturbed, and a great international treaty which we had sent envoys across the ocean to secure, was frustrated by so insignificant a creature as a pig. What M. de Saligny intended as an injury, proved a fortunate deliverance for Texas. We were poor, but still freemen.[16]

Troubling News in Gonzales

James Morrell, at age seventeen, presented himself as a candidate for baptism, having professed his faith in Christ. The little assembly in Gonzales, pastored by Z. N. Morrell, rejoiced at the news and planned a baptismal service for the next day, which would be the first Sunday in March, 1842.

But late Saturday evening, a messenger galloped into Gonzales. A Mexican force had just invaded Texas! About a thousand strong, the enemy had approached San Antonio and demanded surrender. The Texans there had evacuated and fled up the Guadalupe, sending messengers to alert the citizens.

Zechariah Morrell conferred with the other men. What should they do? The consensus was to send the families of Gonzales east, out of harm's way. The baptismal service was postponed, and when the sun rose on Sunday morning, the Baptist preacher's little blacksmith shop was soon surrounded by wagons that needed repairs. Morrell repaired wagon wheel after wagon wheel, and still they kept coming. Finally, that evening, the residents of the little town and its environs were ready to pack.

The next morning, animals were collected, and the people departed for the Colorado River to the east. The bleating and lowing of the stock reminded Morrell of the biblical patriarchs who moved from place to place.

Texas was certainly a land of promise, but it would not be taken easily, nor held without determination. Despite the Hero of San Jacinto now at the helm, "Scenes of blood must yet be passed over before we could in peace worship beneath our vine and fig-tree."[17] So recorded Z. N. Morrell, at the time never guessing what grief would soon be his.

Struggling to Hold the Reins

When news of the treatment of the Texans captured by Governor Armijo had first reached Texas and the United States, the cruel treatment of the prisoners overshadowed the stupidity of the undertaking.

The New Orleans *Picayune*, whose editor had joined the expedition, declared, "...our country is too proud of its glorious birthright and the rank it holds within the pale of nations, to submit, at this year of its history, to insult and injustice."[18]

President Houston tried to go through diplomatic channels to intercede for the captives. Even though he had not supported the venture, and Congress had rejected Lamar's proposal, Houston argued that the Texans had surrendered on promises of safety and liberation; they were entitled to honorable treatment.

Dealing with Santa Anna was one thing, but the Texas Congress was something else. In fact, Houston had stayed up all one night, trying to figure out how to respond to the rage of Congress, which had resulted in a sweeping legislative takeover of all of New Mexico, Chihuahua, Sonora, Upper and Lower California, and parts of four other Mexican states. The bill claiming this territory for Texas authorized war to accomplish this annexation.

This was ridiculous. For one thing, an invasion would cost tons of money, and at present, the government was barely functioning for want of funds. With these facts in mind, Houston vetoed the bill, reminding Congress that the area they were proposing to annex consisted of two-thirds of the Republic of Mexico, inhabited by at least two million people. Surely other nations would regard this measure as a "legislative jest."[19]

Congress passed the bill over Houston's veto just before they adjourned, without making specific provisions for how such a war would be financed or carried out.

Houston rode home to Margaret, this time on a chestnut-colored mule named Bruin. As the dependable animal slogged its way through mud or picked its way over rough ground, the president pondered his situation.

Demands for war echoed around him from every direction. One letter from a group of citizens pleaded with Houston to respond to the will of the people and use his "discretion" to make war on Mexico. He had responded that his duties were "defined by the Constitution..."[20] and that "No calamity has ever befallen Texas, from the commencement of the Revolution up to the capture of the Santa Fe Expedition, but what has been caused by a disregard of law and substituting in its place a "wide discretion."[21]

It was also a bad idea from a military standpoint. Invading a country required much more effort and resources than simply defending one. Texas needed peace to gather her strength and to prosper.

> The true interest of Texas is to maintain peace with all nations and to cultivate her soil... if she should be invaded, the husbandman could be easily converted into the soldier. Then the flag of Texas would be displayed only in defence of her own soil and liberty...[22]

But Houston's emphasis on the rule of law and common sense seemed to fall on deaf ears. Mexico retaliated with a quick "hit and run" strike, advancing as far north as San Antonio and retreating after capturing one hundred men. Could this be the start of a serious invasion? Because the president had no way to tell, he sent orders to General Somerville.

Volunteers poured in from the United States, ill-equipped, and causing more hindrance than help. Insubordination caused problems, and Texas was in chaos.

Threats to Houston's Life

The sweet notes of a piano spilled out into the humid evening air. Houston City had shut down for the day, and Houston the man had likewise retired to his home, newly constructed and newly inhabited by his wife, Margaret. Hoping to regain her health, she had spent a couple of months in Alabama with family, and now she had returned, to the delight of her husband.

Her piano had been transported to Houston, and now the wife of the President of the Republic of Texas filled her home with joyful sound. But all was not joyful.

Houston's life had been threatened.

A special session of Congress had been called here in Houston City, and grumbling over the tacit move of the capital, the legislators came and legislated.

On a miserably hot and sweaty day in July 1842, these men passed a bill declaring war against Mexico. The president was granted sweeping powers with which to make war, and popular opinion raged everywhere that he do so. Texans had not yet forgotten the chopped-off ears, the bodies thrown to the wolves, and the other atrocities committed by Salezar.

But Sam Houston refused. After dark groups of angry men marched past his house, friends of the president entreated him to post guards, but he and his wife continued to act as if all were well, while Margaret's piano music wafted through the open windows of their home.

In his veto message, Houston tried to communicate the enormity and huge cost of the undertaking, especially with the way things were in Texas. He wrote to Congress, "The Executive has indeed a show of power but he is helpless and destitute for want of means."[23]

Then the president discussed the powers granted to him by the bill:

> "If it would be wrong to clothe an individual with powers, who might, by their exercise, bring ruin upon his country; it is equally at war with principle that a man should exercise powers improperly granted, though it were intended for the salvation of his country."[24]

Because Houston stood against the tide of passion, holding tightly to the rule of law and his own common sense, he lost friends. George Hockley went so far as to resign from his post as Secretary of War and Marine. But slowly the tide subsided, and the citizens of the Republic of Texas began to realize that they had been narrowly saved from folly.

Andrew Jackson had been following matters from the Hermitage, and in a shaky hand, the old patriarch wrote Houston, approving his stand. "By your veto you have saved your country and yourself from disgrace."[25]

A Message for Morrell

It was a warm September day. Zechariah Morrell regarded his wagon full of corn. Finished. He and his son, Allen, had finished harvesting their corn crop near the Guadalupe River. The settlers in the Gonzales area had still not returned to their homes, but many of the fields were still tended, their owners making the trek to work them.

Morrell and his son would now haul their wagonload of corn back east to the Colorado River. They got ready to go and were just starting out when someone rode up.

It was Matthew Caldwell, who showed Morrell a message:

> "Colonel: General Woll has arrived at San Antonio with thirteen hundred men. The court, -- judge, jury, lawyers, -- and many citizens in attendance, are prisoners in the hands of the Mexicans, I made my escape, and came round under the mountains to Seguin.
>
> John W. Smith."[26]

Colonel Caldwell said, "Something must be done quick, and you must go with me."[27]

The preacher made excuses. My health is not good, and I'm a cripple. The horse I am riding is borrowed, and it's wild and untrained.

But Caldwell pressed him, explaining that he would be of great service in controlling the young men who would be with him. He appealed to his patriotism.

Allen Morrell, a capable youth, was sent home alone with the wagonload of corn.

A Battle with Sad Results

Houston's fears had been realized: more troops had poured over the Rio Grande and invaded San Antonio. Mexican General Woll commanded more than a thousand men, and the volunteers who had gathered to resist him only numbered about two hundred at first, but their leaders were determined.

Captain Jack Hays, who'd been elected their commander, sat on a dark bay horse in front of his men. The flash of his dark eyes spoke purpose as he addressed the men. And as the Mexicans approached, several other men spoke encouragement as well.

Morrell and the other men listened as Matthew Caldwell declared that he would never surrender to General Woll. He had just returned from the Santa Fe expedition and urged the others to fight to the death. He then asked Zechariah Morrell to address the men, who encouraged them, saying,

> "Gentlemen -- We are now going into battle against fearful odds—eight to one—and with artillery all on the enemy's side. The artillery can't harm us under this bank. We have nothing to fear as long as we can prevent them from coming to a hand-to-hand fight. Keep cool; let us not shoot as they advance on us till we can see the whites of their eyes; and be sure to shoot every man that has an officer's hat or sword. This will prevent them from coming into close quarters. Let us shoot low, and my impression before God is, that we shall win this fight."[28]

Just as he finished those remarks, the Mexican artillery fired. Grape shot rattled through the tops of the trees. The Mexicans advanced, their ornaments, guns, and spears glistening, while music accompanied them. Captain Jack Hays directed some men to head off a flanking movement of the enemy; the rest of the men waited until the Mexican *soldados* were very near, finally letting loose with a salvo.

All of the approaching infantrymen fell to the ground, though some, as it turned out, were merely wounded.

Unable to use his artillery against the sheltered Texans, whose position under the brow of a hill protected them, and suffering the loss of his men, General Woll sounded the horn for retreat. The Texans did not pursue.

Then, firing could be heard from the other side of the retreating Mexican army. The Texans realized that reinforcements had come, but before they could go to the relief of the other group, the firing stopped.

Captain Dawson had received Colonel Caldwell's dispatch and had raised a company of fifty-two men, who acquitted themselves well with their firearms against Woll's men. But in this case, the Texans were in range of the Mexicans' artillery, and after the Mexican soldiers withdrew from rifle range, cannon fire rained down on the volunteers.

Unable to escape and realizing that no good could come of their situation, Captain Dawson raised a white flag. The Mexicans continued to fire upon the little group as if oblivious to their surrender. Dawson died with the white flag in his hand. Only fifteen of the group survived, and they were soon taken as prisoners.

General Woll's army went back to San Antonio, and the Texans camped where they were. Then someone informed Morrell that his son Allen had been part of Dawson's crew. For the anxious father, the night was very dark. Was Allen dead? Was he a prisoner in the hands of their cruel oppressors?

Before daylight, three men volunteered to go with Morrell to the grove of mesquites where Dawson had made his stand. By sunrise, the stricken father had arrived at his destination.

Bodies lay strewn everywhere, some horribly mangled by grapeshot, a few past any recognition. Morrell stared at the corpses. Heads of families, promising sons of neighbors; nearly every man was familiar to the Baptist preacher.

But he did not see Allen. Some bodies had to be turned over before they could be identified. A few could not be identified at all, and these Morrell examined, looking at their feet. Allen had a scar on his foot. No, none of these men was his son.

Looking up, Morrell saw that only one man remained with him. The other two had left, not able to bear the gruesome scene. Well, Allen was not here. The preacher drew a pencil from his pocket and proceeded to list the names of those before him. Someone would have to tell the families.

The Texans pursued Woll as his army moved south. They were determined to rescue the prisoners, and when they came upon the rear of the Mexican army, Captain Jack Hays decided to charge the cannon that was planted in the road in defense of the retreating army. Caldwell asked Morrell to speak to the men to raise volunteers for this dangerous assault.

Morrell galloped to the lower end of the line, his old fur cap in his hand, recognizing almost every man he passed. The men knew that his son was among the captives, just up on the next hill. An indescribable pathos gripped their hearts. Waving his cap, Morrell addressed the men, trying to convince them that the task was possible. "Besides, the prisoners—"

"Come, boys, we will go with him." Voices swelled and rose, and volunteers gathered, Henry McCulloch serving as captain. Once in position, they awaited the command, and finally the shrill, clear voice of McCulloch pierced the air: "Charge!"[29]

The Mexicans fired the cannon, but the deadly shot went over the Texans' heads. The Texan yell had unsettled the artillerymen, and they were unable to get off an accurate shot before the distance to the cannon was closed. In minutes, every artilleryman was dead. The assault was a resounding success.

But the main attack was postponed until morning, when General Mayfield made a speech to the men. He told them that they were outnumbered in the enemy's territory and that General Woll was expecting a large reinforcement. Mayfield was obviously trying to discourage the attempt, and listening, Morrell became incensed.

The Baptist preacher interrupted the general. Despite Mayfield's rank, he had no command, and so Morrell considered them equal soldiers.

He spoke with passion. "The time has passed for long speeches. I for one would prefer to hasten to the fight and recapture the prisoners."[30]

Morrell pointed to the baggage wagons and cannon they had captured the evening before. It was possible! But despite the encouragement of Morrell, Colonel Caldwell, Captain Hays, and a number of men became discouraged. Needing all their numbers to even think of attacking such a foe, the Texans finally withdrew.

As they broke up into small companies and left for home, Morrell dreaded the unenviable duty of informing his neighbors of the loss of husbands and sons. At one point on the ride home, General Mayfield approached Morrell in a friendly manner.

But the grieving pastor was too stricken to be kind to the man he saw as an enemy. He laid both hands on his gun and told the man not to speak another word.

Morrell had vowed to "spend and be spent" for Texas, but the price had suddenly become very high.

Chapter 13

One Last Battle

CAPTAIN CHARLES ELLIOTT was satisfied with his new position as British chargé d'affaires to the Republic of Texas. True, Texas was not the world center of culture and civilization, but the conscientious British officer had offended certain commercial interests in the opium trade during the Chinese "Opium War." Being transferred to the diplomatic service solved the problem in a manner that did not displease him. In fact, this able and intelligent man soon formed a keen interest in the new republic and its current president, Sam Houston.

At first, Elliott served as the British "commercial agent," a position established when Britain signed a trade treaty with Texas. But during the summer of 1841, Great Britain officially recognized Texas as a sovereign nation, and Elliott was appointed chargé d'affaires, a diplomatic position just below the status of ambassador.

In a report to his government, Captain Elliott described Sam Houston. In his younger days, the path of this young man had been stormy, but recently, he had made "a new connextion with a young and gentle woman brought up in the fear of God." In Elliott's opinion, Houston had "conquered" her "no doubt... by a glowing tongue..." And his new wife "in good revenge [made] conquest of his habits of tremendous cursing, and passionate love of drink."[1]

Then, in November of 1842, Elliott wrote a wry description to a friend, the Undersecretary of Foreign Affairs in London.

> ...the President has convened Congress to assemble at Washington on the Brazos, where there are 12 or 13 wooden shanties...
>
> The President writes to me in a private Note a few days since, that He finds things at Washington rather raw and as He has been accustomed to the elaborate comforts of an Indian wigwam, I presume he must be living in a commodious excavation.[2]

Now Elliott prepared to visit Houston at the new capital. The "cradle of independence," where the Texas Declaration of Independence had been signed, Washington-on-the-Brazos, was about one hundred miles east of Austin, and by some accounts, "24 hours from nowhere." The British official would soon see for himself what kind of "commodious excavation" the president and his wife inhabited.

The Need for Forgiveness

How do I obtain forgiveness of sins? And how do I bring my heart into total submission to Christ? Between the mounting pressures of the presidency, the clamoring of favor-seekers, and the more prosaic problems of life, such as finding comfortable shoes to wear, Sam Houston felt the need of his soul.

The footwear question was more easily settled. A pair of russet shoes, casually worn without strings, accommodated his high instep and did not irritate the old San Jacinto ankle wound, which still troubled him a little. And these shoes readily matched Houston's casual attire, usually consisting of a linsey-woolsey hunting shirt and cotton pantaloons.

But how to find peace with God? Earlier in the year, Houston had expressed himself to his wife in a letter:

> Dearest, I do feel as tho' I would not, could not survive unless I have some hope in the atonement of the son of God. I am assured that tho' I admit the awful realities of eternal life and eternal death, yet I do not realise that confident & abiding hope that I will be accepted of my God & thru His death be happy hereafter! One consolation to me is my Beloved, that I am communing with a being on earth who will not ridicule my expressions or withhold the kind sympathies of a Christian believer in Christ Jesus! I will try and meditate upon His Holy and Divine character, His boundless and almighty love for mortals, His wise and sacred precepts. Yes, the soothing influence of his mild and holy spotless example!
>
> Dearest, I would be truly happy on earth while in possession of your Love, and confidence if I could only feel assured that I possessed the favor of my God into

> everlasting life! I will seek the redemption promised in the Holy Scriptures... I know Dearest that I have your prayers daily and Hourly and to them I will add and renew mine. But every hope is vain unless Jesus will interpose in my behalf![3]

Houston's intemperance in drink and conduct had been curbed by Margaret's gentle influence. He sought to walk as a Christian, but he did not believe that he possessed that "evangelical change of heart,"[4] which was characteristic of every child of God. How could he be forgiven? Somehow, his heart could not grasp the answer.

Fisher's Plans

A cool breeze ruffled the feather in William Fisher's hat. Houston's former secretary of war balanced himself easily on the flatboat as it crossed the swollen Rio Grande. Fisher and another man, Thomas Jefferson Green, had gathered up about three hundred sixty men and were headed south into Mexico.

What a loser. That's what Fisher thought of his commanding officer, General Somerville, who was, at that moment, leading the rest of the army north to Gonzales, planning to disband the group.

The flatboat bumped a bit as it nosed along the south bank of the rain-swollen river. Fisher and others aboard jumped onto the shore. His other men likewise crossed on flatboat or horseback, and soon they were making camp.

That chilly December evening, Captain Fisher had made plans. He was an "adventurer," true, but because he was also experienced in military matters, he decided to send a patrol to scout the Mexican town of Mier, just seven miles south.

It was a day of beginnings—that much was certain in this unstable region that drained into the Rio Grande. But Houston had proved to be wimpy. True, the current president of the Republic of Texas had sent General Somerville to the Rio Grande, but not to do anything. And now Somerville had retreated—gone home to mama. How could this have happened? Texans languished in Mexican prisons; Mexican troops crossed the Rio Grande at will. Sure, Texas had no money, but the spoils of war were there for the taking.

A year before, Fisher had written a letter to Felix Huston, pouring out his discontent and outlining the military situation. He described a personal plan to "Command the valley of the Rio Grande... and strike... whenever the opportunity presents... I will receive no Commission or authority from the Government of Texas and will be governed alone by the fixed principle of... rewarding those who serve under me with the riches of the land and the fatness Thereof—and in conclusion will have a potential voice in the disposition of the Conquered Country—"[5]

Adventure. Spoils. Influence. These were Fisher's goals.

Houston meets with Elliott

The Texans in Mexican prisons. Annexation to the United States. These were the two main problems of state that presented themselves to Sam Houston's consciousness again and again: intricately difficult, seemingly insoluble problems. How could he obtain the release of those men now suffering in Mexico City? And though the present political situation argued against the possibility, the president of the new republic knew that Texas must join herself to the United States.

President Houston stepped outside his one-room, newly constructed office, when he learned that a newcomer had made an appearance in town. It was Captain Charles Elliott, the British chargé d'affaires, of whom Houston was rather fond. He approached the visitor.

Captain Elliott looked about him. Washington-on-the-Brazos must have grown, for "12 or 13 shanties" was truly an inadequate description. Indeed, perhaps there were twelve or thirteen saloons and gambling establishments! "Raw" was certainly a valid adjective, but there were several hundred inhabitants settled here, at least.

Houston greeted the British consul and conducted him to his home, which was actually just a spare room in the home of Judge and Mrs. Lockhart. A door had been cut to the outside to give the Houstons the ability to come and go with privacy.

Captain Elliott enjoyed the company of Sam and Margaret Houston before the fireplace of their little apartment. But despite the Houstons' hospitality, Elliott was not impressed with the little town, which he thought much too primitive.

He later related his impression of President Houston to the British Foreign Office.

> Whatever General Houston has been, it is plain that He is the fittest man in this Country for his present station. His education has been imperfect, but he possesses great sagacity and penetration, surprising tact in his management of men trained as men are in these parts, is perfectly pure handed and moved in the main by the inspiring motive of desiring to connect his name with a Nation's rise.[6]

Sam Houston liked Charles Elliott and counted him for a friend. But the captain also represented his government, the government of Great Britain, mistress of a world empire. Houston had difficult problems of state, yet there were great possibilities here. He turned all these things over in his mind.

And now there was one more thing to consider: his wife's condition. Houston wrote up a list of needed supplies for the Texas consul in New Orleans to ship to them. Guitar strings for Margaret, calico, handkerchiefs, socks, "4 Bolts of linen Diaper."

He looked over the list again. He made one small change. "4 Bolts of linen Diaper for towels."[7] There. That seemed a little more discreet.

An Injured Thumb

At first, William Fisher did not know what had happened. Initially, there was a shock, then a horrible burning pain rode up his arm. Morning light was filtering through the clouds to illuminate the housetops of Mier, where Fisher and his men were fighting *soldados* led by General Ampudia. Fisher looked down at his wound. The bullet had split his thumb from the tip all the way to the base. Overwhelmed by the pain and the sight of the wound, Fisher threw up. Thomas Green was going to have to take command.

Things deteriorated from then on. At first, the town of Mier had seemed like an easy target. The mayor had acquiesced to the Texans' demand for supplies, a huge order of clothing and foodstuffs that the local population struggled to gather. But no one had considered that the supplies would need to be transported. The Texans had no wagons, and wagons would be necessary to handle the mountain of shoes, blankets, flour, coffee, and other items that the townspeople had donated.

It was then that a Mexican force of over seven hundred men arrived under Generals Ampudia and Canales. They captured the mound of supplies as well as the handful of men guarding it.

The rest of the Texans were camped a short distance away, on the other side of Alcantro Creek. After making the decision to attack, Fisher led his men through the icy water of the creek and on into town. Although the Texans were outnumbered, they fought well and seemed to be winning. Then Fisher was wounded.

Then they saw a man approaching. *Who is that?*

It turned out to be Dr. Sinnickton, one of the Texans who captured with the mass of supplies. As they watched, he slowly approached the Texan position, carrying a white flag. This was great! Undoubtedly, the Mexicans were appealing for mercy.

But no. The doctor carried a different sort of message. General Ampudia was demanding that the Texans surrender! Surrender or die! The promise was made that if the Texans surrendered, they would not be sent to Mexico City but would be kept "on the frontier until an exchange or pacification could be effected."[8]

Thomas Green wanted to continue fighting, but Fisher, now in excruciating pain from his wound, no longer had the heart to fight. Assured by Fisher, who knew Ampudia, that the Mexican general was an honorable man, the men decided to surrender. They stacked their arms in the plaza of Mier.

Now prisoners, the Texans learned from their comrades captured previously that the demand to surrender had been a desperate act of dissimulation by the Mexicans. Their officers had saddled horses with which to make their escape should the ploy not work, but it was too late now for the Texans to change their minds.

William Fisher must have felt great bitterness of heart as he watched his men being tied together with lariats. General Ampudia, whose character he had vouchsafed to his men, had already broken his promise. They were going to be marched to Mexico City.

Decimated

Captain Ewing Cameron opened his eyes. It was early; darkness still reigned over Haciendo Salado. Fisher's men had marched one hundred miles past Saltillo on their forced march south, arriving at this place the day before. It was time.

Cameron's small group of conspirators prepared themselves. As light spilled into the pale sky from the east, these Texans attacked the Mexican guard, and seizing horses and weapons, made their escape.

But except for a few who made it back to Texas, Cameron's men were soon recaptured and marched back to Haciendo Salado. But not tied with lariats; instead, they were chained in pairs by the wrists. Rejoining the rest of Fisher's men, they soon learned the awful truth: Santa Anna had instructed General Canales to execute one in ten of the Texas prisoners.

The choice of who should die was made by lot. There were 159 prisoners, so a corresponding number of beans was placed in a pot; most were white, but 17 were black. Those who drew a black bean would be executed. Canales wanted to get rid of the leaders, and by putting the black beans on top and making the officers draw first, he hoped to achieve that end.

Cameron protested. Kill me instead! He offered his life for the others, but his request was denied.

One by one, the officers approached the pot. They each reached deep into the pot, and all obtained a white bean. Canales must have been disappointed.

Then the other Texans took their turns. Some came up with black beans. When the drawing was complete, the doomed Texans were led to an adjoining courtyard. The Mexican soldiers shot them, using as many as fifteen bullets to kill each man, and the slaughter affected at least one of Canales' own men, who fainted.

The next morning, the surviving Texans were made ready to resume their march to Mexico City. They were led out past the gruesome spectacle of their comrades' mangled bodies.

They were told that anyone who tried to escape would be shot. Thus threatened, the Texans marched to Mexico City to be imprisoned in the gloomy prison of Perote.

A Letter to Elliott

Sam Houston sat at his desk in his office and looked at the flaming red Turkish robe hanging from a piece of oak branch he had whittled into a hanger. The Sultan of Turkey had sent the President of Texas an ensemble of Turkish clothes, including this robe, baggy pantaloons that tapered down to a soft pair of leather shoes, and a cylindrical fez, which Houston perched on his head and modeled for his wife.

Margaret had thought it funny, and the tasseled hat was quickly put aside. Houston gave expression to his poetic nature in the clothes he wore, but he did not want to look *ridiculous*. He did not even try on the baggy pants. But the red silk robe had caught his fancy. It was something to wear around the office.

But he did not feel like wearing it now. Reports had filtered in about a renegade group of Texans under William Fisher that had fought the Mexicans at Mier and been captured. When Houston had sent Somerville south to patrol the Rio Grande, largely to calm public demand for action, he had feared that such a thing might happen.

Unfortunately, the population of Texas was infested with irresponsible adventurers—lawless men—and glory-seekers like Fisher. Houston remembered Somerville's face as he had stood before him in this very room, not long ago. The general's disgust with the whole affair had prompted him to resign his commission. But truly, the man had done his duty and was not to blame. Houston was able to find him a position collecting customs.

And that was not all. To the east, in Shelby County, lawlessness reigned. Two warring factions, the "Regulators" and the "Moderators," were each supposedly trying to prevent crime, but were burning down houses and killing people in the process. It had all started when one man killed his political opponent. The entire area divided itself into friends of one man or the other, and the judge presiding over the murder trial fled. The rule of law disintegrated, and Houston watched helplessly, knowing that he did not have a large enough military force to bring order to the area.

Annexation to the United States was the solution in Houston's mind. If the strength of the whole Union stood behind the government of Texas, this lawlessness could be dealt with. But politicians in Washington, D.C., argued that Texas should not be annexed because of its lawless elements.

The fact that these ruffians had emigrated from the U.S. was forgotten. Then there was the slavery question, which ebbed and flowed across the American political scene. It all seemed so impossible—except...

Houston gathered together his writing materials. He had two problems: the prisoners in Mexico City and annexation. He wrote a letter to Captain Charles Elliott. The mighty British Empire might use her influence on behalf of her Anglo-Saxon cousins... and if so, how might the U.S. view such a development?

Like a she-tiger jealously guarding her territory, the young United States had already staked out her claim to the North American continent, declaring through the "Monroe Doctrine" that the time for new European colonization was past. The appearance of a close alliance between Texas and Great Britain would excite the fears of many in Washington...

A Messenger

James Robinson arrived in Washington-on-the-Brazos, seeking President Houston. The hungry, flea-bitten man had brought a letter from Santa Anna. Desperate to escape the wretched conditions of the prison of Perote, Robinson had written a letter to the Mexican dictator shrewdly suggesting that Texas might be open to reconciliation with Mexico.

Santa Anna's interest was piqued, and he sent Robinson to Texas with a proposal. He would return all prisoners and grant amnesty for the past acts of the Texas government in return for the acknowledgement by Texas of the absolute sovereignty of Mexico.

Houston received the dark-eyed Robinson, now thin from his sufferings. He opened and read Santa Anna's missive.

Robinson watched Houston's face. First, indignation, then astonishment, stole over the president's face. Finally, Robinson noticed Houston's features relax and his mouth curve into a smile.

Santa Anna was only clutching at straws, but Houston had an idea, which he explained to Robinson.

The Trick

Santa Anna pondered the letter he had received from James Robinson. Truly, it was of doubtful veracity—did he detect the craftiness of that backwoods drunkard, Sam Houston, in the composition of this report?

Robinson had stated that most Texans were diligently working their farms, some with their thoughts turned toward the possible invasion of Mexico. Apparently, Texas was not so torn by faction as might be perceived, since many of the handful of troublemakers had newspapers at their disposal. And the number of men who might be assembled for an invasion of Mexico amounted to about ten thousand, plus another forty thousand from across the Sabine.

Robinson had concluded, "I will not be so presumptuous as to advise your excellency about anything; but... I feel bound to inform you as such facts as result from my observation."[9]

Santa Anna knew that the population of Texas had grown since 1836, when he had suffered a humiliating defeat at the hands of this Houston. But an army of ten thousand? Perhaps the Mexican dictator suspected the truth: that Robinson had simply copied a carefully crafted composition of Houston's. But how much was exaggeration?

It was time to meet with the British minister, Richard Pakenham. The consul was ushered into the room, with each man choosing his words carefully. This was interesting. Pakenham as mediator? For the purpose of negotiating an armistice between Mexico and Texas? Santa Anna listened. There were, after all, some good reasons to stay on the good side of Great Britain...

Two Joyful Events

Houston swept about his desk, cutting a bright figure in the sultan's red robe. He needed to respond to Charles Elliott's recent letter.

The British chargé d'affaires had written to congratulate Houston on two events: a successfully negotiated armistice with Mexico and the birth of his first son, Sam, Jr., who had entered the world on May 25, 1843. The fifty-year-old president, his hair receding and shot through with gray, was a father for the first time.

And the surviving prisoners would eventually be coming home, including a young man by the last name of Morrell, whose arrival in Texas would cause his father great and inexpressible joy.

Houston took up his pen. He wrote that the value of peace with Mexico was "greatly enhanced" by having a son. "A son of mine without a country would cut but a shabby figure and indeed, his father would have toiled in vain."[10]

Publicly, Houston gave credit to Great Britain for arranging the armistice. He neglected to mention his own contributions. He was still playing the game, as his problems of state were not solved yet.

Jackson's Last Days

Andrew Jackson dipped his pen in the inkwell and commenced.

"Hermitage, June 7, 1843."

"In the name of God Amen, I Andrew Jackson Senr. being of Sound mind memory and understanding, and impressed with the great uncertainty of life and certainty of death..."[11]

He continued writing. Since leaving Washington, debts had plagued him. These must be settled first; then most of whatever was left would go to his adopted son, Andrew Jackson Junior. Finally, his last will and testament was complete.

Jackson sat back in the chair in which he spent his time. His body had no strength, and it seemed to some that it was merely the strength of his spirit that now kept him alive. The Hermitage was falling into grave disrepair. Financially, Jackson was not prospering, and his situation was not improved by the help he had given his son, who was a poor money manager.

The shadows were growing very long, but the silver-maned statesman was not discouraged. Upon the writing desk in front of him sat a Bible and a hymnbook. His Shepherd would conduct him through the valley of the shadow of death. And now, his house was set in order.

Somehow, Jackson managed to live through the year. Early the next year, thanking a man who had helped him financially, he wrote that he did not know how long Providence would permit him to remain in the land of the living; but he would depart without any regrets, sure of his destination, where the "wicked cease to trouble and the weary are at rest."

Not long after he'd finished the letter, a visitor arrived at the Hermitage, by the name of William D. Miller, a bright young man who happened to be the private secretary to the President of the Texas Republic. Jackson warmly received him.

Miller handed the aging patriarch a letter marked "Private," in the recognizable handwriting of Sam Houston.

Jackson eagerly opened the seal. Holding the sheets close to his feeble eyes, he read.

A Dark Year

The year 1843 was a dark one for Texas. Z. N. Morrell wrote in his old age, "Clouds of gloom hang so heavily around all the recollections of 1843, in the west, that I must leave its records to others. I can't write them."[12]

Rain fell incessantly until what was normally a blessing became a curse. Not only did mud clog the roads, but burgeoning numbers of mosquitoes flourished throughout the abnormally wet summer, carrying diseases such as yellow fever and malaria. Sickness began to spread across the land.

The lawlessness of idle adventurers and outlaws became a curse to honest, hard-working people, whose goods were appropriated by these wandering men. Shelby County and its environs suffered from the "Regulators" and the "Moderators." In the south, Mexican soldiers had invaded several times; in the northern frontier, Indians scalped settlers. Women mourned their husbands, and children their dead fathers.

Ironically, the news of the armistice with Mexico was not regarded as good news by all. There were many Texans who still wanted to fight, and their contempt for Mexico was such that some had conceived the notion to march south and conquer it! These firebrands incited the people while criticizing their president.

The fact that Great Britain had helped to secure the armistice with Mexico was another thing. Britain was not generally seen as a friend in those days; the aging Jackson still carried the scar on his forehead where a red-coated British officer had struck him with his saber during the Revolution. Americans—and Texans—were still wary of their former enemy. So why was Houston so cozy with the British?

Charges Fly Against Houston

Fanciful charges began to fly, alleging that Santa Anna had bribed Houston, or that Great Britain had required that Texas abolish slavery in return for her help.

The New Orleans *Picayune* absorbed all these rumors and concluded that "[Houston] is demented and the people over which he presides should no longer suffer themselves to be disgraced by the mad acts of an imbecile or a lunatic."[13] The newspaper recommended impeachment.

It is doubtful that many Texans thought this way, but the reticent Houston broke his silence and defended himself. In a church in Huntsville, he described the fierceness of his political opponents:

> "Every arrow has been shot that... could wound, and [the arrows were] poisoned by rancor and malice. Have I deserved this, my countrymen?... I am a traitor to my country; '*bribed* by Santa Anna's gold.' I am denounced as a villain, a blackguard and a wretch... I cannot but view them [these charges of treason and other vices] with astonishment."[14]

In Houston City, the president addressed another crowd, explaining to them that when faced by any decision, his one consideration was: "Would this benefit my country?"[15] If the answer was yes, he did it. His remarks so moved his audience that at the close, the people surged around him, cheering and even openly weeping.

Texas sided with him over these issues, but in many ways, Houston was walking a precariously narrow path. Early in 1844, he spoke with members of the Texas Senate, so they could understand what he was doing. He wasn't playing Britain and the United States off each other as part of some kind of underhanded machination, but rather, there were practical considerations that made his course essential.

If Texas openly clamored for annexation, and the United States failed to respond, it might prejudice England and France against them, whose help they might need. Plus, "If we evince too much anxiety it will be regarded as importunity, and the voice of supplication seldom commands... great respect."[16]

Then Houston turned to his old friend, Andrew Jackson. Despite the old chieftain's age and infirmity, he still had great political influence. Houston needed to use his friend's influence on behalf of Texas. But he did not want to deceive him.

Sam Houston took up his writing materials and thought carefully. Jackson was already on the "side" of annexation; the ex-president believed that the acquisition of Texas was necessary for the security of the borders of the U.S., but not because of Mexico. The Hero of New Orleans was watching Great Britain as a hound would watch a lion.

The President of Texas took up his pen.

> Now, my venerated friend, you will perceive that Texas is presented to the United States, as a bride adorned for her espousal. But if... she should be rejected, her mortification would be indescribable... this is the third time she has consented. Were she now to be spurned, it would forever terminate expectation on her part,

> and it would then not only be left for the United States to expect that she would seek some other friend...[17]

By some other "friend," Houston meant Great Britain, and he knew that Jackson was already concerned with Houston's association with that nation. Was it right to play on his old mentor's concerns in this way? Houston hoped that Jackson would be able to discern his true intentions. Any help Texas had received or would receive from Great Britain was simply of purest necessity, and her sovereignty would not be relinquished to that nation's influence. Annexation to the United States had always been Houston's hope and purpose.

He made a decision. He spoke to his personal secretary, William Miller, who was to deliver this letter. He authorized him to disclose the motives underlying this letter if it seemed necessary.

Houston had used subterfuge to guard the morale of his men during the Revolution in 1836, but his conscience would not allow him to manipulate Andrew Jackson.

Jackson's Response

There was one more battle to be fought while he still could draw breath. Texas. To secure her borders for the glory of her posterity, the United States must have Texas.

Andrew Jackson pondered as he laid the letter on his desk. There was a reference to another "friend." Of course, he knew what Houston meant, and he didn't like it. So far, Jackson had defended his friend against "pro-British" charges. But he knew his friend well. Houston was a tactical man. Wily, but honorable. Yes, he would support him. One thing was for sure: this letter could light a fire under some people.

Jackson prepared a copy of Houston's letter to be sent to a certain senator in Washington. Then, as Miller watched, the old statesman wrote a letter to a man close to President Tyler. Then Jackson sent Miller and the letters on to Washington, D.C.

Later, he responded to Houston, explaining that he was optimistic about the chances for annexation; most of the Senate was in favor of it. And then he fired a shot across Houston's bow. Britain already held sway over the West Indies. Should she acquire both Oregon and Texas as well, she would form "an iron hoop about the United States." This would mean war, for the United States would "burst asunder" that restraint though "it cost oceans of blood & millions of money....yr. friend, Andrew Jackson."[18]

Keep clear of Britain. Strong words from an old friend.

Artful Negotiations

George Gordon, Earl of Aberdeen, laid down the ivory-handled paper cutter on his desk, which was stacked with various papers of state. He rose and received the Texas envoy, Dr. Ashbel Smith, whose arrival he had been expecting. It was June 24, 1844.

In this very room, in the British Foreign Office, Lord North had, years earlier, signed the papers relinquishing control of the American colonies. It was even the same desk. Matters of war and peace had been decided here and would be decided here again. The matter of Texas seemed to be coming to a crisis.

Just recently, the application by Houston for annexation to the United States had cast suspicion and doubt into the diplomatic machinery here. But Dr. Smith had explained artfully that the President of the Republic of Texas was merely responding to public opinion, which had forced him to adjust his course.

But all that was academic now. President Tyler's annexation treaty, now before the U.S. Senate, was not going to pass. Good. Great Britain did not want Texas to become part of the United States, and she was prepared to help keep that from happening.

Dr. Ashbel Smith listened as Lord Aberdeen examined his proposal. Aberdeen was pleased but astonished. This could mean war.

Behind the Scenes

"It's a forgery!" exclaimed Andrew Jackson. "Mr. Van Buren never wrote such a letter."

Two friends had come to the Hermitage with news. Martin Van Buren, an associate of Jackson and current presidential candidate, had taken a position against the annexation of Texas. Henry Clay, his opponent, had already taken such a position, but Jackson did not mind observing, "Clay [is] a dead political Duck."[19]

But Van Buren? Impossible. Jackson's friends placed a copy of a newspaper into his feeble hands and retreated, allowing the old general to read in private.

It was true.

When his friends returned, Jackson spoke quietly. "Mr. Van Buren must write a second letter explaining himself."[20]

That would do no good, they said.

The Democratic National Convention would be meeting soon to formally select a candidate for president, which everyone had supposed would be Van Buren. But whatever else "Jacksonian democracy" may have meant to historians, it did mean this: Andrew Jackson was still a major player in the political process.

And Texas meant too much to Jackson to allow this.

The old statesman's eyes were wet. Van Buren had to go.

A few days later, he explained in a letter to a friend,

> "I am quite sick, really, and have been even since I read V. B. [Van Buren's] letter... Political matters out of the question, Texas [is] the key to our future safety... We cannot bear that Great Britain have a Canedy on our west as she has on our north... Some good democrat must be selected..."[21]

Campaigning in Texas

As political fires raged in the North, Texas endured a maelstrom of mudslinging as Anson Jones and Ed Burleson fought for the prize of the office Sam Houston would soon be vacating. The president of the Republic of Texas was constitutionally limited to two non-consecutive terms, and Houston was forever ineligible to run again.

Anson Jones was Houston's not very popular Secretary of State, but when the Hero of San Jacinto publicly endorsed him a month before the election, it was enough to elect him. Despite the small but vociferous anti-Houston crowd, "Old Sam" was still quite popular with most Texans.

But Jones had a strange twist to his personality, of which Houston was not fully aware.

The Stakes Rise

After the election in September 1844, President Houston worked at his desk, with several months of his term to complete before Jones took over the reins in the spring.

One day, a messenger delivered an envelope from the Texas envoy to Great Britain, Ashbel Smith, who had sent a report that President Houston opened with great interest. After President Tyler's proposal for the annexation of Texas had failed before the Senate, Houston had declared publicly that the Republic must consider herself free from all "involvements and pledges."[22] He had turned to Britain and France for protection and help.

Houston read carefully. Lord Aberdeen had made an interesting proposal, a diplomatic act between five countries: Great Britain, France, the United States, Mexico, and Texas. It would require that Mexico formally recognize the independence of Texas, but would also require that Texas maintain her independence forever. Since Mexico did not desire the United States to annex Texas, this agreement might just work.

But Lord Aberdeen had assured Dr. Smith that neither the cooperation of Mexico nor the United States would be necessary. In fact, Britain and France were willing to go to war, if necessary, to force Mexico and the U.S. to comply.

Sam Houston must have had mixed emotions. His true desire had been for annexation to the United States. But as president, he had to see to the interests of the people of Texas. For the third time, the United States had refused to annex Texas, so Sam saw this as an amazing opportunity. The strongest nation on earth had taken an interest in the feeble Republic of Texas, and though he would have liked to please his friend Andrew Jackson, he must now make a decision.

Signing the Act would close the door to annexation... but there was little hope of that anyway. He had played the game and lost.

Houston spoke to Anson Jones, who, as president-elect, was still Secretary of State. He instructed him to write to Smith and tell him to sign the act on behalf of Texas.

A Mandate

"Let us suppose that Britain seeks a colonization, or offensive and defensive alliance with Texas, and then ask what, in such a contingency, is our duty? Our reply is annexation: with the consent of Mexico if it can be obtained, and without such consent, if it not be obtainable."[23]

So had written the editor of the Philadelphia *Ledger* on March 26, 1844. Even before the defeat of Tyler's annexation treaty in the Senate, Americans had begun to change their minds. Houston's game had produced the intended results. Concern for the security of her borders caused the young nation to divert her attention from internal squabbles, including the slavery issue, at least to a degree.

Suddenly, the annexation of Texas was *the* hot political issue. James Knox Polk, summoned to the Hermitage after Van Buren's fatal misstep, was now running for the highest office on a pro-annexation platform.

For a while, the opposing party, the Whigs, protested annexation and warned of the evils that would follow. Daniel Webster argued that financial issues such as banking and tariffs should not be ignored, but Texas remained the dominant issue of the presidential campaign.

The winds had shifted, and the Whig candidate for president, Henry Clay, realized he was going the wrong way. Because he had wanted to be president for a long time, the sensible architect of the "Missouri Compromise" decided to change his mind on annexation, but it didn't work. Members of his own party turned on him.

In Great Britain, the tumultuous campaign was viewed with interest and concern. A correspondent for the London *Times* sent home the warning that "the project of annexation would be promptly carried into execution by an overwhelming majority..."[24] if Americans believed that Britain was intriguing against them. Some already did.

From the Hermitage, the feeble Jackson sent letters. Too weak to fight with weapons, the Hero of New Orleans fought against the redcoats one more time. With his pen.

And he won. When James K. Polk was elected President of the United States on November 4, 1844, everyone knew that the election of Jackson's man was a mandate for the annexation of Texas.

Two-Faced

Anson Jones was a two-faced man. As Secretary of State, he had obeyed the president and fallen in line with Houston's views and purposes. But privately, he distrusted Houston and viewed him with jealousy. Now, as president-elect, Jones may have found it hard to remain compliant.

He was wary of this diplomatic act constructed by Lord Aberdeen. What were Houston's motives in this? Jones somehow imagined that this diplomatic act would serve to destroy his own forthcoming administration.

With this in mind, the Secretary of State neglected to write and instruct Smith to sign the Act. Houston reminded him, but instead, without informing the president, Jones wrote Smith and instructed him to come home.

A Wise and Benign Providence

Sam Houston faced the crowd gathered before him, once more realizing what a relief it would be to return to private life. A relief to lay down the burden of care he had carried these past three years as president. Today, December 9, 1844, Anson Jones would be sworn in as the new President of the Republic of Texas.

What the future would bring, Houston did not know. Annexation looked very likely, the way sentiment had turned in the United States, but he had been disappointed before.

Houston began his valedictory address, the sum of his heart and hopes for Texas. He first expressed his gratitude for the support of his countrymen.

Then his remarks turned to the subject of annexation, which was on everyone's mind.

"If Texas goes begging again for admission into the United States, she will only degrade herself..."

But annexation was still possible, "...If the United States shall open the door and ask her... But let us be as we are until that opportunity is presented..."[25]

Houston exhorted his audience to promote learning and education as a means of safeguarding their freedoms. These civil and religious freedoms, together with increasing prosperity, were "ascribable to that wise and benign Providence which has watched over our progress and conducted us to the attainment of blessings so invaluable..."[26]

Houston stepped down and observed as his successor was inaugurated. Retirement sounded so good. Of course, he would still be obligated to make a living, and he had some ideas on the subject. But now he looked forward to the normal "cares" of life, enjoying his wife and his little son.

Soon, he wanted to make a trip to the Hermitage to bring his son, so that Jackson might bless him. And they had many things to talk about.

A Problem with Jones

Andrew Jackson Donelson, the nephew of Andrew Jackson, had been appointed chargé d'affaires to Texas. He was now watching for Sam Houston's arrival.

Donelson was puzzled. Seeing the popular support for annexation expressed in the election of James K. Polk, President Tyler had decided to go ahead and push annexation through before he had to leave office in the spring. Congress was now willing, and Donelson had been sent to Texas with an annexation proposal for President Jones.

But for some reason, Jones was unimpressed. In fact, he had refused to call the Texas Congress into special session to consider the offer. Donelson had no way of knowing that British consul Charles Elliott was now in Mexico through the agency of Great Britain and France. Unknown was the fact that Anson Jones wanted Texas to remain independent.

Nobody in Washington-on-the-Brazos knew where Houston was, so Donelson went to Huntsville. Finally, he discovered where the ex-president had gone and managed to contact him.

After the high spring waters receded, Sam Houston arrived in Huntsville and spoke with Donelson. He objected to many of the terms of annexation, including one demanding that huge amounts of property be ceded to the United States. This was unfair.

Houston was just being sensible. But his political enemies, who controlled much of the press, painted him as being opposed to annexation and even accused him of treason.

Before Houston left with his family to visit his in-laws and Andrew Jackson at the Hermitage, he addressed a crowd in Houston City. He defended himself against the charges brought against him, and also explained his political "game," which had caused so many to misunderstand:

> "...Supposing a charming lady had two suitors. One of them she is inclined to believe would make the better husband, but is a little slow to make interesting propositions. Do you think if she was a skilled practitioner in Cupid's court she would pretend that she loved the other 'feller' best?" [Laughter and cheers].
>
> If ladies are justified in making use of coquetry in securing their annexation to good and agreeable husbands, you must excuse me for making use of the same means to annex Texas to Uncle Sam" [Laughter and cheers].[27]

Houston obviously saw annexation as a "done deal." The details could be worked out. Right now, he had more important concerns.

Andrew Jackson was not well.

Jackson's Death

"Death has no terrors for me. When I have suffered sufficiently, the Lord will take me to himself..."[28] Jackson was ready.

For several months, the old chieftain had suffered from intestinal hemorrhage and bleeding in the lungs. Often, severe headaches and a painful racking cough troubled him. Still, he would take up his pen and write. Annexation was still his care, as well as managing the little world of the Hermitage.

Then one day, Jackson received good news about Texas. "All is safe at last."[29] The last battle had been won. It was time to go home.

Houston received news in New Orleans that Jackson was dying. There was no time to lose. With his wife and son, he hurried to Nashville.

Meanwhile, Jackson was rapidly declining. On Sunday, June 8, 1845, the old statesman said his goodbyes to family members and the household servants. "My dear children, and friends, and servants, I hope and trust to meet you all in Heaven, both white and black—both white and black."[30]

People collected in the yard outside. The field hands formed their own group a short distance from the house, where they were heard to chant and pray. The household servants held vigil on the porch.

The shadows began to lengthen. Sobs and groans from outside caught Andrew Jackson's attention as he lay on the bed. "What is the matter with my children? Have I alarmed them? Be good children and we will all meet in heaven."[31]

The Hero of New Orleans spoke no more.

Houston Races to the Hermitage

Sam Houston, Margaret, and little Sam Junior, just two years old, endured the swaying of the coach as the horses galloped toward the Hermitage. Suddenly, the horses slowed.

Someone was coming this way. It was Dr. Esselman, Jackson's physician. He stopped his team and gave them the awful news.

Houston's heart must have ached when he heard of the loss of his old friend. The coach resumed its course, but at a slower pace now. It was not much farther to the Hermitage, and soon they arrived. The horses pulled the coach around the driveway and stopped in front of the house.

By the time Sam Houston helped his wife and son down, darkness had already fallen. Houston picked up his son and carried him inside, where he was shown to the couch that had served as the old general's deathbed.

He was just an hour too late. Houston knelt, put his head on Jackson's breast, and wept.

Jones Foiled and the Way Cleared

On June 3, 1845, Captain Elliott presented the protocol, signed by the current dictator of Mexico, to Anson Jones. Under Britain's sponsorship, peace with Mexico was within their grasp. Peace without the help of the United States. The way was clear for Texas's independence.

Except that Texas didn't want it. The Texas Congress voted against President Jones's plan and voted for annexation instead.

But of course, it wasn't that simple. Details had to be taken care of, such as writing a state constitution. The terms of annexation had to be worked out between Texas and the United States; this, finally, was accomplished, with Texas receiving better terms than originally proposed.

Then the United States Congress had to vote to receive Texas and approve its constitution, which it finally did, after some turmoil and debate, in December.

Texans couldn't help but rejoice.

The Republic of Texas is No More

Noah Smithwick was in Bastrop, where court was in session. Then the news came in. *Annexation passed! Polk signed it!* The celebration began, led by godly Judge Baylor. There were no cannon available, so humble anvils took their place; gunpowder was sprinkled upon them to create an indescribable din.

Smithwick decided that any Indians nearby would flee in "short order." The blacksmith wrote, "We felt something like the children of Israel probably did, when Jehovah flung the Red Sea betwixt them and their foes."[32]

The first state legislature met on February 16th, 1846. Several days later, at the Capitol, the Lone Star flag of the Republic of Texas was taken down from its place of honor. President Anson Jones furled it carefully, reverently, amidst a breathless silence, and said, "The Republic of Texas is no more."[33] Smithwick recorded the scene:

> Many a head was bowed, many a broad chest heaved, and many a manly cheek was wet with tears when that broad field of blue in the center of which, like a signal light, glowed the lone star, emblem of the sovereignty of Texas, was furled and laid away among the relics of the dead republic. But we were most of us natives of the United States, and when the stars and stripes, the flag of our fathers, was run up and catching the breeze unrolled its heaven born colors to the light, cheer after cheer rent the air. Methinks the star in the lower left hand corner should have been especially dedicated to Texas.[34]

TEXAS
Co. A
RANGERS

Chapter 14

War and Peace

Ranger Captain John "Jack" Coffee Hays took a final account of his appearance. He was slim and fair, about five feet nine and one hundred fifty pounds, not the physically imposing type people normally associated with acts of daring on the frontier. Young, intelligent, handsome, and quiet, he was regarded as a gentleman of good character by the inhabitants of San Antonio. But Jack Hays, a surveyor from Tennessee, was the esteemed leader of the band of local volunteers that defended Texas settlers from marauders, whether Comanche or Mexican.

His hair was dark and carefully parted on the side. Well, it would have to be good enough. He wasn't extremely fastidious—who could be, on the Texas frontier? But today he was meeting with a prince. Prince Carl of Solms-Braunfels, from Germany. It was March of 1845, a green spring in San Antonio.

Last summer, Hays had met the German nobleman, a young and handsome man dressed rather formally, accompanied by a retinue of servants and even a "professional hunter." As a surveyor and Texas Ranger, Hays possessed a great deal of knowledge of the areas north of San Antonio. This had interested the prince, who was looking for land on which to settle a coming migration of German immigrants. But the nobleman had a problem.

The Comanches. The land grant purchased by the German immigration committee — the *Adelsverein* — was smack dab in the middle of Comancheria. This huge chunk of land, almost two million acres located northwest of present-day Fredericksburg, had been purchased sight unseen, and Prince Carl was just doing the best he could. Not only was the land in Comancheria, it was a far trek from the coast. The German nobleman needed a place to settle immigrants who were already arriving on Texas shores. Somewhere in between the coast and the land grant.

Jack Hays was going to visit Prince Carl and maybe work something out. He knew of a tract of land fifteen miles north of Seguin that had belonged to the Veramendi family, Jim Bowie's deceased in-laws. The relatives who now owned it had put it up for sale. It was over one thousand acres, right on the Guadalupe and Comal Rivers, between San Antonio and Austin.

There were already some Germans living in Texas, having emigrated earlier, attracted by the possibilities of land as well as civil and religious freedoms. They were mostly decent and hardworking people, though Hays wasn't so sure about this prince fellow. So fancy! But the nobleman seemed to mean well. In any case, the Texas Ranger had no objection to German farmers settling the area. Except—the Comanches. What would happen to these farmers?

Unconsciously, Hays felt for the Colt revolver under his right hand. He possessed two of Samuel Colt's five-shooters. What a great invention. Young Samuel Colt had been whittling while on a ship bound for Calcutta, and out of the wood had sprung the first model of what Hays now valued above gold. The Rangers had seen the possibilities of this new kind of firearm immediately, and soon Captain Samuel H. Walker departed east to visit Colt and make some suggestions for improvements on the design. These were implemented, and now "Walker's Colt" was beginning to change the balance of power on the frontier.

Hays had trained his Rangers to fight with them. Riding like Comanches, his men were deadly with the rifle and the two Colt pistols they each carried. Before, they had to dismount to reload their rifles, whereas the Indians carrying bows and arrows had no such hindrances. Now, a Ranger was more than a match for any Comanche. After one encounter between the force of Rangers and a larger band of Comanches, Hays and his men routed the Indians, chasing them for three miles. The chief, having lost half his warriors, was recorded to say, "I will never again fight Jack Hays, who has a shot for every finger on the hand."[1]

But what about the Germans? Certainly, they would be in danger if they tried to settle their original land grant. Enchanted Rock, a site sacred to the Comanches, was located there. Captain Hays recalled an incident in 1841, when he had inspected this huge outcropping of granite and a small party of Indians had attacked him. Single-handedly, the Ranger captain had driven them off.

But without these Colt revolvers, Hays would not have survived. Would the Germans?

Houston in Washington, DC

Spring had come to the nation's capital once again. No cherry blossoms yet; the famous cherry trees would not be planted for many years. But there was mud in abundance, since few roads were paved.

The White House had been completed, looking much as it does today, except that the grounds behind it were still swampy. The Washington Monument had not yet been built. The Capitol building, where the United States Congress met, would not have been recognizable to us, as the two large wings on either side had not yet been added; the dome was smaller and lower than it is now. But there were fewer congressmen to accommodate than there are today; the Senate chamber was made to seat sixty members, and that was sufficient, even with the addition of two more senators from the new state of Texas.

It was March 30, 1846. In his room in Brown's Hotel, Sam Houston inspected himself briefly in the mirror. Today would be his first day in the United States Senate representing Texas. Having just arrived on Saturday's train, he had rested from his long journey and then paid his respects to President Polk late yesterday afternoon.

Polk was in a difficult place; that he could see. Before the U.S. had annexed Texas, Mexico had threatened war should such an event take place. So as part of the annexation agreement, the U.S. had sent troops to Texas to help guard its borders while the process was completed.

Then, when the annexation of Texas was official, the Mexican consul in Washington had gone home, and the American consul in Mexico City had been asked to leave. As promised, Mexico counted the annexation of Texas—*her* territory—as a hostile, aggressive act by the United States.

President Polk had tried to resolve the situation peacefully, having tried to purchase both Texas and California from Mexico, but negotiations were futile. And Mexico was not his only problem. There was a dispute about the Oregon Territory, to which both the U.S. and Great Britain laid claim. This territory encompassed all of present-day Oregon and Washington, extending east into Idaho and Montana, and extending north into present-day Canada.

Plus, the ever-present slavery issue colored all questions regarding territory acquisition. President Polk had to take these internal debates into account as he struggled to deal with the overriding concern of national security. The United States was not a world power, and the threats to its borders were still very real.

The president also faced much opposition and criticism from Congress. On top of that, he had some sort of digestive ailment. Feeling compassionate, Houston resolved to support the beleaguered man. He could see that the president's judgments were sound, and with war closing in over Texas, Polk needed support. Houston knew what it was like to be the chief executive of a nation.

Perhaps the new senator mulled over some of these issues in his mind as he walked to the Capitol building that morning, his gold-headed cane serving to support his weak ankle. Or, maybe he reminisced. It had been twenty years since he had served as a congressman from Tennessee. Then there was the trial for his beating of Stanberry. Certainly, there were many memories here.

Perhaps Houston noticed the corral full of black slaves near the Capitol as he approached. Here, Virginia-bred slaves waited to be shipped south. Sam Houston's views on slavery were not unusual for a Westerner, or even a Southerner. He disliked slavery, but he owned slaves. If he could eliminate the evil of slavery, he would, but things were never that simple. And making it such an issue did not seem right to him. Northern abolitionists simply made things worse with their arrogant self-righteousness...

Arriving at the Senate chamber, he looked around to see purple hangings decorating the circular room, which had four tiers of seats, above which presided a gallery extending around the room to accommodate spectators. The seats were divided by an aisle, and the senators tended to seat themselves according to party; Whigs congregated on one side, Democrats on the other.

Senator Thomas Rusk, Houston's friend and fellow senator from Texas, introduced him. To some, he was already well known.

Looking around the chamber, Sam recognized Daniel Webster, dressed neatly in fine linen; he also noticed tall and gaunt John C. Calhoun, who was still blessed with an abundance of hair. The senator from South Carolina regarded the Texan coolly.

At first, Houston just listened to the debate. But day after day, certain things began to become apparent: the great learned men in this place didn't always know what they were talking about. And everything was so—*political.*

The Baron Comes to Neu Braunfels

Baron Otfried Han Freiherr von Meusebach decided that such a name as his would be rather unwieldy in Texas. During the long, cramped, and uncomfortable sea voyage, he had time to think, having read about this new land of promise for several years before that. Texas was no place for German titles of nobility.

After some deliberation, he decided to call himself by the English equivalent of

"Han," which was short for "Johann." John O. Meusebach. Yes, that would do nicely.

Meusebach was traveling to Texas under the auspices of the *Adelverein*, or Society for the Protection of German Immigrants. This society had grand aims: to provide land for German farmers who were straitened by difficult economic conditions, and to provide markets for German industry. It was the same idea that had sent English colonists to America: land for the landless and eventually profits that would accumulate back home.

The *Adelsverein*, capitalized by German noblemen, had promised immigrants land: 320 acres for a married man, 160 acres for a single man. By Texas standards, these were small plots, but by German standards, they were large farms. And back in Germany, when a German farmer had several sons, dividing a small farm among them became problematic. Truly, Texas sounded like the proverbial promised land, and many made the ultimate decision to pack up their things and leave their family and homeland, probably for good.

Prince Carl had decided to go back to Germany after having established the village of Neu Braunfels on the Guadalupe River as a settlement for those immigrants who were already arriving. Meusebach was coming to take his place. Having read much about Texas, he was excited about the possibilities, but he also knew that the problems were many.

And though John O. Meusebach was only thirty-three years old, he was willing to tackle problems head-on.

Taylor's Problem at the Texas Border

A grim-faced General Zachary Taylor received the report. There were two casualties at the fort on the Rio Grande, including Major Jacob Brown. Manning the little earthen fort had been a dangerous assignment, but Major Brown had served bravely, raising the stars and stripes each morning with full military honors. The Mexicans, predictably, had attacked.

Taylor commanded nearly half of the entire United States Army—the regular army, that is. Some people still esteemed volunteer militia as the American way, but the task at hand required the discipline of a "real" army. The annexation of Texas to the United States had added not only this huge piece of land and its population, but also its myriad political problems. Mexico had made it very clear that annexation meant war. From the Mexican point of view, Texas was a rebellious Mexican province, and for the U.S. to claim it was an act of war.

General Taylor had been sent to Texas to guard its borders as part of the annexation agreement. He had stationed his large force at Corpus Christi, on the Gulf coast, but things had passed the point of no return. And now Taylor and his men had relocated to the Rio Grande River and were attracting Mexican troops like honey and nectar attract bees.

Taylor was in a contemplative mood. Ranger Samuel Walker had done a good job as a scout, carrying messages to the besieged fort, but the Texan was—well, *irregular*. Short, spare, even slouchy, the red-haired, blue-eyed man was quiet. And another thing—these Texans did not wear uniforms.

In fact, it almost seemed as though they were *trying* to dress as individually as possible. In truth, Taylor really hadn't wanted to accept the help of the Rangers, but politically, he had not been in a position to refuse. Texans wanted to be involved. And though he still didn't want them, perhaps they wouldn't be totally useless.

Disaster on the Beach

What do I do now? John O. Meusebach studied the camp before him. Downwind, the smell was disgusting. Indianola, a site purchased by the *Adelsverein* on the coast to receive German immigrants, was a town in name only. Single men, couples, and families had camped out as best they could, digging holes in the sand and fashioning tents for protection from the elements. Many people were sick. Some had become sick on the voyage over —Meusebach remembered well his own three months in a cramped, smelly ship—and exposure to the elements here on the coast certainly did not help matters.

Furthermore, by the time Meusebach arrived and traveled up to Neu Braunfels, he discovered that mismanagement of the *Adelsverein*'s money had basically bankrupted the society. Could anything else go wrong?

The German nobleman focused his mind. First of all, he knew it was vital that these people leave the disease-ridden coast and go inland. *We need transportation; with wagons, we can move them to Neu Braunfels.*

Meusebach found some teamsters, and they began to talk money.

The E Street Church

Sunday morning, at the E Street Baptist Church in Washington, D.C., Reverend G.W. Samson looked down from the pulpit. Near the front, to Samson's left, sat a hunched figure wearing a brightly colored serape. Was he paying attention to the sermon?

Samson thought he probably was; he was happy to have Senator Houston here every Sunday and considered that his habit of whittling, beyond making a royal mess for the sexton, probably did not distract his attention much.

Houston was indeed listening. Every Sunday afternoon, he wrote Margaret a letter which included a synopsis of the morning's sermon. His habit of whittling helped him when he was troubled or turning an issue over in his mind.

Inspired by the Christian example of his wife, Houston began and ended his day with prayer and attended church each week as well. But he struggled with eternal issues; he did not feel worthy of Christ. Perhaps it was his own habit of self-reliance that kept him from the Savior. He was not sure.

And then there was another thing—if he did profess faith in Christ falsely, and chose to take communion unworthily, what then? He remembered a sermon from his childhood, which had threatened eternal damnation for those who partook unworthily...

The Pastor of E Street Baptist Church continued to preach as Houston listened, whittling the soft pine into the shape of a heart.

Suffering on the Coast

Once again, rain pounded Texas. The coastal marshes were underwater, providing good breeding grounds for mosquitoes and thus a variety of mosquito-borne diseases. For the German immigrants arriving in Indianola, the rain was a mixed blessing. It was a source of fresh water, but it also brought disease. Malaria and a kind of dysentery spread among them.

The teamsters, who were supposed to help transport immigrants to Neu Braunfels, deserted, finding that the U.S. Army would pay more for their services. General Taylor's army, to the south, was regularly siphoning off men and resources.

The Germans did the best they could. They hunted wild ducks and caught fish for food. After the rains tapered off, those who could loaded up and left for Neu Braunfels. Many left behind household goods, as well as sick and dying relatives.

Letters were sent to Germany, describing their suffering. But they had known suffering in their homeland, too. Once, a German poet, Heinrich Heine, asked a fellow countryman why he was leaving Germany. The emigrant responded, "I swear... if France had suffered just one-tenth of what these people in Germany have suffered, it would have caused 36 revolutions in France, and 36 kings would have lost their heads to the guillotine!"[2]

McCullough's Rangers in Mexico

After defeating Mexican troops at Palo Alto and Resaca de la Palma, General Taylor set his sights on Monterrey. But none of his officers knew the country. Well, except the Texans. Taylor decided to have some of these ragged Texans scout out the country and find a route for the army.

Ben McCulloch was a taciturn man. His blue eyes revealed little. He gave few orders, but his men obeyed them. At Taylor's request, he gathered forty Rangers and headed south to scout. They soon found out what the general needed to know, avoiding the Mexicans by night marches and wily maneuvering.

They were, in essence, Taylor's cavalry. There really was no formal American cavalry unit, only men on horseback who preferred to fight on the ground. They did not have Colt revolvers, and on horses with single-shot rifles, they were no match for Mexico's trained lancers.

With their Colt revolvers and superb horsemanship, the Texas Rangers became the eyes and ears of Taylor's army. There was only one problem. Some of these men had been to Perote, captured by General Woll or by General Ampudia after the debacle at Mier. These men had suffered greatly at the hands of the Mexicans, and those who had not still remembered the Alamo. They had old scores to settle. As a result, certain Mexicans were found shot or hanged, and Taylor did not know what to do about it. To his mind, the Rangers were a lawless bunch.

But these tall, bearded, cool-eyed men were not unfriendly and did not harbor antipathy toward all Mexicans. A few times, they even showed up at Mexican dances. But the local inhabitants were terrified of Texas Rangers, and their appearance tended to break up the party. Women screamed at the sight of "*los diablos Tejanos.*"

Heading to Neu Braunfels

Wilhelm listened to the creak of the wagon wheels as he trudged along the track. Ahead, others in the caravan headed to Neu Braunfels led their families and livestock to the hope that lay ahead, trying to forget the nightmare of the coast. He was glad to have a wagon, now that Elise had become ill. He worried about her. So many had succumbed to illness in Indianola, but he could not bear to think of that now...

The young immigrant glanced about him. To the side of the rutted trail was a slope blanketed with blue. He has never seen flowers like this before—and in such number! Earlier, he had noticed other colors in the ditches along the way. Little red flags announced spring like visual poetry. No, they weren't red exactly. Not pink, either. Their shapes, how could he describe them? Paintbrushes! He would call them paintbrushes. He knew Elise wouldn't laugh.

What was that up ahead? Buzzards were circling some point along the trail. He shuddered at the thought of what he might soon see. Texas was such a place of contrasts. Life and hope; misery and death.

Meusebach's Idea

The German nobleman, who stood six-feet-two inches tall and wore a heavy beard, took a deep breath of morning air. It was a good site. John Meusebach stood outside the dwelling he had inherited from his predecessor, Prince Carl.

The Veramendi grant consisted of 1,265 acres and included both springs and a river. The soil was rocky in places, but good to the southeast. The local Indians seemed peaceful enough, although stories of ritualistic cannibalism had startled some of the settlers. All in all, Neu Braunfels promised to be a very good place to live.

But it was quickly filling up with people. A steady stream of immigrants from the coast kept everyone busy. Houses were being built, but not fast enough. And soon there would not be enough acreage for everyone.

Plus, there was another problem. The huge Fisher-Miller grant that the *Adelsverein* had purchased would be lost if it were not settled soon. It was an empresario grant, and legally, it could be retained only if settled. He did not have much time left.

Meusebach knew all about the Comanches, but he also had some ideas.

Margaret at Home

Margaret gathered her writing materials. It was late, but she did not want to close her eyes in sleep until she had written to her husband. She breathed a sigh. On the way to Washington, Houston had written several times, but after a letter from Louisville, she had received no word. The mails could be so irregular. Often, they relied on friends who were coming or going.

Despite the presence of her son, her husband's namesake, little Sam Junior, and another child most definitely on the way, Margaret Lea Houston desperately missed her husband. Her general health (she suffered from asthma) and her current *situation* had prevented her from accompanying her husband to Washington. Sometimes she became downright depressed.

There were servants to do the menial work, such as scrubbing, washing clothes, cooking, and baking, but there were still many responsibilities that fell on Margaret's shoulders. The Houstons employed an overseer to manage the enslaved people who did the outside chores on their little plantation near Huntsville, which the general had named "Raven Hill." But ultimately, the young wife of Senator Houston was in charge.

Light from the lamp illuminated the pensive face of the dark-haired young woman, seated near the sleeping form of little Sam. She picked up her pen and wrote to her husband:

> Huntsville, May 1st, 1846
>
> Ever dearest love,
>
> No letter yet, since the one from Louisville. My anxiety is almost more than I can bear, but it can not be interminable, and I have some fortitude with it, and a little pateince [sic], which I hope will not desert me at this trying season. . . . I am now writing to you at a late hour of the night, but am cheered by the soft breathings of our sleeping boy. He is truly a comfort to me, but my concern for his future well-fare is indescribable. I fear my affections are too much engrossed by earthly ties. Should the Lord call me away, they would cause me some sad struggles, but oh who can resist the fascination of those sweet words husband and child! I will try to prepare myself for any event, and if it should be his gracious will to call my spirit home, will endeaver to leave my dear ones entirely in his hands. . . .
>
> Ever thy devoted wife,
>
> M. L. Houston[3]

Battle at Monterrey

General Taylor gave instructions to his officers to halt and make camp. What an awesome sight. He and his six thousand troops had not seen mountains in a while. But they had come to Monterrey, and the hills above the town were the beginnings of higher elevations beyond.

He gave more orders. Ranger Jack Hays was part of his plan. One of his companies would move out first.

Ben McCullough's men moved out at six in the morning. On horseback, the Rangers followed their captain as they advanced toward Monterrey.

Suddenly, Mexican lancers appeared before them, with good, strong horses, smart uniforms, and sharp lances that caught the morning sun. Their leader, Colonel Najera, turned his mount and rode to the front, commanding his men to prepare for battle.

But before the lancers could prepare themselves, Ben McCullough charged. His men tore through the Mexican cavalry, and there was desperate, close-range fighting with both pistols and knives.

Colonel Najera soon lay dead on the road, along with many of his men. Clearly, the Mexican lancers and the infantry behind them could not stand up to the Colt revolver and the fearless, aggressive spirit of the Texas Rangers, and those surviving fled.

Taylor's column did not fare as well, but because of the Rangers at the vanguard of Worth's column, Monterrey surrendered, and a parley was arranged.

Jack Hays was disappointed with the outcome. His men were furious. The Mexican army was allowed to evacuate with full honors of war, under an eight-week truce. Had the battle for Monterrey meant nothing? Well, the Rangers were going home anyway. They had enlisted for six months, and that time was up.

Disgusted, Hays, Walker, McCullough, and the rest of the Texans went home. General Taylor was not disappointed to see them go.

But the American army had just lost its eyes and ears.

Searching for the Comanche

John Meusebach mounted his horse and waited for the others. Finally, the wagons were ready, and they resumed their trek, led by Lorenzo de Rozas, a man who had been kidnapped by the Comanches as a child. He knew the country and the Comanche language, a perfect combination for Meusebach's purposes: to lead them to the Fisher-Miller grant and to make peace with the Indians.

It is not known whether anyone laughed at the German nobleman or called him a fool. Perhaps Meusebach was not fully aware of the nature of the people he sought. He certainly did not have the burden of festering fear and hate that many Texans held because of the constant depredations they had suffered. And the Indian blood spilled by the Texan settlers had left a similar stain on the red man. Was peace even possible?

Since his group of forty men had left the new encampment named Fredericksburg, the Germans had pushed their way slowly northwest. The heavily loaded wagons struggled up the long and rugged hills, and shortly, several things went wrong.

Critically, a campfire burned out of control, forcing Meusebach and his companions to fight the fire for thirty-six hours, and by the time they left the area, the land for miles around was laid waste by the conflagration.

But they pressed on.

Suddenly, Meusebach reined in his horse. Indians. Were these Comanches?

No. It soon became apparent that the members of this small hunting party could not speak Comanche, and the Germans used simple English to communicate. Meusebach himself was fluent in English, and by necessity, almost all the German immigrants had picked up at least a few words of the new language.

These Indians turned out to be Shawnee, who informed them that the Comanches had Meusebach's group under surveillance.

John Meusebach was encouraged. Surely, he would see the Comanches face-to-face very soon.

Missing Messages

At that moment, General Zachary Taylor faced all sorts of problems. His men were getting sick. In fact, he was losing more men to disease than to the Mexican army. President Polk was infuriated at him for sloppy tactics used at Monterrey, and also for his decision to let the enemy retreat.

And without the Texans to scout and deliver messages, Taylor was having some real problems, not to mention a meandering supply line that left him vulnerable...

Where was Lieutenant Richley? Those dispatches... The old general grumbled. He was worried.

The Nine Lives of Santa Anna

Santa Anna smiled as he read the American dispatches. He did not have all the pieces of the puzzle yet, but it was enough to know that many of the American troops would be going elsewhere. Monterrey would be held with only a small force.

What an opportunity. In the capricious, unstable realm of Mexican politics, Santa Anna had been in and out of favor several times. And while he was not dictator of the nation at the moment, the tide could well be turning, and a great military victory might put him on top again.

Knowing he could muster a large force, he issued orders—how could he lose?

Houston's Speech about Mexico

"Polk's war" was becoming unpopular in some places. For once, both Northern abolitionists and Senator Calhoun of South Carolina were on the same side. Abolitionists did not want to see an extension of southern territory, plus they were rather far removed from the situation that had made the war inevitable. Why should young men from New England die of yellow fever under a bungling general in Mexico?

Could this war be won? It seemed very doubtful to some.

Senator John C. Calhoun had a different argument, maintaining that the objectives of the war were already accomplished; the border of Texas was secure. It was a convincing argument for those who knew nothing of the situation.

Sam Houston listened to all the arguments. After the summer recess, he had reluctantly left his wife, son, and new baby daughter to come back to Washington. Politics indeed was wearisome, but perhaps he was needed here.

Houston took the floor and spoke at length. He defended the president and refuted the false arguments that had unsettled the people. He needed to explain that he was against tyranny, not the Mexican people themselves.

> We *can* conquer Mexico....
>
> Penetrate into the interior with your arms. March on! And if you inflict a shock on the mind of Mexico, follow it up with rapidity, and you will be able to dictate peace in the halls of Montezumas, or wherever else you please, even on the sacrificial stone in her capital.
>
> ...Let them know we are not warring against the rights of their citizens — against the oppressed people of Mexico, nor their priesthood, nor their religion. Show them that you will respect their temples, treat their images with deference, and, however much you may differ from their religious opinions, teach them that they will be entitled to freedom of thought, and the most perfect liberty. Show them that you only intend to chastize their tyrants, and oppressors.[4]

Houston's speech seemed to have an effect. The appropriations bill to sustain the war was passed by a comfortable margin.

Scouting for Taylor

Ben McCullough sent five men back to General Taylor to deliver what intelligence they had already gathered, while he and another man waited in the darkness. They were now within the lines of Santa Anna's camp, sent to determine how many men the Mexican leader had mustered.

Tucked in an out-of-the-way spot, the two men sat quietly, their horses tied up nearby. Before dawn, the *soldados* would undoubtedly light their campfires, and by the number of campfires and the light they shed, the two Rangers would be able to obtain a more accurate estimate.

McCullough thought about Taylor. When the Ranger and his twenty-seven companions had shown up at the general's headquarters last month, they had been well received. General Taylor had even violated army regulations and allowed the Rangers to enlist on their own terms. He had discovered rather painfully how much he needed these irregular Texans.

McCullough had not returned as a favor to the general. But the eight-week truce was over, and it was apparent that the war had resumed. Texans were beginning to trickle back to Mexico. In a way, it was *their* war.

McCullough's Rangers' first assignment was to locate Santa Anna's army, a task Taylor's men had been unable to accomplish. In short order, the Texans accomplished this mission and were given another: to determine the size of that army.

They had, so far, been undetected, and though what they were about to attempt was dangerous, it could be done. If they rode nonchalantly through the camp, not getting too close to any one campfire, no one would suspect them, at least not immediately—and they only needed a few minutes. Then they would disappear into the early morning darkness...

Flames flickered in the night air. The first fire. The two Rangers waited. After a while, other campfires dotted the terrain. There were a lot of men here; that they already knew. Ben McCullough mounted his horse, and his companion did the same.

Luckily, the campfires were smoky, allowing no one to see the buckskins they wore. McCullough carefully directed his horse, and the two rode through the smoke, deftly counting and observing.

Escaping notice, they shortly disappeared into the darkness. Santa Anna had at least fifteen and as many as twenty thousand men. Not the best news for General Taylor.

Arriving at camp, McCullough made his way to headquarters, tired and dusty, where the general received him, and the taciturn Ranger made his report.

"Very well, major, that's all I need to know. I am glad they did not catch you."[5]

The Impossible Happens

So, this was a Comanche. Speaking through his interpreter, Lorenzo de Rozas, John Meusebach assured the leader of his peaceful intentions. This small group of Indians had approached them with a white flag, and soon they were all seated and eating together.

Then the Comanches led Meusebach's expedition to their main camp on the San Saba River. Staring, the Germans took in the sight. A large number of Indians were approaching from the village on horseback, all decked out in colorful array.

The men sported long braided queues of hair decorated with silver; shells and pearls dangled from ears and necks. Their slim but tanned and muscular biceps glinted with brass rings. Greetings consisted of guns firing skyward and handshakes all around.

Meusebach soon came to understand that there were three main leaders. He gazed for a moment at Buffalo Hump, one of the chiefs. Unlike many of the other Comanches, this man refused the dress of the white man but stood before the German nobleman with only the skin of a buffalo wrapped around his hips.

Old Owl wore a dirty cotton jacket and didn't look very distinguished. Then Meusebach caught his eye. This old man was sharp, craftier than he looked—definitely the political leader. Then there was another man, very powerfully built, but this chief, Santana, seemed to wear a benevolent expression.

With Lorenzo serving as interpreter, Meusebach began to negotiate with the chiefs. His honest, earnest face and his willingness to walk about the Comanche camp unarmed had won a degree of respect from the Indians, who now listened.

After discussing more basic things, Meusebach explained,

> "When my people have lived with you for some time, and when we know each other better, then it may happen that some wish to marry. Soon our warriors will learn your language. If they then wish to marry a girl of your tribe, I do not see any obstacle, and our people will be so much better friends.... I do not disdain my red brethren because their skin is darker, and I do not think more of the white people because their complexion is lighter."[6]

The Comanches understood that these white men were different from the others, a different "tribe." Buffalo Hump considered. He understood the cost of war. It was good to have friends and allies. This white chief, whose name he could not pronounce, had even spoken of marriages. This white chief seemed like a real *person*, not like some of the others...

There were many things to consider. The chiefs conferred for a time before at last coming to a decision. There would be peace. Neither people would molest the other; they would live as brethren.

For many years afterward, the German immigrants and the Comanches lived in peace. It seemed John O. Meusebach had done the impossible.

A Strategic Retreat

Taylor knew he and his small force were vulnerable. Unfortunately, many of his men had been sent to the coast to join General Scott's force. Now with only forty-six hundred largely untested men, he knew they would be doomed on level terrain, and therefore, he had retreated to the mountains. What about the pass? Yes, here in the pass of Angostura, they might stand a fighting chance. The Mexicans would not be able to turn their flank.

The Texas Rangers kept him informed of Santa Anna's movements. Taylor never truly liked them, but he appreciated their invaluable insight. They would make great soldiers if only they had discipline.

While Taylor was not surprised by the Mexican advance, Santa Anna was unprepared when the Americans did not act like men in retreat. He had been expecting whipped puppies, not aggressive guard dogs. The blue-coated American soldiers mowed down his unwary army.

Once again, Santa Anna had defeated himself. The blood of his troops watered the ground. Broken, his army struggled back across the desert.

Soon, the word was out that General Taylor had beaten a superior force at Buena Vista, and Americans everywhere rejoiced.

Ben McCullough and his men returned home. The war in northern Mexico was essentially over.

Scott's Goal

Winfield Scott was the titular head of the United States Army. But unfortunately, politics just had to get mixed into everything. It was clear that President Polk didn't like Scott; perhaps he liked Taylor even less. There was one man Polk seemed to get along with—that Texas fellow, Sam Houston.

Senator Houston's name had been tossed around, but rumor had it that Houston had refused a commission because his *wife* didn't want him to go. General Scott smiled. Maybe there was some truth in that. Houston's reformation was a well-known fact, and his wife was given the credit.

Anyway, things had finally worked out in Washington, and here he was in Mexico, his troops disembarking. Scott had just landed near the Mexican city of Vera Cruz, which was east of the capital of Mexico City. His plan was to take Cortez's route west, capture Mexico City, and force the government to surrender.

It was an ambitious undertaking, the largest American invasion ever orchestrated. But Scott was optimistic. He had West Point engineers and the very latest in artillery. The whole problem with artillery was that it took time and energy to move, and before you knew it, your position could be overrun or flanked. But recently someone had developed a more practical, lightweight cannon that was easily moved from place to place. Well, this would be the ultimate test. Real war.

A Search for a Dime

Samuel H. Walker reined in his horse, his men slowing to a stop behind him. The stone edifice before him stirred up memories painful and deep. This was the prison of Perote.

Walker had gone with Fisher on the ill-fated Mier expedition. He remembered the long march, the privation and humiliation, and then the cruel slaughter of seventeen of his fellow Texans at Haciendo Salado.

Those who survived had been imprisoned here, and somewhere inside was a dime that Walker had hidden just in case he ever returned. And now here he was. Thanks to General Scott, the stars and stripes now flew over this hated fortress. But the battle was not yet over.

Walker dismounted and walked inside. He wanted to find that dime.

Rangers Needed Once Again

After finishing his research, Captain Robert E. Lee of the Army Corps of Engineers reported to General Scott. The route over the volcanic ridges southwest of Mexico City had been scouted and a strategy planned. It could be done.

The general was pleased. Santa Anna, recovering from his defeat in the north, laboriously defended his nation's capital, but since the terrain to the southwest was so rugged, it seemed to need no fortifications.

Thanks to his engineers, Scott now knew how he could take the city.

However, he still had other problems. His supply line, for one thing. Food and supplies for his huge army of eleven thousand men came by wagon from the coast. And in the hills and defiles to the east, groups of *rancheros* were harassing and killing his men.

Plus, General Scott was fully aware that his flanks would need protection at all times. He had already stationed men for that purpose, but they might not be enough. This Walker fellow was training his own company of men, and perhaps they would be able to help.

Then the general received a message from President Polk, who had heard about the supply line problem. He wrote back to Scott that Jack Hays was the man for the task, and he would be coming to guard the road with his Texas Rangers.

General Scott was not pleased. How did Polk know what was best out here in the field?

Maybe Scott didn't realize that Sam Houston was a friend of the president. And Houston knew exactly what Jack Hays and his men could do.

Ranger Tactics

With great satisfaction, Ranger Captain John S. Ford handed out "Walker Colts" to his men. A shipment had come in from the East Coast; Samuel Colt had filled a government order for one thousand of these beauties. Now, all the Rangers who had come to Mexico with Jack Hays were fully armed and ready.

The large contingent of Rangers fell in with Lane's Brigade — regular army— for the march inland.

Guerrillas. A guerrilla is, in essence, a soldier without an army. "Real" soldiers mass together and fight other "real" armies on "real" battlegrounds. But when there is danger, and there is no army to fight for you, what do you do?

Some of the citizens of Mexico responded to the threat of the American army by becoming guerrillas. Because good horsemen were well-suited to the task, *rancheros* banded together secretly and attacked the American soldiers and their wagons coming up from the coast.

Their prey never knew when they would strike; afterward, the guerrillas would disappear like magic, leaving the Americans' morale at an all-time low.

Samuel Walker understood the situation. A Texas Ranger was something of a guerrilla himself. And since it was impossible to guard the whole supply line adequately, Walker took the battle to the enemy. He and his men scouted the brush and the hills and the *ranchos*. Sometimes he was able to recapture supplies, but curiously, he never brought back any prisoners.

Walker knew that with his small force, he could not make the supply line secure, but he could make it as dangerous as possible for the Mexican guerrillas.

Mexico City Captured

One more obstacle lay between General Scott's men and Mexico City. The Castle of Chapultepec rose before them on a hill, like a fortress guarding the city beyond. It was guarded by cannon and *soldados* stationed in entrenchments.

Well, one option was to surround the place and lay siege. This would be the safest way, but with his long supply line having been harassed all this time, supplies were low. No, General Scott decided, we will have to attack. Once in Mexico City, supplies could probably be purchased. He had no intention of "spoiling" the city. Nothing would be taken without compensation.

On September 13, 1847, Scott's army attacked, with several generals leading different columns against the castle. One general decided to split his artillery into two groups.

Captain Magruder, in charge of this artillery unit, instructed his right-hand man, Lieutenant Thomas Jackson, to take the guns and men under his command to the northwest side of the castle, while he would direct the action of the rest.

The lieutenant did so, and the maneuverable horse-drawn cannons under Jackson's care were soon hammering away at the enemy. But soon, a necessary change of position found Jackson located straight across from some of the Mexican guns at almost point-blank range.

Very quickly, most of his horses and many of his men were struck down or driven away. But the brave lieutenant remained. Later on, he would acquire the nickname "Stonewall."

General Worth saw the brave man's predicament and commanded him to withdraw, but Jackson sent word that to retreat would be more dangerous than to remain, and if he could have help, he would attempt to capture the guns that had just inflicted such heavy losses.

Magruder saw Jackson's situation and galloped to the scene. As he approached, his horse stumbled and fell dead, pierced by an enemy bullet. The captain kept low and made his way to the ditch where Jackson still labored alongside a sergeant. The faithful lieutenant had pulled one of the cannons by hand to a point where it could be fired against the enemy. His captain assisted him, and soon they had two guns roaring in their ears as they loaded and fired, again and again.

The artillery fire had its intended effect, and the Mexicans across from them were driven from their guns. The rest of Scott's army had similar success, and soon the enemy was in retreat.

On September 14, 1847, General Winfield Scott's army entered Mexico City and met little resistance from the people.

Walker's Legacy

Walker was dead. After the battle, his men even gathered around his body and wept. Jack Hays, who had been called into the battle with Lane's Brigade, heard about what had happened.

Santa Anna had attacked Scott's exposed flank after the Americans entered Mexico City. Samuel Walker and his men had formed the vanguard that charged some Mexican soldiers at Huamantla on October 9th. They fought well until Santa Anna's main force arrived. At that point, things looked very grave until Lane's Brigade and Hays' men arrived. Then the tide of battle turned, and Santa Anna lost all his artillery to the Americans and was driven from the field.

Jack Hays mourned. He looked upon the body of the red-haired man he had personally trained as his lieutenant. Well, "Walker's Colt" was this man's legacy, as well as his brave deeds and cool leadership. Clearly, everyone would miss him.

Hays mounted his horse. There was work to do, especially with Walker gone. It was time to find some guerrillas.

Repercussions

Ranger Captain Jack Hays led his men into Mexico City, along with some prisoners. The whole city was stirred, and soon men and women thronged the streets, fearful of the "*diablos Tejanos,*" yet eager for a peek at these dark legends on horseback.

But it was not long before Hays was called on the carpet. General Scott summoned the Ranger captain to his headquarters.

Before Jack Hays walked into the room, he already had a good idea of what was wrong. Now, some of the incidents were minor. A pickpocket stole a handkerchief, and the victim, an angry Ranger, responded with a bullet. A stone thrown was answered with another bullet.

Then there was the funny story about the waiter in the National Theater. Several Rangers had entered the place, and when a waiter caught sight of them, he dropped his trays and fled, unwilling to risk offending a Texas Ranger!

But there was more, Hays knew, as he gave his respects to the general. "Old Fuss and Feathers," his men called him, behind his back, of course. Today, General Scott was fussing about eighty Mexican bodies in the morgue that the Rangers had slaughtered in revenge for the murder of one of their own.

Hays listened as the general protested. What could he say? He wasn't sure if he could *defend* the actions of his men. As a rule, the Rangers were not lawless ruffians. In fact, many of them were quite well educated; some were even known to speak Greek and Latin around their campfires.

They were raised, by and large, in the West and South, imbibing the code of honor of the gentleman, but they had been thrust into a situation where kill-or-be-killed was a fact of life. The Rangers were part of the American militia tradition, volunteers who were defending the lives of others, protecting the helpless, most notably, those of women, children, and the elderly. It had been a guerrilla war in Texas, fought on two fronts, north and south, against Comanches and against Mexicans, both of whom, in the hearts of Texans, were the "bad guys." And the word was that if you weren't careful, the next turn in the road could be your last.

Captain Hays stood up to General Scott. He couldn't explain, but in a mild tone of voice, he stated that no one should "impose" on the Rangers.

Scott wisely decided to drop the issue. Instead, he arranged for the Texans to be relocated to a place outside the capital.

Political Ramifications

As a treaty was being negotiated between the United States and Mexico, Sam Houston took to the stump. In New England, those who had opposed the war now opposed any additional territory that the treaty might include. In February 1848, Senator Houston spoke to a crowd in New York. He saw a bigger picture, a nation from sea to sea, under the hand of a directing Providence.

> ...I cannot regard as fellow-citizens the men who array themselves against the cause of their country, who defame its armies and the glory they have acquired for the nation; who array themselves against the administration of their country, and seek to strengthen the hands of the enemy. Such people do not reflect, or they have lost all wisdom of the mind... while they reserve all their feelings and piety for "poor Mexico" and care nothing about... their own country...
>
> I do not think the war with Mexico is such a calamity as it has been deplored to be.... The ways of Providence are inscrutable; but I think we may see the finger of God in this war, giving success to our arms, and crowning our forces with victory. I do not deplore it... I say, the Divine Being has been evidently carrying out the destiny of the American race. We give to the Mexican liberal principles; we elevate them far above what their tyrants have done; and the day will come when they will bless the Americans as their friends and liberators until time shall cease....[7]

The treaty was discussed before the Senate. Texas, California, and the area in between the two regions — Mexico's northern half — would be ceded to the United States. But, it was pointed out, Mexico merely *occupied* most of this land. Few Mexicans actually lived there.

Plus, $15,000,000 was being given to Mexico in return, money Santa Anna desperately needed. His government was bankrupt. Also, all Mexican debts owed to Americans were being assumed by the U.S., which amounted to another $3,000,000, which was quite a sum of money in those days.

Some anti-expansionists opposed the "Treaty of Guadalupe Hidalgo," and others thought it was too "easy" on Mexico, but on March 10, 1848, the U.S. Senate approved it by a vote of thirty-eight to fourteen.

W.C.

26th Feby 1848

My Love,

I send one of our dear Boys papers, & as I got Genl Rusk to send you a speech of his, I concluded to write this note, lest his frank might make you feel for an instant, unhappy. To day we interred Mr. Adams, & it is the third day in which nothing has been done.

Tomorrow is Sunday. You will see that there is a Treaty before Congress. I can't tell you any thing about it but what you see. I have only received one letter my Love, and you may judge how I feel in consequence of the fact. I declare that you are the last object, that leaves my mind at night, and the first, that I greet in the morning. You are present to me a thousand times in the day. Dear Sam & Nannie too are often present with us. I would rather see you all for one day, than realise all that this place cou'd afford me in years.

Do my Dearest Love, present me to Ma, and your young companions. Kiss the dear children, and believe me ever thy devoted & faithful husband.

Houston

You see how much my hand is altered. Tho, I am fat,
and I fear becoming much larger than usual, I get no exercise!
Do my Love write me all about your health etc.?[8]

For Sam Houston, the success of Scott's army and the successful negotiation of the treaty must have begotten many thoughts and emotions. Could it be that his beloved Texas might now have peace on her borders? Though it was something for which he had labored for years, could it now be true?

The territory acquired by this treaty was a great boon for the United States. It was a physical manifestation of the Monroe Doctrine, which had seemed slightly presumptuous at its first proclamation.

But holding the vast middle of the continent from sea to sea gave the nation a practical sense of security: it was no longer likely that a new European power would obtain a foothold on the continent. Too bad Jackson wasn't here to see it.

Perhaps Houston even thought back to San Jacinto. If that victory had not been won, would any of this have happened? Would all this new territory have been acquired? Probably not.

Then his thoughts turned back to Margaret. Margaret and home.

Chapter 15

Rising Waters

IT WAS a chilly January evening in 1849. Men filed into the Senate chamber, singly or in groups, until the stuffy room was full. Their formal dress and the formal surroundings clashed with the tobacco juice staining the carpet, but no one seemed to notice. This was a special meeting of senators and congressmen from the Southern states, called by Senator John C. Calhoun, from South Carolina. And the matter before them was already generally known. The cool yet determined Calhoun had written a statement he wanted every Southern legislator to sign. He stood up to read.

> "We, whose names are hereunto annexed, address you in discharge of what we believed to be a solemn duty, on the most important subject ever presented for your consideration. We allude to the conflict between the two great sections of the Union, growing out of a difference of feeling and opinion in reference to the relation existing between the two races..."[1]

John C. Calhoun seemed weak in body, but his blue eyes flashed under stern brows as he continued to address the assembly. He began to review the history of the question of slavery in relation to the Constitution. Slavery had been an issue back in the days of the Founding Fathers, as every educated man knew.

The problem had been circumvented by certain guarantees to protect the property of slaveowners, including a guarantee to return escaped slaves. Speaking of these guarantees, Calhoun brought home the point.

> "It was well understood at the time, that without them the Constitution would not have been adopted by the Southern States, and of course that they contained elements so essential to the system that it never would have existed without them. The Northern States, knowing all this, ratified the Constitution, thereby pledging their faith, in the most solemn manner, sacredly to observe them. How that faith has been kept and that pledge redeemed we shall next proceed to show."[2]

Calhoun continued to speak. He went from point to point, explaining how the Northern states were at fault for their "aggression" toward the Southern states. Abolitionists were enticing slaves to abscond from their rightful masters, and it was now very difficult for a slave owner to recover his property when a slave would flee to a Northern state.

But Calhoun's main focus was the Constitution. Originally, each state had decided for itself whether to permit the institution of slavery within its borders; but now, when new territory was acquired by the United States, the federal government claimed the authority to decide whether states formed by that territory would be "slave" or "free."

The Fear of Southerners

Finally, the white-haired senator brought forth the most emotional argument. If the North had its way, the slaves would be emancipated, in a manner that would cause the "prostration of the white race."

> "[The] people of the North... would not stop at emancipation. Another step would be taken — to raise [the former slaves] to a political and social equality with their former owners, by giving them the right of voting and holding public offices under the Federal Government.... The blacks, and the profligate whites that might unite with them, would become the principal recipients of federal offices and patronage, and would, in consequence, be raised above the whites of the South in the political and social scale. We would, in a word, change conditions with them — a degradation greater than has ever fallen to the lot of a free and enlightened people, and one from which we could not escape, should emancipation take place (which it certainly will if not prevented), but by fleeing the homes of ourselves and ancestors, and by abandoning our country to our former slaves, to become the permanent abode of disorder, anarchy, poverty, misery, and wretchedness."

The men in the Senate Chamber were hearing the worst fears of the South voiced in sure and awful certainty. And many were in basic agreement with the Senator from South Carolina.

"We, then, are of the opinion that the first and indispensable step, without which nothing can be done, and with which everything may be, is to be united among yourselves, on this great and most vital question..." Calhoun was calling the men in the room to place the issue of slavery as the first and foremost issue: "...you must prove by your acts that you hold all other questions subordinate to it."

Perhaps the North would see this unity and determination of the South and back off. If not, "the time will then have come for you to decide what course to adopt."[3]

So that was it. Most of Calhoun's address was not new, except for the last part. In fact, Calhoun had just drawn a line in the dirt with his toe, and he was calling the leadership of the South to stand with him and *dare* the North to cross that line. He was replacing the *Union* of the United States with the *Union* of the South.

Some of the men in the room were angry, including heavy-set Robert Toombs of Georgia, who clashed with Calhoun, standing firm in his support for the Union. The discussion and debate continued for hours. Finally, out of eighty men who attended, forty-eight stepped forward to sign Calhoun's "Southern Address."

But the South was hardly unified. There were many men who had not even attended, protesting the action by their absence. Some of them were very influential, like Senator Benton of Missouri, whose fiery, verbal darts often flew in Calhoun's direction. Neither senator from Texas had shown up tonight, though both Texas congressmen had come and signed the document. After thinking it over, Calhoun decided Sam Houston was the real problem. His patient but moving oratory always carried enormous weight.

Then again, maybe Houston wasn't such a problem. It had been easy to stir up the loyal Southerners of Texas against him after Houston had betrayed the South by voting for the anti-slavery Oregon bill. Even his own constituents had called him a traitor. No, the general was walking on treacherous ground, and if he didn't change his course, that ground might well fall from beneath his feet.

Calhoun's Dangerous Reasoning

In his room, Sam Houston read a copy of Senator Calhoun's Southern Address. His brow furrowed as he analyzed every sentence.

What was this? He read it again. "What then we do insist on, is, not to extend slavery, but that we shall not be prohibited from migrating with our property, into the Territories of the United States, because we are slaveholders."[4]

He coughed, then cleared his throat. His cold was better, but it was not done with him yet. This statement by Calhoun was nonsense. Slavery could only exist in areas where it was protected by law. For slaveholders to retain their "property," their "property" had to be recognized as such by the state in which they lived. Therefore, those territories mentioned by Calhoun would be required to recognize and allow the institution of slavery for slaveholders to bring their slaves!

And here, at the close of the address, Calhoun made his threats: "...the time will then have come for you to decide...." Everyone with a brain knew what he meant by that.

Secession. Calhoun had tried it before—well, not exactly secession. Twenty years ago, South Carolina had "nullified" a federal tariff law, claiming the right to stand between the federal government and its citizens. Nullification was a repudiation of the Constitution, the republic, and the *Union* itself, because if the individual states could accept or reject federal laws at will, the federal government was, in essence, powerless to enforce laws.

Calhoun, as Jackson's vice-president, had initially kept his involvement in the nullification movement behind the scenes, hoping to attain the presidency. *Everything with this man was politically motivated,* thought Houston.

After Senator Calhoun had publicly attacked Houston for his vote on the Oregon bill, the Texas senator had quietly researched the career of this man he feared was a demagogue. His fears were confirmed in his research, which revealed an ambitious man who was pushing the nation toward disunion—even war.

And there was not a single Southerner who had really stood up to him. Some did oppose him on the floor of the Senate, but no one had really *taken him on.*

Secession. That's where Calhoun was leading. Houston thought about the Hartford Convention that had occurred during the War of 1812, when opponents of the war in New England had gathered together. There was even talk of New England seceding from the Union, but Jackson's victory in New Orleans had made all such talk moot.

The nullification controversy had been solved without bloodshed as well, but now—well, there was a lot at stake. Otherwise, he would not endure this separation from his wife and family.

Houston's thoughts turned to home and Margaret. He had not heard from her for an entire month. Was the baby well? A second daughter, Maggie, named after her mother, had been added to their family circle. And how was the new overseer working out? Sam gathered his writing materials.

Bear-That-Walks-Like-Man

Ranger John S. Ford followed his friend, Major Robert S. Neighbors, into Comanche territory. "Old Rip" Ford was not nervous. Rangers didn't get nervous. But Ford was used to fighting, not talking, and their mission now was to talk to these Indians. He really wasn't sure there was much good in it, but he respected his friend, whom everyone simply addressed as "Major."

Ford glanced at Major Neighbors, riding silently ahead of him on a tall, clean-limbed bay horse. Others called this man an "injun-lover," basically a traitor to the white race, but Ford knew differently. Neighbors was an honorable, honest man who was doing a good job as an Indian agent, a job that was really impossible to begin with.

How can a man be responsible for seeing that the Indians keep treaties? The only way Ford knew how to deal with a Comanche was with a fully loaded Walker Colt, like the one now tucked in his belt. But his friend wasn't the type to sit in an office and collect salary for basically doing nothing, as some agents were known to do. Neighbors knew some of these Comanches by name, and they had even come up with a Comanche name for this white man: Bear-That-Walks-Like- Man.

The Ranger had to grin. It was a good description. Neighbors possessed a powerful, six-foot-two frame and a large amount of reddish-brown hair. Yes, he looked like a bear, and he was certainly a brave man, having spent two years in that Mexican prison after General Woll had captured him along with the whole court-house in 1842.

He was a good partner for the job ahead of them: finding a route west for the Americans now flowing west to California, to the gold fields. Well, not everyone heading west in 1849 was seeking gold, but the discovery of the precious metal last year had swollen the trickle of settlers to a flood, and one of the routes west was through Texas.

Gold-seekers filled the hotels and saloons of San Antonio, ignorant of the Comanches that awaited them. The United States Army was supposed to protect these travelers, but to do that, they needed a planned route along which they could build forts.

And the major knew that the Comanches would see this as an invasion of sorts, an excuse for war.

Suddenly, Neighbors reined in his horse, and the Ranger drew up alongside him. "Buzzards," indicated the major.

Ford simply nodded. They must be drawing near to the Comanche camp.

He wasn't nervous. But he suddenly felt glad that Neighbors was a praying man.

Preserving the Union

Sam Houston thought long and hard about what he was about to do. He had decided upon a letter, instead of a Senate speech, and since many of his constituents had opposed his vote on the Oregon bill, he needed to justify his actions.

But this was not going to be just a letter to his constituents. The contents would be spread abroad, he knew. Houston had decided to do something that no other Southerner had done. He would take Calhoun apart and expose him for what he was.

He dipped his pen in the inkwell.

"To My Constituents: Soon after the close of the last session of Congress, my conduct in relation to an important public measure was called into question by Mr. Calhoun."[5]

The pen scratched across the page. The Oregon bill was the immediate reason for this letter, but it was only the beginning. Now for a deeper question—upon what authority did Calhoun presume to speak for the South? By divine right? For services rendered? Houston dipped the pen in the inkwell again and proceeded to ask his constituents those same questions.

Then, bringing forth the public record of the Senator from South Carolina, Houston carefully exposed Calhoun's political motives and ambitions. Houston was no stranger to ambition, and he was no stranger to a lack of it. His heart dwelt with his wife in Huntsville, no longer esteeming the pomp and pride of the political realm, and so with a penetrating insight, he made these statements:

> "...this vigilant guardian of Southern rights, who... was ever ready to barter them, to attain his selfish ends, is now laboring to make more intense than ever the excitement of the question of slavery... both at the north and the south upon new and most ultra grounds...."
>
> "...To embody this engine of revolution, has ever been in the scope of Mr. Calhoun's dismembering machinations. ... agitation in the North is looked to by Mr. Calhoun as an indispensable preliminary to effectuate his *revolutionary movements at the South*....in his late address he renews the idea that the North's interference with Southern rights '*would be, among independent nations, just cause of war,*'

and makes the effort to '*place the several States in the relation to each other of open enemies.*'[6]

Houston finished the letter by taking a personal stand: "if opposition to all the schemes of mad fanaticism at the north and mad ambition at the south, which would embroil the country in civil war, provoke assault upon me, there is no man living who will give them a heartier welcome."

Professing his love and fealty (fidelity) to the Union, he explained, "This feeling has been impressed upon my heart by the instruction and example of the great man whom, when a boy, I followed as a soldier... and from whom as a statesman I never separated, until I wept over his yet warm remains at the Hermitage. The great trophy of his history will be the stern purpose with which he maintained the watchword of his administration, 'The Federal Union, it must be preserved.'[7]

Houston laid down his pen. He had given full and careful expression to his thoughts, and the turbulent pressure in his heart was now relieved. But this letter would cause him problems in Texas — those under the sway of Calhoun's doctrines would not readily change their opinions. Oh well. And then there was the tension currently building up in the Senate. He had more work to do here before he could go home to Margaret.

Deal Made

Sanaco passed the ceremonial pipe to Yellow Wolf, who then passed it to Buffalo Hump. Major Neighbors waited his turn, the smell of the pipe blending with the smell of the bear grease the Comanches used on their bodies. Then Neighbors drew on the pipe, thus sealing the deal they had made, much as the white man would use a signature.

It had not been easy. Sanaco was still suspicious, but the other chiefs were enticed by the thought of gifts from the Great Father in Washington. The major decided that if trinkets would prevent bloodshed, so be it. And though the Comanches would never agree to forts on their hunting grounds, they had agreed to allow the trail to be marked. In fact, one of their chiefs, Guadalupe, would accompany them as a guide.

After the other chiefs had gone, Neighbors made Sanaco a gift of tobacco, lead, and powder, all of which were real gifts, not simply trinkets. And though the big, burly Indian agent knew that no gift would totally erase the glint of suspicion in the red man's eyes, he simply did his best. If only they were treated as *men*... if only his own people would treat them according to what was *right*... if only. The major sighed and went to find Ford.

They had a long ride ahead of them.

John Barleycorn

Sitting in his seat in the Senate chamber, Houston began a letter to his wife. It was already late in the evening of March 3rd, 1849, and it looked like they would all be there for quite a while yet. The debate was fierce and getting quite rude. Houston wrote,

> "If we live to meet, I will tell you that I do not intend,... to be absent from my family longer than a few days, with my own consent. I cannot forgo, voluntarily, the happiness of your society, or the noise of the children. For really, I would not consider it perplexing, if they were with me, or I with them. The noise which I endure here from the grown children, is ten times more annoying to me, than all that I know you hear at home, from the children."[8]

Grown children, indeed. The Senate was in major turmoil. Calhoun had surreptitiously engineered a plan to guarantee slavery in the states that would be formed from the territory acquired from Mexico. The Senator from South Carolina and his supporters had persuaded a young Democrat from Wisconsin to introduce an amendment to extend the laws of the United States to the newly acquired territory.

Mexican law forbade slavery. The laws of the United States allowed it south of the Missouri Compromise line. This amendment, therefore, provided for slavery in this huge southwest territory. But few senators realized this, and Houston was among those who had mistakenly voted for the innocuous-sounding amendment.

Then Daniel Webster stood up and explained the significance of the amendment before the Senate. Could this amendment be reconsidered? Houston was among a handful of members who desired to change their vote. This issue came up for debate on March 3rd, and the battle raged.

Houston did not give many details of the debate in his letter to Margaret. "... matters here to me, are very uninteresting to me, and were I to take them to you, I can not believe that they would be very charming to you. My love, & howda to all."[9]

He could not describe with profit what was going on, and though he did not *hide* things from his wife, there was no point in going into detail. Just the day before, he had explained that it was the custom of some of the members to get full of "John Barleycorn," and that would be sufficient for his discerning wife to get the gist of things happening there.

He signed his name with his full and distinctive script. Then he looked up, wondering if things would come to blows. They eventually did. Curses had already defiled this chamber devoted to the highest offices in the land.

Sam Houston, alias "Big Drunk" in former days and present-day Temperance lecturer, was horrified. Many of the senators had visited a certain drinking establishment during their afternoon break and returned for a lengthy evening debate in a state of inebriation. Now it was after midnight, and members had been slipping out to obtain more infernal inspiration. A few were falling down drunk.

Finally, it was too much. Houston rose and stated that though he was familiar with the license and turbulence of the frontier, the present spectacle filled him with shame. He was anguished to see his fellow senators so agitated and discomposed.

Apparently, his speech had some effect, and a measure of order was restored. Houston remarked, "I will not rebuke the Senate. Every Senator upon this floor is capable of instructing and teaching me. But I can express my joy at the return of system and order."[10]

But they did not accomplish much that night, and finally, bleary-eyed, the tired senators adjourned at six-thirty the next morning. Soon the spring session would be over, and Houston longed to go home.

Neighbors Fired

Major Robert S. Neighbors was angry. He strode out of the building into the harsh glare of the July sun. Washington was always hot in the summertime, but the steamy discomfort barely touched the major's mind as he thought over what he had just learned.

The newly inaugurated president, Zachary Taylor, was a Whig, not a Democrat as Polk had been. Taylor had won the presidential election of 1848 on the strength of his military victory at Buena Vista, which had given him somewhat of a hero status. Now the Whigs were in power, and Neighbors was not a Whig.

He was a Democrat, as most Texans were. In fact, politics in Texas largely consisted of spats between Democrats. There seemed to be two basic groups of Democrats in Texas: pro-Houston "Jacksonian" Democrats, and anti-Houston, Calhoun-type Democrats, who were currently taking Senator Houston apart for his Unionist stand in Congress.

Whigs were now in favor for federal offices, and Neighbors had just been summarily replaced as Indian agent by a man who didn't know anything about the Indian situation, but who was qualified in another way: he was a Whig. Being summoned to the War Department's Indian Affairs Bureau, the major had been tempted to throttle the bureaucrat who had just, well, *fired* him. It wasn't the money. He had land and money both. But what would happen to Texas?

Anglos were constantly immigrating into the new state, pushing back the frontier. The "tame" Indians retreated before them, sometimes being deprived of their land by unscrupulous whites. Now these small tribes, such as the Caddos and Tonkawas, were leading a precarious existence between the whites and the Comanches, sandwiched between two powerful enemies.

Plus, statehood was not solving anything. Sure, there were now federal troops stationed in newly erected forts, but so far, they were ineffective. Many of the Rangers had dispersed after the Mexican War, and they were the only ones who really knew what they were up against.

Neighbors prepared to go back home to San Antonio. Maybe something good would come of this. Time to settle down... could he dare hope for a wife and family?

Raven Hill

Houston picked up his youngest, little Maggie, and set her on his lap. It was nice to be home. Raven Hill, his small estate, was his private domain, away from the bickering of Washington and even the mud wallows of local Texas politics. His refuge from the world.

Actually, though, the Houston home was a world in itself. Relatives visited and sometimes stayed for lengths of time, often a good thing for Margaret when her husband was far away in Washington. At present, Margaret's mother also lived with them, and the Houstons were caring for a teenage girl, a ward of Margaret's brother, Vernal, whose wife had died.

A number of enslaved persons were also employed at Raven Hill. Eliza served the family inside the home, and several others worked outside, caring for the animals and tending to the crops. Joshua, a mature black man with skill as a blacksmith, held a place of authority and was responsible for certain tasks about the place. The rest of his time he was free to use to earn money at his trade. Other slaves were hired out to other families from time to time, if their help was not needed at Raven Hill. Mr. Gott, the white overseer, was responsible for the management of the farm, an important job with Houston absent so much.

These days at home were simply too few. Houston had done some traveling this summer on business, trying a few cases as an attorney, and then returning home. Now it was autumn, and once again, the day approached when he needed to leave. The Thirty-first Congress of the United States would soon convene, and he knew he needed to be there. The whole slavery issue festered like a boil. A boil that needed to be lanced—peacefully, he hoped.

The Great Compromiser

Henry Clay felt the passing of time. He was seventy-three years old, and his body gave testimony to the years that had flowed past him; important years, formative years for the young Republic of the United States. And here he was back again in the Senate, the Kentucky Legislature having seen fit, in its wisdom, to return him to the turmoil of national politics, an unhappy turmoil, which had its unfortunate roots in generations past.

It was January of 1850, and the Senate chamber was warm with the heat of several fireplaces, stuffy and smoky and not always comfortable. From his seat, Senator Clay could see the bright Mexican blanket Houston wore about his shoulders to ward off the chill. Houston, the earnest friend of Clay's old enemy, Jackson. Well, Houston would probably be an ally in the battle at hand, as he was a reliable Union man. That was kind of ironic.

Henry Clay had formulated another compromise, for what was politics but compromise? Everyone remembered his Missouri Compromise of 1820; indeed, it was still an important part of what was going on now. But great skill and care were needed at this critical juncture in their nation's history: both North and South felt strongly, and not only did they feel strongly, but a *moral* sense on both sides fed the fires of self-righteousness.

He knew that some, like Calhoun, were past compromise, wedded to their own path and would take as many down that path as they could. And then there were Northerners, who were just as rigid, proclaiming that a "higher law" than the Constitution demanded the immediate end of slavery in the South.

Clay looked about him, at the fancy purple hangings, the gold snuffbox on the vice-president's desk, then down to the dribbles of tobacco juice on the carpet. Would there be enough wisdom in the men seated here to band together and prevent the calamity that hung over their heads? He certainly hoped so.

Finally, his turn came, and he was given the floor. He gave only a brief speech, announcing his intentions to introduce certain resolutions that he hoped would quell the talk of disunion.

He sat down. There was a low murmuring in the chamber.

A Nation Divided

The woman emerged from the carriage, her gloved hand supported by her escort. Stepping down, she blinked in the sunlight and, with one smooth motion, opened her parasol and lifted it above her head. It was only a short walk to the Capitol, but every lady of fashion regarded sunlight as an enemy. A suntan was fine for farmers' wives, but not for the genteel.

There was quite a crowd here today. Senator Sam Houston was scheduled to speak, and the news had reached folks in Washington who wished to attend. It was not unusual to have visitors in the galleries of the Senate chamber, and of course, there were the members of the press, who would record the senators as they spoke, but from time to time, there were national issues so pressing and momentous that the popular interest was kindled, and then the crowds gathered.

Houston rose to speak. He did not get far before he was interrupted by a colleague, who asked for a suspension of the rules of the Senate regarding visitors. The galleries were already packed, and there was not enough room for all who wished to hear Houston speak.

Before long, the request was approved, and people poured onto the floor of the chamber. Finally, every bit of room was occupied, with ladies sitting on stools between the desks of the senators.

Calhoun was absent and reputed to be ill. Houston expressed regret, both for his physical sufferings and for the fact that he would be addressing Calhoun's position on various issues. Then he launched into his main theme: that the discord between North and South was not incurable.

"But I call upon the friends of the Union from every quarter, to come forward like men, and to sacrifice their differences upon the common altar of their country's good, and to form a bulwark around the Constitution that cannot be shaken...."

Ever practical, Houston suggested a committee of men to take the task in hand:

> "I have no doubt six Senators here could be designated, without reference to party, [or section], ...who would act as a committee of conference, and sit down together as wayfaring men, and produce satisfactory reconciliation, thereby diffusing universal peace, and calming the agitated waves that are lashing at the base of our Capitol, and speak comfort and solace to millions of freemen."[11]

Houston excoriated the Southern Address as intended to cause division. After outlining the basic claims of North and South, he suggested his own compromise:

that the Missouri Compromise line of 1820 be extended to the Pacific coast. Then he gave a heart-rending appeal:

> "I beseech those whose piety will permit them reverently to petition, that they will pray for this Union, and ask that He who buildeth up and pulleth down nations will, in mercy, preserve and unite us. For a nation divided against itself cannot stand. I wish, if this Union be dissolved, that its ruins may be the monument of my grave, and the graves of my family. I wish no epitaph to be written to tell that I survive the ruin of this glorious Union."[12]

A Letter from Home

Houston opened his wife's letter with interest and mild trepidation. Margaret was expecting their fourth child and had recently sprained her ankle. Both circumstances tended to weigh down her sensitive spirits, and he longed to be home with her. He began to read.

The fifty-six-year-old senator started and took a deep breath. Virginia Thorne, Vernal's teenage ward whom they had been housing, had run off with the overseer! The girl had been a trial to the family, but at least now they were relieved of this responsibility, though in a way they had not anticipated nor desired.

Amazingly, Margaret's spirits seemed fine. The Lord had sustained her through these trials, and she even encouraged her husband, writing, "Go on beloved from strength to strength, from grace to grace, and the Lord will give you more and more light."[13]

He needed to be home. He would make excuses to his colleagues. Margaret and his family came before the nation, indeed, the entire world.

Before he retired, Houston pulled out his New Testament, as was his habit, and read a chapter, then knelt on the floor to pray. He had much on his heart, and he could not carry it all himself.

Calhoun's Last Speech

Having left for Texas, Houston was not in the Senate chamber the morning of March 4th, 1850, when a feeble John C. Calhoun entered upon the arm of a stronger South Carolinian, General James Hamilton. The Senate was stunned. Calhoun looked terrible, his cheeks sunken. Both enemies and friends surged about him in welcome.

Later that day, Senator Calhoun rose. He had written a speech in reply to the recent proposals by Mr. Clay. Formally, he thanked his colleagues for their consideration and announced that Virginia Senator James Mason would read his speech. He returned to his seat.

Everyone knew that Calhoun was dying, and so they gave rapt attention to his last effort.

Mason cleared his throat and began. He gave voice to Calhoun's thoughts that the North had become so strong that the rights of the South were being trampled. In fact, the original compact between the states was now replaced by a tyranny like that of Russia. Strong words, but nothing new here. Finally, Mason concluded and took his seat.

Calhoun had given the Senate his last speech, which merely reiterated his basic opinions. Calhoun, in his unbending constancy, had tacitly rejected Clay's compromise measures. Along with these great names, there remained another who had seen many years pass over his head: Daniel Webster. What would the great and wise Webster say to this issue? He was a Whig from New England, an orator few could even hope to equal, and a man who had shared, with these two other men, some hopes for the presidency.

On the seventh of March, the world finally heard Webster speak in support of the Union through Clay's compromises. However, these compromises included a more stringent Fugitive Slave Law. Coming from abolitionist New England, Webster had just cut his own political throat. His hopes for the presidency were dead. Like Houston, this statesman had sacrificed his political standing for the sake of the Union. Like Houston, he would meet bitter criticism upon his return to his home state.

Several weeks later, Webster's voice would echo again, this time at the funeral service of John C. Calhoun, as he delivered a eulogy. Even Texas Senator Thomas Rusk delivered an expression of respect. But Thomas Hart Benton from Missouri refused to say a single positive word. He would explain that Calhoun was dead but that his vicious principles would live after him.

A Mother Sits Down to Write

The woman tucked an errant wisp of hair behind her ear and sat down at her writing table. The younger children were asleep. Their mother adjusted her skirt and the lamp on the table, then drew her writing materials closer.

A deep breath. Her thoughts were continually interrupted by the cares of a household, and she needed to gather the threads of meditation, which she had been nursing for some months now.

Last year, when Webster had backed down on the issue of slavery by endorsing a tougher Fugitive Slave law, Harriet Beecher Stowe had received a letter from her sister-in-law: "If I could use a pen as you can, I would write something that will make this whole nation feel what an accursed thing slavery is." Reading these words, the housewife remarked, "I *will* write something... I will if I live."[14]

There was a market for women's writing, both prose and poetry, in various magazines. Mrs. Stowe had already sold something before; her husband was a theologian with a small salary, which she worked hard to stretch, and selling her writing was simply a variation of the "egg money" farmers' wives would earn. Perhaps she could write a serial.

Harriet, or "Hattie," as she was known to her family, dipped her pen in the inkwell and began to paint pictures with the quill. She used her imagination to flesh out the outlines of things she had heard about or even seen with her own eyes —stories of cruelty and hardship, yet not without sympathy for the masters of these bondmen and bondwomen who poured out prayers night and day for deliverance.

As a Christian, she could not stop at the outward institution. The gospel lived in her heart and would find expression in the life of her main character. His name would be Tom. "Uncle Tom."

> And suiting the action to the word, the door flew open, and the light of the tallow candle, which Tom had hastily lighted, fell upon the haggard face and dark, wild eyes of the fugitive.
>
> "Lord bless you! — I'm skeered to look at ye, Lizy! Are ye took sick, or what's come over ye?"
>
> "I'm running away — Uncle Tom and Aunt Chloe — carrying off my child — Master sold him!"
>
> "Sold him?" echoed both, lifting up their hands in dismay.
>
> "Yes, sold him!" said Eliza, firmly; "I crept into the closet by Mistress' door to-night, and I heard Master tell Missis that he had sold my Harry, and you, Uncle Tom, both, to a trader; and that he was going off this morning on his horse, and that the man was to take possession to-day."
>
> Tom had stood, during this speech, with his hands raised, and his eyes dilated, like a man in a dream. Slowly and gradually, as its meaning came over him, he collapsed, rather than seated himself, on his old chair, and sunk his head down upon his knees.
>
> "The good Lord have pity on us!" said Aunt Chloe. "O! it don't seem as if it was true! What has he done, that Mas'r should sell *him*?"

> "He hasn't done anything, — it isn't for that. Master don't want to sell, and Missis— she's always good. I heard her beg and plead for us; but he told her 't was no use; that he was in this man's debt, and that this man had got the power over him; and that if he didn't pay him off clear, it would end in his having to sell the place and all the people, and move off. Yes, I heard him say there was no choice betwen selling these two and selling all, the man was driving him so hard. Master said he was sorry; but oh, Missis — you ought to have heard her talk! If she an't a Christian and an angel, there never was one. I'm a wicked girl to leave her so; but, then, I can't help it. She said, herself, one soul was worth more than the world; and this boy has a soul, and if I let him be carried off, who know's what'll become of it? It must be right: but, if it an't right, the Lord forgive me, for I can't help doing it."[15]

A Small Victory

As the members of the Texas state legislature debated, Robert Neighbors leaned back in his seat and sighed. The compromise bill being discussed wasn't as good as the original, but it was at least a step in the right direction. His efforts to have a large tract of Texas land set aside for the Indians had gone nowhere, but finally, a bill had been drafted that had hope of passage.

It would grant the governor the right to set aside lands in north Texas for Indian settlement. North Texas was far away, and since the lands weren't specified, it wouldn't cost any of these men political capital.

For white Texans who viewed all Indians, even peaceful ones like the Caddo tribe, as subhuman and dangerous, granting them the right to anything was a step that required courage. But Neighbors had some friends in Austin. Sam Maverick was also a member of the legislature, as was John "Rip" Ford. These men did not see themselves as "Indian lovers," but they knew fairness when they saw it.

Neighbors glanced at Maverick. It was this old San Antonio native's behind-the-scenes work that had gathered support for this bill. The major was grateful, because he wasn't a true politico himself. No, he was always a little too blunt when it came to the Indians. He felt for them. It was hard, knowing what Charlie Two Blankets' band must be suffering, now that white settlers had "legally" stolen their land on the Brazos River.

The burly man with the scratchy red beard shifted in his seat as the debate drew to a close. He understood the animosity of the white man toward the Comanche. Tales of torture, rape, murder, and theft were almost commonplace.

But the Indian problem was complex. Comanches ranged far and wide to hunt buffalo, whose range was shrinking, mainly because of the white man. Their raids not only affected white settlers, but other Indian tribes as well. Lipan Apaches, Tonkawas, and Caddoes were trying in vain to stay out of the way of both the Comanche and the white man, but they were caught in the middle, with little land or game to hunt. White men did not discriminate between a Caddo and a Comanche, sending bullets flying at both. But perhaps death from a bullet was kinder than the slower death of starvation.

Neighbors looked up. The Indian bill had come up for a vote. He was glad that Sam Maverick had talked him into running for office. At least he could do some good while he waited on the sidelines. Yes! The bill had passed. There were other items on the agenda, but they did not interest him much.

Soon, he and Maverick would be back on the road to San Antonio. Neighbors thought of his young wife's face, her beautiful brown eyes. He had left her behind on their little ranch on Salado Creek, just south of San Antone. He counted on his fingers. Only six more months. He couldn't wait to be a papa.

Little Jeff

Things were bad. The cold wind came whistling in through the gaps in the walls of the cabin, if indeed the tiny hut could be dignified by such a name. Little Jeff curled up next to his brother and two sisters as his mother banked the coals in the fireplace, trying to keep warm. He felt his mother's eye on him. Puny for his age and sickly as well, Jeff garnered a bit of extra care and attention from his huge mother.

"Aunt Big Kittie," as this large, enslaved woman was known, did not owe her large size to the generosity of her current owner, a certain Mr. McKell. They subsisted largely on cornbread and sowbelly, which, if it must be known, was the staple diet not only of enslaved people but also of many white settlers.

But Aunt Big Kittie had known better days. It was in the gorgeous blue-grass region of Kentucky, under the shelter of a kind and wealthy master, that this woman had attained her size and girth. Jeff could not remember Kentucky, for their master had moved to Texas when he was only three years old, but his Mammy often spoke of the good treatment and plentiful food they had enjoyed.

After moving to Texas, their former master, Mr. Gibson, was tragically killed in an expedition against marauding Indians. Then, Mrs. Gibson was courted by a handsome, but morally bankrupt man named McKell. Her friends advised against it, but she married him anyway, with disastrous results. McKell drank and gambled away their money and treated the slaves cruelly.

Mammy settled down to sleep, her bulk helping to block the frigid air that threaded its way like icy fingers through the little hut. After a time, Jeff's bare feet finally began to feel warm, and he drifted off to sleep.

One Fateful Sunday

Sam Houston entered the E Street Baptist Church, as was his custom on Sunday morning, and sat down in a pew near the front. He adjusted his Mexican blanket about his shoulders.

Pastor Samson introduced a text from Proverbs: "He that is slow to anger is better than the mighty; and he that ruleth his spirit than he that taketh a city." He proceeded to expound upon its meaning.

Houston fixed his gaze upon the preacher, with no thought of whittling, as was his custom in the past. This verse from Proverbs was like a barbed arrow sprung from a supernatural bow. Unlike the poisoned arrow Houston had endured at Horseshoe Bend, this shaft was intended for good, even though it pricked the very core of his being.

Yes, he already knew that he was a sinner, in need of salvation, in need of Christ. He had known this from his boyhood, his godly mother having taught him this truth many years before. His dear mentor and father figure, Andrew Jackson, had died with the vibrant hope of eternal life, having embraced the truth that is in Jesus after the passing of his godly wife, Rachel. Houston had known and seen all these things and even desired salvation for himself, at least in an intellectual way. But now he saw his need and his true condition as never before.

Samson noticed Houston's fixed gaze. Something was happening in the senator's heart and mind; that was certain.

After church, Houston walked back to his hotel. He had a lot to think about.

Chapter 16

Broken Promises

MAJOR NEIGHBORS URGED his sorrel colt faster. The beautiful Tennessee-bred animal kicked up clouds of August dust as it broke into a canter. After the sickness and poverty he had seen in the other Indian camps along the upper Brazos, the newly reappointed Indian agent was in a hurry to see the condition of Charlie Two Blankets' camp. He feared what he would see.

For one thing, he'd heard the news of Charlie Two Blankets's death, killed while defending his small band against Comanche raiders. Without a wise leader, even the relatively "civilized" Caddo Indians were vulnerable to settlers who stole the Indians' land and to traders who sold them whiskey.

Neighbors slowed his horse as he approached the camp. He saw that there were fewer tepees than he remembered. Had smallpox or cholera depleted their numbers? It was not unlikely. But the real shock came as he entered the camp and observed the faces of the Indians. Men lay under trees in a drunken stupor. A few tired women weeded neglected fields. Thin, dirty children ambled about or sat, too hungry to play.

The major looked for Mary Two Blankets. Perhaps she could explain. There she was. Neighbors dismounted, but he already knew the problems: lazy agents and crooked traders. Something had to be done about a certain trader he knew was selling whiskey to the Indians. It wasn't illegal, but it ought to be.

Neighbors tried to be patient and trust in God, but the sight of these pathetic children made him so angry! He decided to visit this trader. And he sighed. He wanted to be home, enjoying the company of his wife and cute little red-haired daughter, but it was not to be just yet.

Jeff for Sale

A loud thumping threatened the integrity of the fragile slave cabin door.

"Send Jeff over to the house right away!" Mr. McKell yelled. "The rest of you hurry up and get to your cotton picking!"[1]

Soon, Aunt Big Kittie had breakfast ready, cornbread and sowbelly fried over the fireplace. Thirteen-year-old Jeff noticed the fear in her face. What was going on? Mr. McKell had been drunk the night before, and that never resulted in anything good. Would Jeff be whipped for some imagined transgression?

Opening the cabin door, the boy saw two mules that were harnessed to a wagon in the yard. The master ordered Jeff to "pile in," and soon they were off. The scrawny youngster turned and caught a last glimpse of his mother, who was standing at the cabin door, sobbing into her apron.

The wagon clattered along the dirt trail that passed for a road, first ducking under the foliage of the trees near the Trinity River, then bouncing along the rolling hills, until finally master and slave entered the town of Huntsville.

It was October, but the morning sun was warm. An auction block was set up near the courthouse square, in front of the general store, and soon Jeff found himself on top of this platform, attracting the attention of passersby as his master called out, "Here's a little nigger for sale – cheap!"

McKell needed to pay for several kegs of whiskey purchased on credit, and auctioning off his wife's slaves was a favorite way of getting himself out of a financial tight spot.

A crowd gathered. "Make me a bid on this little nigger. He is a strong and willing worker," proclaimed McKell. "He's only eight years old and will make a husky field hand!"

This was an outright lie, of course, but there was no market for gardeners or houseboys. As it was, there were no serious bids for the scared boy. Time wore on, and the sun grew hot. Some white boys tormented Jeff, threatening to strike him, and when he drew back in fear, they jeered and laughed. Tears made tracks down his dusty face.

Finally, a man named Moreland agreed to pay $500 for Jeff, but he had to go and obtain the money. He mounted his horse, promising to be back in a few hours.

Jeff watched his future master depart, wondering what would happen to him now. Then, he saw a buggy approach, drawn by a fine black horse. The tall man driving the buggy stopped his horse in front of the store and then tied the reins to the hitching post. Something about the man caught Jeff's attention.

"What's all this excitement about?" asked the tall man.

Someone responded, "Nothing at all, General. Just a little nigger boy being sold."

Sam Houston regarded the child. Then he said to McKell, "My friend, don't you know it is against the law to block the plank-walk in this way? If you want to put on a show, why don't you move the slave-block to the courthouse square where it belongs?"

McKell was intimidated. He finally tried to speak, but he was interrupted.

"This little Negro isn't old enough to have any sense, and these white boys are scaring him. What sort of offer have you had for the boy, anyway? Has he a father or a mother?"

McKell said that Jeff had a mother, brother, and two sisters, and told him about Moreland's offer.

"Do you mean to tell me that you would take this half-starved child away from his mother and sell him to a yellow dog like Moreland?" Houston's blue eyes flashed with cold fire.

The other man explained that he had whiskey debts to pay.

"McKell, I wouldn't be guilty of separating the family. Rather than see this happen and let this fellow fall into the hands of a slavedriver like Moreland, I'll take him myself, if you will knock $50 from the price, and sell me the rest of the family, too."

A few more words were spoken, and the arrangements were made.

Jeff felt Houston's strong arms help him down from the auction block. In a daze, he followed his new master into the store, where Houston directed the owner, Mr. Gibbs, to give the boy something to eat. He also bought Jeff some candy.

"Jeff, you little squirrel, stay here and eat your candy. Don't get scared and cry any more, as nobody is going to hurt you. Joshua will come for you. I have a little boy almost as old as you with whom you can play."[1] Houston left the store.

After devouring his plate of food, Jeff looked around him. The store was full of strange and interesting things. Mr. Gibbs watched him, and later remarked to a customer that the child was a lucky little devil to have caught the attention of "Old Sam."

Jefferson Davis's Idea

Jefferson Davis sat back in his chair and thought about Texas. Davis, a former Mississippi senator, had recently been appointed as Secretary of War by President Pierce, which meant that he was now in charge of the army. And right now, the U.S. Army had the impossible task of defending Texas settlers against roving bands of Indians.

Davis was a former army man himself, having graduated from West Point and having served on the western frontier much as these soldiers were now doing in Texas. But there was a difference here. Texas was a state, not a territory, and as such, certain legal proprieties had to be observed. The U.S. Army was allowed to defend settlers, but it was not allowed to pursue and attack the Indians. Comanches were masters of guerrilla tactics, slipping away into the moonlight after killing and stealing; if the Army couldn't pursue them, they would have a hard time.

Secretary Davis was not a man who thought like a politician. He was a soldier, and he knew that the situation in Texas was militarily untenable. In fact, the forts that the Army was building to defend the frontier actually attracted Indians, who were always on the lookout for good mounts. There had to be a better way.

Davis gathered his writing materials. He had an idea, but it would be up to the governor of Texas to carry it out. If only land could be set aside by the state of Texas and put under federal jurisdiction, and the Indians somehow induced to settle on it and remain there, it might work. Knowing Indians, he knew it would not be easy. But "difficult" was a lot better than "impossible." He dipped his pen into the inkwell and began to write.

Jeff's Job

Jeff smiled when his new master handed him the reins. The tall general had already begun training his new slave as a driver. It would not be Jeff's only job: the fourteen servants at Huntsville were often "farmed out" to help elsewhere, to learn a trade, or allowed to earn money on their own. The thirteen-year-old watched the horse's ears as he held the reins; he liked horses.

The buggy pulled up at the house, but Jeff could see they were not staying. The Houstons had several homes, and at times they packed up and took off, the whole household piling into a large yellow coach. It was parked here now, in front of the house, with four horses harnessed and ready to go. Independence was the destination; Margaret's mother awaited them.

Jeff watched as the general's wife stepped into the coach along with two servants and the children. The oldest, Sam Junior, was ten and a playmate on occasion. Nannie was about three years younger; her sisters Maggie and Mary were younger still. The baby, Antoinette, was carried onto the coach with the rest. The handsome coachman, a fellow slave named Tom, cracked the whip, and soon the yellow vehicle was rumbling along.

Houston went ahead with Jeff in the buggy. The road to Independence was dusty, but finally the household arrived. Nancy Lea embraced her family with open arms and a fine supper.

Many years later, Jeff Hamilton recalled:

> The next morning, the General hunted up his nephew, Major Martin Roysten. He turned over to him some land notes to collect and told him all about me. He asked the major to go and see Mr. McKell at once; as he had no confidence in any promise he made and was afraid that he would sell the rest of my family and separate us forever. This is exactly what happened, and it was over twenty-five years before I saw my mother again. The General explained that he couldn't look after the matter, as he had to go back to the United States Senate in Washington within a few days. The General said that as there were no railroads west of the Mississippi River, it would take him several weeks to reach Washington.
>
> My master then told Major Roysten that he was very much worried about the disputes over slavery. He said that both sides had a great many fanatics and half-crazy people who ought to be muzzled. He said one of the worst things was the way the newspapers, corrupt politicians, and "political preachers" as he called them, were stirring up hate between the two sections. He said that if the real leaders couldn't get together soon, it looked like we would have a senseless war. Such a war he knew would set the country back a hundred years, and wind up with our being divided into a number of little nations, which sooner or later would be gobbled up by foreign countries which hated American institutions.[2]

The Olmsteads' Trip to Texas

Fall segued into winter, and the year 1853 drew to a close. In East Texas, a small company of men, two brothers from New York and their Texan guide, made its way west from San Augustine. John Olmsted was looking for relief from tuberculosis, and his brother Frederick was interested in Texas's agricultural possibilities.

Southern agriculture consisted of subsistence farming plus cotton as a cash crop, and much of the labor, especially in regard to cotton, came from the sweat of slaves. Frederick believed that Texas represented an alternative possibility, a milieu where slave labor did not need to dominate; indeed, it might prove to be a place in which free labor might be even more economical. The brothers went about their travels as if on a scientific expedition, recording everything, even the temperature, in journals.

The men rode under the pines of East Texas, Frederick on a pert roan, their guide on a bony old gray, and John on a high-strung but beautiful chestnut mare named Fanny. Mr. Brown, a hardworking mule who only occasionally revealed the stubbornness of his kind, followed the party with their equipment and supplies. In the evenings, they boarded in homes, inns, or simply camped out under a canvas tent. A candle served as illumination with which to make the day's journal entry.

> Jan. 2. – We came to-day upon the first prairie of any extent, and shortly after crossed Trinity River. After having been shut in during so many days by dreary winter forests, we were quite exhilarated at coming out upon an open country and a distant view. During the whole day's ride the soil improved, and the country grew more attractive. Small prairies alternated agreeably with post-oak woods....
>
> On landing on the west side of the Trinity, we entered a rich bottom, even in winter, of an almost tropical aspect. The road had been cut through a cane-brake, itself a sort of Brobdignag grass. Immense trees, of a great variety of kinds, interlaced their branches and reeled with their own rank growth. Many vines, especially huge grape-vines, ran hanging from tree to tree, adding to the luxuriant confusion.[3]

The Kansas-Nebraska Act

Senator Houston's mind was not totally focused on the Senate committee's report. The area west of Missouri was being organized into a territory, and the necessary legalities were being taken care of. True, such things could erupt into controversy, since there was always the issue of slave versus free, but the Missouri Compromise and the subsequent measures adopted in 1850 had pretty much guaranteed that territory above a certain latitude would remain free, and territory below would allow slaves. The Nebraska territory, which included modern-day Nebraska and Kansas, was above this latitude. Therefore, the issue of slavery was settled. The bill, as it had originally been written, was nothing earthshattering.

First, the bill had been passed in the House of Representatives, then a similar one was introduced in the Senate. This bill was referred to the Senate Committee on Territories, which then tinkered with it. It was now being presented to the whole Senate for a vote.

Houston thought about his wife. Margaret was expecting their fifth child, and he couldn't help fretting about her health and well-being. He thought tenderly of his little ones at home: Sam, Jr., Maggie, Nannie, and the baby, Antoinette. It would be nice if this next child were a boy. He already had a name picked out: Andrew Jackson Houston, in honor of his dear friend and mentor. Well, in the end, he decided he really would not mind another girl, as long as his wife was safe. Childbirth was dangerous. He hoped to be back in Texas in time for his wife's confinement.

Texas. Houston had lost political support over his vote for Clay's compromise of 1850, but the Texas legislature had re-elected him to the Senate last year, nevertheless. At any rate, the compromise of 1850 had had its desired effect, and the nation as a whole had settled down somewhat with regard to the slavery issue. Mrs. Stowe's novel, *Uncle Tom's Cabin*, had become a bestseller, and feelings were running high, but there was a political balance of power that kept the situation stable. At least for now.

Something caught Houston's ear. The bill had been amended. What was this? The people of the territory of Nebraska would be allowed to decide for themselves whether or not they wanted slavery to be legal in their state. That sounded nice, but it did away with the Missouri Compromise and all that Houston had fought for to bring stability to the Union. It was a repeal of an agreement between North and South that had enabled two different opinions to live together. It was as if Calhoun had risen from the dead. Who, indeed, was responsible for this?

The answer was not hard to determine, but it was very surprising. Senator Stephen Douglas was chairman of the Senate committee on territories, and nothing would have gotten past him without his approval. Could it be—a *Northern* senator? Douglas was from Illinois, a Democrat who was known to be ambitious, perhaps even with an eye on the presidency.

It was a given that a Northern Democrat would also need the support of Southern Democrats to be elected president. Or, perhaps it was some other backroom political deal. Houston did not know what was behind it, but he was familiar with political intrigue. He was a master of it himself. But this political compromise could destroy the nation. That was very clear. If this bill passed, it would open the way to bloodshed.

Food and Conversation in Texas

Frederick and John Olmsted looked forward to seeing Austin, the capital of Texas. For one thing, it might mean an improvement in their diet. Because neither one of the easterners was a particularly good hunter, they had to rely on what they could obtain from settlers, shopkeepers, and inns along the way. So far, they had existed on cornbread and pork, with the occasional addition of milk or bad butter, or perhaps venison or wild turkey. Wheat flour or sugar was simply not to be had, at least not in the homes of the average settler.

On the great plantations in East Texas, tables were laden with food of all kinds, but the only thing the poor whites had in common with their rich brethren was the practice of hospitality. The Olmsted brothers sometimes found this hospitality to be surly and reluctant, but it was part of the backbone of Southern culture. What most settlers had to share or sell was little different from food given to slaves on plantations. In fact, slaves often ate better food than some whites: usually, planters made sure their slaves grew vegetables to keep them healthy.

With their minds on food, Frederick and John rode over the last rolling hill and caught their first glimpse of Austin. As they approached, they were impressed with the little city set on a hill. The Capitol Building, which occupied the center of town, was made of soft, cream-colored limestone. Although most of the other homes and buildings were unimpressive, the surrounding countryside was beautiful.

Tired, the men arrived at a hotel that had been recommended to them, but their hopes for better lodgings were soon dashed. The accommodations were dirty. They settled down as best they could for the night, but the outside door to their room had no latch, and a norther that came through that night blew it open. John and Frederick tried to barricade it shut, to no avail. It stayed open until morning.

Hopeful that at least breakfast would prove to be decent, the party responded to the breakfast bell, only to be greeted by the "burnt flesh of swine and bulls," "decaying vegetables," and "rancid butter." Being informed that this was the best hotel in the city of Austin, the men decided to obtain their grub elsewhere, buying provisions from grocers and bakers and basically fending for themselves, as they had in the wilderness.

The brothers did find one consolation, however: there were many cultivated and educated men living in the city. With these folks, Frederick and John struck up some conversations about slavery and found that these men believed the practice to be beneficial to the slaves themselves, fearing, however, that sectional excitement on the issue might be bad for business.

The Olmsteds also visited the legislature, which was then in session, and they were impressed by the "honest eloquence" and "simple manly dignity" of those who conducted the business of government.

Debate in the US Senate

Like magma moving under a dormant volcano, passions began to stir in the United States Senate. The Committee on Territories had thrown a sop to the abolitionists: by dividing the Nebraska Territory into two parts, Kansas and Nebraska, it was imagined that the southern territory, Kansas, would then become slave, and the northern one, Nebraska, free.

Certainly, the slaveholding residents of Missouri did not want a free state next door to which their slaves might flee. Often, a farmer or planter had more money invested in slaves than he did in land, and the loss of a single slave was significant.

But the bill did not state that Kansas would be slave and that Nebraska would be free; instead, it stated that the people living in each region would choose for themselves (through means of the territorial legislatures) whether they would allow slavery. But the population of these areas was in a constant state of flux: in fact, immigrants could easily pour across the borders and change the balance of power. It is doubtful, however, whether the Senate truly realized what a tragedy would result.

Houston was not happy as he listened to the debate. Many Northern senators opposed the measure and argued against it. Senator Douglas was vitriolic and even coarse in his speeches against them. Southern senators were not as passionate. They were content to see the measure pass, seeing as it protected slavery, and most of them did not seem to see that repealing the Missouri Compromise was dangerous to the South.

Senator Salmon P. Chase from Ohio stood up to speak. Tall and dignified, he argued simply and eloquently against slavery. On principle, he opposed the extension of servitude and stood against Douglas on the floor of the Senate. Another man, William Seward of New York, while not as radical in his views as Chase, joined with him in resisting Douglas. His argument against slavery had to do with the idea of "higher law":

> "The Constitution regulates our stewardship; the Constitution devotes the domain to union, to justice, to defense, to welfare, and to liberty. But there is a higher law than the Constitution, which regulates our authority over the domain, and devotes it to the same noble purposes."[4]

Houston shifted in his seat. In a way, the "higher law" idea was correct. There was a God who presided over all the affairs of men, and He had given to man His law in the Scriptures. This, surely, was higher than the Constitution in a sense.

When obedience to man's law conflicted with obedience to God's commandment, then God's law took precedence.

But what "higher law" was Seward talking about? The higher law of his own conscience? Without recourse to Scripture, men differed widely on questions of right and wrong. Even Christians disagreed on some matters of conscience. So whose conscience were we all supposed to follow? This higher law of Seward was no law at all.

That was why the Constitution was so necessary, and respect for the law so essential. Otherwise, there was no rule of law. Houston would resist the Nebraska-Kansas Act, and he would do it on the basis of the rule of law, because the rule of law was the only thing that could hold the Union together.

Sweet Butter in Neu Braunfels

The Olmsteds' guide had gone on ahead of them to San Antonio, and so the brothers made the trip alone, passing through the tiny hamlet of San Marcos and stopping at a couple of settlements along the way. John and Frederick looked forward to seeing the next town of Neu Braunfels. Before arriving, they were totally ignorant of the mass immigration of Germans to Texas and had only recently learned of the fact. What were these settlers like? They were soon to find out.

Accompanied by their faithful mule, Mr. Brown, Frederick astride his roan, and John perched on Fanny, they rode slowly into Neu Braunfels. The street was very wide, but that was not unheard of in Texas. The houses soon caught their attention: small and unpretentious, yet neat and often accompanied by gardens. Most were not simply planks laid bare to the elements, as many other Texas cabins were, but were covered with stucco or painted. Men and women could be seen going about their labors.

The Olmsteds rode along, passing workshops and small stores, and finally came to a place with a sign reading: "Guadalupe Hotel, J. Schmitz."

Entering the hotel, Frederick was in shock. After traveling for weeks with only a canvas tent or the crudest log or bare plank walls to shelter him, and subsisting on the barest of essentials, entering into the Neu Braunfels Inn was like walking into another world. He was in Germany!

He looked about him. The front room of the building had pink walls with pictures hanging on them. A beautiful solid oak table stood before him, with oak benches and chairs about it, and other furniture graced the room, as tastefully decorated as any cottage on the Rhine.

"Good morning," the brothers heard from four bearded men who rose from their chairs to welcome the new guests. A woman entered, who did not understand English, but who did understand the needs of her guests. A white tablecloth was spread, and soon a bountiful breakfast was laid before the men: meat, vegetables, salad, peach jam, coffee with milk, wheat bread, and sweet, fresh butter.

After thoroughly enjoying this repast, John and Frederick went out to attend to their animals but found a man rubbing down the legs of their horses, the first time they had been so cared for in Texas. Even the manger was full of good hay. By this time, the Olmsteds were hoping to spend the night, even though it was early – what a great place!

Thankfully, the innkeeper had a room available. It proved to be a little cottage out back, with blue walls, oak beds, and even curtains! Towels, wash water, even books on a bureau were provided.

The next day, the Olmsteds left Neu Braunfels. As they rode out of town, they observed schoolchildren carrying satchels of books on their way to school.

"*Guten morgen,*" called the children. The travelers would not forget their cheerful, ruddy faces.

A Wall of Fire

It was soon known that Senator Sam Houston was against the Kansas-Nebraska Act. The correspondent for the Richmond *Enquirer* expressed the opinion of many southerners when he wrote, "Nothing can justify this treachery;..." and called Houston's position "treason."[5]

It wasn't as if Houston approved of slavery. True, he owned slaves himself, but like many honest Southerners who saw the institution up close, he also saw its evils up close. In fact, few Southerners would have felt themselves obliged to defend slavery if it had not been for Northern opposition. The agitation of Northern abolitionists pressed the proud South up against a wall. For one of their own to seemingly desert them and stand with Northerners did indeed seem like treason.

On February 15, 1854, Senator Houston rose from his seat and addressed the Senate. He argued against the repeal of the Missouri Compromise with all his powers of oratory and logic, calling it a "solemn compact" between North and South.

His opponent, Stephen Douglas, sat patiently and listened, planning his rebuttal.

Houston continued.

> "... sir, if it were opposing the whole world, with the conviction of my mind and heart, I would oppose to the last by all means of rational resistance the repeal of the Missouri Compromise.... I deem it essential to the preservation of this Union, and to the very existence of the South. It has heretofore operated as a wall of fire to us. It is a guarantee of our institutions.... Repeal it, and you are putting a knife to the throat of the South, and it will be drawn. No event of the future is more visible to my perception than that, if the Missouri compromise is repealed, at some future day the South will be overwhelmed."

Houston's blue eyes scanned his audience. "I do not wish to be regarded as for the South alone... I am for the whole country. If I am, it is sufficient without rehearsing it here. But, sir, my all is in the South."

It was true. From Virginia to Tennessee to Arkansas to Texas, Houston was a Southerner. "My life has been spent there. Every tendril that clusters around my heart, every chord that binds me to love or hope, is there; and I feel that it is my duty to stand up in behalf of her rights ... for her safety and security."

Would his southern colleagues understand? Houston gathered up his strength and continued,

> "The day, I fear, must come in the progress of our country – though God forbid that it ever should – that great trials and emergencies will grow up between the North and the South. The South is in a minority. She cannot be otherwise.... If the South accede to the violation of a compact as sacred as this, they set an example that may be followed on occasions when they do not desire it. . . . If you regard it as a sacred instrument, one to be esteemed and adhered to, you will find that its benefits will inure to you. But if you tear it up and scatter it to the winds, you will reap the whirlwind;..."

Houston's speech caught the attention of the Senate, and his emphasis on the rule of law was not lost on a few. But Douglas was fuming as he sat listening. "Sacred" instrument, indeed.

The senator from Texas brought his remarks to a close.

> "We are not acting alone for ourselves, but are trustees for the benefit of posterity... those who come after us...are to be affected by the action of this body upon this bill. . . .They are either to live in after times in the enjoyment of peace, of harmony, and prosperity or anarchy, discord, and civil broil. We can avert the last. I trust we

shall....so far as my efforts can avail, I will resist every attempt to infringe or repeal the Missouri Compromise."[6]

As Houston took his seat, he knew that his views were in the minority. The bill would probably pass the Senate, but there was still hope. This revised bill had to be approved by the House of Representatives, and from what he had heard, it was less likely to pass there.

The debate continued. Houston continued to write home.

Washington

19th Feby 1854

My very dear Love,

Another Sabbath has passed, and I find myself, as usual, writing to you. I can only express a portion of my love for you, for really I have no news, which I think will interest you. My speech is to be out tomorrow, and of course, I will send it to you, if you can persevere reading it, and when that is done I fear you may think yourself poorly requited for your trouble. . . If the measure is passed, I will deplore the troubles, into which the country will be thrown. I have done all that has been in my power, but I will yet strive against it.

... Indeed my Love, not an hour passes thro. the day, but what you are present to my mind, and my poor heart beats in unison [with] the dear Wife, of my bosom, and my love. Our children too, they are to me every thing. They are <u>ours</u>! My reflections, and my fancy are always busy, and you are all, presented to me most vividly. When I kneel, every night, and invoke the Father of all mercies in our behalf, and beseech Him to pardon our sins, and bring me "from Darkness, to His marvelous light," I do not feel my dear Love, that God through Christ Jesus, has pardoned my sins, or that he is reconciled to an object so unworthy as I am. I am not by any means discouraged, for in the Gospels, which I read every night I find His promises, of Grace and mercy. Thus through faith, in the Savior, and the promises of mercy, and free Grace, I hope for salvation. It is my duty, to use the means, appointed, in Gods word, and that I will try, and perform to the saving, of my soul. I know that for all my efforts, I deserve nothing but condemnation, and that, if I am saved, it will be thro' the merits, of Jesus Christ, and him crucified....

Thy faithful and ever affectionate

Houston[7]

Back in Texas

The trader opened the whisky jug and poured some of the amber liquid into a glass – not the watered-down version he sold to the Indians, but the good stuff. He swirled a bit around the glass before he sipped it, then threw the rest of it down his throat. He welcomed the raw fire that burned his throat and slid into his belly.

That Neighbors! What right did he have to tell him what to do? Trading with Indians was perfectly legal, and that high-falutin' Methodist ought to keep his beliefs in church where they belonged. That Injun-lover ought to be hanged...

Too bad Neighbors had friends. Rangers like "Rip" Ford, hard men who didn't kowtow to savages like Neighbors, but who defended him, nonetheless. Never mind, he had friends, too . . . and the majority of Texans on his side. One of these days, Neighbors would take a wrong step.

Until then, the sunburned trader would bide his time.

Verbal Blows in the Senate

Senator Fessenden of Maine raised his fist, but the blow never landed. He and Senator Butler of South Carolina were separated by several of their colleagues, but still, tempers flared. During this late-night session, a number of senators had slipped out to the Hole in the Wall, a nearby drinking establishment, for liquid fortification. Some of them were beginning to show the effects, and this did not help the situation in the Senate chamber. The Kansas-Nebraska Act was the source of the contention.

The chair recognized Senator Weller of California, but the man was half drunk. Even though he spoke in support of the Kansas-Nebraska Act, Douglas soon interrupted the man's incoherent speech, telling him to sit down and not mix in a fight that was Douglas's own.

For it was truly a fight. The bitterness of the speeches and the ungentlemanly demeanor of the participants reminded Houston of a similar uproar in 1849. Douglas was about to speak at eleven-thirty when Houston interrupted.

"It is now half-past eleven o'clock. I cannot see any particular necessity for going on tonight, and therefore we might as well adjourn."

"No! No!" cried some of the senators.[8]

Houston then announced that he would speak after Douglas. But that was not to occur for a long while. Under a circle of flickering candles, the senator from Illinois tore apart his opposition. He did not attack Houston, instead preferring to vent his spleen on Senators Sumner and Chase.

Sitting in the gallery, the correspondent from the New York *Tribune* was tired, but Douglas' verbal assault kept him awake. He later wrote that it was impossible to give more than a faint idea of the man's vulgarity and violence. Douglas accused his opponents of corruption and falsehood, claiming that popular self-government was the issue. Plus, Kansas was in no danger of becoming slave territory, he claimed. But others knew differently.

The weary senators endured this harangue all night. Finally, as dawn began to filter in through the windows, Houston rose to speak.

"Mr. President, I can not believe that the agitation created by this measure will be confined to the Senate Chamber. I can not believe, from what we have witnessed here to-night, that this will be the exclusive arena for the exercise of human passions and the expression of public opinions. If the Republic be not shaken, I will thank Heaven for its kindness in maintaining its stability ..."

Houston continued to argue against the measure. "Depend upon it, Mr. President [if this bill passes], there will be a tremendous shock; it will convulse the country from Maine to the Rio Grande. The South has not asked for it. I, as the most Southern Senator upon this floor, do not desire it. If it is a boon that is offered to propitiate the South, I, as a Southern man, repudiate it. I reject it. I will have none of it...."

He continued to argue for compromise. "This much I am bound to declare – in behalf of my country... upon the decision which we make upon this question, must depend union or disunion."[9]

The Texas senator took his seat, and the roll call commenced. Of the Southern senators, only John Bell of Kentucky joined Houston in voting "No." The Kansas-Nebraska Act passed by a vote of thirty-seven to fourteen.

The Olmsteads in Old San Antonio

At the crest of the hill, John Olmsted reined in his mare and waited for his brother to join him. The roan bearing Frederick picked its way through the brush and finally reached the summit, accompanied by Mr. Brown, still faithfully toting their provisions, his long mulish ears flicking this way and that.

In the distance lay San Antonio, their destination. The sun shone brightly on the tightly clustered buildings in the distance, beyond which lay a plain as far as the eye could see. Some trees were visible in and near the city, but otherwise, the Olmsted brothers had entered a dry and rather treeless place, unless you counted the ubiquitous mesquite, whose wiry, twisted branches were good for firewood but not much else.

After a quiet survey of the area, the two men urged their mounts forward, being careful to avoid the worst of the prickly brush along the way.

The first houses they came to were undeniably German in construction. John and Frederick walked their horses along a street and gazed at homes made of creamy-white limestone. Some were small and simple, others much larger, with two stories. Some had balconies or galleries.

Next, the Olmsteds entered a central square. On one side stood the Alamo, an old compound which consisted of several stucco buildings and a church, all connected by a wall. The church opened onto the square and still bore marks of the battle that had occurred less than two decades before. Nearby, the men observed adobe cabins inhabited by men and women with brown-hued skin.

Ambling onward, observing carefully all that they saw, the brothers next made a stop at the river that flowed through town. It was so beautiful that they dismounted for a better look. Pure and blue, the water flowed quietly over a pebbled bottom. They marveled at how the river never varied in height or temperature, due to its local source, a spring not far away. Finally, they tore themselves away from the bridge rail and mounted their horses for a more thorough examination of the town.

Commerce proved to be the main street of San Antonio, and riding along, John and Frederick observed stores and workshops. On this side was a watchmaker, and over there a saddler, while the number of general stores and druggists was impressive. Men of various ethnic backgrounds walked or rode down the streets, and an occasional oxcart, laden with goods from the coast, rumbled along. The shopkeepers appeared to be mostly German, and most of the wealthier inhabitants were Americans. The Mexican portion of the population seemed poorer, and their work largely consisted of transporting goods from place to place, or operating small shops to supply their own needs.

The Olmsteds were mesmerized by San Antonio. It was a backwater place, a city in the midst of the wilderness, surviving on trade with Mexico and government interest to sustain it economically. Despite producing little of its own, it seemed to flourish, being the second largest city in the state after Galveston. The mix of cultures yielded an odd and foreign feel to the place that the brothers would never forget. They wrote down their observations:

> The street-life of San Antonio is more varied than might be supposed. Hardly a day passes without some noise. If there be no personal affray to arouse talk, there is some Government train to be seen, with its hundreds of mules, on its way from the coast to a fort above; or a Mexican ox-train from the coast, with an interesting

supply of ice, or flour, or matches, or of whatever the shops find themselves short. A Government express clatters off, or news arrives from some exposed outpost, or from New Mexico. An Indian in his finery appears on a shaggy horse, in search of blankets, powder, and ball. Or at the least, a stagecoach with the "States," or the Austin, mail, rolls into the plaza and discharges its load of passengers and newspapers.

The street affrays are numerous and characteristic. I have seen, for a year or more, a San Antonio weekly, and hardly a number fails to have its fight or its murder. More often than otherwise, the parties meet upon the plaza by chance, and each, on catching sight of his enemy, draws a revolver, and fires away. As the actors are under more or less excitement, their aim is not apt to be of the most careful and sure, consequently it is, not seldom, passers-by who suffer. Sometimes it is a young man at a quiet dinner in a restaurant, who receives a ball in the head; sometimes an old negro woman, returning from market, who gets winged. After disposing of all their lead, the parties close, to try their steel, but as this species of metallic amusement is less popular, they generally contrive to be separated ("Hold me! Hold me!") by friends before the wounds are mortal. If neither is seriously injured, they are brought to drink together on the following day, and the town waits for the next excitement.[10]

Houston Defends Clergymen

The dark-frocked clergyman drew his finger around the inside of his damp collar as he sat quietly in the dim Senate gallery, listening to the debate. He was a bit nervous, being part of a delegation of clergymen who had submitted a petition against the Kansas-Nebraska Act. The bill had already passed the Senate and was now being debated in the House, but this petition, signed by over three thousand New England clergymen, had finally made it to the floor for consideration.

The pastor took a deep breath. Although slavery was an issue that was being expounded upon, both pro and con, from pulpits across the country, it was a new step to petition the government directly. Wasn't the kingdom of God "without observation"? Yet, when wrong was done, should a Christian remain silent? No, silence would be sin. Somewhere, the spiritual and public lives of a Christian had to merge, and so these clergymen had remonstrated against the repeal of the slavery restriction, "in the name of the Almighty God."

Senators Mason and Butler had already denounced the petition, labeling it as agitation. Then Senator Douglas of Illinois stood and was recognized by the chair.

> "It is presented by a denomination of men calling themselves preachers of the gospel, who have come forward with an atrocious falsehood and an atrocious calumny against the Senate, desecrated the pulpit, and prostituted the sacred desk to the miserable and corrupting influence of party politics. I doubt whether there is a body of men in America who combine so much profound ignorance on the question upon which they attempt to enlighten the Senate as this same body of preachers."[11]

In the gallery, the minister tried to keep calm, but several on the Senate floor could not contain themselves. Senator Sumner rose to speak.

"Sumner, don't speak, don't speak!" cried Houston. "Leave him to me!"

The Northern senator turned. "Will you take care of him?"

"Yes, if you will leave him to me," replied the Texas senator.

Sumner sat down, and Houston took the floor. He explained to his colleagues that clergymen were citizens and as such, had the same right to petition the government as anyone else. His oratory was moving, making Douglas furious.

Houston faced his nemesis and spoke directly to his face.

> "Sir, it comes from the country. I told you that there would be agitation, but it was denied upon this floor. Is not this agitation? Three thousand ministers of the living God upon earth—His viceregents—send a memorial here upon this subject; and you tell me that there is no excitement in the country! Sir, you realize what I anticipated....
>
> "Ministers have a right to remonstrate.... Because they are ministers of the Gospel they are not disenfranchised of political rights and privileges...."

Houston continued, dealing with several angry interruptions from his colleagues. Then Douglas interrupted, protesting that the ministers had called the Kansas-Nebraska bill "immoral."

Houston's quick wit cut down his opponent.

> "Surely that ought not to insult Senators. They are not such paragons of morality that they cannot bear to have their moral character questioned... I pray we may never have another such protest in our body...If we wish to avert calamitous effects we should prevent pernicious causes."[12]

The clergyman in the gallery followed every word, along with several of his colleagues. He was stunned by the gallant defense of their petition given by this bearded senator. This man's name was Sam Houston, from the *Southern* state of Texas. The name of Sam Houston was seared into his brain. Truly, this was an honorable man.

Houston did not know the man seated in the gallery that day, but he would live to be grateful to him eight years later.

Margaret's Trials

Margaret Houston's skirts rustled as she waddled to the cabinet. Her heart was burdened, having recently had to say goodbye to her husband, who had torn himself away from Washington, but had not been able to stay long here in Huntsville. She was finding it a bit hard to maneuver, very swollen with their fifth child, who was expected to make his or her appearance in another month or so. She hoped it would be a boy, for Houston's sake, as he did so want to name a son after his hero.

But most pressing on her mind at the moment was the condition of her youngest, Antoinette. The little one seemed to have scarlet fever, a potentially serious disease. One child was known to have died of it in nearby Brenham.

There it was: the bottle of lobelia tincture. The herb was rather unpleasant to the taste; hopefully, her little babe would not rebel. Margaret went to the bedside of her child with the medicine.

"Now take this my daughter, or Ma will cry as she did when Pa went away." Margaret did not have to make this up. The pain of separation from her beloved husband was close, and the concern over her child stirred similar emotions. Indeed, it was a grief to Margaret how much her emotions ruled her mind. Shouldn't faith in God chase away the dark clouds that so frequently plagued her soul?

Antoinette's eyes opened wide at her mother's entreaty. "Oh Ma don't cry. I'll take it! I'll take it!"[13] Holding the toddler in the crook of one arm, the dark-haired woman administered the medicine with the other. What a blessing her children were to her. In the midst of darkness, God had given her many blessings, both spiritual and temporal, to comfort her heart.

Margaret looked out the window. With their new overseer, a young man named Mr. Sprott, attending to the management of their little farm, the Houstons' place was prospering. The corn was ready for roasting, and the millet and clover were thriving. Roses and dahlias bloomed in their appointed beds, and the servants attended the large vegetable garden. Faithful Joshua had taken little Jeff in hand and tried to make him useful around the barn. Sam Junior was getting some practical experience under the tutelage of Mr. Sprott, who with his mother was in charge of his academic education.

Mrs. Houston sighed. Truly, she wished her husband could be home, not just for her sake, but for Sam's. He was reaching an age where he really needed his father's guidance and example. She knew her husband would not disagree, but it seemed that he needed to be in his place right now; to help steer the whole nation through dangerous waters was his destiny, and it was hers too.

Davis's Idea Comes to Pass

Neighbors closed his Bible and tucked it into his saddlebag. Captain Marcy was now stirring in the pink dawn glow of morning, and the major concluded his devotions with the fervent prayer of his heart, asking God to take care of his wife, who was burdened with her second pregnancy.

Thank You for Anna, he breathed. Anna was a plump, smiling German widow now employed at the Salado Creek ranch, and what a help she had already been to his wife. Thoughts of his little red-haired daughter flitted through his mind. *I have so much to be thankful for.*

The burly man was also thankful for the recent actions of the Texas government. Thanks to the bill passed earlier in the legislature and pressure from the federal government, seventy thousand acres had been set aside for various Indian bands. Neighbors had obtained provisions for the starving Indians on the Brazos, including Charlie Two-Blankets' band, but to survive, these people needed a place to call home. A place with decent land, water, and a guarantee that no white man would chase them out.

Captain Marcy had been sent by the U.S. Army to help Neighbors survey the land that had been set aside for the Indians. There were two parcels, actually, one reserve near Fort Belknap, and another, where they were headed next, just twenty miles to the southwest.

Major Neighbors helped Marcy put on the coffee. The land they had surveyed yesterday was beautiful: rolling country with trees and water. It was perfect. Bringing the Indians was going to be difficult, and he worried a bit about the reaction of nearby white settlers. White hostility to Indians was a given.

The two men cleaned up their campsite and saddled their horses. Neighbors put aside his negative thoughts. He had a job to do, and a Scripture verse came into his mind. "Whatsoever thy hand findeth to do, do it with all thy might." He had to do what the Lord had given him to do at this time and place and leave the results up to God.

Houston's Spiritual State

Once again, it had been hard to leave Margaret. The children were growing; their bright eyes glowed in his memory. Sam Houston thought about his family as he walked to his hotel after church. Washington was usually a dreary place, but somehow today, it seemed even drearier than usual. The other day, the Senate had to disband simply for lack of a quorum. No business was done that day, and what was worse, very little seemed to be accomplished even on the days they did have a quorum.

The House had passed the Kansas-Nebraska bill after all, and there were already rumors that slave owners in Missouri near the Kansas line were going to allow their fellow citizens to set up a free state next door... no, there would be bloodshed soon. How sad that "popular sovereignty" could so often be twisted into mob rule.

Houston shook his head. No, he would not dwell on politics today. He thought again of his wife and tried to gather his thoughts for the letter he would soon write her. He liked to give her a sense of Pastor Samson's sermon each Sunday, along with his own meditations and bits of news.

The Texas Senator rubbed his clean-shaven face with one hand as he grasped his gold-headed cane with the other. Now without a beard, he teased his wife that he had more places for her to kiss, though he still wasn't used to it yet.

The cane tapped its way along the sidewalk. Because his San Jacinto ankle had never fully recovered, the cane was not just for decoration. But overall, his health was good, and Houston had no difficulty traversing the half mile to church and back every week. It was quite warm, but that was to be expected in summer.

Margaret. The baby would be coming any time now. Every evening, Houston prayed for her. Did God hear him? He wasn't sure. Lately, he'd been reading the Scriptures more frequently than he ever had in his life. He wasn't satisfied with a chapter in the morning and a sermon on Sunday.

When Houston was first elected senator and came to Washington, he went to church out of consideration for his wife. His mother has instilled in him a great respect for the Scriptures, yet for so many years, he had had no true interest in God or in the state of his soul.

But now things were different; he felt empty and hollow inside. He wanted peace with God. Intellectually, he had known his need for many years, but now he *knew* his need, and was determined to be reconciled to God through Jesus Christ.

The White Man's Ridiculous Proposal

Sanaco led his warriors back to camp, accompanied by several scrawny cattle and a mediocre horse. The raid was not very profitable, but with buffalo scarce, the Comanches needed to eat, and the cattle would feed their children. The settlers they had raided the night before had all died at the points of Comanche lances and arrows, and their screams still echoed in Sanaco's mind.

He had no compunction against taking what was rightfully his. This land belonged to the Human Beings, as the Comanches called themselves, and the offer made by the Man Who Walks Like Bear was pretty ridiculous. Some of the "tame" Indians, Waco, Tonkawa, and Caddo bands, had agreed to Neighbor's terms and were moving onto the land reserved for them, but they had no pride.

Unbelievably, some of the Penateka Comanches had agreed to the white man's proposal. But Seneca's band would never agree. And they weren't the only ones.

God's Works in Texas

Zechariah Morrell made his way into the church building. This was a day of days, and the old preacher's thoughts were many. Years ago, he had entered a virtual wilderness to preach the gospel and recover from an infirmity of his lungs, and today, though he himself could no longer spend extended time in the saddle, there were many younger men whom God had raised up to take his place.

Brother Creath for one, and of course, Judge Baylor, that faithful man of God. And what about Jonas Johnston, who feared not to preach clearly the doctrine of salvation by grace and God's sovereignty in this grand scheme of redemption? And then there was the pastor of this church here in Independence, Dr. Rufus C. Burleson, a man who had given himself wholeheartedly to the spread of the gospel in Texas and whose charge he had executed faithfully. And there were many more godly men establishing churches and helping form associations between those churches, promoting the cause of Christ, causing flowers and fruits to come forth out of a barren land. It was truly the work of God.

Today was a day of days. Morrell blinked, being moved by the occasion. He was going to preach and needed to control the emotion that welled up inside him. Who would have thought that Sam Houston would embrace Christ? Yes, he was known to be an honorable man and had even married a Christian woman, but his rough-and-tumble background left doubt in the minds of some. Could such a man be saved, especially one well into middle age, when the habits of life were well established?

But Morrell had no doubts. He knew the power of God and had seen greater miracles than this on the Texas frontier. He went into the church and looked up into the bell tower. Here in this wilderness was a silver bell, calling saints to worship, made, as he had heard, from Houston's mother-in-law's silver.

The service began, and the sound of stirring hymns resonated in the wooden church. Happy voices filled the air with music until finally it was time for Morrell to preach. He hobbled up to the platform and began his address. As he spoke, he glanced out over the congregation.

There was Houston, his blue eyes fixed on him. Next to him was Margaret, but he could not look at her long, as the happy tears in her eyes threatened to disturb his own emotional control. She held a babe in her arms, the long-awaited Andrew Jackson Houston. The rest of the children sat near, along with Margaret's mother, a woman whose health was precarious, but whose determination to serve her God was still strong. Members of the church shared the benches with visitors who had come from far away.

After the sermon, Morrell closed his remarks with prayer, and the congregation was dismissed. Chatting, the people gradually made their way outside and down the hill to a nearby creek. When all was ready, Houston took off his hat and laid aside his cane, and he and Burleson waded into the water.

Everyone gathered round. Pastor Burleson made a few remarks before baptizing Houston in the cold water of the creek. The Hero of San Jacinto came up out of the water, dripping wet but happy.

Zechariah Morrell took a deep breath. Truly, God had been good.

Honor

Chapter 17

Man of Honor

THREE MEN slowly rode their horses along the hot and dusty Texas road, the creaking of saddle leather occasionally punctuating their lively conversation.

Suddenly one of the horses stumbled, and its rider bellowed out a curse.

"Brother Houston, do you still swear?"

Houston regarded the Baptist preacher who had thus rebuked him. Cursing was an old habit, which his wife's influences had mellowed but never entirely tamed. But now Christ was the King of his heart, and the man who had verbally eviscerated Stephen Douglas in the Senate did not defend himself.

"Well, what must I do?" he asked.

"Ask God to forgive you!"

"Hold my bridle rein. I'll do it."[1]

Houston dismounted, and removing his hat, knelt in the dust in a fence corner and prayed.

Peaceful Tribes in Danger

In his office at Fort Belknap, Major Neighbors dipped his pen into the inkwell. Another letter. Would anyone listen?

The burly man scratched out a careful argument. Yes, it was true that certain Comanche bands had done atrocious things: killing, maiming, and plundering. But the Wacos, Caddoes, and other peaceful tribes of the Brazos reserve had caused no one any problems. They worked their fields in peace and patience. Nevertheless, the growing white population along the upper Brazos River felt threatened. The horror stories were too near and too recent for most people to act rationally. Any red face was an enemy, not just an enemy but an inhuman enemy...

Neighbors found himself staring into space. He squinted at the half-finished letter and trudged on. He knew who was fanning the flames of hatred here in north Texas, publishing incendiary materials and even planting "evidence" to condemn the reservation Indians. But he couldn't prove it.

Would there be no justice? Would the two small reservations on the Brazos survive?

Neighbors didn't know.

Houston Runs for Governor

Alexander Terrell joined the crowd under the shade of the trees. Sam Houston was speaking on a platform there, and he wanted to hear.

It was a hot day in Lockhart, Texas, but since elections were held in August, campaigning was inevitably a hot and sweaty affair. Houston seemed dressed for the occasion: a shirt unbuttoned at the top, covered only by a light linen traveling coat.

It was 1857, and Terrell was surprised to find himself a candidate for judge, having been encouraged to run by his friends. He wasn't much for politics, but his views had leaned towards those of the current pro-secessionist Democratic candidate for governor, Hardin Runnels, who was expected to win.

Runnel's election would have been guaranteed except for the sudden entry of Houston into the race. Terrell had some inkling of Houston's pro–Union views and wondered what the issue was that had caused him to enter. Maybe he would find out today.

Houston's deep booming voice, posture, and electrifying charisma reminded Terrell of an Old Testament prophet. He had to admit that he admired and respected this man, though he did not always agree with him.

Then he noticed someone he knew drive up. It was Judge Oldham, one of Houston's detractors, who was also planning to speak to the crowd. Terrell managed to make his way through the crowd to join his acquaintance. But his movement distracted the audience, and Houston noticed. "It's only Oldham, only Oldham. I'll tell you what he is doing."

Houston paused for effect: "He is opening some books, but they are not the bank books that he stole and sank in the White River, Arkansas."[2]

Terrell glanced at Oldham and saw him bite his cigar in two. He understood why Houston had dealt the judge such a nasty blow. Recently, the state Democrats had published a paper accusing Houston of being a "traitor-knave" because of his anti-secessionist position. There were a number of names affixed to said document, including Oldham's, and, Terrell was disappointed to learn, his own, without his knowledge or permission.

Houston was going to take them all apart, and Terrell listened, mesmerized. "They say they are going to handle me without gloves."

Theatrically, the old general drew out a pair of heavy gloves.

"This paper is too dirty for me to handle without gloves."

He proceeded to read the handbill aloud, then threw it down.

"Sam Houston a traitor to Texas! I who in defense of her soil moistened it with my blood!"

He moved about the platform so everyone could notice the slight limp he still retained from San Jacinto.

"Was it for this that I bared my bosom to the hail of bullets at the Horseshoe and rode into a bullet at San Jacinto—to be branded in my old age as a traitor?"

Some in the crowd drew out their bandannas to wipe away tears. Terrell found himself needing a handkerchief as well.

Houston roundly scolded each signatory to the offensive document, having begun with Oldham.

Last on the list was Terrell.

"They tell me that this young scapegrace wants to be a judge! A pretty looking judge he would make, this slanderer of a man old enough to be his father!"[3]

Terrell winced inwardly, then mused. It simply would not do to publicly repudiate the handbill now. People might say that he was doing it for political reasons. After the election would be a better time.

Later, under a hot August sun, Texans cast their ballots, and Terrell won his judgeship and promptly published a renunciation of the "traitor-knave" accusation in the newspaper.

Houston lost his bid for governor, but he met Terrell and gained a faithful friend.

Texas Rangers Defeat Comanches

Ranger Captain "Rip" Ford sat his mount and studied the terrain ahead of him. Directly below him flowed the Red River, and he had already sent Indian scouts to search the other side for signs of Comanches.

He had a strong force with him: about a hundred hand-picked men, plus another hundred Indian allies. Among the former was "Sul" Ross, fresh from military school, but Ford knew he'd prove to be a fine Ranger if Sul was anything like his father, Shapley.

They had need of good Rangers just now. While Jefferson Davis had held the post of Secretary of War, the 2nd Cavalry had been stationed in Texas to protect settlers from Comanches. The blue-jackets weren't all bad, Ford mused. Many of them had served in the Mexican War and knew their stuff. He even liked some of the officers. Colonel Lee was certainly a man to be respected. Rode a gray horse...

By the time Ford splashed across the Red with his men, the 2nd Cavalry was gone, and however inexperienced those men may have been, they had provided a buffer against the Indians, a buffer that was now gone. The Comanches were no fools. Now they were back.

Crossing the Red River in pursuit of marauding Comanches was a bold move, in one sense. The Red River was the northern border of Texas, after all, and Ford knew he had no legal jurisdiction outside the state, but he really didn't care. A Texas problem lay a few miles ahead, and he was going to take care of it. End of story.

If they could surprise this band of Indians, it would help. Occasionally, a Ranger would spit, a tin cup would clank, or a horse would snort. Otherwise, they rode silently, the April breeze occasionally ruffling the manes of the horses.

Suddenly, there was a commotion. A scout had spotted two Comanches who had seen him. The Rangers and their allies spurred their horses. If they could catch these two braves, they might not lose the element of surprise.

Ford urged his faithful horse on. For three miles, the men chased the Comanches; then, suddenly, the men came around a bend and saw the Indians' camp. Ford pulled up his mount and studied the ground. They were next to a river, and as the men around him checked their rifles and Colts, he watched the Indians mount their war ponies.

There must be three hundred of them, thought the Ranger, as the Comanche warriors assembled, painted for war. In the forefront, the chief, Iron Jacket, steadied his war pony. The chief's name came from the Spanish breastplate he wore that supposedly made him invulnerable. The crack of a Sharp's rifle cut through the air, then another, and Iron Jacket went down with his horse. The Rangers charged, and the battle ensued.

Up and down the river, little battles were fought under the midday sun. The superior weapons of the Rangers overwhelmed the Comanches, whose bodies littered the ground. Finally, the Texans had to break off the attack through sheer exhaustion, their horses stumbling.

As they regrouped and made camp, Ford evaluated their success. Only two Rangers had died. Any surviving warriors were scattered, and several Comanche women and children had been captured by the Texans, along with several hundred head of horses.

Governor Runnels would be pleased.

Houston's Last Speech in the Senate

Houston rose to his feet, his leopard-skin vest peeking out from beneath his jacket. His blue eyes surveyed his audience, which was larger than usual. Not only did he face his Senate colleagues, but the galleries were especially crowded today: many in Washington knew of the fact that Texas would not be sending the old general back for another term. He only had a few days left. And that was fine with him. He really wanted to retire.

The transcontinental railroad was the object of discussion, and Houston made a few remarks about it. Then he turned to the theme of his heart, the issue which he would speak upon while he yet had breath.

The galleries hung on every word as Houston tore down the notion that the South had special "rights." All states had equal rights! He stood erect as he challenged the forces of "disunion."

Senator Iverson of Georgia gained the floor and produced a scathing rebuttal.

Houston was not dismayed. Indeed, he seemed cheerful, his countenance glowing as he spoke:

...As a Union man, I have ever maintained my position, and I ever shall. I wish no prouder epitaph to mark the board or slab that may be on my tomb than this: 'He loved his country; he was a patriot; he was devoted to the Union.'[4]

Washington lamented when Houston left, never to return.

A Sad Journey

The caravan approached the Red River. Neighbors rode beside the Indians under his charge, watching over those who would soon be his responsibility no more.

Sunlight glinted off the buttons of the neat uniforms of the 2nd Cavalry, which had returned to escort the Brazos reserve Indians to an area north of the Red. The Texas Rangers in their midst looked rather slovenly in comparison.

Neighbors sorted through his feelings. The removal of these Indians had actually been his own idea, which he had gone to Washington to promote. It was no longer merely a matter of prejudice. The white settlers near the Brazos had become so virulently poisonous in their hatred for the red man that six of them had shot and killed seven reserve Indians in their sleep.

Everyone knew who had killed these Indians, but justice would not be served. The man who was instructed to make the arrests, "Rip" Ford, claimed that he had no jurisdiction over the matter.

Neighbors had been incensed when he discovered Ford's "sell-out," but he also understood why his friend had succumbed to the prevailing winds. He knew Ford felt it was useless. No jury would convict those white men.

So here they were. It was better this way: at least "his" Indians would be safe from the white man. Yes, it was better, Neighbors told himself, though when he looked at the thin and ragged Indian children, his throat swelled with emotion.

The Ranger in charge of their removal had not even allowed them to bring their livestock. Too much trouble. So the Indians had thrown their meager possessions into a few Army wagons and left fields and livestock behind on a trek that reminded Neighbors of another journey, long ago...

Later, he wrote his wife:

> I have this day crossed all the Indians out of the heathen land of Texas and am now out of the land of the Philistines. If you want a full description of our Exodus out of Texas... Read the "Bible" where the children of Israel crossed the Red Sea. We have had about the same show, only our enemies did not follow us...[5]

Moving to Austin

The Houston children were used to traveling, but this trip was special. Their father had been elected governor, and they were going to move into the governor's mansion in Austin!

Sam Jr. helped his little brother Andrew, while Maggie, Nannie, Mary, and Nettie climbed into the big yellow coach; two servants helped Margaret with the newest addition, little "Willie." Then Tom Blue, the coachman, took the reins, and they were off. Jeff drove Houston separately, making good time as their lively black mare ate up the miles.

The campaign this time around had been short and simple. Most people knew Houston's views, and he had made just one major speech at Nacogdoches in July 1859, to present himself to the people: "...my conscience has not permitted me to stand aloof from my fellow citizens in this emergency...I have been with Texas in six troubles and in seven I will not desert her."[6]

Agitation over the slavery issue sometimes threatened the rule of law,

Houston knew. Some of the recent laws passed by Congress – or decisions by the Supreme Court – had been hard for Texans and other Southerners to support. He addressed the crowd, "Wherever the will or prejudice of individuals becomes the tribunal for the adjudication of Constitutional rights the Government will fall."[7]

He argued point by point with his hearers to stand by the rule of law and the Union:

> ...If we depart from the Constitution...We will have civil war without end. Make a Southern Confederacy, and there would be a Northern one. These men who have shown a disregard for the struggles of our fathers, will care but little for Union, when their chief end is attained...The scenes that would ensue, I will not shock you by relating. God when He intends to destroy men first makes them mad.... He has maddened these men. Mark me, the day that produces a dissolution of this [Union] will be written in history in the blood of humanity. All that is horrible in war will characterize the future of this people. Preserve Union and you preserve Liberty. They are one and the same, indivisible and perfect.[8]

Newspapers had responded by lashing out at Houston with more of the specious charges that had characterized the campaign of two years before, but this time, Houston had ignored them. Popular sentiment swung his way, and he had gained the office by a modest margin.

Now they were trotting to Austin, the black mare that pulled Jeff and his master outdistancing the heavy yellow coach considerably.

Houston told Jeff to pull over next to a large tree by the side of the road. The shade was inviting, and they took advantage of the opportunity to rest as they waited for the coach to catch up.

The new governor took a keen look at his slave and then asked him to recite the alphabet. The young slave had already learned his letters, so his master progressed to simple words.

Then, reaching into his pocket, Houston pulled out a folded copy of the Telegraph and Texas Register. He showed the newspaper to Jeff, pointing out a few places for him to read, which he did, skipping the harder words.

"Let's hurry on, Jeff. You will be a learned man yet."[9]

Finally, after a long and dusty trip, the whole entourage arrived at their destination. But there was no rest for Jeff. The dust had caused Margaret to suffer a severe asthma attack, and she could barely breathe.

Quickly, the servants gathered leaves and burned them in pans and tins around

Margaret's chair. For hours, Jeff labored to keep the leaves burning until finally his mistress could breathe more easily.

Jeff didn't mind. As he searched out a place to rest, he marveled over his great blessings. Just think, a few years ago, he had been the sorry slave of cruel Mr. McKell, and now look! He was the personal servant of the great Sam Houston, governor of Texas.

A Christian Man Shot in the Back

Fort Belknap was warm and dusty. Neighbors thought about his wife and newborn son as he walked down the street. Soon, he would be going home, his job completed, except, of course, for a little paperwork.

His sharp ears caught an unfriendly sound behind him, the metal scraping sound of a shotgun being readied to fire.

It was the last sound he ever heard.

Rumors of Succession

Houston sat in his office, studying the papers on his desk, while his rambunctious five-year-old son, Andrew, sat nearby, busily drawing on paper. Truly, his father did not mind the presence of an active child, especially when he could help Margaret by minding him.

The office was sparsely appointed. The pro-slavery legislature had dug in their heels at the news of Houston's election as governor, and they had refused to appropriate money for needed furnishings. No matter. The Houstons "made do," and Margaret used all of her womanly skill to make the mansion a comfortable and cheerful place.

The papers in front of the governor were not cheerful, however. There was a letter here from the governor of South Carolina, along with a copy of a resolution passed by the South Carolina legislature stating that any state had the right to secede. In the letter, the governor was asking Houston to send delegates to a "Southern Convention."

Houston pondered while his son drew and played. He would forward this material to the Texas legislature, he decided, along with his own strong commentary.

Following a Trail

A book lay on the trail ahead of them. One of the Rangers picked it up and opened it.

It was Mrs. Sherman's Bible – they knew they were on the right path now. Indians were known to pick up books when they raided cabins; books stashed under a jacket could stop a bullet.

Charles Goodnight was ready. Personally, the young rancher thought the Shermans to be fools, building a cabin within bowshot of the Comanches and not even owning a rifle. But why torture the woman? Poor Mrs. Sherman had been abused, scalped, and shot by arrows, and she did not even die until the next day, after having given birth to a dead child.

"Sul" Ross was leading them to revenge. Well, perhaps not revenge exactly. Ranger Captain Ross, newly commissioned by Governor Houston to deal with the Indians in north-central Texas, was simply meting out justice and keeping order. Likewise, "Rip" Ford and his men patrolled the Rio Grande, trying to break the will of Mexican bandits who broke the peace. But many of the settlers who rode with the Rangers as volunteers had old scores to settle. Where would they draw the line when it came to retribution? So far, few of them had had the chance to retaliate against the Comanches; they were only farmers and ranchers, after all.

The men continued. Soon, a grove came into view, and Goodnight signaled to Ross. He could see some berry bushes underneath the trees.

The rancher rode over to the bushes. Sure enough! Someone had recently been here gathering berries; the signs were very clear.

Goodnight rode back to the group and quietly communicated this intelligence. Ross suspected that the Comanches were extremely close – perhaps on the other side of that sandy hill. Was there a stream on the other side? It would be the perfect place for the Indians to camp.

Ross made his decision. Instead of sending a scout and risking exposure, they would all simply charge over the hill. He spoke to his men, who quietly readied their Colts and rifles.

The Rangers and assorted volunteers spurred their horses at their captain's signal. They gained the top of the hill, where they instantly spotted an Indian camp just a hundred yards away on the edge of a creek.

The Rangers' sudden appearance threw the camp into turmoil. Comanche warriors hurried to grab their weapons and jump on their ponies, but many of them never made it that far. Squaws stumbled about, hindered by the meat, which they had been preparing and packing.

The white men rode through the camp, using their six-shooters to good advantage. Goodnight felled several Comanche warriors in quick succession; then he heard shots behind him. Could it be? Yes, one of them had shot all the squaws.

All but one, that is. He saw Captain Ross direct a man to take charge of a squaw. He also noticed Ross rescue a Comanche boy during the melee, slinging him up behind him, all without dismounting.

Finally, the shooting ceased. Except for those Ross had rescued, the Indians were all dead. The smell of dust, gunpowder, and blood stung Goodnight's nose as he dismounted and looked about. The men were beginning to gather under the trees, and the rancher joined them.

The first thing he noticed was the Comanche woman Ross had protected. She was sitting and weeping, and he couldn't help but be moved by her grief. He walked toward her, wishing he could somehow help her and yet at the same time doubting that he really could. Did she lose family in this fight?

As Goodnight drew closer, he noticed a baby clutched to the woman's bosom. She must have a husband, then. Probably dead.

Then the squaw glanced up, and the rancher gasped. The woman had blue eyes. He looked carefully at her face and hair. Both were dirty, but as he drew nearer and observed carefully, he saw that her hair was blond. But she was so filthy and tanned by the sun that she was almost unrecognizable as a white woman.

Goodnight pointed out to someone else that they had captured a white woman.

"No!"

"Go see for yourself."[10]

The men had difficulty communicating with the grieving woman, as she had forgotten English. But they eventually discovered who she was.

Cynthia Ann Parker had been found.

Defense of the Constitution

Houston was sick, but there were some people who needed encouragement: a meeting of Union supporters had been called, and in these dark days when secession was whispered, nay, was shouted aloud, such folks needed all the encouragement they could get.

The nomination of Lincoln for president by the nascent Republican Party had stirred up a hornet's nest. The newly formed Republican Party supported the prohibition of slavery in the territories, and some northern Democrats had left their own party and joined the Republicans for this reason.

The Democratic Party itself, the dominant political machine of the day, then split. Its northern members could not agree with its Southern members on the issue of slavery, so the Democrats fielded two candidates for president: Stephen Douglas from the North and John C. Breckinridge from the South.

Finally, there were people who had abandoned these parties and set up a new "Union" party, which at first seemed poised to give the nomination to Houston but eventually chose John Bell.

With four candidates in this horse race, anything could happen. Lincoln had strong support in the North and West, Houston noticed, and other Southerners were afraid that the tall man from Illinois might well win the presidency. In fact, many Southerners viewed the possible election of Lincoln as the end of the world.

Houston got dressed as he mulled over what he would say to those who still resisted the siren song of the secessionists. Then he submitted himself to Margaret's inspection. She never nagged, but she did keep a loving and prayerful eye out for the welfare of her husband. Houston gave his children a hearty farewell, peering briefly into the cradle that held little Temple, their most recent addition: their eighth child and fourth son.

Arriving at the meeting, he spoke to his fellow Texans on the subject of the rule of law:

> The error has been that the South has met sectionalism with sectionalism....Because a minority at the North are inimical to us, shall we cut loose from the majority, or shall we not rather encourage the majority to unite and aid us?
>
> ...Let past differences be forgotten in the determination to unite against sectionalism...
>
> But if, through division in the ranks of those opposed to Mr. Lincoln, he should be elected, we have no excuse for dissolving the Union. The Union is worth more than Mr. Lincoln, and if the battle is to be fought for the Constitution, let us fight it in the Union and for the sake of the Union. With a majority of the people in favor of the Constitution, shall we desert the Government and leave it in the hands of the minority?...
>
> Secession or revolution will not be justified until legal and constitutional means of redress have been tried, and I can not believe that the time will ever come when these will prove inadequate...
>
> But,...we have a new party in our midst...what they call a Southern constitutional party...and yet there is scarcely one of them but will tell you that, notwithstanding the fact that Mr. Lincoln may be elected in the mode pointed out by the Constitution and by a constitutional majority, they will not submit. You

> hear it from the stump, you read it in their papers and in their resolution, that if Mr. Lincoln is elected the Union is to be dissolved. Here is a constitutional party that intends to violate the Constitution because a man is constitutionally elected President....[11]

Houston returned home, tired but satisfied. Texas was in turmoil, but he and Margaret were agreed: "...to be honest, and fear not is the right path..."[12]

First Vote for Secession

The South Carolina legislator suddenly jerked awake. He blinked to get the sleep out of his eyes. What had he been dreaming? Something unpleasant...lately he had been having unpleasant dreams, some of them involving freed slaves rampaging over the countryside, killing, burning...

He blinked again. There was a great stir in the front of the room. The Speaker and several other men were conferring. Evidently, more election returns. Although the nation had voted on November 7th, it had taken days for the results to be tabulated and disseminated.

It looked like their fears were finally confirmed. There was no doubt that Lincoln had won the election. He had garnered a majority of the electoral votes.

The South Carolina legislature had stayed in session for this purpose, that they might know the results of the election. An immediate vote was called. The pre-prepared bill was read, calling for a special election of delegates to a convention to decide the course of the state. The sleepy legislator called out "Aye" with the others.

Everyone knew what the result of the convention would be: secession.

Margaret's Thoughts During a Gloomy Time

Margaret sat at her writing table, thinking of her mother. She picked up her pen to write.

> Austin Jan 21, 1861
>
> My Beloved Mother,
>
> My first letter of the present year is to you . . .
>
> Well, I am sure you are anxious to know how we feel about the country. Truly the present appearance of things is gloomy enough, but the Lord can bring lights out of darkness and beauty out of chaos. In Him above is our trust. Gen'l Houston seems cheerful and hopeful through the day, but in the still watches of the night I

see him agonizing in prayers for our distracted country. God's people are offering up the same prayer throughout the whole land. Will He not hear these prayers? I believe that He will. I never had such joyous spirits or such hopefulness. I can not shut my eyes to the dangers that threaten us. I know that it is even probable that we may soon be reduced to poverty, but oh I have such a sweet assurance in my heart that the presence of the Lord will go with us wherever we may go, and that even in the wilderness, we may erect an altar of prayer!

The legislature meets today, and the town is filling up fast. Much depends upon their deliberations and God can incline their hearts to do right. See Br. [Michael] Ross as soon as possible and ask him to make it a subject of prayer that the executive and the legislature may be guided by the hands of God in all they do...

Thy devoted child,
M. M. Houston[13]

The Texas Legislature Votes

Sam Houston sat quietly in his chair, grieving over what was passing before his eyes. A special convention had been called, against his will and despite some delaying tactics. The legislature had simply ignored Houston, and his presence here today was simply that of a guest. He listened as the balloting proceeded.

One after another, delegates stood and proclaimed their votes to the chair, Justice Oran Roberts.

"Aye."

"Aye."

"Aye."

It was like a tidal wave for secession. Houston looked around at the crowds in the galleries, packed shoulder to shoulder, every eye riveted on the drama below.

"Aye."

"Aye."

"No."

The galleries erupted with catcalls for this opposing vote.

"Aye."

"Aye."

Houston knew that only a handful of the men present would vote against secession. He watched James Throckmorton stand and address the chair.

"Mr. President, in view of the responsibility, in the presence of God and my country – and unawed by the wild spirit of revolution around me, I vote 'no!'"

A few in the galleries cheered, but their voices were quickly drowned out by hissing.

Before sitting down, the tall, bearded man made himself heard once again:

"Mr. President, when the rabble hiss, well may patriots tremble!"[14]

Both delegates and onlookers rose up in noisy anger. Finally, order was restored and the voting continued. Only eight men dared to vote against secession, and when the result was official, a Lone Star flag was raised.

The people were now to vote on secession statewide, but the outcome was not in doubt.

Everyone was so happy – except Houston, and the handful of Unionists who had stood with him.

Dark days were ahead.

A Letter from the President

Houston greeted his guests, four good pro-Union friends, including James Throckmorton. It was not a social occasion. Instead, it felt almost as though they were subversives holding a secret meeting. Well, it was a secret meeting.

Events had moved quickly after secession. Union military officers had either surrendered voluntarily or had been arrested. Equipment and stores were being confiscated for the Confederate cause, and the "Committee of Public Safety" subjected Texans to a kind of martial law.

In the midst of all this, Houston had received a letter. Only when his friends were seated did he reveal its contents.

President Lincoln was offering to send military forces to help keep Texas in the Union. What did they think?

The youngest man present proposed they accept the offer, but the others demurred.

"Gentlemen, I have asked your advice and will take it, but if I were twenty years younger, I would accept Mr. Lincoln's proposition and endeavor to keep Texas in the Union."[15]

With that, Houston tossed Lincoln's letter into the fire.

The Vox Populi

Houston walked along the street in Brenham. Evicted from the governorship and Austin, his family had returned to Independence, with the exception of Sam Jr., whom his father had sent to Cedar Point with instructions to supervise things there.

It was clear that his son was itching to join the Confederate Army; Houston's strategy was first to keep him busy, and second, to keep him in Texas should he actually be recruited.

Houston took a very dim view of the Confederacy. Texas had been admitted without even applying for the honor, and the unconstitutional confusion being perpetrated by the new Southern government was not a cause for which he wanted to sacrifice his son's life.

For Texas herself, well, now, that was different. Now that she was adrift from the Union, who could tell? Could she become her own Republic again...?

Up ahead, Houston saw someone he knew. It was Hugh McIntyre, an influential planter and an old friend. McIntyre knew that Houston had been ostracized and evicted from office because he had refused, despite great pressure, to take an oath of allegiance to the Confederate government. The planter had such high regard for Houston that he wanted to know his reasons; not only that, he urged him to speak in public on the issue.

Houston was reluctant, not wanting to stir up strife, but finally he was persuaded. That same afternoon a crowd gathered to hear him speak. Suddenly several voices shouted, "Put him out! Don't let him speak! Kill him! Kill him!"

McIntyre may have been a respectable planter, but he was also an armed Texan. He jumped onto a table and whipped out his Colt six-shooter.

"I and 100 other friends of Governor Houston have invited him to address us. We will kill the first man who insults or in any way attempts to injure him."[16]

He went on to say that although he disagreed with Houston, he had a right to be heard.

In one of his last public speeches, the Hero of San Jacinto pleaded with his fellow Texans.

> ...The Vox Populi is not always the voice of God, for when the demagogues and selfish political leaders succeed in arousing public prejudice and stilling the voice of reason, then on every hand can be heard the popular cry of 'Crucify him, crucify him!' The Vox Populi then becomes the voice of the devil, and the hiss of mobs warns all patriots that peace and good government are in peril...
>
> I protest against surrendering the Federal Constitution, its Government and its glorious flag to the Northern abolition leaders and to accept in its stead a so-called Confederate Government whose constitution contains the germs and seeds of decay which must and will lead to its speedy ruin and dismemberment if it can ever

> secure any real existence. Its seeds of ruin and decay are the principle of secession which permits any one or more of the Confederate States to secede from the parent Confederate Government and to establish separate governments...[17]

Houston went on to explain that the Southern people had been misled: Europe would not support them, as they supposed, and the North would not let them go without bloodshed. In fact, there was a "civil war" now "near at hand" which would be a long and stubborn conflict.

His audience was spellbound by his oratory, and no one was shot by McIntyre's Colt. But even his friends, though sobered by his speech, were not convinced.

Sam Junior in Battle

Young Sam clutched his knapsack. Captain Ashbel Smith had recently delivered a Bible to him from home, a gift from his mother, which he had forgotten in the rush of preparation.

He did try to read his Bible to please his mother, but he did not profess to know Christ...sometimes he thought seriously about his soul, but right now, there was just too much going on.

The oldest son of Sam Houston was eager to go to war and glad to be out of Texas. He could have had a commission if he'd stayed, but he wanted to serve on the battlefield. And if he had waited, the war would be over, and he'd have missed his chance. Word was that it would be a short conflict.

So, he joined the Confederate Army. It was something he needed to do, despite the grief of his mother and the unspoken opposition of his father. Well, maybe it was just his opposition to the Confederacy.

Sam didn't understand his father's feelings entirely, but he did feel from his father a kind of tacit acknowledgment of his manhood, of his right to act according to his own conscience. He hoped to acquit himself with honor before his parents and before his comrades-in-arms.

It was Sunday morning, but Sam's Bible would stay in his knapsack, for it was time to attack Union forces. Sam and his compatriots in gray were ordered to storm the Federal position.

Yelling at the top of his lungs, Sam and the others plunged through the gray dawn, surprising the Yankees who were still cooking breakfast.

Look at this! A good chunk of beef! Sam did not let some Yankee's abandoned breakfast go to waste. The Confederate regiment continued, capturing a Union battery and three thousand men. At one point, Sam felt a solid thunk as something hit his knapsack. A bullet? He may have thanked God, for he was uninjured; the knapsack had taken it.

By the end of the day, the men were weary and collapsed on the ground, utterly exhausted.

Then it started to rain, only the beginning of one long and miserable night.

"Forward, double quick! March!"[18]

Sam jerked awake and packed away his soggy blanket. Despite their exhaustion and lack of sound sleep, the men were in good spirits as they started across a field. Surely today would bring them victory as well.

But where were the Yankees?

Suddenly, a nearby fence became a wall of fire. Union soldiers poured over it so close to him that he noticed the insignias on their uniforms: they were part of the Third Iowa Infantry.

Then there was a thump, a flash of pain from somewhere below his waist, and Sam found himself on the ground, his knapsack beside him.

The Yankees were gone. Only the dead and dying were left in the field. Sam couldn't think straight. He wished he could see his family before he died. What were they all doing?

Was that a doctor? Vaguely, Sam was aware that someone had looked at him, but then moved on.

Later, Sam became aware of another presence. Someone was looking at his knapsack...or was it his Bible? The Bible his dear mother had presented him. He stirred.

"Are you related to General Houston of Texas who served in the United States Senate?" the man was asking. He must have read Sam's name in the front of the Bible.

Sam managed a weak response. "My father."[19]

The man left and returned with another man, who quickly examined him. More commotion. Then Sam was lifted onto a litter and carried off the field.

Later, the young Houston discovered that despite the loss of blood, his wound had actually been minor. He also discovered that his Bible had stopped a bullet from the day before.

And the man who had stopped and looked at his Bible was a Union chaplain who had heard the elder Houston defend the rights of ministers of the gospel on the Senate floor.

Sam never did find out the man's name.

Emancipation

Aunt Liza wiped her hands on her apron and came out on the porch with the other slaves. Margaret and several of the children were outside, along with the general, who, for some reason, was dressed up in his "Sunday suit."

She trembled a bit inside. The Houston family had been through a lot, and what with the war and all…even travel was restricted now. Once, her master had been with Jeff on the road and had been stopped. He had had no "passport" for travel. Jeff had brought back the story that the old general had roared something about San Jacinto being his passport. They had let him pass after all.

Old Liza had taken care of Margaret since she was a baby, and she looked at her mistress. A bit thin, she decided. Sam's enlistment had taken a toll on her. She worried over them sometimes. The Houston family was her life.

Then her eyes turned to the general, who was fishing something from his pocket. Then he wiped off his reading glasses with a handkerchief. Something serious had happened, and Liza stiffened.

Houston looked at the slaves. "I want each one of you to listen very carefully to what I read to you."

Liza listened as her master read some kind of proclamation by President Lincoln, something about "emancipation," which was to take effect January 1st.

But wasn't Jefferson Davis their president? Liza wasn't sure she understood, and it made her nervous. She didn't want to leave the Houstons.

Houston continued, saying something about his having the right to free them whenever he wanted to and that he wasn't going to wait until January.

"You, and each of you, are now free," he continued. "I know I am your friend, and I know you are my friends. I'll always be ready to help you when I can."

Then Houston stumbled over his words. His voice quivered. "If you want to stay here and work for me, I will pay you good wages as long as I can."

Liza saw tears running down Margaret's face. Some of the children were crying, children Liza regarded almost as her own.

Joshua was the first slave to clear his throat and speak up. He would continue working for the Houstons as he had always done.

Others spoke up and said the same thing. But Liza couldn't take it anymore. Too much was changing, and what with the war and all, surely soldiers were going to come and take them all away!

She moaned and stepped up to the slave who held two-year-old Temple, picked him up, and clutched him tightly to her bosom.

"Oh Master!... I don't want no 'mancipation. I'se happy wid you all an' de chillun. I ain't gwine ter be 'mancipated. Glory to God! Hallelujah!"[20]

The family gathered around, comforting their oldest and most faithful servant.

The Tall Stranger

Margaret loved flowers, especially roses, and today she was outside showing Jeff where he needed to plant something new. Joshua was also helping, tending another flowerbed that September evening, while the children played in the yard. Houston had gone over to a neighbor's.

Out of the corner of her eye, Margaret noticed a tall stranger hobble up the walk on crutches. Wounded and furloughed soldiers were a common sight these days. Margaret left the flower bed and approached the skinny, dirty young man.

A dog barked. Then Margaret Houston knew her son, and tears filled her eyes. She threw her arms around him, and the other children crowded up close, crying.

Joshua came around the corner of the house, picked up the six-foot lad in his strong arms, and gently bore him away to the guest room. Jeff went to the kitchen and fetched some soup. Clearly, Sam needed some good food.

Suddenly, in the midst of the domestic hubbub, Houston's horse came clattering up at full gallop. Jeff rushed out and helped his master dismount.

Hurrying into the room where his son lay, the general put his arms around young Sam.

Brokenly, he said, "Sam, all morning something seemed to tell me that you were alive and safe, and that you would come home to us!"[21]

Sam, happy but exhausted, promptly fell asleep.

In the Hands of God

Winter passed, and another summer sun warmed the earth. Now seventy, Houston's old wounds were bothering him, so he went to Sour Lake to bathe in the healing waters there. Then he returned home, but he wasn't well. He seemed to have picked up a cold.

Days passed, and Houston's cold was getting worse. Sometimes he could barely get his breath between bouts of coughing. Though healthy a month ago, he now knew he was failing rapidly.

His eternal soul was in the hands of God, and he had little fear of death. But what of Margaret and the children? What of Texas?

When Texas had joined the Confederacy, it had broken his heart. The turmoil and bloodshed that he had predicted was coming to pass. The war had not been short, and it was still not over.

For a time, the old general had dreamed dreams...dreams of a new Texas Republic, dissociated from the Confederacy...perhaps annexing the western half of the continent to her domain...or perhaps Mexico, which still had no stable government.

But time and reality had eroded those dreams. Now he could only place Texas in the hands of God.

Needing to rest, Houston lay down, chilled despite the July heat. He knew Margaret had summoned the doctor, who was a political opponent but a good friend nevertheless.

Pneumonia was the diagnosis. Houston rested, sometimes aware of Margaret, sometimes not. Jeff seemed to be with him constantly, fanning him when he had nothing else to do. Finally, Houston sent him away to rest. He slumbered again. His last mortal thoughts were of those he most loved on earth.

"Texas!...Texas!"

"Margaret!"

Later, he slipped quietly away.

Man of Honor

The sun was just setting when Margaret Houston and her children were gathered around the still body of her beloved husband.

Gently, the grieving widow removed an old ring from her husband's hand, the ring that his mother had given to him so long ago.

She showed it to her children. There was a word engraved on the inside of the ring that could still be easily read.

"Honor."

Acknowledgments

My boss, Principal Rick Cortez, came to me with a Texas history textbook in his hands. I was not the history teacher in our small Christian school, but apparently he valued my judgment. I was dismayed. This book was so boring!

I looked into the matter. There didn't seem to be much available that was Christian or non-boring. Using primary source materials didn't seem workable. But so much of Texas history was profoundly *interesting*...

Providentially, I was home the next school year: a medical sabbatical. Pat Horner gave me a copy of Fehrenbach's *Lone Star*, the gold standard of Texas history, and I began gathering other source materials. I became well-acquainted with a Toshiba laptop and churned out chapters in time for Mrs. Anna Buitron to field-test them in class.

Several years later, our small school shut down and my materials languished. At one point, author Mary Arant Williams helped to edit the manuscript, but it wasn't until a few years later that my husband asked if he could look into a publisher, Xulon Press.

I soon became acquainted with Scott, Jose, Terry, and Jason the Chick-Fil-A guy who shepherded this newbie author through the process.

I give honor and praise to God through our Lord Jesus Christ, and many thanks to those I have listed here who helped and inspired me along the way.

Postscript:

The book you hold in your hands is the second edition of this book, revised and updated with some original artwork by members of the Avery Johnson family. Many thanks to Shiphrah and Evelyn!

Acknowledgments

Bibliography

The following may be useful for further research and exploration. Other great resources include The Handbook of Texas Online and DiscoverTexasOnline.com.

Pre-History and Texas Amerinds

Holzmann, John, *Incans, Aztecs, Mayans,* Danette Maloof, ed., 5th ed., Littleton: Sonlight Curriculum, Ltd., 2002.

Jeanson, Nathaniel T., *They Had Names,* Green Forest: Master Books, 2025.

Mann, Charles C., *1491: New Revelations of the Americas Before Columbus.* New York: Vintage Books, 2006.

Newcomb, W.W., Jr., *The Indians of Texas: From Prehistoric to Modern Times.* Austin: University of Texas Press, 1961.

Biographies

Cantrell, Gregg, *Stephen F. Austin: Empresario of Texas.* New Haven: Yale University Press, 1999.

Crane, William Carey, *Life and Select Literary Remains of Sam Houston of Texas.* Dallas: William G. Scarff & Co., 1884.

Haley, James L., *Sam Houston.* Norman: The University of Oklahoma Press, 2002.

James, Marquis, *Andrew Jackson: Portrait of a President.* New York: Grosset and Dunlap, 1937.

James, Marquis, *The Raven: A Biography of Sam Houston.* Indianapolis: Bobbs-Merrill Co., 1929.

Neeley, Bill, *The Last Comanche Chief: The Life and Times of Quanah Parker.* New York: John Wiley & Sons, Inc., 1995.

Remini, Robert V., *The Life of Andrew Jackson.* New York: HarperPerennial, 2009.

Shelton, Gene, *Brazos Dreamer: The Story of Robert S. Neighbors.* New York: Doubleday, 1993.

Wisehart, M.K., *Sam Houston: American Giant.* Washington: Robert B. Luce, Inc., 1962.

General Histories

Fehrenbach, T.R., *Lone Star: A History of Texas and the Texans.* New York: American Legacy Press, 1983.

Haley, James L., *Passionate Nation: The Epic History of Texas.* New York: Simon & Schuster, 2006.

Hardin, Stephen L., *Texian Iliad: A Military History of the Texian Revolution.* Austin: University of Texas Press, 1994.

Hodge, Frederick W., ed., *Spanish Explorers in the Southern United States: 1528-1543.* New York: Scribner and Sons, 1907.

Lozano, Ruben Rendon, *Viva Tejas: The Story of the Tejanos, the Mexican-born Patriots of the Texas Revolution.* San Antonio: The Alamo Press, 1985.

Tiling, Moritz, *History of the German Element in Texas from 1820-1850.* Houston: Moritz Tiling, 1913.

Yoakum, Henerson K., *The History of Texas from its First Settlement in 1685 to its Annexation to the United States in 1846,* vol. 1. New York: Redfield, 1856.

Memoirs and Collections

De Vaca, Cabeza, *Adventures in the Unknown Interior of America,* Cyclone Covey, trans. Albuquerque: University of New Mexico Press, 1961.

Hamilton, Jeff, as told to Lenora Hunt, *My Master: The Inside Story of Sam Houston and His Times.* Austin: State House Press, 1992.

Harris, Dilue, "The Reminiscences of Dilue Harris II," *The Quarterly of the Texas State Historical Association,* vol. 4, no. 3, Jan. 1901.

Kreuger, Max Amadeus Paulus, *Second Fatherland: The Life and Fortunes of a German Immigrant,* Marilyn McAdams Sibley, ed. College Station: Texas A&M University Press, 1976.

Morrell, Z.N., *Flowers and Fruits in the Wilderness, or, Forty-Six Years in Texas and Two Winters in Honduras,* 3rd ed. St. Louis: Commercial Printing Company, 1872.

Olmstead, Frederick Law, *A Journey Through Texas, Or, a Saddle-Trip on the Southwestern Frontier.* Austin: University of Texas Press, 1978.

Roberts, Madge Thornall, ed., *The Personal Correspondence of Sam Houston,* 4 vols. Denton: University of Texas Press, 1996-2001.

Roberts, Madge Thornall, *Star of Destiny: The Private Life of Sam and Margaret Houston.* Denton: University of Texas Press, 1993.

Smithwick, Noah, *Evolution of a State, Or, Recollections of Old Texas Days,* comp. Nanna Smithwick Donaldson. Austin: Gammel Book Company, 1900.

Notes

1. Tejas

1. Wisehart, M.K., *Sam Houston: American Giant.* Washington: Robert B. Luce, Inc.,1962, p. 8.
2. Oart, Michael, *Frozen in Time.* Green Forest: Master Books, 2004, p.77.
3. Mann, Charles C., *1491: New Revelations of the Americas Before Columbus.* New York: Vintage Books, 2006, pp. 189-190.
4. *ibid.,* pp. 284-291.
5. Nathaniel Jeanson in *They Had Names* published his latest efforts in research into pre-contact America, but he has a biblical worldview and timeframe.
6. Holtzmann, John, *Incans, Aztecs, Mayans.* Danette Maloof, ed., 5th ed. Littleton Curriculum, Ltd., 2002, pp. 69, 122.
7. Newcomb, W.W. Jr., *The Indians of Texas: From Prehistoric to Modern Times.* Austin: University of Texas Press, 1978, p.280.
8. De Vaca, Cabeza, *Adventures in the Unknown Interior of America,* Cyclone Covey, trans. Albuquerque: University of New Mexico Press, 1961.

2. Trojans and Spaniards

1. Homer, *Iliad,* trans. Alexander Pope, Aeterna, 2011, p. 276
2. James, Marquis, *The Raven: A Biography of Sam Houston.* Indianapolis: Bobbs-Merrill Co., 1929, p.12.
3. *ibid.,* pp. 16-17.
4. Cartwright, Peter. *Autobiography of Peter Cartwright, the backwoods preacher, quoted in James, pp. 17-18.*
5. *Hodge, Frederick W., ed., Spanish Explorers in the United States:1528-1543. New York: C. Scribner and Sons, 1907.*
6. *ibid.*
7. *ibid.*
8. *El Requerimiento* by Juan López de Palacios Rubios (1513), translation, https://en.wikipedia.org/wiki/Spanish_Requirement_of_1513
9. *Hodge.*
10. *Crane, William Carey, Life and Select Literary Remains of Sam Houston of Texas. Dallas: William G. Scaff & Co., 1884, p. 19.*

3. Celts and Comanches

1. James, *The Raven,* p. 27.
2. Wisehart, p. 4.
3. Wisehart, p. 4.
4. Haley, James L., *Sam Houston.* Norman: The University of Oklahoma Press, 2002, p. 12.
5. Wisehart, p. 15.
6. Remini, Robert V. *The Life of Andrew Jackson.* New York: HarperPerennial, 2009, p. 80.
7. Wisehart, p. 19.

4. Men of Destiny

1. James, Marquis, *Andrew Jackson the Border Captain.* Garden City Publishing Co., Inc., 14 West 49th Street, New York, NY, 1940, p. 19.
2. Wertenbacker, Thomas Jefferson, *Patrician and Plebeian in Virginia.* Charlottesville: The Mitchie Co., 1910, p.180.
3. Remini, p. 8.
4. Haley, *Sam Houston,* p. 26.
5. *ibid.,* p. 29.
6. James, *The Raven,* p. 48.
7. Haley, *Sam Houston,* p. 37.
8. Cantrell, Gregg, *Stephen F. Austin: Empresario of Texas.* New Haven: Yale University Press, 1999, p. 56.
9. *ibid.,* pp. 73.
10. *ibid.,* pp. 74-75.
11. *ibid.,* p. 80.
12. *ibid.,* pp. 80-81.
13. *ibid.,* pp. 80-81,
14. *ibid.,* p. 82.
15. *ibid.,* p. 82.
16. *ibid.,* p. 86.
17. *ibid.,* p. 87.
18. *ibid.,* pp. 88.
19. *ibid.,* p. 90.

5. La Casa Blanca

1. Haley, James L., *Passionate Nation: The Epic History of Texas.* New York: Free Press, A Division of Simon & Schuster, 2006, p. 50.
2. Fehrenbach, T.R., *Lone Star: A History of Texas and the Texans.* New York: American Legacy Press, 1968/1983, p. 75.
3. Cantrell, p. 93.
4. *ibid.,* p.116.
5. *ibid.,* p.130.
6. *ibid.,* p.130.

6. Trial by Fire

1. Wisehart, p. 35.
2. *ibid.* p. 30.
3. *ibid.,* p. 42.
4. *ibid.,* p. 46.
5. *ibid.,* p. 45.
6. *ibid.,* pp. 43-44.
7. *ibid.,* pp. 46-47.
8. Haley, *Sam Houston,* p. 63.
9. Wisehart, p. 93.
10. Cantrell, p. 182.
11. Yoakum, Henderson K., *The History of Texas from its First Settlement in 1685 to its Annexation to the United States in 1846,* vol. 1. New York: Redfield, 1856, p. 243.

12. Wisehart, p. 96.
13. Crane, p. 40.
14. Wisehart, p. 62.
15. James, *The Raven*, p. 177.
16. Cantrell, p. 217.
17. *ibid.*, p. 216.
18. Wisehart, p. 103.
19. *ibid.*, p. 65.
20. *ibid.*, p. 66.
21. *ibid.*, pp. 67-68.
22. *ibid.*, p. 69.
23. *ibid.*, p. 70.
24. *ibid.*, pp. 73-75.
25. *ibid.*, p. 76.
26. *ibid.*, p. 76.
27. *ibid.*, p. 76.
28. *ibid.*, pp. 76-77.
29. *ibid.*, p. 79.

7. Come and Take It

1. Haley, *Sam Houston*, p. 95.
2. Cantrell, p. 266.
3. Smithwick, Noah, *Evolution of a State.* Austin: Gammel Book Company, 1900, p. 83, p. 81.
4. Cantrell, pp. 267.
5. Cantrell, pp. 270.
6. *ibid.*, pp. 271.
7. *ibid.*, p. 271
8. *ibid.*, p.271.
9. *ibid.*, p.282.
10. Wisehart, p. 118.
11. *ibid.*
12. Wisehart, pp. 119.
13. *ibid.*, p. 121.
14. *ibid.*, p. 122.
15. *ibid.*, p. 124.
16. *ibid.*
17. Smithwick, p. 102.
18. Hardin, Stephen L., *Texian Iliad: A Military History of the Texas Revolution.* Austin: University of Texas Press, 1994, p. 12.
19. Smithwick, pp. 102-104.
20. *ibid.*, pp. 114-116.

8. Victory or Death

1. Hardin, p. 46.
2. *ibid.*, p. 61.
3. Cantrell, p.323.
4. Hardin, p. 217.
5. *ibid.*, p.78.

6. *ibid.*, pp.79-80.
7. *ibid.*, p. 85.
8. *ibid.*, p. 86.
9. *ibid.*, p. 89.
10. *ibid.*, p. 90.
11. *ibid.*, p. 91.
12. *ibid.*, p. 108.
13. *ibid.*, p. 108.
14. Wisehart, p. 151.
15. Wisehart, p. 152.
16. *ibid.*, pp. 156.
17. *ibid.*, pp. 157-158.
18. *ibid.*, p. 162.
19. Hardin, p. 127.
20. *ibid.*, p. 129.
21. Lozano, R. R., *Viva Tejas: The Story of the Tejanos, the Mexican-Born Patriots of the Texas Revolution.* San Antonio: The Alamo Press, 1985, p. 35.
22. Hardin, p. 129.
23. Wisehart, pp. 165-166.
24. *ibid.*, p. 167.
25. *ibid.*, p.168.
26. Hardin, p. 159.
27. Hardin, p. 161.
28. *ibid.*, p. 136.
29. *ibid.*, p. 139.
30. Wisehart, pp. 168-169.

9. Retreat to Victory

1. Hardin, pp. 155-156.
2. *ibid.*, p.155.
3. Wisehart, p. 173.
4. *ibid.*, p. 180.
5. *ibid.*, p.188.
6. Hardin, p. 167.
7. Wisehart, p.189.
8. Hardin, p. 172.
9. Wisehart, p.192.
10. Fehrenbach, p. 226.
11. Wisehart, p. 202.
12. *ibid.*
13. Wisehart, pp. 203-204.
14. *ibid.*, p. 204.
15. *ibid.*, pp. 204-205.
16. *ibid.*, p. 209.
17. *ibid.*, p. 211.
18. *ibid.*, p. 224.
19. Hardin, p. 209.
20. Wisehart, p.237.
21. Hardin, p. 213.
22. *ibid.*, p. 214.

23. *ibid.,* p.215.
24. Wisehart, p. 244.
25. Haley, *Sam Houston,* p. 154.
26. Wisehart, p. 251. This conversation was reconstructed from the memories of various eyewitnesses and is thought to be more or less accurate.

10. Sam Houston's Republic

1. James, *Andrew Jackson,* p. 412.
2. Fehrenbach, p. 239.
3. *ibid.*
4. Harris, pp. 167-168.
5. Hardin, p. 286 (note 42).
6. Wisehart, p. 252.
7. *ibid.,* p. 254.
8. *ibid.,* p. 259.
9. *ibid.,* p. 262.
10. Morrell, Z. N. *Flowers and Fruits in the Wilderness,* 3rd ed. St. Louis: Commercial Printing Company, 1872, p. 23.
11. Wisehart, pp. 271-272.
12. *ibid.*, pp. 272-273.
13. *ibid.,* p.274.
14. Smithwick, p. 145.
15. Morrell, p. 20.
16. Wisehart, pp. 275-276.
17. *ibid.,* p. 279.
18. Crane, p.120.
19. Morrell, p. 23.
20. James, *The Raven,* p. 268.
21. Wisehart, p. 291.
22. Wisehart, pp. 289-290.
23. *ibid.,* p. 291.
24. *ibid.*
25. Morrell, p. 28.
26. *ibid.,* p. 29.
27. Wisehart, p. 300.
28. *ibid.,* pp. 294-295.
29. James, *Andrew Jackson,* p. 427.
30. Wisehart, p. 295.

11. Margaret

1. Wisehart, p. 326.
2. Morrell, pp. 39-40.
3. *ibid.,* p. 40.
4. Smithwick, p.173.
5. Morrell, p. 42.
6. *ibid.,* p. 43.
7. Smithwick, pp. 177-178.
8. *ibid.*, pp. 178-179.

9. *ibid.*, pp. 180-181.
10. *ibid.*, pp. 190-191.
11. *ibid.*, p. 188.
12. *ibid.*, p. 189.
13. *ibid.*, p. 194.
14. Fehrenbach, p. 453.
15. Wisehart, p. 349.
16. Roberts, Madge Thornall, ed., *The Personal Correspondence of Sam Houston, vol 1.* Denton: University of North Texas Press, 1996, pp. 2-3.
17. Wisehart, p. 349.
18. *ibid.*, p. 346.
19. Roberts, Madge Thornall, *Star of Destiny: The Private Life of Sam and Margaret Houston.* Denton: The University of North Texas Press, 1993, p. 26.
20. James, *The Raven*, p. 313.
21. Roberts, *Star of Destiny*, p. 29.
22. Roberts, *Correspondence*, 1:16.
23. *ibid.*, p. 52.
24. *ibid.*
25. Roberts, *Correspondence*, 1:52.
26. Wisehart, p. 360.
27. Roberts, *Correspondence*, 1:22.

12. Blood and Tears

1. Fehrenbach, p. 458.
2. Morrell, p. 65.
3. *ibid.*
4. *ibid.*
5. Roberts, *Correspondence*, 1:96.
6. *ibid.*
7. Morrell, p. 77.
8. Wisehart, p. 385.
9. *ibid.*, p. 386.
10. *ibid.*, p. 369.
11. *ibid.*, p. 374.
12. Roberts, *Correspondence*, 1:96.
13. Wisehart, p. 387.
14. *ibid.*, p. 390.
15. *ibid.*, p. 378.
16. Smithwick, p. 253.
17. Morrell, p. 82.
18. Wisehart, p. 391.
19. *ibid.*, p. 393.
20. *ibid.*, p. 396.
21. *ibid.*
22. *ibid.*
23. *ibid.*, p. 409.
24. *ibid.*
25. *ibid.*, p. 411.
26. Morrell, p. 84.
27. *ibid.*

28. *ibid.*, pp. 89-90.
29. *ibid.*, p. 93.
30. *ibid.*, p. 95.

13. One Last Battle

1. Wisehart, p. 421.
2. *ibid.*
3. Roberts, *Correspondence,* 1:252.
4. Wisehart, p. 57.
5. James, *The Raven,* p. 316.
6. *ibid.*, p. 341.
7. Wisehart, p. 447.
8. *ibid.*, p. 430.
9. *ibid.*, p. 450.
10. *ibid.*, p. 451.
11. James, *Andrew Jackson,* p. 470.
12. Morrell, p. 99.
13. Wisehart, p. 452.
14. *ibid.*, p. 455.
15. *ibid.*, p. 456.
16. *ibid.*, p. 458.
17. *ibid.*, p. 460.
18. James, *Andrew Jackson,* p. 479.
19. *ibid.*, p. 481.
20. *ibid.*, pp. 481-482.
21. *ibid.*
22. Wisehart, p. 464.
23. *ibid.*, p. 468.
24. *ibid.*, p. 470.
25. *ibid.*, p. 471.
26. Morrell, p. 117.
27. Wisehart, p. 480.
28. *ibid.*, p. 482.
29. James, *Andrew Jackson,* p. 499.
30. *ibid.*, pp. 499-500.
31. *ibid.*, p. 500.
32. Smithwick, p. 282.
33. *ibid.*
34. *ibid.*, pp. 282-283.

14. War and Peace

1. Fehrenbach, p. 476.
2. Block, W.T., "Death March to Comal County," http://www.texasescapes.com.
3. Roberts, *Correspondence,* 2:37-38.
4. Wisehart, p. 510.
5. Fehrenbach, p. 488.
6. Tiling, Moritz, *History of the German Element in Texas from 1820-1850.* Houston: Moritz Tiling, 1913.

7. Wisehart, pp. 516-517.
8. Roberts, *Correspondence,* 2:270.

15. Rising Waters

1. Calhoun, John C., "Southern Address," https://www.civilwarcauses.org/saddress.htm.
2. *ibid.*
3. *ibid.*
4. *ibid.*
5. Wisehart, p. 527.
6. *ibid.,* pp. 529-530.
7. *ibid.*
8. Roberts, *Correspondence,* 3:86-87.
9. *ibid.*
10. Wisehart, p. 531.
11. *ibid.,* p. 533.
12. *ibid.,* p. 535.
13. Roberts, *Correspondence,* 3:146.
14. Fields. Anne, ed. *The Life and Letters of Harriet Beecher Stowe,* Boston: Houghton, Mifflin and Company, 1898, https://utc.iath.virginia.edu/articles/n2esafa1t.html
15. Stowe, Harriet Beecher, *Uncle Tom's Cabin,* New York: Hurst & Co., 1893, pp.40-41.

16. Broken Promises

1. Hamilton, Jeff, *My Master: The Inside Story of Sam Houston and His Times.* Austin: State House Press, 1992, pp. 3-9.
2. *ibid.,* pp. 21-22.
3. Olmstead, Frederick Law, *A Journey Through Texas,* Austin: University of Texas Press, 1978, pp. 89-91.
4. Seward, William H., "Higher Law," speech, March 11, 1850, https://www.ohiocivilwarcentral.com/william-h-seward
5. Wisehart, p. 543.
6. *ibid.,* pp. 544-545.
7. Roberts, *Correspondence,* 4:115-116.
8. Wisehart, p. 544.
9. *ibid.* pp. 544-556.
10. Olmstead, p. 158.
11. Wisehart, pp 560-561.
12. *ibid.*
13. Roberts, *Correspondence,* 4:130.

17. Man of Honor

1. Haley, pp. 339-340.
2. James, *The Raven,* p. 389.
3. *ibid.,* p. 390.
4. Wisehart, p. 575.
5. Fehrenbach, p. 505.
6. Wisehart, p. 580.
7. *ibid.,* pp. 580-581.

8. *ibid.*, p. 582.
9. Hamilton, p. 44.
10. Neeley, Bill, *The Last Comanche Chief: The Life and Times of Quanah Parker.* New York: John Wiley & Sons, Inc., 1995, p. 46.
11. Wisehart, p. 590.
12. Haley, p. 335.
13. Roberts, *Correspondence,* 4:380-382.
14. Fehrenbach, p. 344.
15. Haley, p. 393.
16. Wisehart, p. 618.
17. *ibid.*, pp. 619-620.
18. *ibid.*, p. 630.
19. *ibid.*, p. 631.
20. Hamilton, pp. 100-101.
21. *ibid.*, p. 109.

www.ingramcontent.com/pod-product-compliance
Lightning Source LLC
LaVergne TN
LVHW081313110826
845149LV00006B/1500

* 9 7 9 8 9 9 4 2 3 0 5 5 8 *